Revisiting Slavery and Antislavery

Laura Brace · Julia O'Connell Davidson
Editors

Revisiting Slavery and Antislavery

Towards a Critical Analysis

palgrave
macmillan

Editors
Laura Brace
School of History, Politics and International Relations
University of Leicester
Leicester, UK

Julia O'Connell Davidson
School of Sociology, Politics and International Studies
University of Bristol
Bristol, UK

ISBN 978-3-030-08057-0 ISBN 978-3-319-90623-2 (eBook)
https://doi.org/10.1007/978-3-319-90623-2

Cover design: Fatima Jamadar

Printed on acid-free paper

This Palgrave Macmillan imprint is published by the registered company Springer International Publishing AG part of Springer Nature
The registered company address is: Gewerbestrasse 11, 6330 Cham, Switzerland

Acknowledgements

We are much indebted to the co-organizers, speakers and participants at the British Academy Landmark Conference, 'Slaveries Old and New', March 2014, which inspired this volume, in particular, Bridget Anderson, Karen Bravo, Nathaniel Coleman, Mark Johnson, Nicolas Lainez, Tommy Lott, Samuel Okyere, Srila Roy, Nandita Sharma, Charlotte Sussman, and Zoe Trodd, as well as to the British Academy for funding the conference. Many thanks are also due to Lucy James for her invaluable support, and to colleagues who so generously gave their time to reviewing the contributions and providing such helpful feedback. Julia O'Connell Davidson is grateful to the Leverhulme Trust for the award of a Major Research Fellowship (MRF-2012-085), which made it possible for her to work on this edited volume.

Contents

Part I Past

1 **Slavery and the Revival of Anti-slavery Activism** 3
Laura Brace and Julia O'Connell Davidson

2 **Contextualizing Slavery's Wrongness** 35
Tommy Lott

3 **The Liberty of Naming** 65
Mary Nyquist

4 **Historicizing Freedom of Movement: Memory and Exile in Political Context** 97
Charlotte Sussman

5 **Immigration Restrictions and the Politics of Protection** 123
Nandita Sharma

Part II Present

6 **Prison Labour, Slavery, and the State** 151
Genevieve LeBaron

7 **From Victims of Trafficking to Freedom Fighters: Rethinking Migrant Domestic Workers in the Middle East** 179
Mark Johnson

8 **"Back Home, It Would Have Been Worse Anyway…": Vietnamese Wives' Perspectives on Their 'Arranged' Marriages with Chinese Men** 207
Caroline Grillot

9 **Moral Economies and Child Labour in Artisanal Gold Mining in Ghana** 231
Samuel Okyere

Part III Revisiting the Politics of Antislavery

10 **Abolitionist Anti-politics? Capitalism, Coercion and the Modern Anti-slavery Movement** 263
Neil Howard

11 **Empowering Women: The Contradictions of Feminist Governance** 281
Srila Roy

12 **Abolition Terminable and Interminable** 305
Jared Sexton

Index 327

Notes on Contributors

Laura Brace is Associate Professor in Political Theory at the University of Leicester, UK. Her research interests include the politics of property, self-ownership and the social, sexual and racial contracts, and the political thought of Locke, Rousseau, Wollstonecraft and Hegel. She is author of two books, *The Politics of Property: Labour, Freedom and Belonging* (Edinburgh University Press, 2004) and *The Politics of Slavery* (Edinburgh University Press, 2018) and numerous articles and book chapters on the eighteenth century self, citizenship, Hegel, Wollstonecraft, wet nursing and migration.

Caroline Grillot is a social anthropologist (Paris X-Nanterre University) and a sinologist (INALCO). Her research has mainly focused on social margins if China and Southeast Asia. She has obtained a joined Ph.D. in social anthropology from Macquarie University (Australia) and the Free University of Amsterdam (The Netherlands). Her research topic concerned cross-border marriages between Vietnamese women and Chinese men in borderlands, a topic on which she had previously published a book (*Volées, Envolées, Convolées*, 2010). She has updated her earlier findings on cross-border marriages with a comparative approach and additional fieldwork in collaboration with Elena Barabantseva at the University of Manchester (2016–2017). In 2017, she has started a new research project with the support of the Ecole Française d'Extreme Orient on Chinese transhumant beekeepers; a project she is now pursuing with the Lyon Institute of East Asian Studies (France).

Neil Howard is Prize Fellow in International Development at the University of Bath. His research focuses on the construction and governance of 'unfree labour'. He combines ethnographic research with those defined as victims of trafficking, modern slavery and forced labour, and political anthropological work with the institutions seeking to 'protect' them. He is also Founding Editor of the Beyond Trafficking and Slavery platform publishing at openDemocracy.net. Research for this essay was funded by European Union Marie Curie Actions, and by the EUI's Migration Policy Centre. He is grateful for this funding, and for the generous editorial assistance provided by this volume's editors, as well as by Asha Amirali. Portions of the essay were previously published as media articles with Al-Jazeera and openDemocracy.

Mark Johnson is Reader in Anthropology at Goldsmiths, University of London. His research interests and writing are focused broadly around the issues of gender/sexuality, landscape and material culture, movement and transnationalism. Recent research includes British Academy funded research (2016–2018) that investigates ordinary people's awareness of and perceptions about the different sorts of surveillance they encounter during their travels and explores the connections between care and control in processes of watching and being watched. He was also principle investigator for the AHRC funded *Curating Development* project (2016–2018) that investigates Filipino migrants' contributions to development in the Philippines and co-investigator on previous AHRC funded research on the place of religion in the experiences of Filipino migrant workers in the Middle East and Saudi Arabia in particular.

Genevieve LeBaron is Professor of Politics at the University of Sheffield. She is also Co-Chair of Yale University's Modern Slavery Working Group and a UK ESRC Future Research Leaders Fellow (2016–2019). Her current research focuses on the global business of forced labour and the politics and effectiveness of governance initiatives to combat it. She has held visiting positions at Yale University, the International Labour Organization, and the University of California, Berkeley and has published in some of the world's leading political science journals, including *Regulation & Governance*, *Review of International Studies*, and *Review of International Political Economy*.

Tommy Lott is Professor of Philosophy at San Jose State University. He is editor of *Subjugation and Bondage: Critical Essays on Slavery and Social Philosophy* (1998), co-editor with John Pittman of Blackwell's *Companion to African–American Philosophy*, and author of *Like Rum in the Punch: Alain Locke and the Theory of African American Culture*, as well as numerous articles.

Mary Nyquist is Professor at the University of Toronto, where she teaches in the Centre for Comparative Literature, the Department of English and the Literature and Critical Theory Program. Her research centres on intersections among early modern and enlightenment literature, Euro-colonialism, law and political philosophy. Awarded the Milton Society's title of "Honored Scholar" in 2011 (an achievement award not confined to Milton studies), she recently published *Arbitrary Rule: Slavery, Tyranny and the Power of Life and Death* (Chicago University Press, 2013). She is currently at work on a number of projects that explore the semantic complexity and ideological import of interrelations among 'freedom', 'slavery' and 'tyranny'.

Julia O'Connell Davidson is Professor of Social Research in the School of Sociology, Politics and International Studies at the University of Bristol. She has researched and written on employment relations, prostitution, 'trafficking', childhood and recently held a Leverhulme Major Research Fellowship for a project on 'modern slavery'. She is author of *Modern Slavery: The Margins of Freedom*, London: Palgrave Macmillan (2015).

Samuel Okyere is Assistant Professor of Sociology and Criminology at the University of Nottingham in the United Kingdom. Sam's work critically interrogates policy and popular perspectives on child labour, forced labour, human trafficking, prostitution and other phenomena described by some actors as modern slavery. This preoccupation prompted his research on children's involvement in artisanal gold mining in Ghana and informs his publications examining the interplay between dominant liberal human and child rights discourses, social justice, power, precarity, inequality, exploitation, (un)freedom and domination under conditions of globalization.

Srila Roy is Associate Professor of Sociology at the University of the Witwatersrand and Honorary Assistant Professor at the University of Nottingham. Her long standing research interests lie in the constitution of political subjectivity at the intersection of gender, caste-class, and sexuality in postcolonial contexts, especially India/South Asia. She is author of *Remembering Revolution* (Oxford, 2012); editor of *New South Asian Feminisms* (Zed, 2012) and co-editor of *New Subaltern Politics* (Oxford, 2015).

Jared Sexton teaches African American Studies at the University of California, Irvine. He is the author of *Amalgamation Schemes: Antiblackness and the Critique of Multiracialism*, *Black Masculinity and the Cinema of Policing*, and *Black Masculinity: Lucifer's Nocturne*, as well as various articles and essays on political culture and cultural politics.

Nandita Sharma is Associate Professor in the Department of Sociology at the University of Hawaii at Manoa (Honolulu) and the Director of the University's International Cultural Studies Program. Her research interests address themes of human migration, migrant labour, national state power, ideologies of racism and nationalism, processes of identification and self-understanding and social movements for justice. Amongst numerous publications in journals and edited volumes, she is also the author of *Home Economics: Nationalism and the Making of 'Migrant Workers' in Canada* (University of Toronto Press, 2006).

Charlotte Sussman is Associate Professor of English at Duke University. She is the author of *Consuming Anxieties: Consumer Protest, Gender and British Slavery, 1713–1833* (2000), *Eighteenth-Century British Literature* (2011) and the co-editor of *Recognizing the Romantic Novel: New Histories of British Fiction 1780–1830* (2008). She has published on issues of mobility, population, and memory in the work of Jonathan Swift, Mary Shelley, Walter Scott and others.

Part I

Past

1

Slavery and the Revival of Anti-slavery Activism

Laura Brace and Julia O'Connell Davidson

Slavery had been legally outlawed everywhere in the world by the end of the twentieth century. Yet as the millennium dawned, there was a revival of anti-slavery activism. In 2000, the long-established, British-based NGO Anti-Slavery International acquired a new US-based sister organization, Free the Slaves (the two have since severed their links), and many more anti-slavery NGOs were founded over the next twelve years in the US, Australia, and Western European countries, including Stop the Traffik, Not For Sale, End Slavery Now, CNN Freedom Project, Alliance Against Modern Slavery, and Walk Free Foundation. Building on claims about 'human trafficking' as a vast and growing organised criminal business that have been widely made by

L. Brace (✉)
School of History, Politics and International Relations,
University of Leicester, Leicester, UK
e-mail: lb21@le.ac.uk

J. O'Connell Davidson
School of Sociology, Politics and International Studies,
University of Bristol, Bristol, UK
e-mail: julia.oconnelldavidson@bristol.ac.uk

L. Brace and J. O'Connell Davidson (eds.), *Revisiting Slavery and Antislavery*,
https://doi.org/10.1007/978-3-319-90623-2_1

governmental and intergovernmental actors since the 1990s, and equating 'trafficking' with slave-trading, this 'new abolitionist' movement insists that slavery is not merely a persistent, but also an expanding global problem (Batstone 2007: 5).

In 1999, Kevin Bales, co-founder of the anti-slavery NGO, Free the Slaves, estimated that some 27 million souls were affected by 'trafficking' and other forms of 'new slavery'. In 2013, the Walk Free Foundation, assisted by Bales, launched a report titled *The Global Slavery Index* (GSI), which enlarged that estimate to 29.8 million. The following year, the GSI set the number of 'modern slaves' in the contemporary world at 35.8 million. The 2016 GSI expanded the estimate to 45.8. Figures like these are used to support the claim that there are now 'more slaves than at any time in human history' (McNally 2009).

The discourse of 'new' or 'modern' slavery invokes the past to frame the present not just in the sense that it identifies certain contemporary forms of oppression as equivalent to historical practices of enslavement, but also as a means of stressing the urgency of the present problem. The quantum of human suffering implied by 'new slavery' is even greater than that imposed by 'old slavery'. Other differences between new and old slavery are also asserted. 'Today's slavery focuses on big profits and cheap lives. It is not about owning people like before, but about using them as completely disposable tools for making money' (McNally 2009), and we are also told that whilst 'ethnic differences' were important to 'old slavery', today's slavers are 'colour-blind'. It is said to be poverty, not racialised identity that renders individuals vulnerable to enslavement (Bales 1999, 2004). And unlike old slavery, new slavery is said to be a clandestine phenomenon. In an article for the *Telegraph* in 2013, British Prime Minister Theresa May (who was then the Home Secretary) asserted that 'modern slavery' is 'hidden in plain sight. It is walking our streets, supplying shops and supermarkets, working in fields, factories or nail bars, trapped in brothels or cowering behind the curtains in an ordinary street'.

The task for contemporary anti-slavery activists is thus not so much to proselytise against slavery (which is now regarded as self-evidently wrong), but to expose crimes taking place in a concealed underworld, and to work with governments and civil society to prevent such crimes and to support their victims. The new abolitionists seek to 'shine a light on slavery' (Kristine 2012). Their goal is to raise public awareness such that, as Theresa May (2013), quoting from William Wilberforce, said when introducing her Modern Slavery Bill, 'you may choose to look the other way but you can never again say that you did not know'.[1]

By quoting from Wilberforce, May inserted herself into a narrative that constitutes a particular relation between pasts, presents, and futures (Scott 2004: 45). The story of 'new' or 'modern slavery' promulgated by most politicians, policy makers, and journalists, as well as anti-slavery activists represents slavery as part of the barbarism of the past, abolished by modern liberal states in the nineteenth century; it appears as inimical to the present of liberal societies, and as something that will be entirely vanquished in the future when all the world is guided by liberal values. This is a linear tale that takes the idea of rupture with the past as its starting point and in which liberalism incrementally extends freedom to all. The 're-emergence' of slavery in the twenty-first century does not disrupt that narrative, it simply allows for a kind of abolitionist sequel in which the same liberal superhero is called back to vanquish the old enemy one more time.

This edited volume challenges the dominant discourse on 'new' or 'modern slavery' by initiating an interdisciplinary dialogue between scholarship on the pasts of slavery and abolitionism, and research on phenomena that the new abolitionists discuss under the rubric of modern slavery (such as debt, child labour, forced labour, forced marriage), as well as on restraints on freedom typically overlooked by the new abolitionists (such as imprisonment). It critically interrogates the way in which the new abolitionism portrays the past as well as the present, not only because that portrayal is at odds with serious scholarship on slaveries historically, and on contemporary forms of exploitation, but also because it lends support to policies that are far from benign in their effects. In fact, the response of most governments—especially in the affluent world—to the new abolitionist campaign against 'modern slavery' has been to promise tighter policing, tougher sentencing, harsher immigration policies, and ever-stricter border controls. In other words, in the name of combatting modern slavery, states are pursuing policies that imply heavy restrictions, sometimes extremely violent restraints, on the freedoms of many migrants, and that do almost nothing to change the condition of those unable to move from contexts in which their rights, well-being, and even their lives are under threat. The policy response often further includes measures to suppress prostitution or eliminate child labour, again strengthening the punitive powers of states, and restricting the livelihood options available to women and teenagers without ensuring them realistic or sustainable alternatives.

'The past of slavery has its many presents, and the present of exploitation its many pasts', Alice Bellagamba (2016) observes. Given this, and the extent and wealth of the available literatures on slaveries and on contemporary systems of domination, the volume necessarily provides only a very partial and incomplete survey of research on restraints on human freedom past and present. Because the discourse of 'new' or 'modern slavery' that is under critique takes transatlantic slavery as the archetype of 'old slavery' and a wrong that was righted by abolition, the volume attends to Atlantic world history, rather than to the histories of slaving in the ancient world or in other regions. Our aim in keeping this focus is to move away from the idea of rupture and from the ahistoricism of 'modern slavery' discourse. However, we hope that the contributions to this volume will serve to invigorate further debate on the theory and practice of representing slavery and related systems of domination, and more rigorous interrogation of the binary between slavery and freedom in different historical and political contexts. This introductory chapter contextualises those contributions by exploring how the multiple pasts of slavery and exploitation have been, and are, selectively remembered and forgotten in abolitionist thinking.

From Slavery to Anti-slavery

Different forms of slavery are known to have existed in prehistoric societies and to have been present historically in most regions of the world. Slavery was 'a major institution in antiquity', and one that did not disappear with other ancient institutions at the end of the Roman Empire (Thomas 1997: 25). Throughout the early Middle Ages, 'slaves constituted a highly prized section of the population of Europe' and though the institution of slavery withered in North West Europe during the eleventh century, it persisted in other regions (Thomas 1997: 34). Indeed, the Mediterranean slave trade of the twelfth to fifteenth centuries, through which mostly Venetian and Genoese merchants supplied sugar-producing Crusader states with enslaved Slavs from the Dalmatian Coast (and others from the Black Sea region), is said to have foreshadowed the transatlantic trade in terms of its organization (Angela Davis 2003).

Robin Blackburn (2011: 8–9) reminds us that whilst slaveholding has 'been quite common in human societies', it has not always been 'of structural importance to the ruling group'—in fact, 'fully fledged slave societies have been quite rare'. Nonetheless, considered against slavery's ubiquity in human history, the contemporary global consensus on its wrongness is remarkable. The fight against it is now 'one of the very few human rights imperatives that attracts no principled dissent' (Hathaway 2008: 7). As Thomas Haskell observes, though many free people in slave societies had pitied slaves, and philosophers and moralists had long acknowledged that slavery was ethically difficult, until the middle decades of the eighteenth century, it was generally regarded '*as nothing worse than a regrettable but necessary evil*' (1998: 302, emphasis in the original). Then:

> in little more than a century, slavery was suddenly transformed from a troubling but readily defensible institution into a self-evidently intolerable relic of barbarism, noxious to decent people everywhere. On a historical scale of reckoning, this reversal of opinion occurred overnight (Haskell 1998: 302).

So great was the *volte face*, in fact, that where in the seventeenth and eighteenth centuries, European colonial ventures in the Americas were widely understood to necessitate slave trading and chattel slavery, by the end of the nineteenth century, European and North American colonial ventures in Africa were legitimated, in part, as necessary to cleanse the 'dark continent' of barbaric practices such as slavery and slave trading. Even King Leopold II's deadly regime in the Congo was initially authorised as a humanitarian and philanthropic intervention (Quirk 2011).

The reasons for this relatively abrupt shift in perceptions of slavery in Western Europe and North America have been much debated. Eric Williams' (1944) now classic *Capitalism and Slavery* opened one strand of debate by arguing that the exigencies of capitalist economic development, not humanitarian high thinking, were the primary impetus for the abolition of slavery in the West Indies. The idea of an association between the rise of capitalism and the fall of Atlantic world slavery is now widely accepted, but the exact nature of the link is disputed. David Brion Davis has made particularly important interventions through his focus on how, 'by defining slavery as a unique moral aberration, the [antislavery] ideology tended to give sanction to the prevailing economic order', namely, a capitalist order in which 'free' wage labour was to play a central role (1992: 63; see also Ashworth 1992; Davis 1966, 1975, 2014; Foner 1995; Genovese 1965). The abolition campaigns of late eighteenth-century England were highly political, with a great deal to say about slavery and property, and owning a property in the person, and about the rights of free-born Englishmen and how to preserve them from encroaching despotism. Their selectivity in focusing on natural rights and on the slave trade (rather than on slavery) allowed reformers to project 'the social costs and amorality of growing capitalism onto slavery in politically safely remote West Indian colonies' (Miller 2012: 7).

In the period when anti-slavery thought developed its support, there was also growing public knowledge of the extremely harsh conditions experienced by wage labourers in Europe and North America. Chartists and labour rights activists spoke passionately against the abject squalor in which wage labourers lived, hungered, and died in industrial cities, depicting their 'freedom' as but the liberty to starve, sometimes describing their situation as 'white' or 'wage-slavery'. As Tommy Lott points out in Chapter 2 of this volume, the distinction between slavery and drudgery was not always easy to draw, and slavery always overlapped with other forms of servitude. Yet the key figures of the original British abolitionist movement were not also agitating on behalf of servants and wage workers. In fact, many of them were themselves employers with strong views on the need for servants to be industrious, diligent, sober, faithful, and respectful to their Masters–their 'denunciation of colonial slavery… implied no taste for a freer or more equal society' (Davis 1992: 95). This was true in relation to racial (and gender) as well as class, inequalities.

Through the transatlantic slave trade, 'slavery became indelibly linked throughout the Western Hemisphere with people of African descent… the dishonor, humiliation, and bestialization that had universally been associated with chattel slavery now became fused with Negritude' (David Brion Davis 2003: 29). The history of that fusion is more geographically and chronologically varied than sometimes assumed (Jennison 2012; Midlo Hall 1998), but ultimately, blackness came to signal an incapacity for rights and freedom. In the West Indies and the American South, tropes of enslaved Africans and their descendants as 'evasive, disguised, lazy, childlike, lying, thieving, distrustful, capricious', yet also kind and cheerful 'songsters' were deployed to support the argument that people racialised as black were, by nature, unfit or unready for liberty (Hall 2002: 102; Kendi 2016). Such tropes were not uniformly rejected by slavery's opponents, but were instead often re-worked in abolitionist campaigning to produce a vision of 'the black slave' as nothing but a suffering body, empty of subjectivity, will, and voice. These representations spoke much more closely to the concerns of a white European audience than they did to the experience of the enslaved (Lively 1998: 61). Indeed, as Mary Nyquist (Chapter 3) explains, slavery carried exceptional rhetorical power in defining the status of freeborn Englishmen from the seventeenth century onwards. We are talking here, as Jared Sexton says in Chapter 12, about how status is made.

In anti-slavery literature, 'the black slave' became a screen upon which to project and explore European sensibilities, in particular, the European's reaction to the violence enacted on the bodies of the enslaved, for 'sensibility is exemplified by the ability to suffer along with the suffering of others' (Lively 1998: 75). The idea of slavery, especially 'the brutality of domination', appeared to 'derive some its elemental intensity as a kind of distillation of the helplessness and isolation underlying the radical individualism of modern life', Miller (2012: 5) argues. As part of this elemental intensity and the quest for consolation, anti-slavery narratives also frequently offered their audience moral salvation. In Harriet Beecher Stowe's *Uncle Tom's Cabin*, for example,

Tom functions as 'a Christ figure' whose humiliation, suffering, and death promises the reader redemption, if only she will repent her own spiritual impoverishment and commit herself to the anti-slavery cause (Lively 1999: 87).

Certainly, white Euro-American discourse on slavery allowed for a desire to act on behalf of the enslaved against the cruelties they suffered without simultaneously finding it necessary to acknowledge them as equals. Indeed, the European abolitionist campaign initially focused its concern on the abolition of the slave trade rather than of slavery, which many believed should be gradually ameliorated rather than immediately outlawed. Its efforts mostly centred on the '*abuse* of the practice, not the practice itself, hence… pangs of sympathy and empathy sit side-by-side with the securely entrenched belief in the necessity and justness of the practices' (Pleasants 2010: 204). For the early British abolitionists, slavery was not so much an affront to the inherent dignity and equality of every human being as to the 'traditional' English values and laws that constructed all individuals—whether master or servant, man or woman, adult or child, white or black—'as *subjects* of the king;… bound by the king's laws and… entitled to the king's protection' (Davis 1992: 94, original emphasis). It was the colonial slaveholder's *unrestrained* power over the slave that was understood as wrong.

Thus, William Wilberforce could campaign against the slave trade, hoping that its abolition would encourage 'a disposition to breed instead of buying' amongst the planter class of the West Indies, as he put it in a diary entry in 1818 (Jordan 2005: 180), rather than bringing an immediate end to slavery. In the struggle for the meaning of freedom, Wilberforce made clear that he could not bear to leave 'these poor creatures sunk below the level of their species', and did not deny that he wished to 'impart to them the blessings of freedom'. He was quick to add, however, that the freedom he meant was 'that, of which, at present, they, alas! are not capable' (Debate 1792: 9).

Wilberforce was not the only anti-slavery thinker, however, and those who spoke against slavery in the eighteenth and nineteenth centuries were a heterogeneous group in terms of their reasons for condemning it and their hopes regarding what would follow its abolition. Wilberforce looked forward to a hierarchical but paternalistic post-slavery social order in which every person observed their religious obligations towards God, and towards their social inferiors and superiors, but the anti-slavery cause also had supporters who envisaged a world in which workers would suborn themselves to the demands of a capitalist free market, rather than those of tradition. They made the case against chattel slavery as a case *for* a market in free wage labour. In the aftermath of the Civil War, American opponents of slavery were often quite explicit about the fact that freed slaves must learn to accept the dominion of employers under the system of free wage labour, and keenly instructed the emancipated on how to abide by 'the new rules of the game: the new requirements and responsibilities of contracting on the one hand, and the new compulsions of necessity and self-discipline on the other' (Berlin et al. 1986: 117). This returns us to Davis' contention that anti-slavery sentiment was able to take hold when and where it did because it 'reflected the needs and values of the emerging capitalist order' (1992: 71).

But in addition to those whose opposition to slavery was grounded in an uncritically positive regard for the market and free labour, Chartists, feminists, and other radical political thinkers, some of whom were themselves fugitive slaves, vigorously campaigned against slavery in the US and Europe. These different groupings of anti-slavery actors were divided on the question of how abolition should be achieved (immediately, gradually, or, in the US context, by means of sending American slaves to colonies in Africa, the Caribbean, and/or Central America), and did not share a common political platform beyond the legal abolition of chattel slavery. Even the views of the radicals were not all of a piece. There were significant divisions between them on issues that would today go under the headings of race, gender, and class (Caleb McDaniel 2013; Kendi 2016).

Last but far from least, we should remember that 'the first major breach in the hugely important systems of slavery to the Americas was opened, not by English or American abolitionists, but by Jacobin revolutionaries and the black peasantry of Saint-Domingue/Haiti' (Blackburn 2011: 176; James [1938] 2001; Bhambra 2016). The Haitian Revolution was a 'turning point in history', Davis (2014: 46) observes, and quotes Frederick Douglass' speech dedicating the Haitian Pavilion at the Chicago World's Fair in 1893, in which he remarked that until Haiti spoke:

> no Christian nation had abolished Negro slavery… Until she spoke, the slave trade was sanctioned by all the Christian nations of the world, and our land of liberty and light included… Until Haiti spoke, the church was silent and the pulpit dumb.

In Britain and America, support for the anti-slavery cause was undermined by the Haitian Revolution in the first decade of the nineteenth century, with abolitionists 'increasingly portrayed as inciters of violence', and the abolitionist movement 'virtually disappeared' in France (Davis 2014: 50). More generally, the Haitian Revolution proved, and continues to prove, difficult to fit into the mainstream white liberal narrative of slavery's abolition. Through the lens of anti-black racism, the Revolution itself appeared as unthinkable and impossible, and was, therefore, condemned to silence, pushed into the past, but never given a history. The enslaved, even as they showed themselves to be 'entities that are fit to reason and manifest socio-political agency' (Jean-Marie 2013: 256) were inserted into history rather than understood and recognised as making it (see also Fischer 2004).

When considering the historical movement from a world in which slavery was regarded as an unalterable feature of human society to one in which it is universally condemned and outlawed, Haskell's (1998) question of what prompted the rise of humanitarian sensibility amongst (some) propertied white European and Americans, allowing them to feel moral responsibility for the suffering of distant strangers, is not the only one that needs to be addressed, then. White-propertied Europeans and Americans were not the only actors involved in actions against slavery. Black men and women (enslaved, fugitive, freed and free), for whom the suffering of slaves was not socially, geographically, or temporally remote, also fought to bring slavery down. And not all white anti-slavery actors positioned the enslaved as distant Others in need of humanitarian rescue—some believed that the struggle for liberation from slavery was intimately bound up with their own struggle for freedom (from colonial, class or male rule).

However, in popular European and North American memory, the politically and socially diverse actors who were involved in anti-slavery campaigns and actions—including revolution—in the eighteenth and nineteenth centuries have been homogenised and slotted into a dominant narrative of Western history 'in which acts of abolition and proclamations of emancipation completed a historical movement from the dark ages to Enlightenment that had been in process since the seventeenth century' (O'Connell Davidson 2015: 13; Wood 2010; Carey and Kitson 2007; Paton 2009). This is a narrative in which legal acts of abolition are equated with 'freedom', and chattel slavery is relegated to the past. Attention to race as a system of domination leads to a rather different story.

Abolition and the Race of Freedom

Before abolition, 'the fact of blackness, the story of "negrosity" in the law' was one in which those racialised as black were 'caught in the impossible position of being object of circulation and subject who is only recognised as such by the law in matters criminal' (Bhandar 2014: 218). This did not end with slavery. Indeed, the anti-black racist ideology that developed alongside slavery was, if anything, strengthened following its abolition. In the US South, for example, while the legal machinery of slavery existed, race was constituted a hereditary, caste-like, social marker. Dismantling the institution of chattel slavery threatened to simultaneously undo the legal, social, and political mechanisms through which racial difference and hierarchy were produced, policed, and perpetuated, thereby, eviscerating whiteness of its privilege (O'Connell Davidson 2015). Though some, both black and white, pursued a radical reconstruction of the Southern political and economic order and achieved some impressive successes (Foner 1990), ultimately such reconstruction was effectively, often murderously, resisted by white Southerners seeking to preserve the racial hierarchy of the antebellum period. White supremacy was maintained in a post-slavery US by mechanisms that differentially restricted and allocated the norms of citizenship by race. These included the Black Codes, Jim Crow, anti-miscegenation laws,[2] and the post-Civil War southern convict lease system, a system that Angela Davis (2003) observes 'transferred symbolically significant numbers of black people from the prison of slavery to the slavery of prison' (see also Haley 2016; LeFlouria 2016). In the words of W. E. B. Du Bois (1992: 30), 'The slave went free; stood a brief moment in the sun; then moved back again toward slavery'.

In her book tracing the history of the Atlantic slave trade, Saidiya Hartman (2007: 133) observes that:

> I, too, live in the time of slavery, by which I mean I am living in the future created by it. It is the ongoing crisis of citizenship. Questions first posed in 1773 about the disparity between 'the sublime ideal of freedom' and the 'facts of blackness' are uncannily relevant today.

With its vision of blackness as implying criminality, animality, irrationality, and dependence, the anti-black racism spawned by transatlantic slavery continues to disfigure, and often also prematurely and violently end, black lives. In the United States (and in a number of Latin American and European countries) transatlantic slavery's 'afterlife' is a present in which those racialised as black are disproportionately liable to be imprisoned, killed by the police, and deported (Alexander 2011; Black Alliance for Just Immigration 2016; Golash-Boza 2012; Childs 2015). The 'particular character of slavery's violence is ongoing and constitutive of the unfinished project of freedom', as Stephen Best and Saidiya Hartman (2007: 10) put it. The process of emancipation after 1865 produced 'national innocence' and at the same time 'enhanced the degradation of the past for those still haunted by… the vestiges [of slavery]' (Hartman 1997: 133). And yet, as Jared Sexton (Chapter 12) notes, the restraints on freedom that are engendered by anti-blackness are as uncannily absent from new abolitionist talk of 'modern slavery' as they are relevant to the contemporary distribution of freedom and unfreedom.

The history of slavery between the fifteenth and twentieth centuries is a great deal more complicated and variable than is popularly assumed. There were significant variations between colonial slave regimes in North America, Latin America, and the Caribbean in terms of legal and social practices surrounding slavery (Blackburn 2011; Rinehart 2016); there was an Indian Ocean as well as a transatlantic trade in slaves from Africa (Collins 2006; Williams 2016); slavery existed on the continent of Africa itself (Hartman 2007; Bellagamba et al. 2016). The links between slavery, race, abolition, and freedom play out in different ways in different regional contexts (see, for example, Colosio 2016) and the specific form of anti-black racism that so powerfully shapes the experience of those racialised as black in North America and Europe does not necessarily feature in every post-slavery society. However, efforts to protect the whiteness of citizenship were a constant theme in European settler colonies, and this links to another sense in which legal acts of abolition did not eradicate, merely led to mutations in, the systems of domination set in place to support Atlantic World slavery. The new abolitionists' insistence on not seeing race in modern slavery reflects their refusal to 'grapple with the ways the past in lived' (Balfour 2005: 802) in these many different contexts, and a failure to recognise 'the continuities of slavery and freedom as modes of domination, exploitation, and subjection' (Hartman 1997: 172). The contributions to this volume call our attention back to these continuities, which are particularly important in the contexts of mobility and migration.

Abolition and Restraints on Freedom of Movement

Since enslavement did not literally transform human beings into objects or things, the enslaved retained the capacity to flee their oppressors. And because slaveholders often had an economic interest in permitting their slaves a certain amount of mobility (allowing them to run errands, transport produce, move between workplaces, hunt for their own food, accompany their masters on their travels, etc.), the enslaved were also often presented with opportunities for escape. To enjoy the property they held in slaves, then, slaveholders relied on the state and slaveholding community to operate a legal system that strictly controlled and constrained the 'physical and social mobility of enslaved people' (Camp 2004: 12). There were fences, walls, slave patrols, pass systems, check points, and laws that criminalised those who offered fugitive slaves succour or assistance, as well as providing brutal punishments for recaptured runaways. While there were enslaved people who managed to evade these controls, sometimes forming 'maroon' communities and sometimes escaping to free territory (Price 1979; Midlo Hall 1998; Camp 2004; Roberts 2015), the price of attempting to claim freedom in this way was extraordinarily high. To fail was to face torture, mutilation, and re-enslavement. To succeed was often to face a life in exile from children and other kin and loved ones (Wong 2009).

Slavery's abolition did not spell an end to restraints on freedom of movement. In the US, the Southern system of peonage relied heavily on vagrancy laws that prevented many people racialised as black from escaping a set of social and labour relations closely resembling chattel slavery (Novak 1978). In Barbados, as Alana Johnson's (2016) research reveals, planters' efforts to force the newly emancipated into the same conditions they had endured when enslaved were supported by laws designed to prevent the formerly enslaved from migrating to British Guiana to seek work on better terms. More generally in the British Empire, it had long been recognised that the abolition of slavery would provoke a shortage of labour in many of its colonies. The solution to this problem was a system of indentured labour, the 'coolie system' (see Sharma, Chapter 5). Between 1834 and 1937, more than 30 million people are estimated to have left India as indentured workers, travelling to Mauritius, Guiana, Jamaica, Trinidad, Fiji, Kenya, Uganda, South Africa and other destinations, and at least another 5 or 6 million workers from other parts of Asia, in particular China, were 'employed under the coolie system to build infrastructure and to produce goods for the world market either on the plantations or in the mines' (Potts 1990: 70–71). Once in situ, the mobility of those workers transported under this system was heavily restricted, by means virtually identical to those employed to control slave mobility, including pass systems to leave plantations.

Alongside, these large-scale movements controlled by colonial states under emigration legislation, however, colonial subjects began to take advantage of opportunities to travel independently within the British Empire. And when 'masterless' Chinese and Indian migrants travelled to what were deemed to be white settler colonies (Australia, Canada, South Africa), their freedom to move came to be regarded as a problem in need of a solution. Just as race marked the line between those human beings who were and were not fit to bear 'the rights of man' in the post-abolition US, so it demarcated those who could and could not 'belong' to the nations 'invented by the bourgeoisie' (Cesaire 1972). In fact, it was the freer movement of peoples deemed to be racial Others following the abolition of slavery that generated 'a state monopoly over migration practices and, via the passport… [created] the specifically modern imbrication of the state, the nation, and race' (Mongia 1999: 528). The justification for excluding Indian and Chinese subjects of Empire from white settler countries was framed 'in terms of national sovereign rights—and conversely the definition of sovereignty as a matter of border control' (Lake 2014: 101). This framing has now been generalised around the world with disastrous consequences for the rights and freedoms of many groups of migrants. Immigration controls disproportionately restrict the freedoms of people of colour in contemporary affluent liberal states, and are very much a part of the future created by transatlantic slavery. It is precisely when migrants' freedoms are restricted in these ways that they become vulnerable to the forms of exploitation and violence that are dubbed 'modern slavery' in dominant discourse on the topic. Yet the rights that contemporary states grant themselves to control movement across their borders go unchallenged by the new abolitionists.

The narrative of liberal modernity as the progressive unfolding of liberty, and of abolition as bestowing freedom, has been subject to extensive and powerful critique from postcolonial, critical race, feminist, and other radical theorists (see, for example, Mills 1998; Bhambra 2007; Noble 2017). Such critique has not, as yet, dented the hegemonic hold of 'the mythology of emancipation' (Wood 2010: 19), a mythology that is reproduced in new abolitionist discourse and subjected to critical scrutiny by the contributors to this volume.

From Anti-slavery to Anti-slavery-by-Another-Name: Problems of Definition

Efforts to define slavery and identify its unique wrongs have long provoked scholarly dispute amongst classicists, philosophers, political theorists, anthropologists, and sociologists (see, for instance, Finley 1964;

Kopytoff 1982; Patterson 1982; Meillassoux 1991; Lott 1998). The definitional conundrums surrounding the term 'slavery' have been, and remain, far from academic for anti-slavery activists, however. The passage of legislation against slavery by European colonial powers and in the US complicated rather than spelt an end to anti-slavery activism, making its object less certain. On the one hand, there were questions about practices traditional in colonised settings that were not named 'slavery' and yet looked, through Western eyes, to be very close to it. On the other, there were questions as to whether Western powers were themselves outlawing chattel slavery only to replace it with equally oppressive labour regimes (Quirk 2011). Was the 'coolie system' of indentured labour with which the European powers replaced slave labour in their plantation economies and powered the expansion of extractive industries and construction projects a new form of slavery (Tinker 1974; Cohen 2006; Sharma, this volume)? Were the systems by which labour was exacted from newly colonised people in Africa slavery in all but naming (Nzula et al. 1979)? Was Du Bois right to describe freed slaves and their descendants in the US as having moved back towards slavery?

Such questions made it increasingly clear that abolishing chattel slavery as a juridical status did not automatically banish from the world everything that all the various abolitionists had argued was intolerable about slavery. Early twentieth century anti-slavery activists, therefore, pressed for more expansive legal definitions and political understandings of the term slavery. As a result, the League of Nations' *Slavery Convention* (1926) not only offered a definition of slavery as 'the status of a person over whom all or any of the rights attaching to ownership are exercised' (in other words, a definition that fitted with what had, till then, generally been understood as 'chattel slavery') but also required states to bring about the complete abolition of slavery 'in all its forms'. It did not, however, list or explicate the different forms that slavery could take, nor did it clearly elucidate the difference (if any) between slavery and forced labour. Forced labour was subsequently defined by the ILO's1930 Forced Labour Convention as 'all work or service which is exacted from any person under the menace of any penalty and for which the said person has not offered himself voluntarily'.

The United Nations' *Supplementary Convention on the Abolition of Slavery, the Slave Trade, and Institutions and Practices Similar to Slavery* (1956) later fleshed out the meaning of 'all forms' of slavery by expressly recognising that certain 'institutions and practices similar to slavery' may be 'covered by the definition of slavery contained in article 1 of the Slavery Convention of 1926'. The institutions and practices it recognised were debt bondage, serfdom, and various practices around children and marriage. All of these present their own problems of definition, as illustrated by chapters in this volume on the social meanings of debt, forced labour, child labour, child marriage and cross-border marriages, which uncover the space between not-slavery and freedom, and expose the risks of relying on broad dichotomies of choice and force. Moreover, aligning 'slavery' with institutions and practices similar to slavery opened up possibilities for further extending the reach of the concept, and the 1956 supplementary convention was followed by 'a whole slew of further conventions and declarations, many of them overlapping', that add to the list of phenomena discussed under the rubric of 'contemporary slavery', including the UN Convention on the Rights of the Child (1989) (Miers 2004: 716–717). There are also some who lobby for the extension of the term slavery to female circumcision, female prostitution, and even abortion (Guenther 2012).

Contemporary anti-slavery activists face a dilemma. They do not wish to restrict the term 'slavery' to the forms of legally or socially recognised chattel slavery that have now been universally outlawed. But nor do they want to see the term inflated to incorporate anything and everything that is judged oppressive, exploitative, or immoral. For them, there is a distinction between metaphorical and *true* slavery in the contemporary world, and their struggle is against the latter, not simply against conditions that some may figuratively liken to it. Real slavery, Bales argues, is an obscenity, 'more closely related to the concentration camp than to questions of bad working conditions' (Bales 2012: 7–8). And, as illustrated by Walk Free's *Global Slavery Index*, they are confident that the line between the two is clear enough that it is possible to count the number of people trapped in 'modern slavery' around the globe. How? The statistics produced and circulated by anti-slavery campaigners are largely generated by totting up estimates of people thought to fall into categories such as 'bonded labour', 'forced labour', 'worst forms of child labour', 'early and forced marriage', and 'human trafficking', which are imagined to describe practices that are 'sufficiently horrendous and/or analogous' to be classified as slavery (Quirk 2006: 578).

Yet as will be seen in contributions to this volume, all of these categories present their own definitional problems. Take 'trafficking', for example. Efforts to produce a definition for the UN *Protocol to Prevent, Suppress, and Punish Trafficking in Persons, Especially Women and Children* (which is supplementary to the *Convention on Transnational Organized Crime* 2000) provoked enormous controversy (Doezema 2010), and consensus was finally achieved at the expense of precision. The Protocol defines 'trafficking' not as a single, one-off event, but a coercive *process* that takes place over time (recruitment, transportation and control) and that is organised for purposes of exploitation.[3] 'Exploitation' remains undefined, and the process of trafficking can be organised in a variety of different ways. Moreover, though 'trafficking' is routinely described as 'modern day slavery and slave trading' in political and anti-slavery NGO rhetoric (US Department of State 2003), the UN Protocol actually lists slavery as but one of a number of possible outcomes of 'human trafficking'. In other words, 'trafficking' does not necessarily lead to slavery, according to the Protocol (Chuang 2013).

'Trafficking' can also intersect with what states categorise as other forms of movement, including 'smuggling' and 'asylum seeking' (Anderson and O'Connell Davidson 2003). Still more problematic for those seeking to count the world's 'modern slaves', the category 'victim of trafficking' overlaps with other categories taken as proxies for slavery. The same individual could be identified as being a trafficked person, and a bonded labourer, and subject to forced labour, and subject to a worst form of child labour, for instance. This is only one of many technical problems associated with the compilation of data on these proxy categories. Others arise from the fact that such data are gathered in different countries, by different agencies, and for different purposes, and so are not necessarily comparable (Andrees 2014; Broome and Quirk 2015; Ghallagher 2016).

An even more fundamental problem is that none of the categories used as proxies for 'modern slavery' straightforwardly match the definition of 'slavery' offered by anti-slavery NGOs and activists. For example, writing of 'slavery' in the abstract, Kevin Bales (1999, 2005) states that it is comprised of three essential ingredients: involuntariness (the slave is totally controlled by the slaver and cannot walk away); non-payment or payment covering just bare subsistence; and violence or its threat. Walk Free (2016) simplifies that definition further by stating that 'slavery' refers to 'situations of exploitation that a person cannot refuse or leave because of threats, violence, coercion, abuse of power or deception.' But what kind of obstacles to refusing or 'walking away' do anti-slavery campaigners count as the contemporary equivalent to slavery? They appear to be highly selective and not always consistent in this respect. When it comes to children in what the ILO terms 'worst forms of child labour', for instance, Walk Free includes them as 'slaves' even though, as Samuel Okyere shows in Chapter 9, such children do not necessarily work without pay, and are not necessarily violently coerced into the work by a third party. For many, the obstacle to 'walking away' is that if they did so, they would be unable to pay their school fees, and/or buy food, clothing, or items necessary to make the transition to adulthood, and/or to support their dependents or contribute to their household's economic survival (Hashim and Thronsen 2011; Howard and Morganti 2015).

When the focus is on adults, however, such economic compulsion is not regarded as sufficient to make a 'slave'. 'We're not talking about bad choices, we're not talking about crummy jobs in a sweatshop', Bales said when interviewed about Walk Free's 2013 Global Slavery Index, 'We're talking about real life slavery—you can't walk away, you're controlled through violence, you're treated like property'. Yet when state actors deprive adults of their liberty and contain them by means of threatened and actual violence through imprisonment and immigration detention, they are not automatically counted as 'slaves' by anti-slavery organisations like Walk Free and Free the Slaves. Those held captive by the North Korean state and the People's Republic of China are described as slaves, but immigration detainees and prisoners in Western liberal states are not, even when they are held in for-profit facilities, and even when their labour is exploited for profit (O'Connell Davidson 2015; LeBaron, Chapter 6 this volume).

Contributions to this volume by Caroline Grillot (Chapter 8) and Srila Roy (Chapter 11) highlight the fact that new abolitionist discourse on restraints on women's freedoms is also selective. Forced marriage and bride trafficking is identified as a form of 'modern slavery' affecting women in the Global South and ethnic minority women in the Global North, but domestic violence affecting white women in Europe, North America, and Australia is not, even though the women affected are frequently unable to leave the situation because of threats, violence, and coercion.

Tryon Woods (2013) has observed that 'trafficking' and 'slavery' are depicted as part of the fabric of everyday life in Nigeria's Edo delta, apathetically accepted by the local people who lack the determination to address the problem. This focus, he continues, disregards how the state has been eviscerated by the multinational energy industry, and provides no political economic context that would link colonization to the present (or to the past and the future). Indeed, the 'gesture to poverty as a cause of trafficking is a component of the cultural racism thesis', suggesting that it is African cultural deficiencies that produce predatory economic processes, which in turn cannot support civilised democracies (Woods 2013: 124). By representing 'modern slavery' as a mundane feature of Other societies, new abolitionist discourse works to dehistoricise and depoliticise the forms of exploitation that it claims to address. Rooted in the liberal narrative of advancement, this is a rhetoric that 'reproduces a disabling historical amnesia' (Woods 2013: 126).

From a policy perspective, one of the most troubling outcomes of this amnesia regarding the history of colonization and its legacies, and of blindness to global political and economic structures, is that it licenses and encourages measures that further restrict the choices open to people at the sharp end of structural inequalities. Indeed, the language of slavery invites interventions to redeem or rescue 'slaves', and to abolish or ban the forms of work or mobility where 'slaves' are found, rather than interventions to extend rights and protections to people *as* workers, migrants, child labourers, wives, and so on. The 'slave' of the liberal imaginary has no voice to be heard, no dignity to be respected, no will or agency to author her or his own life-course.

The Problem of Agency

Vincent Brown (2009: 1235) has remarked that studies of transatlantic slavery 'often divide between works that emphasise the overwhelming power of the institution and scholarship that focuses on the resistant efforts of the enslaved.' The latter approach frequently rests upon what Walter Johnson (2003: 115) describes as a 'misleading entanglement of the categories of "humanity" and (liberal) "agency",' through which 'the bare fact (as opposed to the self-conscious assertion) of enslaved "humanity" has come to be seen as "resistance" to slavery'. However, the former can reproduce an equally problematic vision in which the bare fact of slaves' objectification as legal property comes to be seen as erasing their volition and free will, and so *literally* de-humanizing them (O'Connell Davidson 2015; Rinehart 2016). Slavery, as much as any other social phenomenon, presents us with the problem at the heart of all sociological enquiries, namely the relationship between structure and agency.

The problem is made all the more politically troubling by the racialization of the categories of freedom and agency as white in dominant liberal thought, for these are the categories through which the normatively human was, and is still, imagined and socially recognised. In this context, it is difficult to stress the restraining violence of slavery without suggesting that its victims were reduced to mere bodies, the passive objects of structural forces, and therefore, also hard to avoid reproducing the racist association between blackness, dependency, and dishonour. And yet to attempt to counter this by emphasising the agency, courage and ingenuity of those who led or participated in revolts and revolution, or who made daring escapes from slavery, also carries its own risks. What space does it leave to acknowledge the quiet valour of those women, men, and children who somehow managed to make their lives within the confines of the institution (Brown 2009; Wong 2009)? And what kind of moral judgement does a story in which the enslaved were heroes pass on those who capitulated to, or were even complicit with, the power of slaveholders? Where do slaves who served as soldiers and suppressed the revolts of other slaves fit in these stories (Buckley 1979; Morgan and O'Shaughnessy 2006; Lambert 2016; Lott, this volume)? What of the slaves who exercised de facto powers of ownership over other slaves, or bought their own freedom by accepting the role of overseer or even executioner with regard to other slaves, or the maroons who secured the safety of their own community by assisting in the capture and return of other fugitives (Price 1979; Beckles 1987; Midlo Hall 1998)?

Such theoretical, ethical, and political dilemmas are equally, if not more, marked in relation to the contemporary phenomena discussed under the heading 'modern slavery', not least because of significant differences between past and present. Unlike transatlantic slavery, what is today described as 'slavery', in the vast majority of cases, follows from an arrangement that was initially actively desired and pursued by the individual concerned. Whether we are talking about people accessing credit to be able to feed their family or fund their labour migration, or setting off on journeys either to escape desperate circumstances or to pursue a dream, or taking up a job offer, we are not talking about human beings snatched, manacled, and transported as *objects*. We are talking about people moving as *subjects*, albeit subjects whose choices are framed by the limited alternative options open to them.

Anti-trafficking and anti-modern slavery discourse hinges on an imagined line between those who have actively chosen to move and consented to the type of work they will undertake and the conditions under which it will be undertaken (cast as agents), and those who have been tricked, cheated, bullied, and trapped (cast as non-agential victims). It conceives of migrants, child labourers, debtors, wives, and sex workers, as *either* willing selves, acting on the basis of their own freely made choices, *or* as forced to submit to the will of another. 'Modern slaves' are described as having 'lost' their agency along with their freedom. One problem with this is that it transports us onto territory that is profoundly gendered and aged: adult men are regarded as almost by definition authors of their own destinies, whereas women and children's grip on their own wills is understood to be already fragile and tenuous. They are readily imagined in the garb of victimhood. Another is that it reflects a preoccupation with the form of compulsion produced by the exercise of direct, personalistic power, and so a very narrow and distinct understanding of 'force'. It reproduces a liberal vision of a world in which people are *either* abject, passive objects, and slaves *or* freely contracting subjects, thereby missing the unseen, structural factors that force fates on men as well as women and children under the social relations of capitalism. It privileges a very particular kind of 'freedom'—what G. A. Cohen described as the 'the bare bourgeois freedom which distinguishes the most abject proletarian from the slave' (1995: 101).

Yet the liberal model of people as *either* objects *or* subjects also works to obscure the agency that people (women and children as well as adult men) exercise in choosing between the narrow range of fates available and working them as best they can to meet their own interests and goals. In this regard, neither Marxist nor feminist critiques always provide a clear counterpoint (O'Connell Davidson 2015). Representations of exploited workers of the Global South found in some Marxist writings, and of female migrant sex workers found in radical feminist writings, can sometimes look uncomfortably like the representations of 'victims of trafficking' and 'modern slaves' found in dominant liberal discourse. But when other commentators react against this by celebrating the action of such workers as a form of resistance against the exclusionary forces of neoliberal capitalism or patriarchal norms, it returns us to the dangers of entangling 'the categories of "humanity," "agency," and "resistance",' that Walter Johnson (2003: 115) identifies.

It is important to remember Marx's basic insight about the relationship between structure and agency—people make history, but not in circumstances of their own choosing–and to connect that to a different vision of the relation between agency and force, one that recognizes the human will as inalienable, and approaches agency 'as the capacity to act—differential, context specific, and always, in some fashion extant', as Svati Shah (2014: 199) puts it. The chapters in this volume on migration and domestic work (Mark Johnson), child labour (Okyere), and marriage (Grillot) all work with such a model of agency, exploring the ways in which agency is relationally constituted and related to the idea of 'compulsion by necessity'. They are based on ethnographic studies that do not reduce their research subjects to abject victims and suffering bodies, nor romanticise them as 'heroic subalterns'. They do not insist on a gendered and aged division between willing subjects or will-less objects, or attempt to correct for this by seeking to find liberalism's rugged individual subject wherever they look.

Volume Themes and Structure

The slave of contemporary anti-slavery concern, as much as the slave of anti-slavery discourse of the eighteenth and nineteenth century, remains a figure who illuminates the difference between 'a progressive modernity and its stagnating Others' (Purtschert 2010: 1049). 'Modern slavery' talk tells us much more about liberal understandings of modernity and Otherness than it does about the lived experience of those it names as 'slaves' (Kempadoo 2015). It shines a light on the way in which liberal modernity is imagined against particular understandings of race, nation, gender, labour, property, and freedom, all of which are core concerns of this book.

Approaching slavery as both a symbolic and a substantive issue, this volume is concerned with how slaveries were bound up in European imperialism, colonialism, and sovereignty in ways that continue to play out in the multiple and complex afterlives of slavery (Bhambra and Shilliam 2009; Hartman 2007; Bellagamba 2015). Its first section addresses the philosophical, theoretical, and definitional problems presented by the term 'slavery' and its imagined opposite, 'freedom'. Tommy Lott explores the historical development of the discourse in which slavery appears as uniquely and self-evidently morally wrong. He elucidates the overlaps between, on the one hand, various forms of slavery in the ancient and modern worlds, and on the other, servitude and other forms of drudgery in the same societies, highlighting the implications of these overlaps for analyses of phenomena grouped under the heading of 'modern slavery'. Mary Nyquist then examines the historical distinctions, dating back to the ancient world, between 'slavery' as a rhetorical figure and slavery as an economic institution; and between figurative 'freedom' and the privileges that actually did (or did not) attach to being legally 'free'. It is only when these different registers of 'slavery' and the complex relations that have developed historically between them are open to view that we can appreciate the ways in which 'slavery' past shapes the present in which we live, including its contribution to the white supremacist discourses inaugurated by Euro-colonialism.

Continuing Lott's concern with the overlaps between slavery and other systems of domination, Charlotte Sussman begins from the observation that European migration into indentured servitude in the Americas in the eighteenth century entailed such heavy and serious restraints on freedom that it is mistaken to imagine it as the opposite of slavery. Rather, 'slavery was the limit case at one end of a continuum of coerced movement and servitude'. Through a particular focus on the use of the term 'exile' to describe both emigrants and slaves, her chapter elucidates the way in which slavery and European migration came to be imaginatively untangled. Sussman suggests that the British Empire's dependence on the mobility of devalued populations, such as landless labourers, emigrants, and soldiers, necessitated the creation of the concept of 'freedom of movement,' and illuminates the role of abolitionist discourse in constructing that ideal.

Nandita Sharma's contribution takes as its starting point two ordinances regulating and restricting human migration by the local Council of the British colony of Mauritius, passed in 1835, soon after Britain's 1833 *Slavery Abolition Act*. These ordinances, she argues, 'were the beginning of the end of the regime of unrestricted human mobility of co-imperial subjects within the British Empire'. By detailing how a large-scale, state-controlled system of regulating and restricting the movement of workers emerged, Sharma reveals the 'coolie' labour system as the bridge between what Radhika Mongia calls the imperial-state 'logic of facilitation' and the nation-state 'logic of constraint' of human mobility. That national 'logic of constraint' on human mobility remains central to the reproduction of world capitalist markets for exploitable bodies, and yet it is left almost entirely uncontested in state- and NGO-driven discourse on 'trafficking' and 'modern slavery'. Today, as in past talk of 'protecting coolies', she concludes, the discursive practices of 'anti-trafficking' spectacularly fail the needs of people by failing to call for their free mobility across space and their freedom within nationalised labour markets.

The second section of the book moves to detailed studies of some of the present-day phenomena discussed under the heading of 'modern slavery'. It draws out the historical and political complexities and ambiguities of slavery by paying attention to contexts where the line between slavery and freedom has long been, and remains, most elusive. Through a focus on imprisonment (LeBaron), migrant domestic work (Johnson), marriage (Grillot), and child labour (Okyere), contributors examine restraints on freedom that are socially sanctioned, as well as those often dubbed 'modern slavery', and reflect on slavery and freedom as relative, not essential, categories. In this section, the problem spaces in between slavery and freedom are laid bare, as contributors explore the fuzziness of the lines between categories, the 'choice by default' (Grillot) that emerges from thinking about the complex and ambiguous realities of life worlds shaped by the pasts, presents, and futures of slavery.

The final section is oriented to the future. It considers anti-slavery activism past and present in relation to other political projects seeking to transform systems of domination, namely, class (Howard), gender (Roy), and race (Sexton). These contributions remind us both that calls to end 'slavery' are not the same as calls for freedom, and that the dominant ideal of universal human freedom today is rooted in interlocking histories of slavery, capitalism, patriarchy, and colonialism. It is an ideal of freedom that has separated and continues to separate 'some people whose liberties matter from others not to be included in that favoured category' (Sen 2009: 116), and that remains capable of producing unfreedom in its own name (Roy, this volume). In a world that is built upon but refuses to remember racial slavery, abolition is 'a protracted, perhaps interminable, process' (Sexton, this volume).

Notes

1. The Bill came into law in 2015.
2. Emancipation made interracial marriage and 'miscegenation' into urgent political questions in the US. They formed an important part of the ground on which the question of 'what freedom would for former slaves was to mean, what sort of citizenship African Americans would possess, what power they would hold relative to other free people' was debated (Rosen 2005: 291).
3. The UN Trafficking Protocol defines trafficking as: The recruitment, transportation, transfer, harbouring or receipt of persons, by means of

threat or use of force or other forms of coercion, of abduction, of fraud, of deception, of the abuse of power or of a position of vulnerability or of the giving or receiving of payments or benefits to achieve the consent of a person having control over another person, for the purpose of exploitation. Exploitation shall include, at a minimum, the exploitation of the prostitution of others or other forms of sexual exploitation, forced labour or services, slavery or practices similar to slavery, servitude or the removal of organs.The Protocol further provides that the consent of a VoT to the intended exploitation is irrelevant where any of the means set out above have been used.

References

Alexander, M. (2011). *The New Jim Crow*. New York: The New Press.

Anderson, B., & O'Connell Davidson, J. (2003). Is Trafficking in Human Beings Demand Driven? A Multi-Country Pilot Study. *IOM Migration Research Series*, No. 15. Geneva: IOM.

Andrees, B. (2014). http://www.theguardian.com/global-development-professionals-network/2014/jan/31/child-slavery-legal-definitions-ilo.

Ashworth, J. (1992). The Relationship Between Capitalism and Humanitarianism. In T. Bender (Ed.), *The AntiSlavery Debate*. Berkeley: University of California Press.

Bales, K. (1999). *Disposable People: New Slavery in the Global Economy*. Berkeley: University of California Press.

Bales, K. (2004). *New Slavery: A Reference Handbook*. Santa Barbara, CA: ABC-CLIO.

Bales. K. (2012). Slavery in Its Contemporary Manifestations. In J. Allain (Ed.), *The Legal Understanding of Slavery*. Oxford: Oxford University Press.

Balfour, L. (2005). Reparations After Identity Politics. *Political Theory, 33*(6), 786–811.

Batstone, D. (2007). *Not for Sale: The Return of the Global Slave Trade–And How We Can Fight It*. New York: HarperCollins.

Beckles, H. (1987). *Black Rebellion in Barbados*. Bridgetown and Barbados: Carib Research & Publications.

Bellagamba, A. (2015). Living in the Shadows of Slavery. *Beyond Trafficking and Slavery*. https://wwwopendemocracy.net/beyondslavery/alice-bellagamba/living-in-the-shadows-of-slavery.

Bellagama, A. (2016, July 18). Living in the Shadows of Slavery. *Beyond Trafficking & Slavery, openDemocracy*. https://www.opendemocracy.net/beyondslavery/alice-bellagamba/living-in-shadows-of-slavery. Accessed 20 Dec 2016.
Bellagamba, A., Greene, S., & Klein, M. (2016). *African Voices on Slavery and the Slave Trade*. Cambridge: Cambridge University Press.
Berlin, I., Hahn, S., Miller, S., Reidy, J., & Rowland, L. (1986). The Terrain of Freedom: The Struggle Over the Meaning of Free Labor in the U. S. South. *History Workshop Journal, 22*(1), 108–130.
Bhambra, G. (2007). *Rethinking Modernity*. London: Palgrave Macmillan.
Bhambra, G. K. (2016). Undoing the Epistemic Disavowal of the Haitian Revolution: A Contribution to Global Social Thought. *Journal of Intercultural Studies, 37*(1), 1–16.
Bhambra, G., & Shilliam, R. (Eds.). (2009). *Silencing Human Rights*. Houndmills: Palgrave Macmillan.
Bhandar, B. (2014). Property, Law, and Race: Modes of Abstraction. *U.C. Irvine L. Rev*. No. 4, 211.
Black Alliance for Just Immigration. (2016). *The State of Black Immigrants*. www.stateofblackimmigrants.com.
Blackburn, R. (2011). *The American Crucible: Slavery, Emancipation and Human Rights*. London: Verso.
Broome, A., & Quirk, J. (2015). The Politics of Numbers: The Normative Agendas of Global Benchmarking. *Review of International Studies, 43,* 813–818.
Brown, V. (2009, December). Social Death and Political Life in the Study of Slavery. *American Historical Review, 114*(5), 1231–1249.
Buckley, R. (1979). *Slaves in Red Coats: The British West India Regiments, 1795–1815*. New Haven: Yale University Press.
Caleb McDaniel, W. (2013). *The Problem of Democracy in the Age of Slavery: Garrisonian Abolitionists and Transatlantic Reform*. Baton Rouge: LSU Press.
Camp, S. (2004). *Closer to Freedom*. London: University of North Carolina Press.
Carey, B., & Kitson, P. (Eds.). (2007). *Slavery and the Cultures of Abolition: Essays Marking the Bicentennial of the British Abolition Act of 1807*. Basingstoke: Boydell and Brewer.
Cesaire, A. (1972). *Discourse on Colonialism*. New York, NY: Monthly Review Press.
Childs, D. (2015). *Slaves of the State*. Minneapolis: University of Minnesota Press.
Chuang, J. (2013). Exploitation Creep and the Unmaking of Human Trafficking Law. American University, *WCL Research Paper*. http://ssrn.com/abstract=2315513.

Cohen, G. A. (1995). *Self-ownership, Freedom and Equality*. Cambridge: Cambridge University Press.
Cohen, R. (2006). *Migration and Its Enemies: Global Capital, Migrant Labour and the Nation State*. Aldershot: Ashgate.
Collins, O. (2006). The African Slave Trade to Asia and the Indian Ocean Islands. *African and Asian Studies, 5*(3–4), 325–346.
Colosio, V. (2016, July 19). Memories and Legacies of Enslavement in Chad. *Beyond Trafficking & Slavery, openDemocracy*. https://www.opendemocracy.net/beyondslavery/valerio-colosio/memories-and-legacies-of-enslavement-in-chad.
Davis, D. (1992). The Problem of Slavery in the Age of Revolution, 1770–1823. In T. Bender (Ed.), *The Antislavery Debate*. Berkeley: University of California Press.
Davis, D. B. (1966). *The Problem of Slavery in Western Culture*. Ithaca, New York: Cornell University Press.
Davis, D. B. (1975). *The Problem of Slavery in the Age of Revolution*. Ithaca, New York: Cornell University Press.
Davis, A. (2003). *Are Prisons Obsolete?* New York, NY: Seven Stories Press.
Davis, D. (2003). *Challenging the Boundaries of Slavery*. Cambridge, MA: Harvard University Press.
Davis, D. (2014). *The Problem of Slavery in the Age of Emancipation*. London: Penguin Random House.
Doezema, J. (2010). *Sex Slaves and Discourse Masters*. London: Zed Books.
Du Bois, W. E. B. (1992). *Black Reconstruction in America*. New York: The Free Press.
Finley, M. (1964, April). Between Slavery and Freedom. *Comparative Studies in Society and History, 6*(3), 233–249.
Fischer, S. (2004). *Modernity Disavowed: Haiti and the Cultures of Slavery in the Age of Revolution*. Durham and London: Duke University Press.
Foner, E. (1995 [1970]). *Free Soil, Free Labor, Free Men: The Ideology of the Republican Party Before the Civil War*. New York: Oxford University Press.
Foner, E. (1990). *A Short History of Reconstruction, 1863–1877*. New York: Harper & Row.
Genovese, E. (1965). *The Political Economy of Slavery: Studies in the Economy and the Society of the Slave South*. New York: Pantheon Books.
Ghallagher, A. (2016, June 28). Unravelling the 2016 Global Slavery Index. *50:50, openDemocracy*. https://www.opendemocracy.net/anne-gallagher/unravelling-2016-global-slavery-index. Accessed 21 Dec 2016.
Golash-Boza, T. (2012). *Due Process Denied*. London: Routledge.
Guenther, L. (2012). The Most Dangerous Place: Pro-life Politics and the Rhetoric of Slavery. *Postmodern Culture, 22*(2).

Haley, S. (2016). *No Mercy Here: Gender, Punishment, and the Making of Jim Crow Modernity*. Chapel Hill: The University of North Carolina Press.
Hall, C. (2002). *Civilising Subjects*. Cambridge: Polity.
Hartman, S. (1997). *Scenes of Subjection*. Oxford: Oxford University Press.
Hartman, S. (2007). *Lose Your Mother: A Journey Along the Atlantic Slave Route*. New York: Farrar, Straus and Giroux.
Hashim, I., & Thronsen, D. (2011). *Child Migration in Africa*. London: Zed.
Haskell, T. (1998). *Objectivity is not Neutrality*. Baltimore: Johns Hopkins University Press.
Hathaway, J. (2008). The Human Rights Quagmire of "Human Trafficking". *Virginia Journal of International Law, 49*(1), 1–59.
Howard, N., & Morganti, S. (2015). (Not!) Child Trafficking in Benin. In M. Dragiewicz (Ed.), *Global Human Trafficking* (pp. 91–104). London: Routledge.
James, C. L. R. (2001). *The Black Jacobins*. London: Penguin.
Jean-Marie, V. (2013). Kant and Trouillot and on the Unthinkability of the Haitian Revolution. *Souls, 15*(3), 241–257.
Jennison, W. (2012). *Cultivating Race*. Lexington: University Press of Kentucky.
Johnson, W. (2003, Fall). On Agency. *Journal of Social History, 3*(1), 113–124.
Johnson, A. (2016). Stealing Freedom: Attempts to Re-enslave Blacks in Post-emancipation Barbados. *Beyond Trafficking and Slavery*. https://www.opendemocracynet/beyondslavery/alana-johnson/stealing-freedom-attempts-to-re-enslave-blacks-in-post-emancipation-barb.
Jordan, M. (2005). *The Great Abolition Sham*. Stroud: Sutton.
Kempadoo, K. (2015, January 11). The White Man's Burden Revisited. *Beyond Slavery and Trafficking*. https://www.opendemocracy.net/beyondslavery/kamala-kempadoo/white-man's-burden-revisited.
Kendi, I. (2016). *Stamped From the Beginning*. New York: Nation Books.
Kopytoff, I. (1982). Slavery. *Annual Review of Anthropology, 11*, 207–230.
Kristine, L. (2012, January). Photos That Bear Witness to Modern Slavery. *TEDx*. http://www.ted.com/talks/lisa_kristine_glimpses_of_modern_day_slavery. Accessed 16 Mar 2015.
Lake, M. (2014). "The Day Will Come": Charles H. Pearson's *National Life and Character: A Forecast*. In A. Burton & I. Hofmeyr (Eds.), *Ten Books that Shaped the British Empire* (pp. 90–111). London: Duke University Press.
Lambert, D. (2016). *Slaves to Soldiers*. https://blogs.warwick.ac.uk/asua/entry/slaves_to_soldiers/. Accessed 20 July 2016.
LeFlouria, T. (2016). *Chained in Silence: Black Women and Convict Labor in the New South*. Chapel Hill: The University of North Carolina Press.

Lively, A. (1998). *Masks: Blackness, Race and the Imagination*. London: Chatto and Windus.
Lively, A. (1999). *Blackness, Race and the Imagination*. London: Vintage.
Lott, T. (1998). Early Enlightenment Conceptions of the Rights of Slaves. In T. Lott (Ed.), *Subjugation and Bondage* (pp. 99–130). New York: Rowman and Littlefield.
May, T. (2013). Theresa May: The Abhorrent Evil of Human Trafficking Taking Place on London's Streets. *Metro Blogs*. http://metro.co.uk/2013/10/14/theresa-may-the-evil-of-modern-day-slavery-taking-place-on-londons-streets-4144671/. Accessed 10 Jan 2015.
McNally, T. (2009, August 24). There are More Slaves Today Than at Any Time in History. *Alternet*. http://www.alternet.org/story/142171/there_are_more_slaves_today_than_at_any_time_in_human_history./. Accessed 10 Sept 2016.
Meillassoux, C. (1991). *The Anthropology of Slavery*. London: Athlone.
Midlo Hall, G. (1998). *Africans in Colonial Louisiana*. Baton Rouge: Louisiana State University Press.
Miers, S. (2004). Slavery: A Question of Definition. In G. Campbell (Ed.), *The Structure of Slavery in Indian Ocean Africa and Asia* (pp. 1–16). London: Frank Cass.
Miller, J. C. (2012). *The Problem of Slavery as History: A Global Approach*. New Haven and London: Yale University Press.
Mills, C. (1998). *The Racial Contract*. Ithaca: Cornell University Press.
Mongia, R. (1999). Race, Nationality, Mobility: A History of the Passport. *Public Culture, 11*(13), 527–556.
Morgan, P., & O'Shaughnessy, A. (2006). Arming Slaves in the American Revolution. In C. Brown & P. Morgan (Eds.), *Arming Slaves: From Classical Times to the Modern Age*. New Haven: Yale University Press.
Noble, D. (2017). *Decolonizing and Feminizing Freedom*. London: Palgrave.
Novak, D. (1978). *The Wheel of Servitude: Black Forced Labor after Slavery*. Lexington, KT: University Press of Kentucky.
Nzula, A., Potekhin, I., & Zusmanovich, A. (1979). *Forced Labour in Colonial Africa*. London: Zed.
O'Connell Davidson, J. (2015). *Modern Slavery: The Margins of Freedom*. London: Palgrave Macmillan.
Paton, D. (2009). Interpreting the Bicentenary in Britain. *Slavery and Abolition, 30*(2), 277–289.
Patterson, O. (1982). *Slavery and Social Death*. Cambridge, MA: Harvard University.
Pleasants, N. (2010). Moral Argument is Not Enough: The Persistence of Slavery and the Emergence of Abolition. *Philosophical Topics, 38*(1), 159–180.

Potts, L. (1990). *The World Labour Market*. London: Zed.
Price, R. (1979). *Maroon Societies: Revel Slave Communities in the Americas*. Baltimore, MA: The John Hopkins University Press.
Purtschert, P. (2010). On the Limit of Spirit: Hegel's Racism Revisited. *Philosophy and Social Criticism, 36*(9), 1039–1051.
Quirk, J. (2006). The Anti-Slavery Project: Linking the Historical and the Contemporary. *Human Rights Quarterly, 28*(3), 565–598.
Quirk, J. (2011). *The Anti-Slavery Project*. Philadelphia: University of Pennsylvania Press.
Rinehart, N. (2016). The Man That was a Thing: Reconsidering Human Commodification in Slavery. *Journal of Social History, 50*(1), 1–23.
Roberts, N. (2015). *Freedom as Marronage*. Chicago: University of Chicago Press.
Rosen, H. (2005). The Rhetoric of Miscegenation and the Reconstruction of Race: Debating Marriage, Sex, and Citizenship in Postemancipation Arkansas. In P. Scully & D. Paton (Eds.), *Gender and Slave Emancipation in the Atlantic World*. London: Duke University Press.
Sen, A. (2009). *The Idea of Justice*. Harvard: Harvard University Press.
Scott, D. (2004). *Conscripts of Modernity*. Durham and London: Duke University Press.
Shah, S. (2014). *Street Corner Secrets: Sex, Work, and Migration in the City of Mumbai*. London: Duke University Press.
Shilliam, R. (2012). Forget English Freedom, Remember Atlantic Slavery: Common Law, Commercial Law, and the Significance of Slavery for Classical Political Economy. *New Political Economy, 17*(5), 591–609.
The Debate on a Motion for the Abolition of the Slave Trade in the House of Commons, 1792.
Thomas, H. (1997). *The Slave Trade*. London: Picador.
Tinker, H. (1974). *A New System of Slavery: The Export of Indian Labour Overseas, 1830–1920*. London: Oxford University Press.
US Department of State (2003). *Trafficking in Persons Report*. http://www.state.gov/documents/organization/21555.pdf.
Williams, E. (1944). *Capitalism and Slavery*. New York: Putnam.
Williams, K. (2016). An Introduction to the Indian Ocean Slave Trade. *MediaDiversified*.
Wong, E. (2009). *Neither Fugitive Nor Free*. New York, NY: New York University Press.
Wood, M. (2010). *The Horrible Gift of Freedom: Atlantic Slavery and the Representation of Emancipation*. London: University of Georgia Press.
Woods, T. (2013). Surrogate Selves: Notes on Anti-trafficking and Anti-blackness. *Social Identities, 19*(1), 120–134.

2
Contextualizing Slavery's Wrongness

Tommy Lott

Notions of slavery are employed in various ways, mostly to indicate wrongfulness, yet the question of why slavery is wrong turns on a somewhat elusive definition of the concept. In this chapter, I highlight the existence of overlapping cases involving various forms of unfree labour, such as indentured servitude and debt bondage, which are sometimes indistinguishable from slavery as an important reason to be sceptical of any definition based on a peculiar injustice unique to slavery. Given that there are cases involving forms of unfree labour analogous to slavery, proponents of the idea of 'modern slavery' often suppose this to refer to an underlying social injustice that multifarious instantiations share in common. I want to extend my earlier view to include a critical examination of the term slavery, suggested in part by Thomas Hobbes and John Locke, which has an application to a variety of unjust practices often cited in literature on human trafficking. I oppose using the term 'slavery' when this is meant only as a metaphor for analogous unjust

T. Lott (✉)
San Jose State University, San Jose, CA, USA
e-mail: tommy.lott@email.sjsu.edu

L. Brace and J. O'Connell Davidson (eds.), *Revisiting Slavery and Antislavery*,
https://doi.org/10.1007/978-3-319-90623-2_2

practices we wish to condemn—especially when the metaphorical usage functions largely to supply a justification for the condemnation.

Previously, I have argued that conceptions of slavery that rely on the idea that it involves a violation of natural rights, while not wholly misguided, fail to specify an injustice peculiar, or unique, to slavery (Lott 1998). On this occasion, I want to reconsider this particular shortcoming of the definitions presented by Hobbes and Locke in the light of current anti-human-trafficking policies regarding transoceanic labour exploitation—sometimes referred to as 'modern slavery' (Bales 2005; Kapstein 2006). My earlier view aimed to show that, given the overlap of slavery with certain forms of servitude, both practices should be condemned as unjust. I now want to consider whether both should count as slavery.

I begin with a consideration of some of the implications of the practice of selling oneself into slavery that was legally permitted early on in Greek and Roman law, and governed by a set of rules in the *Bible*. I take this practice to represent a challenge to the assumption that slavery is inherently evil. Sometimes, philosophers who believe that slavery is an unjust social practice, nonetheless allow it as morally permissible because it is 'less unjust' than its alternative (Rawls 1971: 248). This is a sign that, with regard to slavery's wrongness, there are shades of gray. Throughout my discussion, I treat the concept of slavery as inherently ambiguous on the question of whether it is always wrong.

Next, I examine more closely the social and political significance of a contract in definitions of slavery offered by Hobbes and Locke. Human trafficking cases involving migrant labour often involve questions regarding the voluntary status of a contract and whether it is sufficiently consensual. Locke appeals to a contract to ground his re-categorization of self-selling into slavery as drudgery. I respond to this by first indicating the importance of having the definition formulated at the 1926 League of Nations Convention on the Abolition of Slavery because it was meant to apply to unfree labour that counts as de facto slavery. I champion the appropriateness of a legal response to the legal re-categorization of unfree labour with a broader concept of slavery.

Hobbes' definition of slavery comes very close to the definition of serfdom proposed at the 1956 Convention, which focuses on the sense in which a serf is bound to the land. The second response that I employ in response to Locke's view of drudgery is to consider whether serfdom (or, debt peonage in nineteenth-century Mexico) is a form of slavery? I defend the overlap of serfdom and slavery against criticisms tendered by G.E.M. Ste. Croix and Orlando Patterson. I point out why Patterson's recent definition (Allain 2012) only re-instates his earlier account, on which serfdom was, at times, indistinguishable from slavery (Patterson 1991). With regard to serfdom and other forms of unfree labour, I bring in Hegel's account of domination to shed light on their inter-relations and intersections with various forms of slavery.

On what criteria do we decide whether an overlapping case of unfree labour, that literally intersects with slavery in time and locale, should count as slavery? To draw comparisons between indentured servants and slaves, I critically examine a case involving Chinese indentured servants, who worked side by side with African slaves on plantations in nineteenth-century Cuba. I insist that, to count as virtual slavery, a de facto case must be *indistinguishable* in all relevant respects.

Kevin Bales' concern with consenting 'victims' of sex trafficking involves, more broadly, a question of whether voluntary self-selling into slavery is morally wrong. I ask whether marriage is a version of a self-sale slavery contract. I then discuss Mill's view of marriage as a form of enslavement to examine the idea of a slavery contract. I employ Robert Nozick's libertarian view that un-coerced slavery contracts are valid to make plausible Mill's argument that, because marriage constitutes lifelong domestic servitude, it is a form of slavery for women. The lesson I draw from reflecting on Mill's view is that the concept of slavery accommodates a consent-based paradigm, as well as a coercion-based paradigm (Ellerman 2010; Drescher 2012).

The Dominance of Pro-Slavery in Antiquity

The permissiveness of earlier Judeo-Christian views of the wrongness of slavery contrasts sharply with the abolitionist stance later associated with the Enlightenment. Two main sources of slaves in antiquity were debt bondage and war captives. Although both were initially conceived as forms of slavery, a changing socio-historical context in Greece and Rome occasioned a re-categorization of debt bondage. Solon's reforms in early seventh-century Athens aimed to reduce an over-abundance of debt-slaves, many of whom were farmers who had been driven into slavery by the growth of a propertied aristocracy (Plutarch, 75 A.C.E.). In the early Republican period, not all slaves were war captives, and many debt-slaves were Roman citizens—a practice later abolished in the fourth century. Bernard Jackson characterizes debt bondage in the classical context as a temporary enslavement of Greeks and Romans, whereas permanent enslavement was largely reserved for foreigners (1988: 87–91).

Free citizens in antiquity sometimes voluntarily enslaved themselves to wealthy masters for the opportunities this would provide. Jackson describes this version of Roman debt bondage in third century AD as 'voluntary self-sale', whereby a debtor could voluntarily enter into bondage to a creditor and share the profit (1988: 90).[1] In the Roman context, debt slavery was not only a way to survive, for some, it also afforded a means of seeking economic gain. What should we say about slaves who belonged to slaves—a practice the Romans permitted (Martin 1990)? Although, technically, such slaves were legally owned by the masters of the slaves that bought them, nonetheless, they were possessions that could eventually be used to purchase freedom. The Roman abolition of debt bondage as a form of slavery is reflected in Biblical law as a distinction between temporary and permanent slavery.[2]

Locke on Slavery and Drudgery

In different ways, Thomas Hobbes and John Locke relied on the idea of a contract to distinguish servitude and slavery. They employed the paradigm, from antiquity, of a war captive, to whom a contract is extended on the condition that he obeys the master, and he, thereby, becomes a servant, or he is not granted this option and becomes a slave. Their paradigm of a slave is a trans-historical 'servant taken in wars' who does not have a labour contract (Hobbes 1642). Although their views of slavery have an application in the current discourse on human trafficking, it is important to note here that their respective definitions of slavery were not modelled on the trans-Atlantic slave trade, of which, both had a direct hand. Locke was an investor in the Royal African Company and authored, *The Fundamental Constitution of Carolina* (1670). Hobbes attended meetings with administrators of the Virginia Company (Malcolm 2002). Rather than addressing directly the slavery, they condoned in their personal lives; they were preoccupied in their writings with a critique of Aristotle's account of authority in the household. Ironically, their social contract theories provided a basis for rejecting Aristotle's claims regarding natural slaves. Nevertheless, the anti-slavery stance represented in different ways by their respective theories, contrasts sharply with their exclusion (and evasion) of any application of their accounts to the stark racism that grounded the European enslavement of Africans (Uzgalis 1998).

Locke defines slavery as being subject to the 'absolute, arbitrary power' of a master (Locke 1689: 4.22). A contract sets a limit on the amount and duration of service. Once a slave enters into a contract, his condition is changed from slavery 'only to drudgery' (1689: 4.24). Locke explicitly rejects a self-sale agreement as a valid slavery contract and insists that a voluntary slavery contract is inherently invalid because 'no man can, by agreement, pass over to another that which he hath not in himself, a power over his own life' (Locke 1689: 4.24) The subtlety of this claim is elusive because he allows unjust aggressors, when taken as war captives, to yield such power, as a matter of *forfeiture*. This suggests that, for those who violate the Law of Nature, liberty and a right to life are not inalienable.

It is really the nature of the contract granted to servants that distinguishes slavery and servitude on Locke's account. A servant's contract explicitly limits the master's power, whereas the slave's tacit no resistance-no death agreement, is an acknowledgement of the master's absolute power. When Locke stipulated that, to count as only drudgery, a contract must limit the duration of service, he wanted to rule out counting self-sale agreements—which are temporary—as slavery contracts. Long before he drew this distinction between slavery and drudgery, the idea that slavery can be distinguished from debt bondage by an agreement that establishes a time limit had already been employed in antiquity for ideological reasons (Jackson 1988: 86). The re-categorization of debt slavery, which could be voluntary and temporary, as debt bondage aimed to distinguish it from the permanent slavery reserved for war captives who were outsiders. According to this policy, a debt bondsman could only be sold into permanent slavery by being sent abroad. If the difference between a slave's implied contract and a servant's explicit contract is that, in the former, the duration of service is life-long, while in the latter, it is temporary, this amounts only to a distinction between a permanent and a temporary slave.

As a substitute for enslavement, Locke appears to allow war captives the option of becoming a servant with rights. His concealment of the coercion involved in the captive's election of servitude, however, is revealed when this choice is juxtaposed with immediate death, or lifelong enslavement, as alternatives. The nature of the servitude is also concealed. How different is the condition of the servant from that of the slave on Locke's view? Although he never conceives the slave as property, with regard to reparations for costs incurred by war, the servitude option includes a consideration of the victor's property-loss that could result in lifelong servitude for war captives. In the case of a costly war, the possibility that a captive will have a lifelong labour contract is entirely consistent with Locke's account. Despite the potential overlap of plight shared by a slave and a servant in this regard, Locke would rely on the idea of a contract to distinguish a servant's identical situation as, nonetheless, only drudgery. In such cases, servants are really 'statutory slaves' and the function of a contract is to legitimate this (Gorsuch 2012: 162).

Slavery and Drudgery in International Law

Locke's appeal to the existence of a contract to distinguish between drudgery and slavery is problematic for reasons that have a bearing on two central issues—coercion and exploitation—that are often cited in anti-human trafficking legislation in the US.[3] I shall have more to say below regarding the use of force and fraud to obtain labour contracts in cases of indentured servitude and debt bondage. Here, I want to point out that Locke's distinction between slavery and drudgery was called into question at the League of Nations convention on slavery in 1926. Slavery was defined as 'the status or condition of a person over whom any or all of the powers attaching to the right of ownership are exercised' (Allain 2012). Notice that this definition does not require legal ownership. Instead, it only stipulates that a master exercises power over another person that is normally associated with ownership. Moreover, with greater emphasis on power relations, it is a conception of slavery that extends readily to various forms of unfree labour—whether, or not, a contract exists. To what extent, however, are we entitled to include different forms of unfree labour under the rubric of slavery?

At the Geneva Convention in 1956 *Debt Bondage* Was Defined as '[T]he status or condition arising from a pledge by a debtor of his personal services, or those of a third person under his control, as a security for a debt, where a value reasonably assessed of those services rendered is not applied towards the liquidation of the debt, or the length and nature of those services are not respectively limited and defined' (Allain 2012).

Ste. Croix takes this to mean that, while the debt bondsman's labour is at the disposal of his creditor, he remains a free citizen and regains his original status when he works off his debt. If a debt bondsman can remain in lifelong bondage, as Ste. Croix admits many did, this 'freedom' appears to be only a legal technicality that prevents the bondsman from being *referred* to as a slave. The significance of this distinction of being free 'in principle' depends on whether the status of debt bondsman, in fact, allows greater access to freedom than the status of chattel slave. Nonetheless, Ste. Croix's distinction between a debt bondsman and a slave in antiquity seems inconsistent with his acknowledgement that Aristotle thought manumission should be offered to slaves as an incentive (Ste. Croix 1988: 24).

With the idea of physical constraint in mind, Hobbes defined slavery as the denial of corporal liberty (e.g., to be held in chains, or bonds), or the denial of freedom of movement (e.g., imprisonment) (Hobbes 1652/1994: 131). This notion of slavery is reflected in the Geneva Convention's definition of *serfdom*. It is defined as 'The tenure of land whereby the tenant is, by law, custom, or agreement bound to live and labor on land belonging to another person and render some determinate services to such other person, whether for reward or not, and is not free to change his status' (Allain 2012). The serf's services are rendered to the lord, with the inability to move away, or to liberate himself. For Hobbes, this level of physical constraint on serfs is not sufficient to count as slavery. Although, perhaps, serfs had limited travel, their 'denial of corporal liberty', otherwise, included no physical constraint to prevent escape. There are two conditions, cited by Ste. Croix, that further distinguish serfs. His first has to do with Locke's stipulation regarding a limit on the quantity of labour, but is mitigated by his admission that serfs were unlikely to refuse a demand for additional labour.

The second condition Ste. Croix cites to distinguish serfs from slaves is the right to marry. Perhaps, in the case of Greek chattel slavery, slaves rarely were granted a legal right to marry. However, in the slave system of the American South, marriage was an important incentive and slaves were permitted to marry. Many free blacks married slaves with the expectation of someday purchasing their freedom. Slave families faced a dreaded threat of members being sold, for, even if this was no further than twenty miles, the difficulty of travel for slaves rendered the maintenance of contact impossible (Fields 1987: 23). Even though slaves had families, due to their being denied freedom of movement, when sold elsewhere, often they would be permanently separated from their families.

The conception of serfdom as always vastly different from chattel slavery seems to ignore the overlap of different forms of slavery, as well as the intersection of multiple forms of slavery with various forms of unfree labour. The employment of agrarian slave labour sometimes involved both chattel field slaves, and household slaves who were domestic servants. There was more than status attaching to these different positions. A plantation in the US would include the personal slaves of the master and mistress, which, in some states, had a fairly strong tradition of granting manumission to personal slaves, at the death of a master (Jacobs 1861). After the Civil War changing socio-historical conditions brought about a legal transformation of former chattel field slaves, with no families, into serfs (sharecroppers) with families, to perpetuate bonded labour. Marriage and manumission are not features that distinguish serfdom and slavery, rather a closer look at their role in slave systems can reveal the interplay of slavery and other forms of unfree labour.

Coerced Wage Labour and Voluntary Serfdom

In his study of unfree labour in Latin America between 1500 and 1800, Alan Knight has identified an intermediate, hybrid category of serfdom that he refers to as 'debt peonage' (Knight 1988). He points out that, in the nineteenth century, Mexico had 750,000 chattel slaves and five million debt peons. There were three distinct types of debt peons. In type (1) pay advances that resulted in debt were an incentive to lure subsistence peasants on to plantations. Coercion was 'superfluous and counter-productive' given the emergence of free wage labour that was employed mostly on a voluntary basis. In this case peasants were induced by a market-supply mode of exploitation to become proletarians. Type (2) peonage was a more traditional serfdom that had flourished in colonial Mexico. In this case debt functioned as part of a labour contract. When the supply of labourers favoured employers, land owners curtailed debt, often against the wishes of peons. Knight maintains that 'These were, in effect, "voluntary" peons in the same sense that proletarians are "voluntary" wage labourers' (Knight 1988: 109). The desire to replace peonage with a system of pure wage-labour was regularly thwarted by peasants who preferred peonage as a better option.

Type (3) peonage was much more servile and coercive. This type developed in regions where labour supply was scarce. Labourers were 'dragooned' on to estates and maintained there by coercion. It warrants the question of whether debt peonage was, in some cases, a form of de facto slavery.[4] It also raises concerns regarding the moral implications of the manner in which debt peonage functioned in a context where slavery continued under another form of unfree labour long after formal slavery had been abolished. Knight raises the question of whether we should view debt-peons as surrogate slaves, or as a surrogate proletariat. He argues that the crucial factor that marks the difference is a consideration of whether extra-economic coercion—physical and political—is required. What complicates sorting this out in the case of Mexico is the fact that there were several types of debt peonage, which included coerced wage labourers (type (3)), *and* voluntary serfs (type (2)).

It was, in fact, a reconsideration of 'convergent serfdom' in Europe that led Orlando Patterson (1991) to give up his claim that natal alienation is the essential ingredient uniquely peculiar to slavery. With regard to the convergence of serfdom and slavery in the Middle Ages Patterson claims that 'Freedmen status was so circumscribed, and the continued dependency on the ex-master, now patron, so similar, that there was little objective socioeconomic difference between the freed tenant and the domiciled slave' (Patterson 1991: 354). He cites the fact that, in the sixth century, European serfs were predominantly foreign-born and that, for this reason, they were also natally alienated. According to Patterson, 'The element of slavery that in ancient times had been most constitutive of the relation, natal alienation, was increasingly shared with the bonded person. The only real difference between serfs and slaves pertained to the element of honor, of which slaves had none and serfs some, however small'. Under feudal serfdom there was a shift toward recognition by the ruling class that serfs had natal rights (Patterson 1991: 357). He then points out that feudal serfs were 'characterized by the two slave-like attributes of degradation and powerlessness'. Under this 'proprietary' form of serfdom 'serfs were bought and sold all over western Europe.... They were slaves in all but name'. He acknowledges several transitions, and the possibility of evolving coexistence and recombinations of slavery and serfdom, beginning with the substitution of slaves for serfs in antiquity, whose status shifted gradually into a proprietary serfdom that in the feudal period 'changed to convergent serfdom and was rapidly on the way to becoming pure slavery once again' (Patterson 1991: 358–362).

Patterson abandons the definition he presented in *Slavery and Social Death* to propose, instead, a definition that allows other overlapping forms of unfree labour to share the three features that define slavery—dishonour, powerlessness, and natality. He insisted that slavery is distinguishable in that, unlike other forms of unfree labour, only it has all three features at once (Patterson 1991: 351). Patterson can be taken to have replaced his earlier conception of slavery, which specified natal alienation as a uniquely peculiar injustice of slavery not shared with other forms of unfree labour, with a multiple component concept.

In a more recent discussion of slavery and human trafficking Patterson rejects the League of Nations definition as mistaken. He revives his argument from *Slavery and Social Death* that, because legal ownership is not unique to slavery, it is not a defining feature. He fails to consider that legal ownership per se is not stipulated by the League of Nations definition. Rather, what is regarded as slavery, according to the definition, is the exercising of the powers that *attach* to ownership. The emphasis is on the treatment of humans, *as if* they are owned. This conception of slavery is entirely focused on the abuse of power to which slaves are subjected; especially, their treatment by their masters as having no rights whatever.

As a better offering, Patterson presents his own polythetic definition. According to Patterson, '[W]e define slavery as the violent, corporeal possession of socially isolated and parasitically degraded persons' (Patterson 2012: 6). He tells us that this definition is derived from a paradigm of the female slave. By allowing this definition to refer 'to a class of objects which have many but not all properties in common', he seems to avoid the need for a definition that has universal application to all the diverse forms of slavery. However, it is not clear whether he meant to *replace* his original universal definition from *Slavery and Social*

Death entirely, or whether he only intended to *subsume* his polythetic definition under a rejuvenated version of his universal definition—as one among many paradigms of slavery, each of which has its own polythetic definition. This approach, of course, raises a question of whether all the different paradigms can be subsumed under a monolithic concept of slavery? What about paradigms of slavery involving social mobility? The paradigm of 'self-selling' into slavery, cited above, involved Greek and Roman citizens entering slavery voluntarily. There is a similar paradigm of military slaves, involving slaves and their offspring intermarrying into nobility, that Patterson's universal definition cannot accommodate (Eaton 2005; Chanana 1960).

Patterson wants his polythetic definition to extend the concept of slavery to include sex trafficking as an analogous case that may not fully satisfy a formal definition. The polythetic definition of slavery that he extends to sex trafficking, nonetheless, reflects the three defining features of his earlier universal definition. Natal alienation has been replaced with 'social isolation', and there is an added Hobbesian feature of 'corporeal possession'. His strategy of relying on a paradigm-based definition of slavery commits him to count, as slavery, any analogous unjust practice with a sufficiently similar configuration of properties. His inclusion of sex trafficking, using this criterion, also commits him to an inclusion of identical configurations shared by slaves and wives.

In his well-known parable, 'Of Lordship and Bondage' Hegel characterizes the master-slave relationship by abstracting certain ingredients from notions advanced earlier by Hobbes and Locke (Hegel 1976). There is no state of nature or contracts, but there is a struggle for power that involves a Hobbesian risk of death by the master and a fear of death by the slave. For Hobbes, conquest is a ritual that establishes an agreement to submit to the authority of the conqueror, but only as long as the conqueror can maintain a monopoly on power over his subjects. The vanquished retain a right of nature that is inalienable. No agreement with a conqueror overrides a right to resist—which is understood by both parties to always be in play, even after submission. Hence, the act of conquest is justified as a right of nature and resistance to conquest is justified as a right of nature. The fact that Hobbes allows both parties to act, with justification, on this basis sets up a dynamic similar to the dialectical transactions between master and slave that Hegel employs in his parable.

On Hegel's view, domination is exhibited in terms of recognition by the slave of a master as an independent subject, while the slave views himself as a dependent non-subject. Hegel follows Locke to the extent that the slave's will is subjected to the master's will, and, repeatedly re-subjected, in an ongoing series of dialectical exchanges between them. Unlike Hobbes and Locke, Hegel was not concerned with spelling out a definition of slavery. Nonetheless, the League of Nations' definition follows his more abstract view of the master-slave relationship. Unlike proponents of the idea of modern slavery, Hegel had European serfdom in mind, and not the chattel slavery of the trans-Atlantic trade. The broad scope of the League of Nations' definition allows an application to human trafficking cases in which issues pertaining to coercion and consent are often ambiguous. We saw how this binary breaks down in the case of debt peonage in Mexico. In the case I examine next I explore further the ambiguous nature of contracted labour with regard to coercion and consent.

The Overlap of Slavery and Servitude in Practice

Even with definitions of various forms of unfree labour, that stipulate the existence of a contract in each case, and which *in principle* distinguishes them from slavery, there remains a question of whether they can always be distinguished from slavery *in practice*. What accounts for certain indistinguishable cases is the fact that some forms of unfree labour, as a source of slaves, have been historically interconnected with slavery. The ancient practice of selling debt bondsmen into slavery to pay off the debt accompanied a common practice of free and unfree labourers working side by side (Ste. Croix 1981: 133). In their study of the trafficking of Chinese coolies into Cuba, Lisa Yun and Ricardo Laremont (2001) present a case from the mid-nineteenth century involving the literal overlap of Chinese indentured servitude and the enslavement of Africans *in practice*. They report that on smaller plantations, Chinese indentured servants could be 50% of the labour force. This case raises not only the question of whether, as exploited labour, African slaves and Chinese indentured servants received the same treatment, but also raises a question regarding the dubious nature of coolie contracts. Given the absolute power that planters had over labourers, the ambiguous nature of coercion and consent was an important factor in negotiating and enforcing contracts. Yun and Laremont tell us that, by extending the coolie's debt, contractual obligations were 'engineered against the possibility of freedom' (Yun and Laremont 2001: 115).

Several of the parallel features are quite striking. There was a 'middle passage' for coolies that resulted in 16,400 dying on European and American ships during the 26 years of trafficking—a much higher rate than the African middle passage to Cuba. Some of the coolie ships, with names like *Africano* and *Mauritius*, were formerly used in the slave trade. They report that the primary traffickers of Chinese indentured servants were the same top six countries who were the leaders in the trafficking of slaves (Yun and Laremont 2001: 111) On arrival in Cuba, coolies were sold at some of the locations where slaves were auctioned—usually at much less than half the price of a slave. On the sugar plantations that used both, coolie trafficking was more profitable, because, as wage labourers who were used as slaves, coolies were much less costly.

If we shift our attention away from the actual physical treatment of coolies and slaves, as well as from the question of whether they were equally coerced by their owners, towards a consideration of the legal status of coolies, perhaps there remains a significant difference between them. According to Yun and Laremont, however, over 50% of coolies in Cuba died before the end of their eight-year contracts and the percentage of coolie attrition due to voluntary exit was negligible (2001: 115). The slave labour, to which Chinese coolies in Cuba were subjected, would count as only drudgery on Locke's conception of slavery, because they were legally wage-labourers under contract. The contracts in this case, however, were obtained through the use of deception and were difficult to enforce on behalf of labourers. To the extent that Chinese coolies and African slaves were 'persons over whom any and all of the powers attaching to the right of ownership are exercised' by a master, both should count as slaves.

On the League of Nations' definition of slavery, the Chinese indentured servants in Cuba can provide a paradigm of what I have deemed virtual slavery—but only to the extent that they can be understood to be under the absolute, arbitrary power of a master without *enforceable legal restrictions on this power*. An important difference between African slaves and Chinese indentured servants in Cuba was, perhaps, that Chinese indentured servants could legally appeal their case to the Chinese government, as citizens engaged in contracted labour abroad (Knight 1970). Whether Chinese indentured servitude was convergent slavery, of course, depends on the extent to which these appeals actually influenced the recognition by Cuban authorities of the status of coolies as contracted labour. If, however, as Yun and Laremont suggest, this influence had 'negligible' results, then, in this case, it is a distinction that applies 'in principle' only.

Human Trafficking and Virtual Slavery

The case of Chinese indentured servants in nineteenth-century Cuba represents an overlap of slavery and servitude, whereby an indentured servant, unlike a slave, is understood, from a legal standpoint, to be a contracted labourer. In other cases of overlap there is a similar distinction in legal status that facilitates the acceptance, as not wrong, of certain forms of unfree labour, some of which may qualify as virtual slavery. Shortly after the abolition of American slavery, in many southern states, there was mass incarceration of ex-slaves for prison labour. There also developed a share-cropping practice involving former slave-masters lending land to their former slaves and thereby indebting them permanently. Just as debt bondsmen have been, since antiquity, a source of slaves, similarly, in the wake of the global spread of abolition in the nineteenth century, the British fostered the idea of using indentured servants as a replacement for slave labour (Williams 1944). In moments such as this, the overlapping cases, which can go in either direction between slavery and other forms of unfree labour, will often have starkly similar features.

Given the difference in the legal status of indentured servants, it appears to be a stage between slavery and freedom that is an improvement over being a slave—to the extent that the indentured servant (or debt bondsman, or serf) has a set of rights denied to the slave. What if we conceive this case of slavery-servitude overlap as involving wage labour, as well as indentured labour—with the following alteration, the wage-labourers are hired-out slaves (whose wages are returned to their masters)? How do we gauge the difference between wage-labour and slavery in cases involving contracted indentured labourers working side by side with slaves who are hired out to work for wages? Think, for example, of Frederick Douglass's experience of working in the shipyards of Baltimore as a hired-out slave (1855/1969: 328–329). In contexts where there is a juxtaposition of free and unfree labour, we can further imagine a situation involving non-wage earning slaves, hired-out (wage-earning) slaves, and (wage-earning) indentured servants. As exploited labour, all three legally distinguishable groups are engaged in such a manner that 'wage-earning' in this case seems to signify the existence of a proletariat that counts as virtual slavery. The distinction Locke would make between drudgery and slavery does not clearly apply to overlapping cases involving a hired-out slave who earns wages, given that he is, at once, slave and wage-earner. With regard to Locke's distinguishing criterion, it is further confounded, as I discuss below, if slaves and unfree labourers in the imagined situation are all subject to the arbitrary will of a master.

Analogous Cases and the Slavery Metaphor

The similarity of overlapping cases, from the slavery that precedes them to other forms of unfree labour that follow, is often a basis for drawing the analogy that justifies using the term 'slavery'. In the nineteenth-century Cuban case of indentured servitude, the question is whether both slave and indentured servant working side by side were, in accordance with Locke's definition, equally subject to the absolute, arbitrary power of a master. Despite the fact that Chinese indentured servants were duped by traffickers, they, nonetheless, voluntarily entered into an agreement that created a legal obligation. The more coercive tactics came into play once they had been transported overseas. In antiquity, what I refer to as 'virtual slavery' occurred during the waiting period when a debt bondsman had been sold abroad as a slave. According to Jackson, at that stage of the transition, the bondsman's status of remaining a citizen who has a debt to pay lapsed and he was treated no differently than a chattel slave (Jackson 1988: 89). A decisive determination of whether Chinese indentured servants in nineteenth-century Cuba were virtual slaves is complicated by a consideration of what to count as a coerced contract. A contract entered into under coercion can be distinguished from a contract entered into voluntarily, and afterwards extended, and maintained by force. In the latter case, there seems to be a quasi-legitimate claim, as well as a completely illegitimate use of coercion, by the indentured servant's employer.

This pattern of subjugation is frequently cited in reports on human trafficking and modern slavery (Bales 2005; Kapstein 2006). The type (3) peons in some regions of Mexico and Latin America in the late nineteenth century, that Knight has studied, were coerced in this manner, with the use of fraud to lure peasants on to estates and then, by force, keep them there—ostensibly until their debts were paid. Does contracted labour, that initially poses as free, become virtual slavery when coercive tactics used to maintain slavery are brought into play at some later stage?[5] Recent news reports indicate a similar pattern of fraud and force being used by landowners who employ coerced labour to clear forest in the Amazon region of Northeast Brazil. Peasants typically come to the region voluntarily seeking work. While employed, they accrue a debt to repay the employer for food and lodging. At that point, armed guards are required to keep workers from attempting to escape. Some escapees are sold to labour recruiters, who pay off their debt. The top anti-slavery official in Brasilia put the number of these 'modern slaves' at 50,000 (Hall 2004).[6]

There are two factors that complicate the easy acceptance of this case as slavery. First, the coercion seems directed at the enforcement of a contract between worker and employer—albeit one that is illegal and unfair to the worker. Second, we are told that these 'modern slaves' are 'unpaid until their employer declares their season ended' (Hall 2004: 15A). The harsh labour and inhumane working conditions to which these exploited workers are subjected, is nonetheless wage labour in lieu of the receipt of wages, even when delayed and when a huge amount is deducted for living expenses. This case has elements of both servitude and slavery, with accrued debt facilitating the transition from the former to the latter. The illegal use of coercion by non-state agents to enforce a contract in this case, however, suggests that an alternative to counting this as slavery would be to view it as a form of involuntary servitude—in the sense intended by the 13th Amendment (Carter 2012: 209). The analogy with slavery, in this case, is drawn on the basis of the use of force to deny the corporal liberty of workers. For this reason it seems similar enough to qualify as slavery on Hobbes' definition. But why is there a need for special anti-trafficking laws specifying this as a form of modern slavery, rather than the alternative of simply dealing with this type of injustice by filing charges of kidnapping, false imprisonment, etc. against violators under existing criminal law?

Slavery as the Best Option

Julia O'Connell Davidson has raised objections to some of the anti-trafficking policies that ignore the role of un-coerced consent (O'Connell Davidson 2006). Her research on migrant sex workers in London critically examines immigration policies that do not distinguish between consensual and non-consensual contractual agreements for 'trafficking victims' working in the sex industry.[7] Kevin Bales (2000: 6) defines modern slavery as 'the total control of one person by another for the purpose of economic exploitation'. However, he fails to consider (or simply discounts), that what appears from his standpoint to be unjust exploitation, could be a matter of choice for many in certain contexts, and, hence, elected as the best available option. O'Connell Davidson shifts our attention to the 'victim's' standpoint, from which it is difficult to overlook the choices made by consenting adults as irrelevant, especially when none of the other options bode as well.

Bales expresses the difficulty of his having to acknowledge that 'victims' of sex trafficking are consenting to their own oppression. From his moral perspective he is unable to imagine that, when given a choice, 'victims' of trafficking who become migrant sex workers may have a preference for prostitution, rather than marriage. From a 'victim's perspective, in such cases, the choice would be between two forms of unfree labour, with each amounting to enslavement. The decision to become a sex worker, rather than opt for migration marriage, may be simply a matter of determining which provides the best option regarding access to freedom. 'Sexual slavery' would be a preferred option for its instrumental role, and its higher probability, in gaining access to freedom.

There appears to be a noticeable difference in moral attitudes towards prostitutes and brides that inhibits treating marriage as domestic slavery and facilitates treating prostitution as sexual slavery. Should John Stuart Mill's remark in *On Liberty*, that marriage enslaves half of humanity, be taken as a metaphor for the subjugation of women in the household (Mill 1859)? Or, should it be taken to mean that wives are literally slaves? Although Mill is very clear in *The Subjection of Women* (1869) that he means to draw a comparison between the oppression of women and the oppression of African slaves as deriving from a common source of domination, it should be noted here that he does not consider the plight of women who were wives *and*, literally, slaves.[8] Comparisons of the important differences between wives and slaves by feminist scholars suggest a more complicated result. While analogous in certain ways, O'Connell Davidson has cautioned against making comparisons between wives and slaves too strongly. She highlights the continuities and discontinuities involved in trying to understand the parallel feminists have often drawn. She points out that 'white women occupied a position that was simultaneously similar and dissimilar to that of chattel slaves, and similar and dissimilar to that of white men' (O'Connell Davidson 2015: 179). This observation indicates why marriage fails to satisfy the condition of being indistinguishable from slavery, a condition that must be fulfilled to count as virtual slavery.

There is nonetheless an important lesson to be gleaned from examining more closely a difference O'Connell Davidson cites regarding white women being socially connected, through marriage and motherhood, with two lines of kinship. Although white women were excluded from the public sphere, they carried out a very important social function that allowed them to have a sense of inclusion and belonging that slaves were denied. With regard to Davidson's concept of slaves as marginalized and not belonging to society, it is important to note that, while she acknowledges the many difficulties slaves had managing kinship ties, she does not buy into Patterson's view of natal alienation. Nonetheless, the notion of belonging she advances to distinguish wives and slaves is consistent with the idea that slaves were excluded and lacked a sense of belonging because they were structurally marginalized as a source of economically necessary alien labour. This conception of slavery does not apply to the social position of white women, even though, as wives relegated to lifelong domestic servitude, there may be other analogous features that marriage shares with slavery.

Mill understood the oppression of women to be a case of de facto slavery. However, his reflections on the Greek practice of slavery avoids dwelling on the overwrought war captive paradigm. Instead, with women's oppression in mind, he points out that the Greeks practiced *domestic* slavery. He emphasizes the fact that the rule of men over women is accepted by women as voluntary and tells us that 'They make no complaint and are consenting parties to it' (Mill 1869: 139). His explanation of this observation is that, being brought up 'in a culture that constantly prescribes that women submit to others', women are raised to be domestic servants (Mill 1869: 156).

Bernard Williams has informed us, regarding the Greek practice of slavery, that Aristotle's view was that 'if slavery were properly conducted, slaves would become what women actually were' (Williams 1998: 13). The consent of many women to their domination by men, a phenomenon on which Mill comments, was the key aspect of women's oppression that led Aristotle to employ the conventional Greek view of the role of women in households as his model of a master-slave relationship.

Hence, the subordination of women, as lifelong domestic servants, was Aristotle's model for the management of enslaved war captives. His idea was to get enslaved captives from abroad to *accept* their inferior status within Greek society. Rather than marginalized foreigners who are natally alienated, on the analogy with women, Aristotle meant by this that, through proper acculturation, slaves would develop a sense of belonging and acceptance of their lot as lifelong servants, just as uncomplaining wives have done. It was not only the barbarian races of Tracians and Asiatics that Aristotle viewed as natural slaves. According to Williams, he employs the domestic servant paradigm of women in the household to show that 'there are pairs of people naturally related as master to slave' (Williams 1998: 10). This reading of Aristotle suggests that women were the first to be subjugated on the basis of having a different nature. Barbarian war captives, with slavish natures, were to be enslaved afterwards and managed on the model of women. He envisioned Greek society functioning at its best when slaves have accepted their lifelong servitude, as women have.

Mill's domestic servant paradigm of marriage can be mapped on to Aristotle's vision of a well-managed slave system. Beginning at birth, society seeks to acculturate women to an early acceptance of their servile position in the household. Marriage, then, is a re-categorization of the domestic servant status of women by means of a marriage contract that is, in fact, a lifelong domestic servitude contract. According to Mill, 'When women are merely slaves, to give them a permanent hold upon their masters was a first step towards their evolution' (Mill 1832). He employs this aspect of his analogy between wives and slaves to qualify marriage as a case of de facto slavery. What is noteworthy here is that it was this lifetime domestic servant paradigm of the de facto enslavement of women in the household that provided the model for Aristotle's view of how slavery should be understood to function best (Williams 1998: 12–13). Although, O'Connell Davidson has given us reasons to be sceptical regarding a too-tightly drawn comparison of wives and slaves, there seems to be more at work than a metaphoric use of the term slavery in the analogy Mill draws. The important lesson to be gleaned from Mill's insight, regarding women's oppression, is his suggestion of an alternative to the coercion-based paradigm of slavery that currently shapes anti-trafficking policies. Gendered forms of de facto slavery that are ambiguously consensual (e.g., debt–bonded migrant domestic servants) elude anti-trafficking legislation, for, without evidence of coercion, there is nothing for anti-trafficking activists to seek to criminalize, abolish, or rescue (Scott 2012).

Would the prostitution, or the marriage, involved in human trafficking cases still be considered slavery if either included an un-coerced contract that was consensual? In opposition to Mill, Robert Nozick and other libertarians have argued that un-coerced slavery contracts should be legally recognized (Nozick 1974). Nozick has maintained that individuals may use liberty rights to contract into slavery. This poses a challenge for Mill's view of slavery's wrongness, for he assumes that to label cases that overlap as 'slavery' is a reason to condemn what has been labelled. On Nozick's view, to label a practice as 'slavery', is not always a reason to condemn it.

Along with the question of slavery's wrongness, also at issue here is the conception of slavery, articulated by Hobbes and Locke, that stipulates that a slave becomes a servant once there is a contract. Mill follows Locke and opposes slavery contracts on the ground that, upon becoming a slave, one loses the freedom to contract out (the liberty of retraction). Whether this is always so is really an empirical question that depends on context. I have already acknowledged above that, in various contexts since antiquity, there has existed an option to contract out of slavery through the mechanism of manumission. The point of contention between Mill and Nozick on the legal enforcement of slavery contracts is much more focused on the question of contracting *into* slavery. Once we acknowledge, however, that slavery can be a relief from the drudgery of a certain type of wage-labour, it becomes less difficult to see that slavery is not always the worst option. In antiquity, a debt slave opting to become a permanent slave was an occasion for celebration, whereas manumission due to the repayment of debt was not (Jackson 1988: 94). For many of today's migrant labourers, temporary enslavement provides a means to escape permanent unemployment (Bastia and McGrath 2011).

The prohibition of self-sale in Greece and Rome aimed to restrict slavery to non-citizens, but there was no such prohibition of other forms of unfree labour such as debt bondage and indentured servitude. The Greco-Roman policy of treating the enslavement of citizens as wrong, while permitting the enslavement of non-citizens as justified, indicates that a justification of slavery is continuous with its condemnation. This policy, which developed in ancient practice and was updated with a social contract ideology during the Enlightenment, amounted to re-categorizing the temporary enslavement of citizens, while justifying permanent enslavement for foreigners. The question of slavery's wrongness is not whether it is *not* wrong in certain cases. The allure of its force as a term of condemnation, simply by labelling, derives from its *inherent* evilness being part of what the term means. A concern with slavery's evilness is, in fact, maintained, not only by those who condemn it, but also by those who justify, or re-categorize, it when it is a legally permitted practice. The fact that slavery, even in permissive contexts, always stands in need of justification, or re-categorization, is an acknowledgement of its wrongness. The function of a justification, or re-categorization, of slavery is to immobilize the demands of justice—usually in contexts where it is an economic necessity. Despite the ambiguity of wrongness created by re-categorization, the League of Nations' definition aims to identify more accurately the exact nature of this wrongness by stipulating the injustice of slavery to be any practice in which someone exercises absolute power over other humans, as if the latter have no rights whatever. On this specific criterion, slavery's wrongness can also be identified in the overlapping de facto cases.

The emphasis on power relations allows the League of Nations definition to accommodate a Hegelian view of domination, along with its implications for the coercion-consent binary, which undergirds the legalistic contractual distinction between slavery and servitude. In keeping with the more abstract view Hegel presents, the definition's broader conception of slavery had the set purpose when it was being drafted of including other forms of unfree labour (Allain 2012: 225). In this regard, it is important to note that it accommodates a practice of self-selling into slavery, as well as overlapping transitions from servitude to slavery and from slavery to servitude, as manifestations of domination.

The meaning of 'ownership' in the League of Nations' definition is important to clarify here. With regard to the significance of Locke's criterion of 'absolute power' in trafficking cases, some legal scholars have raised the question of whether the definition's stipulation regarding the exercise of 'all the powers attaching to the right of ownership' refers to, or includes, an owner's a right to destroy, or to dispose of, what he owns (Quirk 2012: 293). This matter of absolute power, and death, which was permitted under Roman law (Ellerman 2010: 574), is an issue on which the views held by Locke and Hegel are in agreement. For both, domination in the case of slavery involves an ongoing threat of death. There is, however, a major difference between their views. A Hegelian view would include, as a manifestation of domination, obligations created by consent-based contracts, whereas Locke would emphasize the voluntary nature of the servitude contracts to conceal the coercion.

The question of whether slavery is still wrong when it is voluntary and consensual suggests that, perhaps slavery can be justified on the basis of these criteria. I have, so far, taken Nozick's endorsement of the validity of slavery contracts to be consistent with the view that slavery is not wrong, when it is a matter of choice. His support for the legal enforcement of slavery contracts is also consistent with the view that slavery is a permissive evil when it is a matter of choice. Given that, on the libertarian view, individuals are legally permitted to enter into contractual arrangements that are considered to be a form of slavery, it is not clear that libertarians need think slavery is wrong, when consent is taken to be an adequate reason for allowing it to exist.

For non-libertarians, slavery can be wrong for various reasons. Typically the evil, on which I have placed great emphasis, and for which it is condemned, has to do with the right of a master to exercise absolute, arbitrary power such that the slave does not have control of her own body and can be bought and sold, or be killed, if she disobeys. This power of life and death is the most important analogue in overlapping cases of unfree labour. When slavery also involves unpaid labour, coerced labour, debt bondage, or imprisonment, it is wrong for the same reason these unjust practices are wrong. The exploitation of wage-labour in low paying jobs, such as domestic and farm labour, should also be condemned as unjust (Yeung 2004; Bridis 2002). This condemnation, however, usually does not require us to label these practices as modern slavery.

Notes

1. B.S. Jackson (1988), 90. He acknowledges that children were also sold into slavery to pay off a debt.
2. Although Jackson tells us that it is not known whether Rome ever had laws ending debt slavery after a specified time, he cites the tenure specified in the *Laws of Hammurabi*, 117, *Deuteronomy* 15:12 and *Leviticus* 25:40.
3. See Victims of Trafficking and Violence Protection Act of 2000, *U.S. Department of State*, 28 October 2000. http://www.state.gov/j/tip/laws/61124.htm.
4. Knight uses Genovese's criteria for making comparisons between slavery and other forms of unfree labour. According to Genovese, comparisons between Latin Catholic and Anglo-Saxon Protestant slavery are to be made on the basis of day-to-day living conditions, conditions of cultural life, and access to freedom (Genovese and Foner 1969: 202–210). Cited in Knight, 103.
5. I take 'free labourer' to mean a worker's freedom from direct compulsion and freedom to negotiate the sale of her labour power. When domination is reconstituted in this manner, it is really the labour power of the slave that becomes a commodity over which the slave-owner seeks complete control. For Hobbes, this is accomplished through a physical constraint on the slave's bodily movements, whereas for Locke and Hegel this is accomplished by constraining the slaves will to the master's.
6. See K.G. Hall, 'Unpaid Labor: Brazilian slaves help make products that end up in the United States through world trade' *San Jose Mercury News*, 14, September 2004, 1A and 15A.

7. Davidson discusses an interesting situation of some migrant sex workers in Central London who are encouraged by their employer to refuse to provide any services that they do not feel comfortable about providing. There is no loss of business, and the employer does not have high turnover of staff.
8. In 1921, Carter G. Woodson published a statistical report on the free Negro ownership of slaves in 1830. He presented cases in which many free husbands purchased their wives without granting them emancipation. Some put their wives on probation, and, if they were dissatisfied with them, they would sell them as slaves. In one story an unfaithful wife plotted to steal her husband's manumission papers to run away with her lover (Woodson 1924). This case of American free black husbands owning their wives as slaves is literal, with no need for analogy.

References

Allain, J. (2012). *Slavery in International Law*. Leiden and Boston: Martinus Nijhoff.

Bales, K. (2000). *Disposable People: New Slavery in the Global Economy*. Berkeley: University of California Press.

Bales, K. (2005). *Understanding Global Slavery*. Berkeley: University of California Press.

Bastia, T., & McGrath, S. (2011). Temporality, Migration and Unfree Labour: Migrant Garment Workers. *Manchester Papers in Political Economy* (Vol. 6). Manchester: University of Manchester.

Bridis, T. (2002, January 2). Visas for Some Who Are Smuggled in "Slaves" Can Stay If They Would Face Extreme Hardship at Home. *San Francisco Chronicle*, p. A7.

Carter, W. (2012). Toward a Thirteenth Amendment Exclusionary Rule as a Remedy for Racial Profiling. In A. Tsesis (Ed.), *The Promises of Liberty: Thirteenth Amendment Abolitionism and Its Contemporary Vitality*. New York: Columbia University Press.

Chanana, D. R. (1960). *Slavery in Ancient India: As Depicted in Pali and Sanskrit Texts*. New Delhi: People's Publishing House.

Curley, E. (Ed.). (1994). *Hobbes Leviathan* (p. 131). Indianapolis: Hackett Publishing.

Douglass, F. (1855/1969). *My Bondage and My Freedom*. New York: Dover Publications.
Drescher, S. (2012). The Shocking Birth of British Abolitionism. *Slavery and Abolition, 33*(4), 571–593.
Eaton, R. M. (2005). *A Social History of the Deccan, 1300–1761: Eight Indian Lives*. New York: Cambridge University Press.
Ellerman, A. (2010). Undocumented Migrants and Resistance in the Liberal State. *Politics and Society, 38*(3), 408–429.
Fields, B. J. (1987). *Slavery and Freedom on the Middle Ground: Maryland During the Nineteenth Century*. New Haven: Yale University Press.
Genovese, E. D. (1969). The Treatment of Slaves in Different Countries: Problems in the Application of the Comparative Method. In L. Foner & E. D. Genovese (Eds.), *Slavery in the New World: A Reader in Comparative History* (pp. 202–210). Englewood Cliffs: Prentice-Hall.
Gorsuch, A. (2012). To Indent Oneself: Ownership, Contracts, and Consent in Antebellum Illinois. In J. Allain (Ed.), *The Legal Understanding of Slavery* (Chapter 7). Oxford: Oxford University Press.
Hall, K. G. (2004, September 14). Unpaid Labor: Brazilian Slaves Help Make Products That End Up in the United States Through World Trade. *San Jose Mercury News*, pp. 1A and 15A.
Hegel, G. W. F. (1976). *Phenomenology of Spirit* (A. V. Miller, Trans.). Oxford: Clarendon. Ebook Available at: https://www.marxists.org.
Jackson, B. S. (1988). Biblical Laws of Slavery: A Comparative Approach. In Archer (Ed.), *Slavery and Other Forms of Unfree Labor* (p. 90). London: Routledge.
Jacobs, H. (1861). *Incidents in the Life of a Slave Girl*. Boston, np. Ebook Available at: http://docsouth.unc.edu/fpn/jacobs/menu.html.
Kapstein, E. B. (2006). The New Global Slave Trade. *Foreign Affairs, 85*, 103–115.
Knight, A. (1988). Debt Bondage in Latin America. In L. Archer (Ed.), *Slavery and Other Forms of Unfree Labor*. London: Routledge.
Knight, F. (1970). *Slave Society in Cuba During the Nineteenth Century*. Madison: University of Wisconsin Press.
Locke, J. (1689/1960). *Two Treatises of Government*. New York: New American Library.
Lott, T. (1998). Early Enlightenment Conceptions of the Rights of Slaves. In T. Lott (Ed.), *Subjugation and Bondage: Critical Essays on Slavery and Social Philosophy* (99–129). Lanham: Rowman & Littlefield.

Malcolm, N. (2002). *Aspects of Hobbes*. Oxford: Oxford University Press.
Martin, D. (1990). *Slavery as Salvation*. New Haven: Yale University Press.
Mill, J. S. (1832). Early Essays on Marriage and Divorce. In A. Rossi (Ed.), (1970) *Essays on Sex Equality*. Chicago: University of Chicago Press.
Mill, J. S. (1859/1978). *On Liberty*. E. Rappaport (Ed.), Indianapolis: Hackett Publishing.
Mill, J. S. (1869). The Subjection of Women. In A. S. Rossi, J. S. Mill, & H. T. Mill (Eds.), *Essays on Sex Equality*. Chicago: University of Chicago Press.
Nozick, R. (1974). *Anarchy, State, and Utopia*. New York: Basic Books.
O'Connell Davidson, J. (2006). Will the Real Sex Slave Please Stand Up. *Feminist Review, 83*, 4–22.
O'Connell Davidson, J. (2015). *Modern Slavery*. New York: Palgrave Macmillan.
Patterson, O. (1991). *Freedom in the Making of Western Culture*. New York: Basic Books.
Patterson, O. (2012). Trafficking, Gender, and Slavery: Past and Present. In J. Allain (Ed.), *The Legal Understanding of Slavery* (Chapter 17). Oxford: Oxford University Press.
Quirk, J. (2012). Defining Slavery in All Its Forms: Historical Inquiry as Contemporary Instruction. In J. Allain (Ed.), *The Legal Understanding of Slavery* (Chapter 14). Oxford: Oxford University Press.
Rawls, J. (1971). *A Theory of Justice*. Harvard: Harvard University Press.
Scott, R. (2012). Under Color of Law: Siliadin v. France and the Dynamics of Enslavement in Historical Perspective. In J. Allain (Ed.), *The Legal Understanding of Slavery* (Chapter 8). Oxford: Oxford University Press.
Ste. Croix, G. E. M. de. (1981). *The Class Struggle in the Ancient World, From the Archaic Age to the Arab Conquest* (pp. 133–200). Ithaca: Cornell University Press.
Ste. Croix, G. E. M. de. (1988). Slavery and Other Forms of Unfree Labour. In L. Archer (Ed.), *Slavery and Other Forms of Unfree Labour*. London: Routledge.
Uzgalis, W. (1998). The Same Tyrannical Principle: Locke's Legacy on Slavery. In J. K. Ward & T. Lott (Eds.), *Subjugation and Bondage: Critical Essays on Slavery and Social Philosophy*. London: Rowman and Littlefield.
Williams, E. (1944). *Capitalism and Slavery*. Chapel Hill: University of North Carolina Press.

Williams, B. (1998). Necessary Identities. In J. K. Ward & T. Lott (Eds.), *Subjugation and Bondage: Critical Essays on Slavery and Social Philosophy*. London: Rowman and Littlefield.

Woodson, C. G. (1924). *Free Negro Owners of Slaves in the United States in 1830*. New York: Negro Universities Press.

Yeung, B. (2004, February 18–24). Enslaved in Palo Alto. *San Francisco Weekly*, pp. 21–27.

Yun, L., & Laremont, R. R. (2001). Chinese Coolies and African Slaves in Cuba, 1847–74. *Journal of Asian American Studies, 4*(June), 99–122.

3

The Liberty of Naming

Mary Nyquist

In 2015, after years of testimonial witnessing and consultation, Canada's Truth and Reconciliation Commission delivered its report on the residential school system to which First Nations children had been subjected for almost a century and a quarter.[1] The language with which commissioners passed judgement on the residential school system could not have been more unequivocal or controversial: 'cultural genocide'. Scarcely had the words been uttered before objections were raised: since so many First Nations' children survived, 'genocide' was obviously inapplicable to their experience; 'cultural genocide' was unsuitably inflammatory for a state-commissioned report; 'cultural genocide' provocatively appropriated a term coined with reference to the Jewish Holocaust. Why, in brief, use 'cultural' to modify 'genocide', a term that's contentious whenever applied to situations outside Nazism? At the same time, however, many people passionately supported this strongly worded verdict on Canada's residential schools. In articles,

M. Nyquist (✉)
University of Toronto, Toronto, ON, Canada
e-mail: mary.nyquist@utoronto.ca

L. Brace and J. O'Connell Davidson (eds.), *Revisiting Slavery and Antislavery*,
https://doi.org/10.1007/978-3-319-90623-2_3

editorials, and talk-shows, commissioners were commended for voicing such whole-hearted repudiation of colonialist violence. A few supporters mentioned the UN's *Convention on the Prevention and Punishment of the Crime of Genocide* (1948), Article 11 of which specifies at least two criteria that Canada's abduction, institutionalization, and brutal abuse of First Nations children unquestionably meet. Finally, regarding the question 'how can genocide be cultural?' one writer settled the matter by declaring *all* genocide cultural.

I open with the debates 'genocide' has recently sparked partly as a reminder that the higher the stakes, the greater the likelihood that an act of naming will be contested. Even those who applaud applying 'genocide' to the residential school system are often conscious of possible drawbacks. Given mainstream media's fickle engagement with accounts of harrowing abuse, a powerful term such as 'genocide' may divert attention from the prior, historical contexts for a specific instance of state-authorized violence as well as from current practices that perpetuate it under other names. Constructive, proactive responses to the Truth and Reconciliation Commission's report have had vigilantly to guard against these dangers.

Regarding 'slavery', a term with a much longer, more complicated history, these difficulties are multiplied many times over. Categorical references to 'slavery' are equally if not more inflammatory than 'genocide.' Yet what exactly are the sources of 'slavery's' condemnatory power, of its potent rhetorical charge? This question may at first seem a non-starter: slavery is bad, and that is that. In this view, it is self-evident that slavery, legally abolished in contemporary nation-states, should be opposed wherever it emerges. It will be argued here, however, that the act of calling a given phenomenon 'slavery' is not as straightforward as this presumes, and that neither common-sense nor ethical principles are responsible for 'slavery's' rhetorical effects. The term 'slavery' (or its equivalents) designates a socio-economic institution, not a crime. In this respect, it can be contrasted with 'genocide', which, like 'homicide', 'infanticide', 'regicide', or 'parricide', designates an act of killing in its very semantic formation. If not always considered criminal, such acts are generally believed to violate ethical, religious, or social values.

Only very recently—if we take a trans-epochal perspective—did 'genocide' enter international public discourse. By contrast, linguistic versions of 'slavery' have circulated for millennia, while both cross-culturally and historically, the socio-economic relations to which 'slavery' refers have had countless permutations. As a result of this variability, the sociological or legal essence of slavery continues to be debated, as does the appropriateness of using 'slavery' to characterize a broad range of oppressive practices, past and present. These debates are not directly engaged in this chapter, where, instead, I take up the question just posed: what are the sources of 'slavery's' exceptional rhetorical power? In reflecting on this question, I draw attention to the many, often pernicious, legacies that Euro-colonialist usage of 'slavery' has handed down. My aim, firstly, is to create awareness of the continuing hold these legacies have on contemporary political and intellectual formations. Secondly, it is to caution against naming performed from the standpoint of the 'free'. As will be seen, naming that presupposes the supreme value of 'liberty' has its own complex, layered history, which all too frequently erases relevant contexts, stigmatizes those who carry the burden of inherited or newly devised injustices, and perpetuates pseudo-universalizing ideologies of 'freedom' (as explored in Mignolo and Escobar 2010).

In the ancient Athenian and Roman societies from which dominant Amer-European discourses derive—the discourses that inform discussions of 'modern slavery'—the institution of slavery is inextricably bound up with the stirringly emotive, endlessly adaptive deployment of 'slavery' as the antonym of 'freedom'. Social values relating to freedom and slavery were, of course, developed and celebrated by those who were legally free. For the most part, in both ancient and later Euro colonial settler and plantation societies, the experiences and needs of those enslaved went unrecorded; they most emphatically are not represented in dominant discourses of freedom (or 'liberty', from the Roman *libertas*). I hope to persuade readers that it is important to understand the often mystifyingly complex set of relations that have developed historically between 'slavery' as a rhetorical figure and slavery as an economic institution, between figurative 'freedom' and the privileges attached to being legally or by ideological *fiat* 'free'. Until these interrelations are recognized, it will remain all too easy unwittingly to continue validating dominant, often racialized, Euro-colonialist uses of 'slavery'. Put more positively, acknowledging them will open up space for language that might situate injurious practices more precisely in the circumstances of the historical present, in which financialization, neo-liberalism, and new forms of authoritarianism seek to reign.

Whose Slavery? Whose Shame?

From its gradual emergence in archaic Greece, 'freedom' became a highly valued ideal owing to its interrelations with 'slavery' and 'tyranny', conceptual constructs that pertained to both the household and the city-state. When their significance crystallized in democratic Athens, whose adult, free-born men comprised the *polis*, 'freedom', 'slavery', and 'tyranny' developed powerful, multi-layered meanings (Raaflaub 2004; I further explore these meanings as adapted in later historical eras in Nyquist 2013). Athens, it is now agreed, was a city-state the outstanding achievements of which were dependent on the labour of slaves, the majority of whom were barbarians (largely Asiatic non-Greeks) either acquired in war or the unfree descendants of those previously acquired. Unsurprisingly, the Athenian dramatic, philosophical, and political texts that have become central to Europe's own self-conception not only presuppose the inestimable value of freedom but were also authored by members of the slave-holding classes who had 'free' status.

In various Athenian literary and philosophical texts, connections among 'freedom', 'slavery', and 'tyranny' represent social hierarchies in the process of being threatened or overturned. In ethico-philosophical discourse, for example, figurative slavery occurs when reason or some other higher function of the individual self which ought to take the part of the free-born 'master' becomes the helpless 'slave' of desire or addictive pleasure. Alternatively, desire or pleasure can tyrannously usurp reason's role as master, in this way, too, reducing reason to the status of the enslaved. Such inversion of the appropriately hierarchical statuses of 'master' and 'slave' is, of course, to be deplored.

These figurative relationships function independently of an individual's social and legal status. In theory, at least, someone who is formally enslaved could experience ethical conflicts between free and unfree aspects of the self. The Stoics, for example, are fond of hypothesizing the paradoxical but satisfying capacity for inward freedom possessed by the institutionally enslaved. The ideological status of the categories 'free' and 'slave' is revealed by the fact that they do not accurately represent the variety of available legal identities in classical Athens or, later, Rome. At the same time, though, they assume the existence of living, breathing individuals whose worth is determined by legal status. They were deeply meaningful because institutional slavery was a taken-for-granted, all-pervasive feature of ordinary, everyday life which both secured and gratifyingly set off the privileges enjoyed by those who were 'free'.

As elaborated by adult, free males in classical Athens and Rome, the values associated with 'freedom' and 'slavery' intersect with social approbation and disapprobation in affectively powerful codes apportioning honour and shame.[2] From within the elite population of household 'masters' with political standing, slaves are regarded as pre- or extra-political beings without honour. With the exception of ideologically crafted narratives such as Livy's (2002: 229–235) about a slave who reports seditious plans to the authorities and is rewarded with public money, emancipation, and citizenship, actions performed by free women and men are alone considered honourable or shameful.

Fixedly centred in the experience of those legally free, the language of enslavement is often used to induce a fear of shame or to represent a condition of unutterable disgrace. If slaves themselves are supposed to be without shame (an assumption that would likely seem laughable to those enslaved), why should the condition of enslavement be invoked to convey dishonour? For those enjoying free status, why should the mere possibility of enslavement—a possibility determined, when all is said and done, by a nexus of historical and economic forces as well as the vagaries of fortune—bring shame?

Graeco-Roman shame often appears in conjunction with slavery as a condition in which freedom and honour are not so much absent—absence indicates a condition of servility, discussed below—as possibly to be lost, perhaps irrevocably, or in the process of being surrendered. Shame, in other words, attends the potential extinction of freedom and honour, the preserve of citizens who are legally free. In both Greek and Roman literary and non-literary texts, male warriors and citizens are expected to face the prospect of defeat with a dread of the shame associated with figurative, collective enslavement or, more commonly, by displacing this dread on to the wives or daughters whose enslavement it is their responsibility to prevent. In a dramatic work such as Euripides' *Trojan Women*, for example, female chorus and characters face the prospect of imminent enslavement by passionately mourning the deaths of loved ones and the loss of homes, attachments, and social status. Loss itself rather than defeat per se becomes associated with exposure to every conceivable dishonour; female survivors are powerless to stop the ritual sacrifice of their children and anxiously anticipate sexual relations with one of the victors, an inevitable component of enslavement.

Honour and shame generally find their most memorable expression on the battlefield, where defeat is an ever-present possibility. Eloquently mobilized by military leaders, honour accrues to those who courageously fight to preserve freedom, while shame attaches to the ignominy of slavery, the end result of defeat. That individual members of the vanquished population—especially female—might be enslaved is not an idle, fear-mongering fantasy; chattel slavery's kinship with shameful defeat is based on social and material realities. At the same time, military exhortations that raise the spectre of shameful enslavement serve to inculcate martial fearlessness by giving freedom a value higher than life itself. Warriors are encouraged willingly to sacrifice their lives in battle by contemplating the glorious preservation of collective freedom even if preservation results in individual deaths.

This nexus of associations opens up a perspective from which enslavement may be regarded as voluntary or an issue of individual responsibility: to participate in achieving victory is courageously to resist personal and political, interstate slavery, while to survive military defeat as a prisoner of war and potential slave is weakly to have handed life, labour-power, and political honour over to the enemy. Viewed in this way, enslavement resulting from military defeat is similar to the figurative, ethico-philosophical slavery just discussed insofar as it results from either a failure of self-mastery in the form of cowardice or a surrender of masculine agency. More than merely counterintuitive—chattel slavery obviously originates in and is maintained by force—this construction insidiously contributes to the degraded status of the enslaved. By the same token, it perpetuates the identification of individuals who have been enslaved militarily with the nation they have failed. For the Athenian *polis* and the Roman republic or empire, the very prospect of enslavement arising from military defeat threatens not only the integrity of the individual self or the city-state but indirectly, or symbolically, the ordered well-being of the free community.

According to Aristotle's formulation in *Politics* (1988, 1327b: 24–33), barbarians are naturally servile in that, lacking a free, citizen-governed polis, they collectively subject themselves to the rule of a single master-ruler with absolute power. Aristotle's contentious discussion of those (typically barbarians) who are chattel slaves by nature cannot be disentangled from his theorization of political slavery, which is a figurative form of slavery. Unlike ethico-philosophical slavery, which results from a failure of self-mastery, political slavery results from the natural servility of subjects who serve a single, absolute master-monarch or from a tyrannous ruler's attempted reduction of the status of his free citizens. The latter occurs, Aristotle argues (1988, 1225b: 18–20, 1295a: 19–23), when a ruler inappropriately plays the part of a household master who serves the interests of his own household *vis a* community of freeborn citizens who are entitled to rule themselves and capable of ruling for the polity's good. To maintain its distinctively *political* freedom, the polis needs to meet two conditions: first, the intra-state condition of self-rule by citizens acting collectively according to the laws it has produced and, second, the inter state condition of self rule in relation to other city-states. Should either intrastate or interstate freedom be jeopardized, the *polis* risks reduction to a condition of figurative slavery. Though its imperial ambitions did not prevent Athens from ruling other city-states in ways that could be and were considered oppressive, 'tyranny' or political 'slavery' generally represents threats to Athens' own freedom, whether internal or external.

With so many different semantic registers, Greek and Roman language relating to slavery can either strategically conflate or flexibly discriminate among forms of servitude at the same time that it draws, rhetorically, on multiply charged associations, all of them negative. When synthesized with Hebraic and early Christian conceptions of sinfulness, redemption, and service to the Creator, Graeco-Roman language relating to servitude develops even greater semantic plasticity. For post-abolitionist readers in particular, this can create confusion, since facile slippage between or among registers makes it possible to mistake rhetorical invective against figurative slavery for principled objection to chattel slavery as an institution. Contrariwise, as will be seen, what appears to be principled objection to institutional slavery often exploits the pejorative connotations that the entire ensemble of slaveries has accumulated.

Anti-tyranny Invective, National Liberty, and Euro-colonialism

Opposition to political slavery, both internal and external, took centre stage at moments of revolutionary fervour in early modern England, France, the Netherlands, and again in the Age of Revolutions. Proponents of the legitimacy of political resistance against tyranny drew on Athenian and Roman anti-tyranny discourses, which sanctioned actively, even violently, opposing a tyrant's attempt to reduce 'free' citizens to 'slaves'. Today, anyone educated in North American and Western European literature or institutions is most likely to be familiar with anti-tyranny rhetoric as it was taken up in New England's War of Independence or the French Revolution. Like the Netherlands, which fought to deliver itself from the bondage of Spanish tyranny in the mid-sixteenth century, the Thirteen Colonies pitted themselves against external tyranny, the tyrant in this case being imperial Britain. Legislation and taxes imposed by the British metropole government were increasingly regarded as arbitrary, imperialist encroachments on citizens' rightful, inherited privileges. British rule, it was claimed, sought to strip its colonial subjects of their freedom to govern themselves, to treat them, in other words, as nothing but slaves.

As a figure of speech, political slavery operates by means of an identification that is hypothetical, hyperbolical, or both: under tyrannous rule, free citizens are treated *as if* they were about to be enslaved, *as if* already enslaved, or *as if* vanquished and, therefore, potential slaves. Because it is fundamentally polemical, this figure assumes that in reality this should not or cannot be. In postulating injurious, tyrannous treatment that threatens free people with reduction to the status of slaves, anti-tyrannicism postulates two, opposing responses on the part of those so threatened. On the one hand are to be found those who dishonourably tolerate this reduction while on the other are those who know how much their freedom is worth and are prepared honourably to preserve it, if necessary by rising up.

Owing in part to the assimilation of Roman liberty with Christian conceptions of divinely created freedom, in early modern and enlightenment Western European anti-tyrannicism, freedom is increasingly represented as a status inherited by not only the individual members of an entire nation but also nations themselves. Using Graeco-Roman terminology, members of an entire community are said to be 'freeborn', or, alternatively, they can claim freedom as what in Hebraic discourse is a 'birthright'. Whatever the means of inheritance, radical Western Europeans laud freedom's inviolability or contest tyranny's injustices in polemical language that gradually loses its sharp, cutting edge to become the monumental, well-polished cornerstone of liberal capitalist societies. In this perennially pleasing language, citizens of 'free' nations regard 'slavery' as a condition that is simply irrelevant to them (see Nyquist 2013).

As imaginary properties of Western European nations, internal and external political liberty are often subtly, if not confusingly, interconnected, as they were for Aristotle as well as other Athenian and Roman writers. In mid-seventeenth England, for example, when internal, constitutional issues are of paramount importance, radical Parliamentarians assign Charles I every characteristic of the classical Graeco-Roman tyrant. Many of the same radicals, however, give tyranny a foreign, external identity when railing against England's 'Norman Yoke' (Hill 1968: 58–125). England's slavery under its current ruler, it is claimed, goes directly back to the national slavery instituted by the Norman Conquest, which, in addition to a foreign tongue and foreign laws, introduced the absolutist monarchical rule that has been passed on to every one of William's successors. In *Saint Edwards Ghost, or Anti-Normanisme* (1647), John Hare tries to inspire his fellow countrymen to reclaim the ancient Teutonic rights they lost under Norman rule, which violated Britain's native, pre-Norman traditions of self-government. Should they continue to acquiesce in the shame the Conquest has brought them, they might as well give up 'talke of honour, as being a thing that we have least to doe withal, but yielding that and the glory to the Normane Name, reserve unto our selves nothing but the inheritance of shame and confusion of face; yea let us either confesse and professe ourselves for ever, meere vassals and slaves, or else attempt to uncaptive our selves (the end and scope of this whole discourse)' (1647a: 19). Hare ends this tract with a call to rid England of its servile status so it can extend its 'dominion', and announces in the sub-title of his next that at present England 'and every Member of her are no other then *Slaves* properly so called' (Note the slippery hyperbole in 'no other then *Slaves* properly so called' [Hare 1647b: title-page]).

At a later moment in Britain's development as a Euro-colonial power, 'Rule Britannia' (1740) memorably evokes (1) personal, (2) internal political, and (3) external political slavery as a nearly magical, indissoluble trinity. In the song's original lyrics, the exceptional nobility of Britain's hoped-for status as permanently, wondrously free is so ostentatiously on display that its singular conflation of different slaveries has evaded analysis. To generations of later auditors and readers, its refrain, 'Rule, Britannia, rule the waves / Britons never will be slaves' (now 'Rule, Britannia! Britannia, rule the waves!' And 'Britons never, never, never will be slaves') brazenly trumpets Britannia's extended imperial power.[3] The more the empire grew, the clearer it seemed that Britain's rule of the 'waves' was metonymically rule of its extensive transatlantic and transpacific lands and peoples. Though at the time it was composed such an empire was more wishful prospect than reality, even in its own historical moment Britain's colonial holdings are obliquely positioned as Britannia's political 'slaves'.[4]

Appearing at the conclusion of the first verse on Britain's blessed origins, the refrain is sung by guardian angels who give choral voice to an original 'charter of the land':

> *When* Britain *first, at Heaven's command,*
> *Arose from out the azure main;*
> This *was the charter of the land,*
> *And guardian angels sang this strain:*
> '*Rule* Britannia, *rule the waves;*
> 'Britons *never will be slaves.*' (Thomson 1740: 42)

With its stress on 'main' and 'land', this verse foregrounds Britain as a geopolitical entity. Unfurling the charter's promise of future greatness, the refrain thus sings of determination to safeguard Britannia's external, political freedom. The shift from 'Britain' and 'Britannia' to 'Britons', however, inevitably raises the possibility of personal, domestic slavery, that is, of each individual Britons being enslaved to an individual slaveholder. What in this sense Britons will never be is precisely the status that has been instituted for the Africans transported to and forcibly detained in Britain's Atlantic colonies.

Throughout the six verses, there is not the faintest trace of Britain's previous subjection to—that is, political enslavement by—a conquering nation. Indeed, the second verse boasts of the liberty to be enjoyed evermore by Britannia because, unlike other nations, it is essentially invulnerable to tyranny:

> *The nations, not so blest as thee,*
> *Must, in their turn, to tyrants fall:*
> *While thou shalt flourish great and free,*
> *The dread and envy of them all.*

Are the 'tyrants' to whom other nations 'fall' intrastate political tyrants or foreign conquerors? The ambiguity—repeated in a later stanza's 'haughty tyrants' who will never be able to subject Britannia—serves to magnify Britain's capacity to retain and exercise its freedom. Since Britannia would scarcely consider her own rule over nations 'not so blest' to be tyrannous, the primary reference in the stanza just cited is to the internal, civil freedom from tyranny England has enjoyed since the Glorious Revolution. Yet this freedom sparks in other nations not only 'envy' but also 'dread'. If the latter suggests fear of external rule imposed by force, the next stanza shows Britannia becoming 'More dreadful, from each foreign stroke':

Still more majestic shall thou rise,
More dreadful, from each foreign stroke:
As the loud blast that tears the skies,
Serves but to root thy native oak.

The external political servitude Britannia effortlessly repels—each foreign stroke merely strengthening her native freedom—is, by an unexpressed dialectical movement, the external rule she just as effortlessly imposes on subaltern nations. Never overtly martial, the stance 'Rule Britannia' takes up is that of a community of proud onlookers who extol the honour and freedom Britannia courageously defends.

My point, here, is that it significantly diminishes the refrain's semantic range to hear 'Britons never will be slaves' in the sole context of transatlantic plantation slavery, where individuals who are enslaved are considered property of an individual slave-holder. National political freedom and slavery are major preoccupations in early modern and enlightenment Western Europe and in Euro-colonialism generally. They inform early Spanish and Portuguese debates on whether or not Amerindigenes are 'natural' slaves in ways that have not been appreciated owing to the very semantic over-determination we are investigating here. For theorists indebted to Aristotle, an incapacity for internal political self-rule is taken to be a primary signifier of barbarism and the natural servility that attends it. The Hamitic curse in Genesis, which applies to Canaanites, often falls on a similarly undifferentiated geopolitical collectivity by being associated with 'nation' in the sense of lineage or 'race.' That certain nations—the British and the Dutch most prominently—are, like Israel, divinely chosen recipients of special guidance and blessings is an early modern and enlightenment commonplace, as is the corollary, that some nations suffer the withdrawal of divine goodness and truth as a supernatural penalty. For such nations and their inhabitants, servitude of some sort is simply part of the larger, providential order.

Slavery and Abuse

Whether spoken or written, 'slave(s)' and 'slavery' have an unrivalled ability to arrest thought, to rouse passion, to conjure unspeakable abjection and, in a post-abolitionist era, to signify the very nadir of injustice. In late sixteenth and early seventeenth centuries early modern Western European literature, produced in nations within whose borders slavery had no legal basis, the term 'slave' occasionally serves as a signifier of abjection in the form of grossly inferior, baseborn status. Like many of his English and continental contemporaries, Shakespeare uses 'slave' in this sense as well as in expressions of verbal abuse. In direct, abusive address, 'slave' acts as a rank-based slur, which puts the British or European addressee down as a worthless, perhaps lawless, nonentity. Prince Hal uses it in this way when he chides Falstaff for his transparently self-aggrandizing lies: 'What a slave art / thou, to hack thy sword as thou hast done, and then say / it was in fight!' (II.4: 252–254).[5] When not verbally directed at a specific addressee, 'slave' still expresses contempt or disdain. For example, Falstaff refers to the conscripts whose bribes he has accepted as 'such a commodity of warm slaves as had as lief hear/ the devil as a drum' (IV.2: 17–18), and to those he has taken into his charge as 'slaves as ragged as Lazarus in the painted cloth, where/ the glutton's dogs licked his sores, and such as indeed/ were never soldiers, but discarded unjust serving men' (IV.2: 24–26). Whether in direct verbal abuse or as third-person descriptor, a speaker who employs 'slave' thereby asserts, creates, or (in Falstaff's case) magnifies an immense distance in social status dividing him from the one(s) so disparaged.

Both Hal's abusive 'What a slave thou art', and Falstaff's reference to 'warm slaves' indirectly reference attempts to conceal cowardice and, therefore, draw on the affective energies of martial honour and shame codes. The designation 'slave,' however, points to the *absence* of shame in a situation where men of honour would be overwhelmed by it. Falstaff's 'slaves as ragged as Lazarus' has the simpler, rank-related meaning of lowlife or base. Both these registers are relevant to the following passage from Shakespeare's *Henry V*, in which the Duke of Bourbon rallies his troops by depicting a cowardly retreat to the safety of home—the alternative to manfully following their leader into battle—as necessarily leading to (or being the equivalent of) the deserter's taking on the part of his daughter's pimp:

> And he that will not follow Bourbon now,
> Let him go home, and with his cap in hand
> Like a base leno [pimp] hold the chamber door
> Whilst by a **slave** no gentler than my dog
> His fairest daughter is contaminated. (IV.5: 11–15; my emphasis)

A daughter's sexual assault by an anonymous English 'slave', the climax of this vividly developed vignette, is not the randomly selected, gratuitously violent scene of degradation it might at first seem. It obeys the logic of Graeco-Roman codes of martial honour, which dictate that warriors must willingly put their lives on the line in order to protect the freedom and thus the chastity of their womenfolk (Nyquist 2017). Since the battle for which Bourbon musters his men takes place in France, where defeat could result in the plundering of French homes and the raping of French girls and women (invasive violence that Henry V himself threatens earlier), Bourbon portrays a warrior's fainthearted retreat from combat as the prequel to his debasingly permissive involvement in his fairest daughter's rape.

The shamefulness of retreat is not underlined by the daughter's potential enslavement, though, as it might be in Greek or Latin literature. Among Christian Europeans—even those with multi-generational hostilities that go back as far as do the French and English—war slavery is not practiced, a social reality Shakespeare faithfully observes. Shame, which links the individual warrior's flight from battle to his pimp-like management of his daughter's physical accessibility, instead reduces the noble warrior to a servile submissiveness, indicated by 'his cap in hand' as well as the servant-like 'hold the chamber door'. It could be argued that by a process of contamination, the figure of the 'slave' recalls chattel slavery as an institution bound up with warfare. The rapist in this mini-drama—'a slave no gentler than my dog'—is, however, clearly not enslaved but rather a 'free' Englishman so base as to be unworthy of recognition by Bourbon. Animalized as the enslaved are in Graeco-Roman traditions, the rapist 'no gentler than my dog', is, clearly, not 'gentle' at all. Like the abusive 'slave' revealing Prince Hal's clear-sighted penetration of Falstaff's camouflaging lies, the term 'slave' here points up the rapist's essential shamelessness; as presented here, he is immune to the shame that aristocratic codes of honour expect dishonourable actions to induce.

In some early modern literature, then, 'slave(s)' is associated with either shame or a shameful shamelessness in contexts where institutional slavery is not in any way at issue. In the field of early modern political debate and theory, by contrast, invective against political servitude depends on tropes and motifs relating to Graeco-Roman institutional slavery inherited along with anti-tyranny discourse; on familiar representations of Hebrew slavery; or—increasingly in the course of the seventeenth and eighteenth centuries—on references or allusions to transatlantic slavery. Even in the case of political slavery, as was argued earlier, this invective issues from the standpoint of Western European freeborn peoples who assume that their ruler(s) ought not even momentarily to threaten them with intrastate, political enslavement, or to expose them to the indignities of foreign, political servitude. On the part of those who are 'free,' the shameful abjection associated with figurative political slavery is actively to be spurned or resisted.

Racializing Liberty and Slavery

Together with 'to harm, to mistreat', in much pre-modern literature 'to abuse' has the complementary meaning of 'to mislead, to deceive'. I would like to propose that as transatlantic slavery became institutionalized, in the ameliorist discourses that emerged alongside it, and, later, in abolitionism, language relating to servitude could be peculiarly abusive in this sense. It has been argued that inconsistent usage demonstrates how unevenly colonial slavery's racialization developed or that distinctions between indentured servitude and slavery were fundamentally unstable. Anti-Spanish sentiment certainly made English, Dutch, and French rivals uneasy with the institution's novelty, conscious of its lack of jurisprudential grounding, and wary of appearing to replicate Spain's infamous ruthlessness. Yet in the Bahamas, the first quarter of the seventeenth century saw the resulting circumspection lead to the tacit racialization of indentured servitude when terminal dates were assigned only to those of European descent while for Amerindigenes and Africans, the period was ninety-nine years (Bernhard 1999: 49–52). In this case, a single term relating to (implicitly 'free' though temporarily bound) servants clearly obscures the extent to which there was an accepted, racialized distinction in practice. Similarly, penal servitude, understood to be time-limited, could be referred to as penal 'slavery' but with the understanding that such servitude, imposed by European nation-states, was distinct from the 'slavery' endured by Africans. This is a topic that requires more discussion than it can receive here, but a few examples may give an idea of how specific Euro-colonial interests motivate linguistic practice when it comes to 'slavery' or 'servitude' (the Latin-derived term that often acts as a synonym for the later, European term 'slavery', but is also related to the conventionally free 'servant' and the sometimes wholly positive 'to serve').

We can start with the petition Marcellus Rivers and Oxenbridge Foyle present to Parliament and publish along with other materials in 1659 to protest having been sold into 'slavery' in Barbados (Beckles 1998: 230–231; also Guasco 2014: 2–4, 168–172). The 'slavery' Rivers and Foyle vituperate is their own, that of seventy-odd Englishmen who share their plight in Barbados, and also, as the title of their tract announces (a title echoing radical literature of the 1640s), 'Englands Slavery' (Rivers and Foyle 1659). Not episcopal, monarchical, or agrarian-capitalist as it would have been for mid-century radicals, the 'slavery' targeted is the penal servitude of free-born English citizens. Rivers and Foyle, the title-page announces, are 'gentlemen'; they are also royalists who had been imprisoned for conspiring to return Charles Stuart to the throne. This doesn't, however, prevent them from appropriating the rhetoric of Leveller prison pamphlets, as do other royalists opposing the

Protectorate's arbitrary exercise of its power (Murray 2014: 156–158). The petitioners object to having been transported to Barbados—in the degrading company of lowly convicts from Bridewell and Newgate—in spite of the fact they had not been convicted of any crime. That they are all legally innocent is central to the case they make against their 'slavery,' which for that reason is primarily figurative, political slavery. In preceding decades, criminalized inhabitants of the British Isles, primarily Scots and Irish, had so frequently been sent to Barbados to do time as labourers that the verb 'Barbadosed' was coined. In the context of the rapidly expanding population of trafficked and enslaved Africans—by 1653 there were 20,000 enslaved Africans to 8000 indentured servants in Barbados (Blackburn 1997: 231)—the petition opposes their penal 'slavery' on grounds that emphasize their Englishness: not having been convicted, they are identified on the title-page as 'Free-born Englishmen sold (uncondemned) into slavery'.

While they no doubt were exposed to or interacted with enslaved Africans on a daily basis, the petitioners do not once mention them. Absence of overt comparison, however, may heighten the rhetorical import of certain claims, as, for example, that the petitioners were 'bought and sold still from one planter to another, or attached as horses and beasts for the debts of their masters, being whipped at the whipping-posts (as rogues), for their masters' pleasure, and sleeping in sties worse than hogs in England, and many other ways made more miserable, beyond expression or Christian imagination' (Stock 1924: 248). Scarcely a neutral, verisimilar report, this language, found in several other passages, polemically reinforces their self-representation as sub-human chattel slaves. Martin Noell, the wealthy Caribbean merchant responsible for transporting them, contests the petitioners' account of their treatment in Barbados. Noell says they had been indentured for a limited period (in the colonies the period of indenture could be traded or sold), had been treated well, and had even been provided with horses. As for work, indentured servants don't do 'so much as the common husbandman here', Noell says: 'The work is mostly carried on by the negroes' (Stock 1924: 250).

In all sorts of ways, the status Rivers and Foyle enjoy as free-born Englishmen is insisted upon. Parliament itself is addressed as 'the representative of the freeborn people of England' (Stock 1924: 248). More importantly, the petitioners encourage members of parliament to identify with them: if English liberty can so easily be violated, then no free-born English individual is beyond the threat of arbitrary enslavement. Throughout, the language of popular sovereignty is appropriated so as to underline the political stakes of this threat. In the following passage, for example, the petition is said to be presented 'on behalf of themselves and all the free-born people of England, by whose suffrages they sit in Parliament, any of whose cases it may be next, whenever a like force shall be laid on them, to take course to curb the unlimited power under which the petitioners and others suffer' (Stock 1924: 249–250). Despite the danger that Rivers and Foyle pose as adversaries of the Commonwealth, their double-barrelled, polemical charge—that free-born Englishmen are being reduced to figurative, political slaves and treated no better than West Indian chattel slaves under the 'unlimited power' of their enslavers—has a strong impact on some MPs. 'I do not look on this business as a Cavalierish [i.e. anti-Protectorate or anti-Commonwealth] business', declares Sir Arthur Henry Vane, 'but as a matter that concerns the liberty of the free-born people of England' (Stock 1924: 253). Sir Haslerigge expands on the illegality of the whole episode, adding, 'These men are now sold into slavery amongst beasts. I could hardly hold weeping when I heard the petition' (Stock 1924: 257).

The petitioners' plight thus becomes a test of England's political liberties, which, if undefended, leaves every citizen vulnerable to both figurative slavery and enslavement in the West Indies: ('Our case, is but your Touchstone, by which you may discover whether *English*, be Slaves or Freemen') (Rivers and Foyle 1659: 10). Referring to the whipping River and Foyle say they've endured—vulnerability to physical punishment being a Graeco-Roman signifier of slave as opposed to free status—Mr. Boscawen, a self-declared supporter of the Old Cause (that is, the cause of freeing the English from Charles I's tyrannous rule), comments that 'We are miserable slaves, if we may not have this liberty [liberty from disciplinary force] secured to us' (Stock 1924: 256). In the two geo-political contexts the petition cleverly exploits, the phrase 'We are miserable slaves' has primary reference to the figurative, political slavery that results when English political liberty is violated with impunity. The opening 'we' situates both speaker and auditors safely in England amongst freeborn Englishmen. At the same time, however, the shame of being treated as 'miserable slaves' is energized by its association with those who are permanently enslaved in Barbados.

This semantic slipperiness is confirmed when another speaker declares, 'Slavery is slavery, as well in a Commonwealth as under another form' (Stock 1924: 254). While this formulation shows how seriously Parliament takes its responsibility to uphold the rule of law impartially, making no exception for treasonous royalists, rhetorically it conflates figurative, intrastate slavery with the slavery that is burgeoning in England's Atlantic colonies. Far from being naive, 'slavery is slavery' collapses different semantic registers, thereby heightening the significance of jeopardizing the liberty of free-born Englishmen. (Compare Hare's deliberately inflammatory 'Slavery properly so called' of England's 'slavery' under the Norman Yoke.) It also furthers another, unstated agenda, which is the covert racialization of both figurative political slavery and transatlantic chattel slavery. Mr. Boscawen brings this out when he urges consideration of the legality of transporting Rivers and Foyle: 'If you pass this, our lives will be as cheap as those negroes' (Stock 1924: 256).

Unlike this relatively obscure but revealing petition, Daniel Defoe's novels—especially, of course, *Robinson Crusoe*—have been immensely popular since their publication in the second and third decades of the eighteenth century. Half a century or more separates Rivers' and Foyle's petition from Defoe's best-known works, which were published when slavery was securely institutionalized in England's Atlantic colonies and when both liberty and slavery were thoroughly racialized. This increases the significance of Defoe's equally motivated deployment of 'servant' and 'slave' in both his fictional and journalistic prose. Friday's status in *Robinson Crusoe* continues to be debated because Defoe uses 'servant' as well as 'slave' of the figure whose bodily, gestural submission is interpreted by Crusoe to be 'in token of swearing to be my Slave for ever' (Defoe 2010: 204). Here and elsewhere, 'slave' has Friday's position conform to transatlantic practices regarding enslavement, but 'servant', the term applied to 'free' domestic help within Britain, also appears.

As Defoe ingeniously constructs it, both terms are appropriate to the novel's suspenseful presentation of Friday's entrance into relationship with his 'master' Crusoe: Friday *voluntarily* chooses permanently to subject himself to the armed and dangerous European who stands before him. In addition, 'servant' better captures the various domestic parts Friday subsequently plays as Crusoe's companion, son, and catechumen. Yet readers knowledgeable about the New World institution will recognize that in the memorable scene of their first encounter Defoe adapts war slavery doctrine so as to make it compatible with prevailing European notions of consent, and that he has the enslavement of Africans in mind when Crusoe names the Amerindigene 'Friday', a name found among enslaved Africans in apparent imitation of the Akan-derived day-name Cuffee, meaning 'Friday-born.'[6]

When in other novels Defoe's English rogues are transported to the Americas, their condition may be referred to as 'slavery', but often in the spirit of the parliamentary objections to the 'slavery' of Rivers and Foyle. Even the most lowborn, roguish English are, after all, free-born. An inappropriately brutal condition for them, 'slavery' may also be a penal sentence that providentially encourages in those transported either spiritual conversion, the disciplined development of business acumen, or both. In any case, Defoe's free-born English are ever only temporarily bound as indentured servants and find in the colonies countless opportunities for advancement, with the result that their servitude, facilitating upward mobility, serves to advertise the material benefits of migration.

It may be surprising, then, to find Defoe frequently referring to enslaved Africans, together with indentured Christians, as 'servants'. In *Colonel Jack*, for example, 'servants' is often used inclusively of both Africans and Europeans. Closer examination, however, reveals that 'servants' who are African are eventually explicitly designated 'Negroes', and are distinguished from their European counterparts by numerous devices, including the dialect assigned them, the fearful submissiveness they repeatedly act out, and the manipulative disciplinary regime that Jack designs to subject them. At times, casual linguistic practice gives this away, as when Jack is to ride all over the Plantation 'to see Servants and Negroes' at work, taking with him a whip 'to correct and lash the Slaves and Servants, when they proved Negligent, or Quarrelsome' (Defoe 1724: 162). Because Defoe regularly supplies markers of racial distinction, the deployment of 'servants' as an apparently undifferentiated category has the effect of prompting readers to perceive the many consequential differences between enslaved Africans and indentured Europeans. At the same time, its apparent inclusivity reassuringly suggests that Christian planters recognize the equal humanity of all.

Abusive use of the term 'slavery' becomes even more prevalent in the abolitionist discourses that gain traction in the Age of Revolutions. With consensus among radicals on the injustice of 'slavery' of every kind, including the tyrannous 'chains' of civil society excoriated so eloquently by Jacques Rousseau, transatlantic slavery is often only one among a host of objectionable slaveries. It is certainly not the primary or exclusive target of most Jacobins or French radicals, for whom the abolition of transatlantic slavery is one expression of a wide-ranging, multi-focal anti-tyrannicism. William Godwin (1793: 755–756), for example, illustrates the superior humanity of rational persuasion over corporal punishment by equating subjection to the latter with 'slavery': 'It can only be by the most deplorable perversion of reason that we can be induced to believe any species of slavery, from the slavery of the school-boy to that of the most unfortunate Negro in our West India plantations, favourable to virtue'. Though the two 'species' of slavery here (with the 'school-boy' presumed to be English or European) are not exactly levelled, this passage, like many others, has no committed abolitionist agenda (Nyquist 2014: 228–233).

Even when transatlantic slavery is a more central focus, it frequently subserves imperial interests. For politically conservative abolitionists, the need to counter the bad name slavery gives Christianity and English imperialism is sometimes a major motive for entering the abolitionist fray. In her influential 'The Black Slave Trade: A Poem,' Hannah More (1788), for example, praises William Penn for having founded his colony on non-violent principles: 'Thy followers only have effac'd the shame/ Inscrib'd by SLAVERY on the Christian name'. For once, shame attaches to the enslavers not the enslaved. Yet because Britain, for More, is 'where the soul of Freedom reigns', she can go on to claim that it will not forge chains for others or hoard its prize possession. Providentially blessed, Britain, More proclaims, rather 'spreads the blessing wide as human kind'. More's vision of an imperialism revitalized by its beneficient, freedom-bestowing 'Freedom' concludes with a prayer that conveys the view, conventional at the time, that 'Afric,' the abode of 'intellectual night', will be spiritually and intellectually enlightened by Christian England's gift of freedom.

In one of history's great ironies, Britain's comparatively early move to legislate against the transatlantic slave trade and slavery itself is often extolled, as if such decisive, honourable action wipes the record clean. In many ways, however, abolitionism deepened racialization by widely disseminating materials with new visually and emotionally affecting tropes and stereotypes at the same time as repurposing those already in existence (see Midgley 1998: 161–179; Brown 2006). Sentimentalized vignettes of children 'torn' from their families, of passively dominated or tortured Black bodies, of loyal slaves sweetly suffering for or with their enslavers appear alongside the Wedgewood engravings, which feature enslaved Africans begging to be freed by the Europeans who mysteriously hold 'freedom' in their hands. This emphasis on abject victimhood is not merely or simply racist, however. It underwrites an ideologically powerful opposition essential to the polarity free/unfree, namely that between freedom and force, between actions that are voluntary and those that are compelled, between conditions that have been produced by human agency and those that result from human coercion. Though this polarity might seem to possess experiential truth, its reductiveness and ideological implications are especially apparent in the context of transatlantic slavery. As historians have recently argued, an emphasis on the powerlessness of those enslaved produces blind spots regarding not only the many forms of resistance that were undertaken by enslaved Africans but also the vital, collective acts through which communities were created and, against all odds, sustained.[7] I would add that it also risks assuming the standpoint of the always already 'free' and reproducing a racialized fetishization of freedom.

Modern Slavery?

In the context of the *longue durée* I have been outlining, the phrase 'modern slavery' clearly exploits the long-standing, multiply pejorative connotations of 'slavery' and, most importantly, 'slaves'. At the same time, it invites—overtly, at times—comparison with the slavery that immediately leaps to most minds, namely, Euro-colonial slavery in the New World (or, given the USA-centric character of the news and media industries, slavery in the Southern USA). Among the many things this comparison elides is the incremental process, year-by-year, decade-by-decade, stretching over centuries, whereby Euro-colonialist economic interests, ideology, and practices entrenched themselves so as to gain widespread social acceptance of the abduction, trafficking, and enslavement of African women, men, and children, together with their subjection to distinctive disciplinary regimes. While meant to underscore their injustice, stress on the illegality of the practices or phenomena labelled 'slavery' obscures the many differences between these phenomena and transatlantic slavery, which became a diversely regulated institution in numerous Danish, Dutch, English, French, and Spanish colonies in the Caribbean as well as in settler colonies in the Americas. In short, the new abolitionism fails to acknowledge the complex, often historically disjunctive, interrelations between social practices and the jurisprudence or legislation that may or may not later support them.

The new abolitionism also unselfconsciously perpetuates racialized Euro-colonialist tropes. Uncritical appropriation of the aims of earlier White abolitionists basically ensures this result, since the stances they took up were so thoroughly racialized. Humane European benefactors and downtrodden non-European victims re-appear all too often in connection with modern 'slavery'. A TED Talk, 'Free the Slaves', for example, features a glamorous White spokeswoman journalistically exposing the atrocious conditions in parts of Africa and South Asia under which countless men, women, and children are compelled to work without pay (Kristine 2012). Described as 'slaves' and photographed doing arduous tasks, every one of the individuals whose photos appear in stark, visual contrast with the ever-present, compassionate White speaker is either African or South Asian, engaged in demanding, dangerous labour, and captured facially expressing pain, sadness, and/or despair. For even slightly resistant viewers, confidence in the accuracy of the information conveyed is likely to be shaken by the absence of any local, historical, or economic contextualization, by the relentless attention to suffering under unidentified slaveholders, and by the desire attributed to the 'slaves' for 'freedom'—ostensibly a natural human good but functioning, as it has increasingly over the twentieth and twenty-first centuries, as an immaterial signifier of 'Western', that is, Amer-European, hegemony.

For decades, now, activists and scholars have been subjecting Euro-colonialist and neo-colonialist representations such as these to thoughtful, detailed analysis (for example Mohanty and Russo 1991; and for visual representations see Pieterse 1992). In the absence of historically informed self-consciousness or decolonizing critique, racialist stereotypes, tropes, and modes of address are too easily replicated. It matters that many aspects of the centuries-long history of New World slavery first became widely known through abolitionism's popular mass-media representations. The racialization inscribed in the abolitionist project is, as it were, indelibly present in many post-abolitionist discourses, and perhaps nowhere more visibly than in those that revisit that earlier moment. When recently successful cinematic productions such as *Amistad* and *Amazing Grace* perpetuate the abolitionist trope of the enlightened, white crusader benevolently dispensing justice and liberty, it should probably not come as a surprise that some new abolitionists march to trumpets brassily heralding achievements like those of their forebears.

The continuities assumed by the new abolitionists may obscure the new forms of gendered racialism that neo-colonialist economies are in the process of producing. Besides resting on mistaken assumptions about slavery as an ahistorical social institution with identifiable because invariable features—'the beast of bondage' as the TED talk mentioned earlier calls it—'modern slavery' frequently functions as an umbrella term for a variety of oppressive practices that inexplicably occur in far-flung, geo-politically unrelated sites. Trafficking in migrants, in human (largely female) sexuality, in child labour or child militancy can all be brought under this capacious umbrella, as can the varied local conditions of precarious employment that have been established for undocumented workers. Decontextualized as are the many faces of 'slavery' today, these practices appear to be the monstrous effects of human greed and an unbridled taste for tyranny whose victims just happen overwhelmingly to be non-European. It is they, however, who are labelled 'slaves' when their oppression is being named (Kempadoo et al. 2012).

When understood, instead, in the context of neo-colonialism and neo-liberalism, the same practices may reveal unsightly yet vigorous roots in earlier Euro-colonial formations. Severing such practices from their roots may create a satisfied sense of having come to terms with a nasty piece of current reality or recent history but may also prevent the recognition of new growth, especially when it flourishes in the uniquely opaque transnational networks engineered by contemporary finance capitalism. Within European settler societies, interrelations between new oppressive phenomena and inherited Euro-colonial formations may disappear from view in discussions of racism that take for granted the pre-existence of distinct races (as if, for example, calling White people 'Caucasians' mitigates racialization) or by habituation to the overrepresentation of Black and Indigenous women and men in the ever-increasing incidence of state-induced poverty, deschooling, deskilling, subjection to state-sponsored violence, and imprisonment.

From this perspective, it is significant that discussion sparked by the Canadian Truth and Reconciliation Commission's activities concentrated with such intensity on injustices directly associated with residential schools. This focus was, of course, the commission's mandate, established by survivors and survivors' families themselves.[8] Yet the impression created by media reports was that the period in which Indigenous children were forced to reside in these schools was the only or most egregious episode of the last 500 and more years in which European settlers could be said to have attempted 'cultural genocide'. Connections between the residential schools and the Indian Act of 1876—a blatantly colonialist legislative ensemble imposed unilaterally by the Canadian state and, while often amended, still in force—were, for example, seldom stressed. Since most non-Indigenous Canadians receive little or no public education on First Nations, Inuit, and Métis communities or on early modern settler colonialism, erasure of this larger historical context may permit new forms of neo-colonialism to prosper. Jonathan Rudin, head of Aboriginal Legal Services of Canada, observes that the number of Indigenous children currently in the state's care is higher than at any given moment of residential schooling: 'Now we don't have residential schools. What we have is child welfare, and when you graduate from child welfare we have jails' (Wahlquist 2016).

Slavery as Freedom's Aporia

In a brief conclusion, I would like to compare two recent appeals to 'slavery' that differ radically from that of the new abolitionist movement, the first being Kanye West's 'New Slaves'. West's (2013) rap is a powerful revision of anti-tyrannicism, with neo-liberalism and consumer capitalism acting the part of tyrants and both 'broke' and 'rich' African-Americans the part of social or political slaves. Its masculinist language ('You see it's leaders and it's followers / But I'd rather be a dick than a swallower') graphically rejects the conventionally emasculating position occupied by servility, while the refrain, 'Y'all niggas can't fuck with me' throws the 'N' word back against racialized, that is, Amer-European representatives of the tyrannous state, with its private prisons, Drug Enforcement Agency, and promotion of a dizzying array of super-luxury goods, from Alexander Wang clothing to Maybach keys. From the beginning of the rap, West's 'new slaves' are situated both in the racialized consumer culture of the contemporary USA and in historical relation to the enslaved Africans of US plantations societies, of post-Reconstruction lynching (in the echoes of 'blood on the leaves' from 'Strange Fruit'), and of the segregationist practices of the Jim Crow era. Immediately taking a position *within* this history ('My momma was raised in an era when, / Clean water was only served to the fairer skin'), West's rapper (distinct for analytical purposes from the historical West) identifies himself with the 'new' slaves whose social and political slavery he brilliantly protests.

West's 'New Slaves' can be interestingly juxtaposed to the 'slave' and 'slavery' that appear in the concluding paragraphs of David Bromwich's *London Review of Books* piece (2015: 15–16) on the brazen impunity with which U.S. secret services have practiced torture under two different administrations, with the support if not outright collaboration of Britain, Canada, Australia and New Zealand. 'The evidence suggests', Bromwich says, 'that Anglo-Saxon democracies in our time have influenced each other chiefly in the cause of social control and illegal violence'. For the respectability it lent Bush's war-mongering, Bromwich singles out Tony Blair's high-minded eulogy of the 'sense of justice that makes moral the love of liberty'. As testimony to the vigour with which a professed commitment to 'liberty' continues to justify imperialist violence, this declaration is relevant to my exploration of naming. In ways that are not acknowledged, though, it also seems to inform Bromwich's comments on similarities between torture and slavery. Both, he points out, have been defended on the grounds that they have been practiced time out of mind. However, while in the twentieth century both were roundly condemned, Bromwich observes that thanks to Bush, Cheney et al. this is no longer true of torture, which is today implicitly condoned (explicitly and enthusiastically now by Trump).

Bromwich's piece opens by comparing New York City's decision not to indict the police officers who killed Eric Garner with Obama's refusal to hold U.S. secret services accountable for their use of (illegal) torture. Though based on synchronicity—the judicial decision was made only a week before the Senate Intelligence Committee's report on the CIA was released—the comparison is thought-provoking and chillingly apt. Yet I was taken aback by the paragraph with which Bromwich closes his article:

> The object of torture is a slave as long as the infliction lasts; a slave has no recourse against torture so long as the master chooses to inflict it. To suppose that slavery is a matter of ownership is a half-truth that misses the political basis of the oppression. The evil consists in the ability to dominate other persons without check, the ability to do with them what you will, armed with assurance of impunity. Such a custom of acquittal or habit of non-accountability may have broad consequences in the treatment by the state of its own people – the treatment, for example, of a large black man on the streets of New York by a huddle of police who are determined to subdue him. The suspect becomes a rightless subject and not a person who bears the inalienable rights of a citizen.

Why is the victim of torture here not compared with (as the argument has just suggested) but actually identified *as* a slave? Especially if the identification lasts only so long as the torture does? Is Bromwich aware that in classical Greece the testimony of slaves was not admissible in court unless it had been obtained under torture? Although this particular connection between slave-status and torture is not drawn, it might indicate how Graeco-Roman legacies silently haunt modern discourse. Questions about Bromwich's intentions, however, persist.

In Graeco-Roman and transatlantic slave-societies, the status of slaves as property is legally tied to the permanence (with manumission the only way out) of their enslavement, their availability for sale, and the principle of heritability. If ownership or *dominium* is not relevant to Bromwich's torture victim as 'slave', then why introduce slavery? Further, if the victim of torture is rightless only while being tortured and in relation to the torturer's non-accountability, could this victim not with equal plausibility be compared with a prisoner sexually assaulted with impunity by fellow inmates (as happens to the wrongly convicted white male protagonist of the TV series *Rectify*)? Or as a child abused by its parent(s), or perhaps a wife sexually assaulted by her husband—forms of violence which until fairly recently could be practiced with impunity in Amer-European societies? Why merge the victim of torture and, specifically, the *slave*?

The answer, I believe, lies in the final phrase regarding 'the inalienable rights of a citizen', which reproduces the ideologically charged opposition between an individual who is 'free' and one who is a 'slave'. By focussing on the individual victim, Bromwich is able to evoke the single household master conventionally associated with institutional slavery and with the tyrannous political ruler who abuses his citizens with impunity. Both are integral components of the philosophical, political, and theological discourses that derive from Graeco-Roman literature. Owing to its evocatively figurative character, inherited along with the 'love of liberty' invoked by Blair, Bromwich's 'slave' is ostensibly without ethnicity, social rank, and gender—the exact counterpart, in fact, of the ostensibly featureless liberal Euro-colonial subject.

Along the way, though, the paradigmatic 'slave' suddenly assumes Eric Garner's characteristics when victimized as 'a large black man on the streets of New York by a huddle of police who are determined to subdue him'. As if being asked to fall in with the Middle Eastern victims of U.S. sanctioned torture, the previously anonymous, generic 'slave' is unselfconsciously assigned membership in a non-European population vulnerable to oppression owing precisely to the Euro-colonialist legacies outlined here. Bromwich's unwitting racialization of 'liberty' and 'slavery' illustrates how easily the legacies of

Euro-colonialism may dictate the terms of contemporary analysis. If not countered by awareness that rhetorical practices relating to 'liberty' and 'slavery' are a feature of Euro-colonialism, blindsiding of this sort will continue to occur. Or, put, more simply, 'slavery' will go on working as 'liberty's' *aporia*. Among the issues this will obfuscate is the potential *alienability* of any and all 'rights' held by the 'free'.

Notes

1. For the Final Report of the Truth and Reconciliation Commission, see 'TRC Findings', *Truth and Reconciliation Commission of Canada*, http://www.trc.ca/websites/trcinstitution/index.php?p=890.
2. For a discussion of honour, shame and gender in Athenian democracy, see Balot (2014: 256–277) and Foley (2001); for Rome, see Kaster (1997).
3. The lyrics were written by James Thomson and originally published as an ode (Thomson 1740: 42–43).
4. For an analysis of 'Rule Britannia' as part of the emerging ideology of an integrative, Atlantic British Empire, see Armitage (2000: 170–174).
5. William Shakespeare, *1 Henry IV*, in *The Complete Works*, 2nd edn., eds. Stanley Wells, et al. (Oxford: Clarendon Press, 2005). Subsequent parenthetical references are to this edition.
6. Defoe's narrative and ideological strategies, together with his meliorist adaptation of war slavery doctrine, are discussed at greater length in Nyquist (2016: 335–359).
7. Vincent Brown (2009) offers an important critique of Patterson's theorization of slavery as 'social death', and argues that current scholarship on transatlantic slavery often occludes the emergence of both transient and more lasting communities. For a critique of the ways in which an emphasis on the agency of the enslaved may reproduce white-supremacist assumptions, see Walter Johnson (2003: 113–124).
8. For the official mandate of the Commission, see 'Schedule "N" of the Indian Residential School Settlement Agreement,' *Truth and Reconciliation Commission of Canada*, www.trc.ca/websites/trcinstitution/File/pdfs/SCHEDULE_N_EN.pdf.

References

Aristotle. (1988). *The Politics* (S. Everson, Ed.). Cambridge: Cambridge University Press.

Armitage, D. (2000). *The Ideological Origins of the British Empire*. Cambridge: Cambridge University Press.

Balot, R. (2014). *Courage in the Democratic Polis: Ideology and Critique in Classical Athens*. Oxford: Oxford University Press.

Beckles, H. Mc D. (1998). The "Hub of Empire": The Caribbean and Britain in the Seventeenth Century. In N. Canny (Ed.), *The Oxford History of the British Empire* (Vol. 1). Oxford: Oxford University Press.

Bernhard, V. (1999). *Slaves and Slaveholders in Bermuda, 1616–1782*. Columbia: University of Missouri Press.

Blackburn, R. (1997). *The Making of English Colonial Slavery: From the Baroque to the Modern, 1492–1800*. London: Verso.

Brown, C. L. (2006). *Moral Capital: Foundations of British Abolitionism*. Williamsburg, VA: University of North Carolina Press.

Brown, V. (2009, December). Social Death and Political Life in the Study of Slavery. *The American Historical Review, 114*(5), 1231–1249.

Bromwich, D. (2015, January 8). Working the Dark Side. *London Review of Books, 37*(1), 15–16.

Defoe, D. (1724). *Colonel Jack* (3rd ed.). London.

Defoe, D. (2010). *Robinson Crusoe* (E. R. Davis, Ed.). Peterborough: Broadview Editions.

Foley, H. (2001). *Female Acts in Greek Tragedy*. Princeton, NJ: Princeton University Press.

Godwin, W. (1793). *An Enquiry Concerning Political Justice and Its Influence on General Virtue and Happiness* (Vol. 2). London: G.G.J. and J. Robinson.

Guasco, M. (2014). *Slaves and Englishmen: Human Bondage in the Early Modern Atlantic World*. Philadelphia, PA.: University of Pennsylvania Press.

Hare, J. (1647a). *St. Edwards Ghost: or, Anti-Normanisme*. London.

Hare, J. (1647b). *Plaine English to Our Wilfull Bearers with Normanisme*. London.

Hill, C. (1968). The Norman Yoke. In *Puritanism and Revolution*. London: Panther History.

Johnson, W. (2003). On Agency. *Journal of Social History, 37*(1) (Fall), 113–124.

Kaster, R. (1997). The Shame of the Romans. *Transactions of the American Philological Association, 127,* 1–19.

Kempadoo, K., Sanghera, J., & Pattanaik, B. (Eds.). (2012). *Trafficking and Prostitution Reconsidered* (2nd ed.). Boulder, CO: Paradigm Publishers.

Kristine, L. (2012). *Photos That Bear Witness to Modern Slavery.* TED. https://www.ted.com/speakers/lisa_kristine.

Livy. (2002). *History of Rome* (B. O. Foster, Trans.). Cambridge, MA: Loeb Classical Library, Harvard University Press.

Midgley, C. (1998). Anti-slavery and the Roots of "Imperial Feminism". In *Gender and Imperialism.* Manchester and New York: Manchester University Press.

Mignolo, D., & Escobar, A. (Eds.). (2010). *Globalization and the Decolonial Option.* London and New York: Routledge.

Mohanty, C. T., & Russo, A. (Eds.). (1991). *Third World Women and the Politics of Feminism.* Bloomington: Indiana University Press.

More, H. (1788). Slavery: A Poem. In M. Wood (Ed.). (2003). *The Poetry of Slavery: An Anglo-American Anthology 1764–1865* (pp. 101–110). Oxford: Oxford University Press.

Murray, M. (2014). The Liberty of the Subject and the "Pris'ner Samon". In C. Gray & E. Murphy (Eds.), *Milton Now.* New York: Palgrave Macmillan.

Nyquist, M. (2013). *Arbitrary Rule: Slavery, Tyranny, and the Power of Life and Death.* Chicago: Chicago University Press.

Nyquist, M. (2014). Equiano, Satanism, and Slavery. In C. Gray & E. Murphy (Eds.), *Milton Now: Alternative Approaches and Contexts.* New York: Palgrave Macmillan.

Nyquist, M. (2016). Friday as Fit Help. In B. Hoxby & A. Baynes Coiro (Eds.), *Milton in the Long Restoration* (pp. 335–359). Oxford: Oxford University Press.

Nyquist, M. (2017). Base Slave and Roman Yoke. *Oxford Handbook of Early Modern Literature and Law.* Oxford: Oxford University Press.

Pieterse, I. N. (1992). *White on Black: Images of Blacks in Western Popular Culture.* New Haven: Yale University Press.

Raaflaub, K. (2004). *The Discovery of Freedom* (R. Franciscono, Trans.). Chicago: Chicago University Press.

Rivers, M., & Foyle, O. (1659). *Englands Slavery, or Barbados Merchandize; in a Petition to the High and Honourable Court of Parliament, by Marcellus Rivers and Oxenbridge Foyle Gentlemen, on the Behalf of Themselves and Three-Score and Ten More Free-Born Englishmen Sold (Uncondemned) into Slavery.* London: Printed in the Eleventh Year of Englands Liberty.

Shakespeare, W. (2005). 1 Henry IV. In S. Wells, et al. (Eds.), *The Complete Works* (2nd ed.). Oxford: Clarendon Press.

Stock, F. (Ed.). (1924). *Proceedings and Debates of the British Parliaments Respecting North America* (Vol. 1, pp. 1542–1688). Washington, DC: Carnegie Institution of Washington.

Thomson, J. (1740). *Alfred: A Masque*. London: Millar.

Truth and Reconciliation Commission of Canada. http://www.trc.ca.

Wahlquist, C. (2016, February 24). "It's the Same Story": How Australia and Canada are Twinning on Bad Outcomes for Indigenous People. *The Guardian*.

West, K. (2013). New Slaves. *Yeezus* (Def Jam Recordings).

4

Historicizing Freedom of Movement: Memory and Exile in Political Context

Charlotte Sussman

In her poem of 1788, "The Black Slave Trade," the English antislavery activist Hannah More makes the following plea to her British readers:

> …if to you, who voluntary roam,
> So dear the memory of your distant home,
> O think how absence the lov'd scene endears
> To him, whose food is groans, whose drink is tears;
> Think on the wretch whose aggravated pains
> To exile misery adds, to misery chains. (ll. 133–138)

I begin with this passage because of its prominent juxtaposition of memory and mobility. We often think of memory as a function of time, but the history of transatlantic slavery reminds us that memory has a relation to space as well. In More's poem, the rhyming pair 'roam' and 'home' pulls away from each other at opposite ends of the couplet, only bridged, or perhaps even held together, by 'memory.' This placement

C. Sussman (✉)
Duke University, Durham, NC, USA
e-mail: sussman@duke.edu

L. Brace and J. O'Connell Davidson (eds.), *Revisiting Slavery and Antislavery*,
https://doi.org/10.1007/978-3-319-90623-2_4

and the resonance of the words reveal that the struggle to remember the faraway is as difficult as the struggle to remember the long ago. This double nature of memory was driven home to the British during the eighteenth century by both the slavery debates and the contemporaneous debates about British emigration. The definition of memory was up for grabs in these debates, as it still is in our exploration of the archives of these massive less-than-free migrations.

More's modification of 'roaming' with the adjective 'voluntary,' however, creates a distinction between those whose movement is free and those whose movement is coerced—a distinction between the emigrant and the slave—even as it insists that the memory of home is 'dear' to both. The poem asserts both a difference and a commonality between the two forms of mobility. In this essay, I argue that our understanding of both forms of roaming—coerced and free—is historically constructed. Such an understanding, I contend, is vital to understanding the history of slavery. As my attention to More's poem indicates, the essay also claims that forms of representation we now think of as literary rather than political played an important role in forming our concepts of both slavery and 'freedom of movement,' in part because they shaped our ideas about the nature of memory.

The political intent of More's poem is evident in her discussion of memory. The question of what the slave remembers has always been a vexed and painful issue; it was contested in the slavery debates of the eighteenth century, and it continues to be contested in current explorations of the archive of transatlantic slavery. Its very existence is tenuous and hard-won: 'in every slave society,' writes Saidiya Hartman, 'Slave owners attempted to eradicate the slave's memory' (2007: 155). This practice of enforced oblivion explains why More, like many late eighteenth-century antislavery activists, insists that memory of the slave is ineradicable. Her poem imagines the slave in possession of an exile's memory of a lost and beloved 'home.' This kind of memory, More posits, is shared by European 'roamers,' and when these roamers recognize that they share this way of looking backward with slaves, slaves will rise in their eyes to beings worthy of empathy. In other words, the slave's claim to personhood is, in antislavery appeals like More's, contingent on his or her possession not just of memory but of a particular form of memory: a memory of home. To understand the political and historical importance of this appeal, we need to ask why the slave's memory matters so much. Of all the miseries of transatlantic slavery—the physical violence, the sexual depredations, the near impossibility of manumission—why is the slave's relationship to his or her lost home so often foregrounded in the slavery debates? What are the consequences of focusing on the loss of that home? This essay examines the claims More makes for memory, and asks why those claims are bound up with the varieties of human mobility. It argues that the answers to those questions are important not only to antislavery discourse, but also to thinking about human mobility in the eighteenth-century as an affective as much as a political or economic question. Exilic memory—the memory of and longing for a lost homeland—turns out to play a crucial part on both European and African mobility.

Our ideas about European emigration to the new world are retrospectively colored by the vast, voluntary migrations of the nineteenth century, the phenomenon that James Belich (2009) has dubbed the 'Settler Revolution.' We tend to contrast this 'free' mobility with the coerced mobility of the slave trade. But our celebration of the former and our condemnation of the latter have tended to obscure the peculiar status of the long eighteenth century in the history of human mobility. In the Atlantic arena, this era, from approximately 1650 to 1830, was a regime of primarily unfree human movement, for British migrants and slaves alike. As David Eltis has demonstrated, until the 1830s, 'four out of every five migrants from both Europe and Africa sailed with the expectation of being in some kind of servitude at the completion of the voyage,' whether that servitude was indentured labor, a sentence of penal transportation, or slavery (2002: 33). 'Servitude,' writes Aaron Fogleman, is the word 'that best characterizes the status of the vast majority of immigrants' to the new world in the era before the American Revolution (1998: 43). Such research seems to show that, without taking anything away from the horrors of chattel slavery, it is still possible to say that slavery was not the opposite of European mobility in the way we have been taught to think of it. Instead, slavery was the limit case at one end of a continuum of coerced movement and servitude. In order to understand how slavery and European migration were eventually disambiguated, we need first to acknowledge the extent to which they were mutually implicated and intertwined. We need to ask how the slave's absolute lack of freedom of movement helped to define the movement of European emigrants as 'free,' and, conversely, how new ideas about the nature of freedom of movement at the end of the eighteenth century fueled the antislavery movement.

The era of Britain's greatest involvement in the slave trade, from the mid-seventeenth century to the early nineteenth century, was also characterized by a particular set of beliefs about British migration to the new world. This set of beliefs took hold in the mid-seventeenth century, as British immigration to the Americas began to decline, not to rise again until the last quarter of the eighteenth century. These new ideas about migration developed against the backdrop of the tremendous and ongoing need for labor to fuel England's imperial expansion. At the start of that expansion, in the early seventeenth century, it seemed that the demand could be met by moving British laborers overseas. This solution had the advantage of seeming to 'disburthen' Britain of 'its worst people' (quoted in Beier 1985: 150). In the early decades of the century, writes Abigail Swingen, 'it was widely understood that there were always more servants to be had from England, or possibly Scotland and Ireland…[I]t seemed that colonial labor demand could only be met through channeling undesirable subgroups into indentured service' (2015: 15). As the early seventeenth-century pro-emigration tract, "A Good Speed to Virginia," explains:

> Although the honour of the king be in the multitude of people, Pro. 14.28, yet when this multitude of people increaseth to over great a number, the common-wealth stands subject to many perilous inconveniences…[and governments] have sent their overflowing multitudes abroad into other countries and provinces…so we see the husbandman deal with his grounds when they are overcharged with cattell, he removes them from one ground to another, and so he provideth well for his cattell and his ground. (Gray 1937: 5)

Proponents of colonization lauded such human mobility as natural (Chaplin 2001: 121, 130).

As the century progressed, however, attitudes about both the desirability and feasibility of this labor flow began to change: the British poor became less likely to sign on as servants, indentured or otherwise; and social and economic thinkers were less likely to encourage emigration. Explanations for this shift in attitudes vary. The population of Britain contracted somewhat in the second half of the seventeenth century, increasing the demand for labor at home, while at the same time increasing wages. Perhaps not coincidentally, attitudes about the poor also began to change; 'there was a mercantilist strain of thought in relation to the poor [at this time], in which they were regarded as idle resources rather than moral threat' (Braddick 2000: 118). At home, the poor provided both a potential work force and a market for consumer goods: density of population was seen by many as the key to prosperity (Pincus 2012). John Locke believed that 'numbers of men are to be preferred to largeness of dominions' (Locke 1690). The Poor Laws reflected this new interest in harnessing the labor power of the poor for domestic rather than colonial use: those able to find employment were granted the right to settle in the place where they worked; those without employment were 'removed'. Mobility came to be seen not as a natural condition of mankind, but as something that happened to subaltern persons—the "idle poor" and criminals. One opponent of a failed census bill in 1753 demanded, 'To what end then should our number be known, except that we are to be pressed into the fleet and the army, or transported like felons to the plantations abroad?', linking government interest to coerced mobility (*Parliamentary History* 1813 column 1320). In the retrospective light of the 'Settler Revolution,' we tend to think of freedom as it relates to mobility as meaning the freedom to go where one wants—to cross territories or borders. Through most of the eighteenth century, however, liberty meant the freedom to stay put—to not suffer 'removal' under the edicts of the poor laws, impressment, transportation, or, the most brutal form, capture into slavery. Thus, the suicidal speaker of Thomas Day's *Dying Negro*, published in 1773, declares, '...better in th'untimely grave to rot,/The world and all its cruelties forgot,/ Than dragg'd once more beyond the western main,/To groan beneath some dastard planter's chain.' Here, the important register of slavery's lack of freedom is the man's vulnerability to being forced to leave his natal place, to being 'dragg'd' across the ocean, to end up in chains. The lines imply that 'freedom' would mean staying put. And while this is obviously true for slaves stolen from Africa, I would argue that it was true for many other subaltern groups as well.

Only in the last third of the eighteenth century was freedom re-associated with movement. In his *Commentaries on English Law* (1783), William Blackstone records what Edlie Wong dubs a 'right of locomotion': 'personal liberty consists in the power of locomotion, of changing situation, or removing one's person to whatsoever places one's own inclination may direct, without imprisonment or restraint' (Wong 2015). Under this structure of thought, emigration was not a violation of one's rights, but an exercise of them—not the imposition of state power, but autonomy from it. As William Godwin wrote in his retort to Malthus in 1820, *Of Population*,

> As long as there is tyranny and oppression among any of the governments of mankind, as long as it is possible for a human being to come under the burthen of unmerited disgraces, as long as there shall exist a pride in men that disdains servitude, and a spirit of industry anxious to free itself from vexation and constraint, so long will emigration form a feature in the history of our race. (378)

As Bridget Anderson says, with the overhaul of the Poor Laws in 1834, 'There was a rebalancing of the response to the mobility of the poor. Being mobile and moving from one's parish was increasingly about being "free," improving oneself through selling one's labour rather than being "masterless"' (Anderson 2013: 25). Improving oneself could include leaving one's country: 'Emigration assumed a totally new character,' one commentator wrote in 1819, 'it was no longer merely the poor, the idle, the profligate, or the wildly speculative who were proposing to quit their native country' (quoted in Belich 2009: 148). This shift in attitudes corresponded with a huge increase in numbers; 'In the eighteenth century,' writes Belich, 'about half a million people emigrated from the British Isles. In the long nineteenth century, 1815–1914, the number rocketed to 25 million' (2009: 126).

It was between these two developments in the mobility of British labor that British involvement with transatlantic slavery rose and fell, and while the two things did not determine each other, they were intimately connected in a way we do not always acknowledge. British migration and African slavery are not separate phenomenon, but rather part of a complex dynamic of labor and colonial expansion. As Abigail Swingen puts it, 'the turn toward African slavery in the Caribbean colonies was not driven entirely by colonial labor demand but was closely tied to political, economic and social concerns in the metropolis' (2015: 12). Between 1700 and 1775, over 1,000,000 slaves were transported from Africa to the Americas. In 1713, England assumed the Asiento, an agreement granting it a monopoly over the slave trade to the Spanish colonies in the new world, as part of the Treaty of Utrecht that ended the War of Spanish Succession. Although Britain had used slave labor in the Caribbean since the early sixteenth century, this event marked the beginning of its greatest involvement in the trade: 'annual shipments of slaves by the British probably tripled over the eighteenth century, rising from 12,000 to 14,000 before 1720 to 42,000 during the 1790s' (Richardson 1987: 106; Curtin 1969; Lovejoy 1982). For a long time, this profitable practice gave very few moral qualms to British subjects, but by the 1770s and 1780s, more and more Britons had grown dissatisfied with the economic and moral structures that governed the slave trade and plantation culture, and agitation to abolish the trade and emancipate the slaves began to swell. Nevertheless, propositions to end Britain's involvement in the trade were defeated by the West India interest in Parliamentary debates in 1791 and 1792, and despite promises to the contrary, the trade was not abolished until 1807. It took another thirty years for complete emancipation to take effect: West Indian slaves were not granted their freedom until 1833, and many continued to be bound in 'apprenticeship' until 1838.

The emergence of the British antislavery movement is one of the great puzzles of Enlightenment historiography; its eventual success is even less explicable. At the beginning of the eighteenth century, almost all Britons regarded chattel slavery as an unpleasant but necessary requirement for enjoying the benefits of an overseas empire, perhaps the worst of the many existing forms of human servitude, but not an absolute moral wrong. By the end of the same century, that broad segment of the population regarded slavery as a moral outrage that could not be tolerated in a modern nation. From a contemporary perspective, the story is puzzling on two counts. How could so many people have cared so little about the horrors of slavery for so long? But, if that was indeed the case, why did so many people change their ethical ideals so radically in such a relatively short amount of time? Historians have pointed to several key moments in this transition. The Somerset case, decided by Lord Mansfield, in which slavery was declared illegal on British soil in 1772 (Brown 2006: 96–101; Wong 2009); the *Zong* massacre in 1781, in which slaves were thrown overboard alive in order to lighten the load of the ship, and then the ship owners made, and were awarded, insurance claims for the loss (Baucom 2005); and the publication of Thomas Clarkson's *Essay on the Slavery and Commerce of the Human Species* in 1786 (revised 1788), with its infamous image of how slaves were held on board ship.

Until the second half of the twentieth century, historians generally drew upon a Whig narrative of progress and enlightenment to explain the abolition of the British slave trade. The "Saints" theory of antislavery argued that, led by the spiritual insights of Evangelicals like Sharp, Clarkson, and Wilberforce, Britons gradually came to see slavery as a moral wrong (Klingberg 1926). Later scholars proposed, by way of puncturing this narrative, that economic self-interest rather than morality drove the abolitionists, or that their idealism simply masked the sociocultural imperatives of the industrial revolution (Williams 1944; Davis 1975). More recently, historians have focused on the spread of antislavery sentiments through popular culture, and tended to ignore the actions of governmental authorities and parliament (Drescher 1987). To these explanations—moral, economic, ideological—Christopher Leslie Brown's *Moral Capital: The Foundations of British Abolitionism* (2006) added one firmly anchored in the political. Brown argues that abolitionism achieved its moral dominance through the complex political negotiations that characterized transatlantic relationships during the eighteenth century—not least the fierce conflicts over the meaning of 'liberty' during the American Revolution.

Many of these arguments about the rise of British abolitionism rely on the idea of implicit or explicit comparison between the 'freedom' of Britons and the lack of freedom of the enslaved. These comparisons were made primarily in imagination because Britons, by and large, had no direct experience of the slave trade or plantation culture. In this strategy, such arguments follow the lead of the historian David Brion Davis. In 1975, Davis made the influential claim that the abhorrence of slavery newly visible at the end of the eighteenth century was generated by an ideological need to categorically separate free labor from its 'unfree' opposite; the resulting sharp distinction helpfully obfuscated the similarities between wage slavery at home and chattel slavery abroad. 'If British abolitionists could express horror over the iron chains of the slave trade,' he writes, 'their acts of selectivity and definition helped to strengthen the invisible chains formed at home' (1975: 456). Thus, he claims, the deflection of social outrage away from the 'wage slavery' of the new factories in England and toward the physical brutality of slavery in the colonies helped to secure the labor force necessary to fuel the industrial revolution. Since questions of labor were so bound up in ideas about mobility, a similar claim can be made about human mobility during this era. If the industrial revolution depended on 'wage slavery,' the expansion of the British Empire in the decades before the American Revolution depended on the 'voluntary' mobility of devalued populations, such as landless laborers, urban paupers, and soldiers. Such persons needed to contrast their own movement to the coercion of slavery in order to define it as 'free.' We can see this contrast between freedom of movement and slavery developing in the both the discourse surrounding emigration and in the emergent antislavery movement. As C.L. Brown demonstrates, both issues arose from an ongoing 'crisis in British liberty' (2006: 27). This crisis concerned issues such as *habeas corpus* and religious freedom, but it extended to the question of mobility. Wong points out that the first stirrings of antislavery feeling in England arose from the questions of 'freedom of movement' in the Somersett case (2009).

In the last third of the eighteenth century, as the antislavery movement slowly began to gather steam, a new definition of freedom emerged in the discourse surrounding British emigration: freedom of movement. If unmolested settlement was still freedom to the slave, movement began to seem like freedom to the settler. An Irish emigrant to Pennsylvania, writes in 1767, for example,

> I have often wondered at our Countryfolk [who] would rather live in Slavery and work all the year around and not be three pence better at the year's end than stir out of the Chimney Corner and transport themselves to a place where with the like pains, in two or three years, they might know better things. (quoted in Jackson 1992: 78)

For this man, stasis, rather than movement, is slavery and the emigrant who can 'transport' himself is the free man. In a literary work of the same decade, Frances Brooke's 1769 novel, the *History of Emily Montague*, the hero, Edward Rivers, uses the same definitions of captivity and freedom as he explains his reasons for immigrating to Canada in a letter to a friend:

> What you call a sacrifice is none at all; I love England but am not obstinately chained down to any spot of earth; nature has charms every where for a man willing to be pleased: at my time of life, the very change of place is amusing; love of variety, and the natural restlessness of man, would give me a relish for this voyage, even if I did not expect, what I really do, to become lord of a principality which will put our large-acred men in England out of countenance. (3)

Here, Rivers associates movement with freedom, and 'chains' with being held to one place; 'man's' restlessness, his natural mobility, had been seen as a lynchpin of European settlement since the seventeenth century, and Rivers once again sees it as not only natural, but also the key to his economic success, something we also see in the letter from the Irish immigrant.

And yet, we should note that the celebration of freedom here is to some degree rhetorical: Rivers's move to Canada has been subsidized by the eighteenth-century British state, which paid its soldiers for service in the Seven Years War with land in the North American colonies.

His choice was between living on his half-pay pension from the army and immigrating to Canada to live like the 'lord of a principality.' We need to understand his celebration of autonomous movement as being underwritten, and indeed encouraged, by the state, for the benefit of the state, which needed settlers to take possession of the Canadian territory it had gained in the war. It is that state that wants to categorize, and naturalize, such movement as 'free'; in historical retrospect, we need to understand such definitions of 'freedom of movement' as socially and politically constructed.

Ideas about memory, particularly memory of a natal place, play a surprisingly large role in ideas about freedom of movement and the settlement of colonies, something the *History of Emily Montague* makes clear. Brooke's novel is convinced that the colonies are Britain's 'greatest and surest sources of wealth,' and that the nation's 'very being as a powerful and commercial nation depends upon them' (1769: 233). The book also articulates a surprising conviction that,

> England, however populous, is undoubtedly…too small to afford very large supplies of people to her colonies; and her people are also too useful, and of too much value, to be suffered to emigrate, if they can be prevented, whilst there is sufficient employment for them at home. (233)

Significantly, the argument pairs this economic and political dictum—a continuation of mercantile beliefs of the early eighteenth century about the necessity of a dense population of consumers—with a corollary about the emotional structure of Englishness. The English should be prevented from emigrating because they are the 'worst settlers on new lands in the universe' (233). The qualities that make them the 'worst' are both physiological and psychological. Not only are the English 'ill fitted to bear the hardships, and submit to the wants, which inevitably attend an infant settlement,' but also 'Their attachment to their native country, especially amongst the lower ranks of people, is so very strong, that of the honest and industrious few can be prevailed to leave it' (233, 234). The English have bonds to their native soil that cannot be broken without coercion. The solution, according to this line of reasoning, is to recruit Germans to settle British colonies in North America, since they 'have a patience, a perseverance, an abstinence, which peculiarly fits them for the cultivation of new countries' (234)—and presumably lack the emotional attachment to natal place that characterizes the English.

The resolution of Rivers' narrative plays out this view of the English as unsuitable settlers for English colonies. Although Rivers characterizes his time in Canada as 'perpetual exile' on more than one occasion (Brooke 1769: 146), his sojourn in North America turns out not to be 'perpetual' at all. Instead, he ends the novel by returning to England to reunite with his mother, who has been pining for him. Thus, despite Rivers' initial celebration of emigration, the novel eventually becomes a narrative of exile and return. And, indeed, on seeing his childhood home again, Rivers demonstrates the 'strong attachment to [his] native country' supposedly typical of an English traveler, and records the kind of strong emotion in relation to a 'lov'd scene' that More claims for the voluntary English roamer:

> 'Tis inconceivable what I felt on returning to a place so dear to me, and which I had not seen for many years; I ran hastily from one room to another; I traversed the garden with inexpressible eagerness: my eye devoured every object; there was not a tree, not a bush which did not revive some pleasing, some soft idea.
>
> I felt, to borrow a very pathetic expression of Thomson's,
> "A thousand little tendernesses throb,"
> On revisiting those dear scenes of infant happiness[.]. (1769: 318)

Rivers here experiences joys that override the 'love of variety,' the natural restlessness, and even the desire to be lord of a principality that he earlier professes. These joys are the joys of memory, the 'reviving' of scenes of 'infant happiness.' The scene implies that the freedom of movement he celebrates at the opening of the novel is perhaps most fully realized as the freedom to return. It is interesting to note, however, that the line of poetry he quotes comes from a scene of forcible transport and captivity in James Thomson's play, *Agamemnon: A Tragedy*

(1738). In that play, when Cassandra sees her fellow Trojan captives in Mycenae, she exclaims, 'At this, ten thousand images awake/ Ten thousand little tendernesses throb.' Brooke uproots and reroutes these lines about the emotions of exile into a narrative of return. Yet, Cassandra's emotions haunt the passage, suggesting that memories of home derive their greatest strength from the passage away from it.

As a way of understanding why such memories were so valued in the second half of the eighteenth century, I want to make a distinction between the form of memory represented by Rivers's return to his childhood home, a structure I will call exilic memory, and a contrasting form that I will call diasporic memory. This is a distinction that existed before the eighteenth century, but perhaps became more of a binary opposition in that period's increasing investment in literacy and print culture; it persists, I hope to show, in our discussions of the slavery archive today. I will illustrate the division I am talking about with reference not to eighteenth-century texts but rather to something even older: the great epic of imperial relocation, Virgil's *Aeneid*. Virgil's narrative was familiar to late seventeenth- and eighteenth-century Britons through Tate and Purcell's 1672 opera, *Dido and Aeneas*, and John Dryden's (1697) translation of the full poem. Joseph Roach has argued convincingly that the opera's 'narrative of abandonment,' focusing on Dido's self-immolation, crystalizes an important moment in the expansion of Britain's Atlantic empire. It is 'a public performance of forgetting,' Roach claims, that mirrors the way that Africa (Dido is a Carthaginian queen) 'plays a hinge role in turning the Mediterranean-centered consciousness of European memory into an Atlantic one,' even as 'the scope of that role largely disappears'; 'Dido's last words seem to speak for the victims of transoceanic ambitions: "Remember me, but ah! Forget my fate"' (Roach 1996: 45).

In this essay, however, I am less interested in the narrative's depiction of forgetting than its representation of memory, which also has implications for Britain's understanding of its imperial expansion and the settlement of the new world. Aeneas, exiled after the sack of Troy, enters Carthage, and is immediately confronted with a mural of the Trojan War, including his own deeds therein. Dryden's translation of the scene, a scene which does not appear in the opera, reads:

> [Aeneas] saw, in order painted on the Wall
> Whatever did in unhappy *Troy* befall:
> The Wars that Fame around the World had blown,
> All to the Life, and ev'ry Leader known.
> ...
> He stop'd, and weeping said, "O Friend! Ev'n here
> The Monuments of *Trojan* Woes appear!
> Our known Disasters fill ev'n foreign Lands:
> See there, where old unhappy *Priam* stands!
> Ev'n the Mute Walls relate the Warrior's Fame,
> And *Trojan* griefs the *Tyrians* pity claim
> He said, his Tears a ready Passage find,
> Devouring what he saw so well design'd
> And with an empty Picture filled his Mind. [1.638–641, 644–652]

Aeneas's reaction seems to adumbrate Thomson's Cassandra's: 'At this ten thousand images awake/Ten thousand tendernesses throb.' Yet, the mural Aeneas confronts, unlike the living countrymen Cassandra encounters, also resembles what Pierre Nora calls *lieux de memoire*: 'moments of history torn away from the movement of history, then returned: no longer quite life, nor yet death, like shells on the shore when the sea of living memory has receded' (Nora 1989: 12). Unlike Cassandra's, Aeneas's personal history has become a public archive, an object separable from himself. And this, I would propose, is a further capacity of exilic memory—it can be exteriorized and made into an artifact. It can be, like the mural, ekphrastic. Exilic memory is also narrative memory.

Yet, exilic memory depends on content as well as form; it evidences your bonds to your homeland or "native land," as the mural does for Aeneas. Thus, it is usually a memory of lineage (the ancestors one has left behind—or a living person, like Rivers' mother), though it can also be monumental or botanical (the memory of native buildings or plants—as it is for Edward Rivers); sometimes, it is both, as in the well-worn trope of remembering the grave of a family member. But it is always tied to place; it reasserts the sojourner's tie to the home from which he or she has been exiled. Thus, although its archival nature resembles Pierre Nora's *lieux de memoire*, it is bound up with mobility, which Nora does not treat. Aeneas's tears on seeing the mural spring partly from his relief that for all the distance he has traveled, he has not left his previous identity behind. 'Ev'n the mute walls relate the warrior's fame,' he says, 'And Trojan griefs the Tyrian's pity claim.' This is Dryden's translation of one of Virgil's most frequently quoted lines: *sunt lacrimae rerum* (variously understood as 'there are tears for things' or 'there are tears of things'). Robert Fagles's translation makes the importance of transmission of memory outside the self even more explicit: his Aeneas tells Achates, 'even here, the world is a world of tears/and the burdens of mortality touch the heart./Dismiss your fears. Trust me, this fame of ours/will offer us some haven' (Fagles 2006: 1.558–561). Aeneas's claims prove true, although only under the impossible temporality of the epic hero, in which news of his deed precedes his own entrance—something for which most exiles cannot hope. Still, one value of exilic memory is that it seems to promise recognition and acceptance in a new place.

The opposing kind of memory, the one I'm dubbing 'diasporic memory,' is a kind of memory not tied to place, or lineage, but rather to praxis, performance, and cyclical time. This is a memory you can carry with you and re-enact wherever you are. In the *Aeneid*, this form of memory emerges in the funeral games for Anchises, Aeneas's father. Anchises dies on the Trojans' journey from Troy to Italy, and the community remembers and honors him with games on the anniversary of his death. Although the celebrations take place near Anchises' grave, the location is not crucial. 'This wou'd I celebrate with Annual Games,/With Gifts on Alters pil'd, and holy Flames,/ Tho' banish'd to *Getulia*'s barren Sands,/ Caught in the *Grecian* Seas, or hostile Lands' (Dryden 1697: V.65–68). This kind of memory is not a vision of home; it is constructed through repeated performance, through the activity of commemoration. This form of memory resembles what Joseph Roach brilliantly describes as 'kinesthetic imagination': 'the idea of expressive movements as mnemonic reserves' (1996: 26). If the value of exilic memory is as an idealized guarantor of an identity that transcends geographic mobility, a value of diasporic memory is to construct and confirm community in a new place. This is what Aeneas and his followers do in celebrating the funeral games, and this is what, argues Roach, funerals among slave communities in the new world also did, where 'the occasion created by death offered this community an opportunity to affirm its semiautonomous but discretely submerged existence within or against the obligatory rituals of the better publicized fiction called the dominant culture' (1996: 60). Roach dubs these practices 'imaginative' because in the circum-Atlantic arena, 'Displaced transmission constitutes the adaptation of historic practices to changing conditions, in which popular behaviors are resituated in new locales… In this improvisational behavioral space, memory reveals itself as imagination' (1996: 29).

Roach points out that kinesthetic imagination 'exists interdependently but by no means coextensively with other forms of social memory: written records, spoken narratives, architectural monuments, built environments' (1996: 27). And, in texts like the *Aeneid*, exilic memory and diasporic memory coexist. But during the eighteenth century, the two forms of memory were increasingly put into opposition, even conflict—a conflict with significant bearing on our understanding of the history of slavery and antislavery. In this period, exilic memory, memory associated with home, with lineage, with narrative, with artifacts, often print artifacts, is celebrated, while diasporic memory, associated with praxis and performance is denigrated as barbaric and insubstantial, not only among slaves, but also among other, 'less civilized,' people. Here, for example, is Samuel Johnson bemoaning the ephemeral nature of Scottish oral culture during his tour of the Highlands and Islands in 1775.

> In nations where there is hardly the use of letters, what is once out of sight is lost forever…Their only registers are stated observances and practical representations. For this reason, an age of ignorance is an age of ceremony. Pageants, and processions, and commemorations, gradually shrink away, as better methods come into use of recording events, and preserving rights. (Johnson and Boswell 1775/1984: 333–334)

One can imagine what Johnson would think of funeral games. This passage is oft-cited, and out of context, it can seem as if Johnson is predicting that Highland culture will decay in situ. It is worth noticing, however, that his musings arise in the context of his examination of the emigration of

Highlanders to the Americas, a phenomenon he calls an 'epidemic desire of wandering, which spreads its contagion from valley to valley' (Johnson and Boswell 1775/1984: 103) until 'where there was formerly an insurrection, there is now a wilderness' (Johnson and Boswell 1775/1984: 104). Johnson was not imagining this depopulation; the Scots were among the first groups to experience the rise in emigration at the end of the eighteenth century. According to Bernard Bailyn, 'In the years after 1760, transatlantic migration reached levels beyond anything seen before in British America, which is to say, beyond anything seen in the entire history of Europe's and Africa's connections with the Western Hemisphere.' Driven by rising rents, enclosures, and the collapse of traditional social structures, at least 125,000 people emigrated between 1760 and 1776 (Bailyn 1986: 24, 26). Whether such movement was 'free' is debatable; when Johnson asks about 'the general dissatisfaction driving the highlanders into the other hemisphere' and 'whether they would stay at home, if they are well treated,' he is told 'that no man willingly left his native country' (Johnson and Boswell 1775/1984: 58–59). But Johnson also realizes that, 'if [the Highlanders] long for bright suns, and calm skies, and flowery fields, and fragrant gardens, I know not by what eloquence they can be persuaded, or by what offers they can be hired to stay' (Johnson and Boswell 1775/1984: 102).

Emigration has emptied the landscapes Johnson visits, and in passages such as the one above, I would argue, Johnson is as concerned with the loss of cultural memory across space as he is with its loss over time. Thus, we see the idea that 'what is once out of sight is lost forever' in oral cultures recur in another of Johnson's much-cited images of the disappearance of Scottish culture in North America: 'for a nation scattered in the boundless reaches of America resembles rays diverging from a focus. All the rays remain, but the heat is gone. Their power consisted in their concentration: when they are dispersed, they have no effect' (Johnson and Boswell 1775/1984: 131). Migrants with only diasporic memory, the wrong sort of memory—migrants who have only ceremonies, pageants, and processions—are doomed to disappear, or at least to disappear as legible Enlightenment subjects. Unlike Aeneas, they will not be greeted in the new world with a mural depicting their exploits.

Is it any wonder then, that antislavery activists gave their fictional slaves such clear memories of home? Or that they were so keen to imbue them with exilic memories, rather than represent them partaking in the 'barbaric' practices of diasporic memory? The suicidal protagonist of Thomas Day's 'Dying Negro' (1773), for example, laments the suffering that exilic memory has caused him:

> My tortured bosom sad remembrance spare!
> Why dost thou plant thy keenest daggers there?
> And show me what I was, and aggravate despair?
> Thou streams of Gambia, and thou sacred shade!
> Where in my youth's first dawn I joyful stray'd [.]

The poem goes on to detail several scenes from the speaker's childhood in Africa. Its claim that memory causes the slave an almost physical pain, and further that memory's pain is the 'keenest' of all slavery's psychological torments, grants him not only human feelings, but also an identity that persists across his journey from Africa to the Americas, to England itself. The slave's ability to conjure up stories and images of his native land, and then to narrate them, is an important part of what the poet hopes will register his enslaved protagonist as a being worthy of his readers' sympathy—the embodiment of a plight that will rally them to the antislavery cause.

The former slave, Olaudah Equiano, whose *Interesting Narrative of the Life of Gustavus Vassa*, published in 1789, was so important to the antislavery movement, also goes to great lengths to establish his exilic memory of Africa.

> I hope the reader will not think I have trespassed on his patience in introducing myself to him with some account of the manners and customs of my country. They had been implanted in me with great care, and made an impression on my mind, which time could not erase, and which all the adversity and variety of fortune I have since experienced served only to rivet and record; for whether the love of one's country be real or imaginary, or a lesson of reason, or an instinct of nature, I still look back with pleasure on the first scenes of my life, though that pleasure has for the most part been mingled with sorrow. (32)

When we consider that Equiano is attempting to construct a voice that will compel British readers to recognize him as a person with a valid argument to make against slavery, the imagery he choses to describe the formation of childhood memories becomes very interesting. These memories are "implanted" and then "riveted" into his psyche. All the horrors of slavery, Equiano insists, cannot eradicate them. He then equates such memories with love of one's country, defining them as exilic memories. His political and cultural strategy, like Hannah More's, is clear: if writers like Brooke can claim that the English make bad colonists because they love their country too much, then Equiano can claim slavery is wrong in part because slaves love their country, too. If slaves can remember the lands from which they were taken, if they can put those memories into words, into narrative, then they should, like the hero of Brooke's novel, be free to go back. A certain kind of memory is both a guarantor of personhood and of the right to freedom of movement.

In a recent article on the memory practices of slaves in the middle passage, Ramesh Mallipeddi describes 'the memory-work of the opening chapter of *The Interesting Narrative*' as 'Janus-faced, a retrospective account of the past, but also a self-conscious attempt to harness the past to current concerns' (2014: 14). Mallipeddi places Equiano's memories in the context of the eighteenth-century understanding of nostalgia as what Kevis Goodman calls a 'mobility disability' thought to afflict unwilling travelers, particularly sailors, and in which the 'pain of separation from country and friends produces depressing passions of the mind, which, in turn, generate bodily ailments' (2010: 198). Mallipeddi argues that 'it was by tenaciously retaining and cultivating memories of Africa to the point of self-destruction that slaves sought to counter the forces of dislocation. In the process, memory emerged as the principal site of contestation between the slave holders and the enslaved' (13). By foregrounding his memories of childhood, Equiano presents himself as a person whose identity has persisted across both time and space, and a person who should be listened to.

But the contest in the eighteenth century was not merely between memory and forgetting, but between various kinds of memory—or rather, between which representations and practices would be recognized as memory and which would not. The nature of memory was a political problem for slave holders and abolitionists alike. Mallipeddi describes the struggle around slaves' songs in the middle passage:

> While the masters sought to use song to distract slaves from memories of home, the enslaved seized on it as a means to cultivate those very memories…[F]or Africans, melancholic song was not only a 'reaction' to loss, but also a mnemonic instrument in the struggle against obliteration and the erasure of their historical past. Not surprisingly, the slaves' effort at memory and commemoration frequently provoked the wrath of their masters. (243)

Exilic memories, such as the ones Equiano recounts in the opening chapters of his narrative, were legible to abolitionists and parliamentary committees. Diasporic memories, such as the sorrow songs of the slaves, were not legible, until much later, to anyone but the slaves who sang and heard them. Roach describes one European commentator's confusion at a slave funeral in early nineteenth-century New Orleans as, 'the pronounced tendency of the literate observer to misrecognize incorporated memory as spontaneous emotion' (Roach 1996: 63).

Thus, the abolitionist attempt to assert the slave's exilic memory arose not only in relation to the slavery debates, but also in the context of the more general eighteenth-century anxiety about the ephemerality and barbarism of other kinds of memory, particularly the kind of memory associated with ceremony and pageant. Vincent Brown (2010), for example, in his study of the discourse surrounding death in eighteenth-century Jamaica, *The Reaper's Garden: Death and Power in the World of Atlantic Slavery*, documents the slave owners' discomfort with and disgust for the rituals associated with slave funerals—processions, ceremonies, and celebrations outside of plantation discipline. 'European descriptions of expressive styles of movement at funerals as "wild," "frantic," and "ludicrous" "gesticulations" distinguished appropriate—in other words 'white'—decorum from 'negro' lack of restraint' (2010: 74–75). The planter Edward Long, Brown tells us, concluded that '"Their funerals are the very reverse of our English ceremony."' Yet, with a historian's hindsight, Brown draws a connection between slave 'cultures of ceremony' and those within the British isles, the very ones Johnson bemoans: 'If [Long] knew of the customs in the Northern English borderlands—where mourners were compelled to touch corpses because of the belief that the body would bleed at the touch of one guilty of foul play—he was careful not to say (though he did compare black funerals to Highland Scottish and Irish wakes)' (75). The borders between civilized and uncivilized persons, borders to some degree based on memory practices, were constantly being redrawn and strengthened.

Brown himself, like Roach, wants to recuperate such practices as slave funerals as a form of memory, a diasporic memory (or, in Roach's terms, a 'countermemory' [61]) based not on images of home but on the repetition of practices learned in one place and repeated in another, tied not to place, but to life events, associated not with vision, but with performance. Such memories were never exact repetitions, since so many different African cultures with different beliefs came together in the Caribbean. Nevertheless, says Brown, 'Divided though they might be by language, regional identification, gender or occupation, enslaved Africans nevertheless held some common assumptions about death' (2010: 65). These assumptions allowed them to reshape, to re-member, their rituals in a new world.

Conclusion

My argument in this chapter has been two-fold. First, I have been arguing that seeming opposites, like slavery and freedom or mobility and settlement, cannot be understood in isolation from one another. We cannot see slavery as involving only the question of African labor, just as we cannot see the question of British immigration to the new world as only a question about the British. The two phenomena are intertwined in complex ways, and the idea of the European migrant's freedom of movement came to be defined against the coerced movement of the slave. The association of free movement with national identity—first with the claim to be a British subject, and then, for some, the claim to be American citizens—grew over the first three quarters of the eighteenth century until, after the Revolution, the distaste for the coerced mobility associated with servitude was so strong that in 1784 a group of New Yorkers protested the arrival of a shipload of indentured servants because the 'traffick of White People' was contrary to 'the idea of liberty this country has so happily established' (quoted in Fogleman 1998: 65).

New Yorkers, by and large, did not extend their abhorrence of the traffic of people to slaves; freedom of movement was one of the constitutive elements of whiteness. It was this association of freedom of movement with whiteness that British antislavery activists tried to pry open in order to allow slaves access to the concept.

One way they went about that—and this is the second part of my argument—was to endow slaves with the exilic, narrative memory so important to eighteenth-century ideas of personhood, while slave owners, on the opposite side of that debate, reviled the slaves' expressions of (an already denigrated) diasporic, performative, non-narrative memory. Both proslavery and antislavery attitudes were bound up not simply with the economic, the demographic, and the epidemiological, but also with structures of feeling, particularly with the nature of memory as it relates to human mobility. During this era, a particular form of memory that I have been calling 'exilic' memory came to serve as a guarantor of identity and personhood, while other forms of memory were denigrated and disavowed. Attention to it demonstrates the ways that concepts of labor and mobility are conjoined with questions of cognition and subjectivity.

Because memory is so important to the debate, we all, as scholars of transatlantic slavery, and coerced human mobility more generally, continue to wrestle with eighteenth-century assumptions about the relationship of memory, mobility, and personhood. Scholars like Brown and Roach, as we have seen, aim to rehabilitate those forms of diasporic memory denigrated by eighteenth-century writers. Saidiya Hartman, meanwhile, takes a different approach to exposing the consequences of celebrating the exilic memories of slaves. She suggests that such memories, often 'implanted' by antislavery writers, obscure the brutal erasure of selfhood slaves underwent in the middle passage. Hartman describes an herb reputedly given to slaves as they left Africa: this 'made you forget your kin, lose sight of your country, and cease to think of freedom. It expunged all memories of a natal land, and it robbed the slave of spiritual protection. Ignorant of her lineage, to whom could the slave appeal?' (Hartman 2007: 155, 157). Her book, *Lose Your Mother,* is a sustained attempt to try and represent what such a complete loss of memory would look like—what that absence would look like—but note the focus on lineage and place in this passage. What the slave has lost is her exilic memory, and with it, her personhood, and her right to freedom of movement. As Hartman so eloquently documents in her account of the vexed attempts of African-Americans to return to Africa and claim it as a homeland, her own journey among them, one problem with privileging exilic memory, even if you privilege it as an ineradicable loss, is that it promises only a return as a solution.

Another problem with exilic memory and archival study shows up in scholarly interest in Equiano's African past. Perhaps not surprisingly, it is precisely Equiano's exilic memories of Africa that have been questioned by scholars like Vincent Carretta, who seek to show that Equiano was born in South Carolina, not Gambia as he claims (Carretta 1999). Whether or not such challenges are correct, I think we can see the ongoing controversy about the truth of Equiano's childhood memories as testimony both to the importance of exilic memory in eighteenth-century discourse about human mobility, and also as part of our inherited anxiety about the capacity of that structure of mind to grant personhood. Equiano demonstrates a tension at the heart of the eighteenth-century valuation of exilic memory: the very fact that it can be exteriorized, turned into an artifact separable from and longer lasting than the body of the person who lived those memories—in this case, the printed artifact of the *Interesting Narrative*—both imbues such memories with value, and opens the possibility of them being fabricated or transferrable. Equiano's memories are not necessarily his memories.

I will conclude by pointing to a recent example of the problems of memory and mobility, and the capacity of the right kind of memory to grant status to the refugee or unwilling migrant. Such more recent controversies demonstrate our continued investment in the artifactual nature of exilic memory and the problems it causes. Andrew Jefferson (2014) documents the case of Liberian refugees in Sierra Leone who claim that their stories, stories that granted them refugee status in the eyes of the UN and gave them the right to repatriation, were stolen from them and used by others. 'Their claim,' says Jefferson, 'was that stories collected by the relevant authorities and stored in a file for consideration as part of the process of determining their status [as refugees], entitlements and possibilities for resettlement were "sold" by local staff to Sierra Leonean citizens who armed with a new identity (containing the appropriate story of displacement and suffering) were then processed and resettled [to places like Canada] in lieu of the Liberians' (Jefferson 2014: 221). As with Equiano, the capacity to narrate one's memories and exteriorize them—to make them into artifacts that can be stored in a file—both certifies the value of the memories, and persons to whom they belong—and makes them transferrable, makes them liable to being stolen. Even today, then, the memory of the migrant, whether he or she is a slave, or subject to some other form of coerced mobility, remains vulnerable and contested.

References

Anderson, B. (2013). *Us and Them? The Dangerous Politics of Immigration Control*. Oxford: Oxford University Press.

Bailyn, B. (1986). *Voyagers to the West*. New York: Alfred A. Knopf.

Baucom, I. (2005). *Specters of the Atlantic: Finance Capital, Slavery, and the Philosophy of History*. Durham: Duke University Press.

Beier, A. L. (1985). *Masterless Men: The Vagrancy Problem in England 1560–1640*. London: Methuen & Co. Ltd.

Belich, J. (2009). *Replenishing the Earth: The Settler Revolution and the Rise of the Anglo-World, 1783–1939*. Oxford: Oxford University Press.

Braddick, M. J. (2000). *State Formation in Early Modern England c. 1550–1700*. Cambridge: Cambridge University Press.

Brooke, F. (1769/2008). *The History of Emily Montague*. Toronto: McClelland & Stewart Ltd.

Brown, C. L. (2006). *Moral Capital: Foundations of British Abolitionism*. Chapel Hill: University of North Carolina Press.

Brown, V. (2010). *The Reaper's Garden: Death and Power in the World of Atlantic Slavery*. Cambridge, MA: Harvard University Press.

Carretta, V. (1999). Olaudah Equiano or Gustavus Vassa? New Light on an Eighteenth-Century Question of Identity. *Slavery & Abolition, 20*(3), 96–105.

Chaplin, J. (2001). *Subject Matter: Technology, the Body, and Science on the Anglo-American Frontier, 1500–1676*. Cambridge, MA: Harvard University Press.

Curtin, P. (1969). *The Atlantic Slave Trade: A Census*. Madison: The University of Wisconsin Press.
Davis, D. B. (1975). *The Problem of Slavery in the Age of Revolution*. Ithaca, NY: Cornell University Press.
Day, T. (1773/1775). *The Dying Negro*. London: W. Flexney, J. Wilkie and J. Robson.
Drescher, S. (1987). *Capitalism and Antislavery: British Mobilization in Comparative Perspective*. New York: Macmillan.
Dryden, J. (1697/1997). *Virgil's Aeneid* (F. M. Keener, Ed.). Harmondsworth: Penguin.
Eltis, D. (2002). Coerced and Free Migrations from the Old World to the New. In D. Eltis (Ed.), *Coerced and Free Migration: Global Perspectives* (pp. 33–74). Stanford: Stanford University Press.
Equiano, O. (1789/2001). *The Interesting Narrative of the Life of Olaudah Equiano, or Gustavus Vassa, the African, Written by Himself* (W. Sollors, Ed.). New York: W.W. Norton.
Fogleman, A. (1998). From Slave, Convicts, and Servants to Free Passengers: The Transformation of Immigration in the Era of the American Revolution. *The Journal of American History, 85*(1), 43–76.
Godwin, W. (1820). *Of Population: An Enquiry Concerning the Power of Increase in the Numbers of Mankind, Being an Answer to Mr. Malthus's Essay on That Subject*. London: Longman, Hurst, Rees, Orme, and Brown.
Goodman, K. (2010). "Uncertain Disease": Nostalgia, Pathologies of Motion, Practices of Reading. *Studies in Romanticism, 49*, 197–227.
Gray, R. (1609/1937). *A Good Speed to Virginia*. New York: Scholar's Facsimiles and Reprints.
Hartman, S. (2007). *Lose Your Mother: A Journey Along the Atlantic Slave Route*. New York: Farrar, Strauss, Giroux.
Jackson, C. (1992). *A Social History of the Scotch-Irish*. Lanham, MD: Madison Books.
Jefferson, A. M. (2014). Performances of Victimhood, Allegation, and Disavowal in Sierra Leone. In S. Jensen & H. Ronsbo (Eds.), *Histories of Victimhood* (pp. 218–238). Philadelphia: University of Pennsylvania Press.
Johnson, S., & Boswell, J. (1775/1984). *A Journey to the Western Islands of Scotland and The Journal of a Tour to the Hebrides*. London: Penguin Classics.
Klingberg, F. J. (1926). *The Anti-Slavery Movement in England: A Study in English Humanitarianism*. New Haven, CT: Yale University Press.

Locke, J. (1690). *The Second Treatise of Government.* New York: Barnes & Noble Publishing.
Lovejoy, P. E. (1982). The Volume of the Atlantic Slave Trade: A Synthesis. *Journal of African History, XXIII,* 474–500.
Mallipeddi, R. (2014). 'A Fixed Melancholy': Migration, Memory and the Middle Passage. *The Eighteenth Century: Theory and Interpretation, 55*(2–3), 235–253.
More, H. (1788/1856). The Slave Trade. In *The Complete Works of Hannah More.* New York: J.C. Derby.
Nora, P. (1989). Between Memory and History: Les Lieux de Memoire. *Representations, 26,* 7–24.
Pincus, S. (2012). Rethinking Mercantilism: Political Economy, the British Empire, and the Atlantic World in the Seventeenth and Eighteenth Centuries. *The William and Mary Quarterly, 69*(1), 3–34.
Richardson, D. (1987). The Slave Trade, Sugar, and British Economic Growth, 1748–1776. In B. Solow & S. Engerman (Eds.), *British Capitalism and Caribbean Slavery: The Legacy of Eric Williams.* Cambridge: Cambridge University Press.
Roach, J. (1996). *Cities of the Dead: Circum-Atlantic Performance.* New York: Columbia University Press.
Swingen, A. L. (2015). *Competing Visions of Empire: Labor, Slavery and the Origins of the British Atlantic Empire.* New Haven: Yale University Press.
The Parliamentary History of England, from the Earliest Period to the Year 1803. Vol. 14, 1747–1753. (London, T.C. Hansard, 1813).
Thomson, J. (1738). *Agamemnon: A Tragedy.* London: A Millar.
Virgil. (2006). *The Aeneid* (R. Fagles, Trans.). New York: Viking Penguin.
Williams, E. (1944). *Capitalism and Slavery.* Chapel Hill: University of North Carolina Press.
Wong, E. (2009). *Neither Fugitive nor Free: Atlantic Slavery, Freedom Suits, and the Legal Culture of Travel.* New York: New York University Press.
Wong, E. (2015). Bound and Determined: New Abolitionism and the Campaign Against Modern Slavery. https://www.opendemocracy.net/beyondslavery/edlie-wong/bound-and-determined-new-abolitionism-and-campaign-against-modern-slavery. Accessed 6 May 2015.

5

Immigration Restrictions and the Politics of Protection

Nandita Sharma

Introduction

To better understand and historically situate the raging discourses on 'human trafficking' and 'modern-day slavery', we need to examine the period in which state regulations and restrictions on free human mobility were first enacted. This is crucial for at least two reasons. First, without the intense system of contemporary state controls on human mobility, the intermediaries that people currently rely on to facilitate their movement into well-fortified states would become much less necessary and, at least, lose much of their power over people on the move. Secondly, like today's 'anti-trafficking' policies, the initial, nineteenth-century organization of border controls also relied on the discourse of 'rescue' and 'protection' of the very people whose mobility was coming under regulation.

N. Sharma (✉)
University of Hawaii at Manoa, Honolulu, HI, USA
e-mail: nsharma@hawaii.edu

L. Brace and J. O'Connell Davidson (eds.), *Revisiting Slavery and Antislavery*,
https://doi.org/10.1007/978-3-319-90623-2_5

The beginning of the end of free migration, far from being a timeless and integral element of state sovereignty as is often supposed, is, instead, a part of the politics surrounding the abolition of slavery within the British Empire and its replacement with the trade in indentured persons, pejoratively known as 'coolies,' mostly from British-colonized Asia. The term 'coolie' has from the start been imbricated with deeply racist meanings. Hence, my placement of it within quotes. The 'coolie' labour system comprised three forms: indentured labour, the *kangany* system and the *maistry* or contract system. Indentureship was the form of employment relationship that the majority of 'coolie' labourers worked under. Indentured labour consisted of a legal requirement for workers to labour for a contracted period of time (usually five years, but sometimes shorter or longer). During this period, they were tied to the contracting employer and were not free to change either their employer or place of work (Potts 1990: 79).

The 'coolie' system of labour recruitment acted as a bridge between what Radhika Mongia (2007) terms the imperial state 'logic of facilitation' of human movement and the national state 'logic of constraint'. By examining the emergence and growth of regulations and restrictions on human mobility within the politics of anti-slavery, labour control and the growing power of nationalist discourses over both capitalists and workers, we might be better able to evaluate both the claims made and the solutions offered by contemporary 'anti-trafficking' frameworks.

The first restrictions on mobility within the British Empire were enacted in the colony of Mauritius and were indeed done so through a set of conflicting and contradictory concerns. On the one hand, the London Colonial office was intent on constructing a labour recruitment system that would replace slavery and, in the absence of slavery, the local Mauritian colonial authority was intent on sufficiently disciplining the labouring bodies of indentured "coolie" workers. On the other hand, anti-slavery campaigners wished to 'protect' 'coolies' from would-be slavers, and the British Indian colonial office, along with London, was concerned that the new coolie labour recruitment system not be portrayed as slavery by abolition activists.

Of course, no one working in the British imperial state's wide and dispersed apparatus would have known the long-range consequences of regulating the entry of British subjects from one part of its territories—in this case India—into another of its territories—in this case Mauritius—at the start. Such regulations were initially piecemeal strategies in response to economic and political crises of the moment. The coolie system of labour recruitment emerged as the British imperial state's response to the threats to both its power and imperial trade posed by the abolition of the slave trade in 1807 and of slave labour relations in 1833. Nonetheless, the British imperial state's response to end of the slave trade, but even more importantly, to the end of slave *labour relations*, precipitated a new world order of nation-state regulations and restrictions of human mobility, one that has created many crises for many people trying to move ever since, most especially those seeking new livelihoods.

Imperial Logic on Human Mobility

Imperial states ruled by making those subjected to their powers of taxation, levies and forced labour into subjects of its empire. Generally speaking, the more subjects the state had, the more persons whose labour could be exploited, the more wealth that could be amassed and the more power states could wield. For these reasons, imperial states' concerns about borders and boundaries were primarily about preventing people from *leaving*. Holding people *within* imperial territories in order to subject them to the state's coercive power was the *sine qua non* of the imperial project of 'civilizing' people ('civilization' always having been an effect of state power, see Scott 2009). This was no easy task. Many would-be imperial subjects, keen on making an escape, practised what James Scott has nicely termed, 'the art of not being governed' and carved out non-state spaces for themselves where, when and for as long as they could (2009). Thus, in contrast to the Hobbesian story of sovereignty, where states were purportedly created by people to *protect* them from the violent chaos of an 'uncivilized' (i.e. stateless) life, in actuality, keeping people subjected to the state's power was the main purpose of boundary maintenance.

Even for those unable to escape, imperial states were not interested in the wholesale *immobility* of their subjects. Rather, imperial states *facilitated* the movement of people within their empires (Mongia 2007). Indeed, imperial states were actively involved in the movement of people, often on a massive scale. Movements of enslaved persons, of persons pressed into service, of persons caught up in systems of debt-bondage, of persons moved through penal transport, of persons moving as indentured labourers, and, later, the continued movement of (im)migrant workers regulated through border controls, were all *structural* elements of European imperialism (Potts 1990: 204). Indeed, *facilitating* human mobility was central to the ability of imperial territories to be profitable, particularly where colonialism resulted in the high death rates of those the colonizers encountered and often enslaved. The high death rate of enslaved persons from Africa, European and, later, Asian indentured labourers, and, even, of so-called free labour also meant that ongoing labour recruitment into the colonies was necessary for their political and economic viability.

One of the first main systems of moving people within a rapidly globalizing space of imperialism was the trade in slaves largely from the West coast of Africa, a system that was dramatically altered with the introduction of capitalist market imperatives. The British Empire, the first empire to expand through the imposition of capitalist social relations, became, not only the most powerful of the European Empires, but also the largest slave-trading empire from the 1760s onwards, the period in which the Atlantic slave trade peaked. Slightly more than half of the persons from Africa enslaved and transported across the Atlantic to the Americas each year were carried on British slave ships protected by the British navy. By 1780, at the height of the Atlantic slave trade, approximately one slave ship left Britain every other day. Over the course of British involvement in the slave trade, approximately 3.4 million persons from Africa were moved, of whom 2.7 million arrived in British colonies in the Caribbean, South and, to a much lesser extent, North America. In the eighteenth century, the slave trade was the richest part of Britain's trade. Not insignificantly, it was mostly a trade in persons classified not as co-British subjects but as 'foreigners.'

The end of the 'evil trade,' indeed, the world-historical shift that came with the delegitimization of slavery, a shift that contemporary campaigns to "end trafficking" or "end modern-day slavery" explicitly reference with their calls for the "abolition of sex work" or the end of "sexual slavery," was without a doubt the result of the centuries-long and countless acts of rebellion of the enslaved as well as those who joined them in an organized movement to abolish slavery. These latter efforts began in the late-eighteenth century and from within the centre of the British Empire itself—the City of London (Hochschild 2005; Linebaugh and Rediker 2000). With its 25 March 1807 *Abolition of the Slave Trade Act*, the British Empire ended its trade in slaves from Africa.

Yet, due to the heavy reliance on slave labour by plantation owners and the imperial treasury, the *institution* of slavery itself (or the *slave labour relation*) was maintained within the empire for several decades afterwards, indeed in some imperial territories even for several years *following* the passing of Britain's *Slavery Abolition Act* of 1833. A central reason for the decades-long gap between the end of the slave *trade* (1807) and the complete end of slave *labour relations* (1834–1843), was the search for a system of labour recruitment that could replace it and do so in a manner that met investors' demands for a cheapened and weakened workforce. The central issue was that of *rights*. What, if any, rights would the workers recruited to replace enslaved workers have after the abolition of slavery? In this, there was no uniform resolution.

The post-abolition period saw a dramatic increase in persons recruited from Europe for a variety of work. They did not face any restrictions on their movement to the places they came to. However, while many of these workers had been held in some kind of bondage to their employers (or Masters in the parlance of the day),[1] by the early nineteenth century, the numbers of persons arriving from Europe were less and less likely to be employed in unfree employment relations.[2] Moreover, already by the seventeenth century—and certainly by the end of the eighteenth century a racialized division of labour and a differential pay scale between workers racialized as White and those racialized into various categories of non-Whites was well established, especially in the various White-settler colonies (the United States, Canada, Australia, and New Zealand) where the ratio of Whites to non-Whites had been reversed earlier on. This racialized division of labour along with the higher "wages of whiteness" meant that the search for the replacement of slaves did not end with the increase in workers from Europe (Roediger 1999). Plantation owners and other employers were generally unwilling to replace former enslaved Black workers with White workers since their (recently acquired) freedom resulted not only in employers having to pay a higher price for their labour, but also in a substantially decreased ability of employers to control them. Free labour relations were seen to be too costly for employers and too politically empowering to (mostly White male) workers.

The Abolition of Slavery and the Start of 'Coolieism'

The greater 'solution' to investor's 'problems' with the end of slavery was the "coolie" system. That is, the system of recruiting and exploiting negatively racialized people, mostly men and mostly from British-controlled China and India, to work in conditions of indentured servitude.[3] Coolieism became the *dominant* system through which people were moved from approximately 1830 to the 1920s (Potts 1990: 69). While there is no definitive number on the scale of coolieism—some estimate a low of 12 million and even 'an estimate of 37 million or more would not be entirely without foundation'—both the scale and significance of the coolie system were, with the lowest estimates, comparable to those of slavery (Potts 1990: 71–73). The 'coolie' system also surpassed African slavery in its *intensity* as the millions of 'coolies' from Asia were recruited and exploited within the space of slightly less than a hundred years (1830s–1920s) (Potts 1990: 73).

The end of slavery was the basis not only for the demand for 'coolie' labour but also for its supply. Britain's *Slavery Abolition Act* of 1833 was in effect in all of imperial space, thus, persons enslaved throughout British-colonized South Asia were also freed. At the same time, the period of the 'coolie' labour system was a period of major expansion of the British Empire. Between 1815 and 1914, a period referred to by some historians as Britain's "imperial century" but one which could also be referred to as the "century of coolie labour," around ten million square miles (or 26,000,000 km^2) of territory and roughly 400 million people were added to the British Empire.

The plunder of the wealth of the labour in British India, initially administered by the East India Company from 1757 to 1858, resulted in successive famines: 1770, 1784, 1804, 1837 and 1861 in Bengal and northern India, and in 1877, 1878, 1889, 1892 and 1897 until 1900 in other parts of India. Some of these famines were a result of the British insistence that farmers grow cash crops in order to accrue hard currency (silver at this time) in the international trading market. One of these cash crops was opium which was sold in China in an effort to reverse the British imbalance of trade with China. This resulted in the Opium Wars (1839–1842 and 1860–1862) between the British imperial state and the Qing imperial state in China which expanded British imperial control over mainland China and intensified its insertion into global capitalist markets. Thus, by the beginning of the nineteenth century, millions of people throughout Asia had been left dispossessed of any means of production or even of subsistence, making them ripe candidates to be exploited as 'coolies' throughout the British Empire in Asia, Africa and the Americas.

As these people were moved throughout the British Empire, their relationship to the still- or soon-to-be former- slaves, as well as to the institution of slavery, was called into question. Such questions were the foundation for the establishment of regulations and restrictions on the free movement of persons throughout the British Empire. Thus, it was the impending end to slave labour relations which led to the enactment of the very first controls on in-migration. And, it was against 'coolies' from Asia employed on contracts of indenture that a growing list of regulations to monitor the mobility of co-imperial subjects were first ordered (Potts 1990: 68–71). Specifically, as Radhika Mongia's (2007) detailed study on the subject shows, it was in the British colony of Mauritius, an island in the Indian Ocean about 2000 kilometres off the southeast coast of the African continent, where the first efforts to regulate the in-migration of co-imperial subjects took place. This was a monumental shift, one that generated much heated discussion at the time. The local colonial government of Mauritius's effort to regulate and restrict the entry of co-British subjects marked a shift from imperial concerns about exit to new concerns about entry. In retrospect, it was the beginning of the end of the regime of the unrestricted entry of British subjects within imperial territory and, in a sense, the start of ideas of a fragmented imperial space.

Mauritius had first been claimed as a colony by the Dutch (1638–1710), then the French (1710–1810) and finally, the British during its period of great expansion (1810–1968). The Dutch first tried to profit from the island through the export of ebony. For that purpose, 105 slaves from Madagascar were brought to the island. After this failed, Dutch officials introduced sugar cane to Mauritius. Sugar plantations reliant on slave labour from Africa soon became the mainstay of the colonial economy. With the expansion of the sugar trade and the takeover by French imperial administration in 1710, the number of slaves increased. On the eve of British conquest in 1810, there were some 63,000 enslaved workers in Mauritius (Allen 1999: 13). Despite Britain's 1807 *Abolition Act*, the trade of enslaved persons destined for the British colony of Mauritius continued unabated. Indeed, until the mid-1920s, the island was one of the centres of the illicit trade in slaves (Allen 1999: 14).

The real end of the slave trade in Mauritius was linked to developments in international trade relations and coincided with the repeal of the preferential tariff on West Indian sugar entering Britain in 1825 (Allen 1999: 12). As this allowed sugar production on Mauritius to become more profitable, the area planted in cane more than doubled. With the impending abolition of slave labour relations in Mauritius—slated to take place in 1835—local British colonial officials became increasingly concerned about maintaining this profitability.[4] They were particularly worried about the planters' intent to recruit workers from India to replace the soon-to-be freed slaves. Their greatest concern was the possibility that these workers would refuse to work under the harsh working conditions prevalent on sugar plantations. This was related to their concern—also grave—that the soon-to-be-freed slaves would learn from this ability to refuse their exploitation. Together, these concerns led the colonial government to look for some sort of measure to *immobilize* this new workforce. Forcing enslaved people over the age of six to work for another three to five years as "apprentices" tied to their employers accomplished this for the soon-to-be-freed slaves, but the same measure could not 'solve' the 'problem' of the workers from British India.

In 1835, the same year that slaves were freed in Mauritius, two ordinances regulating the migration of people from British India were passed by the local British Council (and ratified in 1837 by the British Parliament) (Mongia 2007: 399). These ordinances were meant to regulate the terms of labour of 'coolie' workers from India by admitting only those who had permission from the Governor of the colony. This placed limits on the hitherto free mobility of 'coolie' labour from British India who, it is well-worth remembering, were co-imperial subjects, theoretically on par with all other British subjects, including those made White. The Mauritius ordinances thus made a break with previous imperial practice concerning migration. Indeed, such interventions were viewed as wholly novel and lacking in legal precedence. The imperial office admitted as much when it stated that 'this practice [of regulating migration] has no foundation in any existing law…' (quoted in Mongia 2007: 399).

Initially, planters in Mauritius were not convinced of the need of such regulations and feared that they might be used to limit the number of workers they could recruit from British India. One such planter, Hollier Griffith, used the argument that any intervention into the movement of workers from India was unprecedented when he wrote to G.F. Dick, the Colonial Secretary of Mauritius (in Mongia 2007: 399–400). Griffith noted that the imperial state might prohibit the departure of a British subject from British territory (but even then only in '*exceptional* cases'), however, he maintained, the state's sovereignty did '…not extend so far as to prohibit the *entrance* into his dominions of any of his subjects' (in Mongia 2007: 400). In other words, regulations and restrictions on in-migration were not the purview of the British imperial state. In response, Mr. Prosper D'Epinay, the Protector General of Mauritius, defended the right of local Mauritian authorities to impose entrance restrictions on each new migrant, and argued that the ordinances were 'a measure of foresight and of internal police…' without which there would be "…tumult and disorder [rather] than [an] increase in [the] industry of the country" (in Mongia 2007: 401).

Clearly concerned about the changes wrought by the end of slavery on Mauritius and the colonial officials' desire for a disciplined labour force, D'Epinay further argued that,

> wise and prudent precautionary measures [should] be taken … when this new population is put into immediate contact with the new apprentices just emerging from slavery, still susceptible of every impression; and to whom it is of importance, at the first step towards civilization, to give [an] idea and examples of order, labour, discipline. This end would be frustrated, if permission were given to associate them with all the vagabonds and all the idlers with which India swarms…. Who can say what influence this medley of individuals, with their manners, their usages, and their vices will have on our indigenous population, especially when it shall become wholly free? … It is the part of a wise Government to give to it serious attention; it is, therefore, necessary to proceed with caution in the new order of things. (in Mongia 2007: 401–402)

His claims for a "new order" were not hyperbolic, for, in retrospect, the Mauritius ordinances represented a striking shift in British imperial policies towards migration. Significantly, while bowing to the still dominant (and formal) notion that British Indian subjects had the same rights as 'those who reside in any possession, territory, or dependency of Great Britain', D'Epinay, in defending the *elimination* of this formal equality, asked whether 'the term British subject, and the privileges attached to it, are not according to places and circumstances, susceptible of important division and modification' (in Mongia 2007: 401).

The view in favour of regulating and restricting the movement of people from British India to British won out and was the start of juridical distinctions between who could and could not freely move across the space of the British Empire. From 1835 to 1838, approximately 25,000 indentured labourers from India had already been shipped to Mauritius—of whom 7000 died. This demonstrated to the planters that immigration ordinances would not harm their profits. To the contrary, one enthusiastic planter, George Arbuthnot, speaking after the first 'coolie' workers had been brought to Mauritius, stated '[t]heir cost is not half that of a slave' (cited in Potts 1990: 63).

Although the Mauritius colonial officials were enthusiastic about immigration controls, both the British Indian Government as well as the London Office remained concerned. In the wake of the success of the slavery abolition movement, it was crucial for both administrative units of the British imperial state that this new 'coolie' labour recruitment system *not* be viewed as a new form of slavery. Instead, it wanted the British Empire to be seen as a defender of freedom. Nonetheless, realizing the singular importance of new labour recruitment for planters, both sets of colonial authorities came to support the Mauritius colonial government's regulations and restrictions on free mobility. Moreover, also in the name of 'protecting' 'coolies', the British Indian Government added *emigration* controls to the immigration controls of the Mauritius colonial government. They presented both as necessary to ensure both that the movement of 'coolie' workers from British India was 'voluntary' and that they were 'freely' selling their labour power. People's free mobility across British imperial territories, such a logic held, had to end in order to ensure that British subjects remained 'free' workers. In the process, the *coercion* inherent in the making and reproduction of a capitalist labour force was obfuscated.

Indeed, in order to deflect challenges from anti-slavery campaigners, "[t]he *hallmark* of state regulation of Indian indentured migration was the appearance of the state-authorized labor contract each emigrant was required to sign" (Mongia 2007, emphasis added).[5] In 1837, the British Indian Government Regulations laid down specific conditions for the movement of people leaving British India from Calcutta, one of the main ports of the 'coolie' labour trade. The would-be emigrant and his (or less often, her) newly minted Emigration Agent were now required to appear before an officer designated by the Colonial British Government of India with a written statement of the terms of the contract. Under 'coolie' contracts of indenture, the length of work (service) was to be five years, renewable for further five-year terms. The emigrant was to be returned at the end of his or her service to the port of departure. Each emigrant vessel was required to conform to certain standards of space, diet, etc. and carry a medical officer. In 1837, this scheme was extended to the city of Madras.

A labour *contract*, often written in English, which "coolies" signed or, most often, marked with an X and, after the introduction of fingerprinting technology in India in 1858, with the labourer's fingerprint, helped the imperial state to make the case that the worker had entered into the arrangement voluntarily. Labour contracts thus provided the documentary proof that the 'coolie' system was not a new form of slavery. So central were such contracts of indenture to the operation—and legitimation—of the coolie labour trade that those recruited through it from British India even referred to each other as *girmit*, a creolized version of "agreement" or contract (Mongia 2018).

The mobilization of the contract as a legitimation device, as Lisa Lowe has cogently pointed out, had a long intellectual pedigree in Europe. For philosophers such as Hobbes and Hegel, contracts were '… the very symbols of humanity and freedom' (Lowe 2006: 202). Hegel, who died in 1831, just as slave labour relations were coming to an end, defined freedom as, '…a condition achieved through a developmental process in which the individual first possessed him-or herself, his or her own interiority, then put his will in an object through labor, and then made a contract to exchange the thing' (Lowe 2006: 201). As C.B. Macpherson (1962) well understood, Hobbes's political theory of 'possessive individualism' was the perverse legitimation of the exploitation of the waged capitalist labour force. It was these contracts of indenture that disciplined 'coolies'. States gave employers access to the power of its courts and prisons to judge, punish and discipline those 'coolie' workers accused of not fulfilling their part of a contract or even for challenging the authority of employers. Employers were given the power to use corporal and other forms of punishment/abuse against resistant 'coolies'. Along with these contracts, which ideologically removed the "coolie" labour trade from the institution of slavery it was designed to replace, it is important to note that it was the state's regulations on both immigration and emigration that were central to not only disciplining 'coolie' workers but also ensuring the legitimacy of the labour system under which they were recruited. Without signing these contracts of indenture, workers from British India were neither permitted to leave nor to enter the British colonial of Mauritius. Ironically, then, while 'coolies' were portrayed as 'free', the very thing—the contract of indenture—that made them 'coolies' also rendered them as *unfree* labour.

With these contracts and these restrictions on the mobility of people who did not sign contracts of indenture, the 'coolie' trade expanded rapidly, as did sugar production. By the mid-1850s, in Mauritius, sugar production surpassed 100,000 tons a year (Allen 1999: 12). A ship transporting 'coolie' labourers arrived every few days in Mauritius and the large number of 'coolie' labourers was causing a backlog in processing. Between 1834 and 1867, it is estimated that between 366,000 indentured labourers from India had entered Mauritius. The 'coolie' trade soon expanded to become part of the global supply chain of workers for the expanding British Empire. By 1844, 'coolies' were shipped to British colonies in the West Indies, including Jamaica, Trinidad and Demerara. Eventually, 'coolie' labourers from Asia were transported throughout the British Empire and, to a lesser extent, to the French, German, Dutch, Danish, Spanish, Portuguese, Belgian and US colonies (Potts 1990: 67).

Yet, despite the official rhetoric, it was clear to anyone interested in looking that neither the Mauritius immigration controls nor the emigration controls of the British Indian government 'protected' 'coolie' labourers. Not only were conditions inhumane and dangerous in this new Middle Passage, but also mortality rates at the places employing 'coolies' were very high. 'Coolies', as Lisa Lowe (2006: 339) notes, '… would be shipped on the same vessels that had brought the slaves they were designed to replace; some would fall to disease, die, suffer abuse, and mutiny; [and those] who survived the three month voyage would encounter coercive, confined conditions upon arrival'. Thus, as soon as knowledge of the new trade in 'coolie' labour became public, comparisons to slavery began to be made and were not without basis in fact. Soon enough, campaigns similar to those fighting slavery arose in both the British metropole and in the British colonies, especially in India. Claims that 'coolies' were moving 'voluntarily' and were 'freely' working came to be challenged.

Convinced that British Indian Government regulations were insufficient to protect workers from India, campaigners successfully pressured the Government to appoint a special committee to inquire into the export of Indian labour. It began to hear evidence on 1 August 1838. However, it was ending *coerced* migration—the kind clearly evident in the Atlantic slave trade—that became the focus of these campaigns. A report in the *Anti-Slavery Reporter* stated, that "[i]t should be observed, that, of all the thousands who have hitherto gone to Mauritius, or other colonies, there is no proof afforded that any of them went voluntarily; but, on the contrary, decisive evidence that they were either kidnapped for that purpose, and by force put on board vessels employed in transporting them, or were obtained by the most fraudulent statements…" (British and Foreign Anti-Slavery Society papers 2014 [1842]: 47).

Such reports were direct challenges to the British imperial state's claims that signed (or otherwise marked) contracts of indentured proved the voluntary nature of the 'coolie' labour system; such a focus worked to valorise a particular notion of freedom, one defined by the absence of direct force. However, while some 'coolie' labourers were undoubtedly pressed into labour, most were caught up in the process of displacement unleashed by British imperialism and sought to replace what they had lost with new livelihoods. Indeed, tens of millions persons were on the move in search for a means of subsistence. Campaigners thus turned to the idea of fraud. A story in the *Anti-Slavery Reporter* on October 20, 1841 stated that 'coolies' were fraudulently '…allured by the [East India] company's servants, under the promise of constant employment, good wages, land for tillage, and ample protection' (British and Foreign Anti-Slavery Society papers 2014 [1842]: 46).

Yet, while alluding to the 'helplessness' of the labourers caused by poverty, the *source* of their impoverishment was avoided. In particular, the vast majority of anti-slavery campaigners paid scant attention to existing imperialist conditions, precisely the conditions that might make moving preferable to staying. Instead, campaigners argued that the *only* way to ensure the freedom of workers from India and prevent their being abused, was to deny them free mobility. Reports about the great hardship brought to the 'wives and children of Emigrant Coolies' by their movement out of India were presented to the special committee established to hear about the 'coolie' labour system. Comments such as the following were part of a common trope arguing for ending the mobility of people from India: 'At present their [the emigrants'] families for want of food, are begging from door to door'; 'family is in great distress for maintenance'; 'starving for want of food'; 'their families have taken menial service (become slaves?) for maintenance'; 'And these remarks are not confined to a family here and there, but are applicable to a great extent to all the families left at home by the Coolies on their shipment for Mauritius'.

For most campaigners concerned with the 'coolie' labour system, then, the 'freedom' of workers in British India depended on their being immobilized. This immobilization was presented not only as a 'protection' for workers, many of whom were dealing with the colonial destruction of the rural economy in India, but also as *the emigrants'* own preference. To buttress such a conclusion, campaigners argued that mobility itself was anathema to people in India. For example, the *Anti-Slavery Reporter* (October 20, 1841), argued, the '…population, so far from desiring to emigrate from their native land to distant and foreign parts, are utterly averse to it. They even object to go to distant and unknown sections of their own country…' (in the British and Foreign Anti-Slavery Society papers 2014 [1842]: 46). Again, this flew in the face of actual events on the ground where tens of millions of people were on the move as part of their strategies for survival.

Initially, the efforts of anti-slavery campaigners were successful. This is reflected in the committee's subsequent report which stated that, 'We conceive it to be distinctly proved beyond dispute that the Coolies and other natives exported to Mauritius and elsewhere, were, generally speaking, induced to come to Calcutta, by misrepresentation and deceit, practiced upon them by native crimps[6]…employed by European and Anglo-Indian undertakers and shippers, who were mostly cognizant of these frauds, and who received a very considerable sum per head for each Coolie imported.' Thus, citing fraud and misrepresentation—and not the difficult plight of people left impoverished by British imperialism—on 29 May 1839, the movement of workers from British India engaged in manual labour was prohibited. Any person effecting their emigration was made liable to a then-substantial fine of 200 rupees or three months in jail. While a few people moved to Mauritius via the French enclave of Pondicherry in southern India, their movement out of India was effectively halted.

Unsurprisingly, the planters in Mauritius and the Caribbean worked hard to overturn the ban, while the anti-slavery committee worked just as hard to uphold it. Under intense pressure from planters and their investors in other parts of the British Empire, on 2 December 1842, the Governors of the East India Company reversed their earlier decision and the emigration of 'coolies' was again permitted from the ports of Calcutta, Bombay and Madras to Mauritius. That year alone, almost 35,000 persons were shipped as indentured 'coolies' from India to Mauritius. Again, as a way to avoid comparisons with slavery, newly minted agents titled Protectors of Emigrants were appointed at each departure point. Likewise, an office of the Protector of Immigrants in Mauritius was established.

Early imperial-state regulation of the movement of labour represented as 'free' took place in the historical conjuncture of the end of slavery and the continued need of investors of capital for a cheapened and legally disciplined workforce. Significantly, especially in light of the present-day politics of rescue, the entire, massive system of 'coolie' labour was legitimized by portraying workers engaged in manual labour as particularly 'simple', 'ignorant' and therefore 'vulnerable' and thus in need of the 'protection' of contracts. The first effort to exert state sovereignty over the *in-migration* of persons into state territories, thus, took place in relation to limiting the mobility of workers in order to limit their power all in the guise of protecting them.

Yet, even after the 1835 ordinances regulating and restricting immigration to Mauritius, imperial states, including the British, still implemented their regulations largely under an imperial state of 'logic of facilitating' movement into state territories. At the time, "[t]he [British] Law Commission felt that *extensive* legislation and regulation were unwise and unnecessary…" (Mongia 2007: 399, emphasis added). This is because the imperial-state was most keen to ensure a stable *supply* of labourers—not to prevent them from coming. Indeed, in retrospect, the regulations enacted on the "coolie" labour trade were quite minimalist. Thus, while there was a marked quantitative and qualitative expansion of migration regulations after about 1850, the spatial mobility of all those *not* captured by contracts of indenture remained, for the most part, very much *unregulated* and *unrestricted* within the British Empire until the early twentieth century. The earliest regulations and restrictions—and even the state category of emigrant—did not apply to those moving outside of the 'coolie' system of labour recruitment (Mongia 2007: 403). The groundwork laid by the Mauritius Ordinances—particularly the idea that separate administrative units of the British Empire ought to be allowed to enact their own regulations and restrictions on the in-migration of co-British subjects—was to form the basis of the modern system of migration controls.

The Logics of Constraining Free Mobility

The contemporary figure of the 'migrant'—the one that contemporary campaigns to end a 'modern-day slavery' wish to protect—was first constructed through the exigencies of an imperial state pondering ways to discipline a plantation workforce from British India while simultaneously trying to represent the emergent 'coolie' system of labour recruitment as a form of 'free' labour. The British imperial state responded to the success of the slavery abolition movement by enacting the first restrictions on the entry of co-British subjects into other parts of its Empire—all in the name of ensuring that their movement was 'voluntary'. In the early- to mid-nineteenth century, being categorized as an 'emigrant' subjected one to the labour market discipline imposed by contracts of indenture which were said to 'protect' them and ensure their freedom. The tropes of 'protection', 'freedom' and 'choice', thus, were central to the rationale for ending free human mobility across imperial state space.

While initiated by the British imperial state, however, it is what Mongia (2007: 403) has termed the nation-state 'logic of constraint' which cemented the 'migrant' as a crucial state—and labour market—category. Mongia shows how the imperial-state 'logic of facilitation' largely left people within the British Empire to move across its different imperial administrative units without the restraint of obtaining permission to enter, but that by the late-nineteenth and into the early-twentieth-century, the pressure for enacting more and more regulations and restrictions intensified. The increasingly popular ideology of nationalism provided the political rationale for doing so. This was especially the case in those former colonies that had successfully transformed themselves into 'self-governing' states with imperialist ambitions of their own, such as the United States in 1776 and, in the beginning of the twentieth century, the "White Dominions," such as Canada, South Africa, Australia and New Zealand which started to undergo the process of nationalizing their sovereignty.

In all of these places, the first imposition of state *restraints* on in-migration was done on the basis of racist criteria of desirability. Determining who was 'desirable' or 'undesirable' was integral to the process of nation-*making*. For those administrative units of the British (and other) Empire(s) trying to break with the imperial-state to which they were politically subordinated, racist definitions of nationhood were integral to the creation of legitimacy for their political independence. With the institutionalization of the idea that 'nations' were units of homogenous 'races', states became intent on regulating and restricting people's movement into their claimed territories (Torpey 2002: 1). The racialization of state spaces was key to the legitimization of constraints to human migration, for negatively racialized people—those defined as outside of the bounds of nationhood—faced limitations on their mobility. These limitations were not only intended to keep them out of state spaces undergoing the process of nationalization. Rather, while negatively racialized people were generally 'unwanted' as co-members of the 'nation,' their labour power was nonetheless very much needed. Immigration regulations and restrictions, thus, worked not only to deny them entry (which they certainly did at particular moments in various national histories) but also to place them into new state categories of 'immigration status' that ensured that their labour power would be cheapened and weakened. Indeed, as Robert Miles (1993: 35) has noted, it is difficult to overestimate the significance of the capitalist world economic system and the political economy of labour migration within it, to the practices of racism.

As with the first British imperial regulations and restrictions on the free mobility of co-imperial subjects from British India, the first national restrictions and regulations on human mobility also concerned those who were recruited through the 'coolie' labour recruitment system. Added to the imperial-state category of '*em*igrant', then, which as we will recall referred only to those moving under labour contracts of indenture, was the new nation-state category of '*im*migrant'.[7] Both initially referred to 'coolies.' For example, the first constraints against 'immigrants' in the United States—the 1875 *Page Act*—expressly barred the entry of two categories of persons: 'coolies', this time from China, and any woman thought to be engaged in sex work (the official term being 'prostitutes'). In a rather perverse use of the abolitionist movement's delegitimization of slavery, U.S. trade unions, whose membership was largely limited to White, male workers, came to represent 'coolie' labour as a 'relic of slavery' (Lowe 2006: 202). And, like the anti-slavery campaigners concerned about 'coolies' in British India, the American 'solution' to this 'slavery' was to halt their migration. Their use of the racialized nationalist discourse insisting that 'Chinese coolies' be kept out in order to 'keep America White' was inextricably linked to their concerns over the relative cheapness of 'coolies' in the labour market.

Rather than calling for an end to conditions of *indentureship* which led to this relative cheapness of 'coolies', the vast majority of the white, male trade union movement (with a notable exception of the Industrial Workers of the World or Wobblies), simply called for—and won—severe restrictions on the entry and on the liberties of 'coolies'—and later 'Asians'. The racialization of immigration controls continued to allow practically *unimpeded* access to the United States of people from Europe while severely restricting migration from Asia. By the late nineteenth century, while male workers had largely escaped the unfree employment relations established by various Masters and Servants Act. In winning their 'freedom' against the continued unfreedom of Others, they insisted on the exclusion of all those who were still labouring under unfree employment relations. As I have discussed elsewhere (Sharma 2006), the process by which free labour was normalized, therefore, was both relational and highly ideological as it was founded in the emergence of national, liberal styles of governance with their racialized and gendered criteria for national subjectivities. Freedom and unfreedom were constituted through the establishment of political hierarchies shaped by now-national immigration policies.

Conclusion

Regulations against 'coolies' were the first contemporary inter-statal regulations on migration. It is when the 'coolie' recruitment system replaced the slave labour system that the figure of the 'migrant' (first the 'emigrant' and, later, the 'immigrant') came into being. The 'migrant' was s/he whose movement across space was regulated, initially in the early-nineteenth century by the British imperial-state eager to facilitate and legitimate the availability of a highly disciplined and therefore cheapened workforce of 'coolies' and, by the end of the nineteenth century, by nationalizing states (such as the United States) intent on legitimizing a racialized view of the now-national political community while simultaneously cheapening a negatively racialized workforce.

The nation-state's 'monopoly of the legitimate means of movement', as John Torpey (2002) puts it, did not target all people on the move but only those grouped together through prevailing ideas of 'race' as well as normative ideas of gender (e.g. restrictions on the entry of women sex workers). The 'migrant' was, thus, from the outset, a negatively racialized and gendered figure. That this figure was deemed 'undesirable' and 'unassimilable' demonstrates the centrality of ideas of nation-ness to the racialization and gendering of immigration controls. Crucially, then, it was through the regulation of the international mobility of 'undesirables' that states nationalized their sovereignty and the subjectivities of those who believed they 'belonged' to the 'nation' that such states purported to rule *for*. The regulation of human movement entailing something we can term a *system of migration* thus came into being with the regulation of workers from various parts of Asia, the vast majority of whom were recruited through the 'coolie' labour system. Neither regulations on emigration nor restrictions on immigration were meant to stop the movement of workers, however, but only to ensure that they were sufficiently disciplined. State regulations and restrictions were not only about numbers but also about the *rights* that various groups of workers on the move would have. Importantly, the regulation of migration arose alongside the growing nationalization of states from the late-nineteenth/early-twentieth and into the twenty-first century. In the process, ideas about mobility and people's movements changed profoundly.

Obscured in efforts to regulate and restrict human mobility was, as Ellen Meiskins Wood cogently acknowledges, the fact that:

> the distinctive and dominant characteristic of the capitalist market is not opportunity or choice but, on the contrary, compulsion. Material life and social reproduction in capitalism are universally mediated by the market, so that all individuals must in one way or another enter into market relations in order to gain access to the means of life. (2002: 7)

The immobilization of persons seeking a livelihood, all the while maintaining, indeed *intensifying* capitalist market practices that entailed expropriation and exploitation, was—and remains—the height of hypocrisy.

Today, we have a globalized system of migration controls in which it is nearly impossible to move freely across now-nationalized borders, particularly for those left with little but their labour power to sell in the capitalist marketplace. As François Crépeau (2003: 174) has well noted, 'We have established all the barriers we could think of to prevent refugees [and other categories of 'migrants'] from coming: imposition of visas for all refugee-producing countries, carrier sanctions, "short stop operations", training of airport or border police personnel, lists of "safe third countries", lists of "safe countries of origin", readmission agreements with neighbouring countries forming a "buffer zone", immigration intelligence sharing, reinforced border controls, armed interventions on the high seas…[,] military intervention…' and, as recently announced, even efforts by the European Union to launch attacks against ships used to carry people attempting to move from Northern Africa to Europe.[8] Notably, this last—but also many other—border control measures have been rationalized as efforts to 'protect migrants' and to 'end trafficking' (Traynor 2015). In this, much was learnt from the earliest imperial efforts to regulate and restrict free human mobility. Now, as then, the trope of 'rescue' is a powerful one in legitimating even the murderous actions against those rendered as 'migrants.'

The abuse and exploitation of the labour power of 'migrants' today result from the plethora of immigration controls people on the move face. Their abuse and exploitation are organized through the logics of the global system of national sovereignties and the equally global system of capitalist social relations that governs and is governed by them. The restriction of people's ability to enter now-nationalized state territories results in the vast majority of people on the move being unable to gain full, legal status in the places they seek to work and live. The coercion of the state as represented in its immigration regulations is part and parcel of how the coercion of the market is enforced against those denied the possibility of moving freely. It is this, beyond all other facts, that results in their overwhelming reliance on private-market intermediaries to facilitate their clandestine migrations.

In short, the greatest danger to people trying to cross national borders is the immigration policies and policing of nation-states. Moreover, the categories that nation-states slot most migrating people into—'illegal' or 'temporary foreign worker' being two of the largest—are the greatest threats to their liberty. Being categorized as 'illegal' or 'temporary' is what entraps a growing number (and proportion) of people on the move into substandard working and living conditions while severely limiting their rights and mobility. In short, national immigration policies legislate the conditions that make some people 'cheap' or even 'disposable'. Quite simply put, without national immigration policies, there would be no such group we know as 'migrants' who could be subordinated, scapegoated and abused—or rescued.

We learn none of these real-life dangers and exploitations from the ever-multiplying accounts of 'human trafficking' and 'modern-day slavery', however. The discursive state practice of 'ending trafficking' or 'modern-day slavery' is wholly reliant on the acceptance of the legitimacy of national immigration regimes and their lack of concern with the gross disparities and exploitation organized by capitalist social relations, relations of which human mobility has always been and remains an integral part. Anti-trafficking policies do a great disservice to migrating people, especially the most vulnerable, and do much to divert our attention away from the practices of nation-states and employers and to channel our energies in support of a law-and-order agenda of 'getting tough' with 'traffickers'—even to the extent of attacking them militarily. In this way, anti-trafficking measures are *ideological*: they render the plethora of immigration and border controls as unproblematic and place them outside the bounds of politics. The reasons why it is so difficult and increasingly dangerous for people to move safely or to live securely in the places they move to are brushed aside while nation-states rush to criminalize 'traffickers' and (largely) deport 'victims of trafficking'. Today, as in past discourses of 'protecting coolies', the discursive practices of 'anti-trafficking' spectacularly fail the needs of people by failing to call for their free mobility across space and their freedom within nationalized labour markets.

Notes

1. Some of the workers brought to replace slave labourers in the New World came from Europe. However, until the abolition of the slave trade in 1807, the number of Africans throughout the Americas outstripped the combined total of Europeans by a ratio of 3: 4: or even 5:1. Between 1492 and 1820, while approximately ten to fifteen million Africans were forcibly brought to the 'New World', only two million or so people from Europe had made the journey. This only began to change after the abolition of the African slave trade and, even then, only in the 1820s. See Steinfeld (1991), and Baines (1994).
2. It is estimated that more than half of all persons moving from Europe to the English colonies of North America during the seventeenth and eighteenth centuries came as indentured servants (Potts 1990).
3. The India Act of 1858, inaugurating the period of British rule referred to as the Raj (or British India), direct transferred authority over most parts of the South Asian subcontinent from the British East India Company (which had ruled it from 1757) to the British Crown. Under the 1842 Treaty of Nanking, the British gained direct control over Hong Kong and Canton, Shanghai, Amoy, Fuzhou and Nigbo were opened up as nodes in the British-organized and controlled trade in opium.
4. With the abolition of slavery on Mauritius, the *planters*, not the enslaved, received a compensation of two million pounds sterling.
5. Contracts for labour (or service) were, of course, not exclusively used against 'coolie' labour from British India. An 1823 United Kingdom Act which bound workers to their employers through labour contracts described its purpose as "the better regulations of servants, labourers and work people". This particular Act influenced employment law in Australia (an 1845 Act), Canada (1847), New Zealand (1856) and South Africa (1856). As with contracts of indenture applied to 'coolies', these Acts were designed to discipline workers and required their obedience and loyalty to their contracted employer. Infringements of the contract were punishable by the courts and the punishment was often a jail sentence of hard labour. Such statutes remained in effect in England until 1875 when criminal sanctions for premature departure from a contracted place of employment were eliminated (Steinfeld 1991: 115, 160).

6. The term 'crimps' appears to have first been used in the Atlantic slave trade and also in eighteenth Century British Navy and Merchant Marine shipping to designate a sub-contractor who secured slaves, seamen or, in this case, 'coolies' for contracted indentured labour.
7. There is, of course, a long history of people moving about the planet in short as well as very long journeys. Indeed, it can be said that mobility—in smaller or larger scales—is part of the practice of being human. Such movements came to be termed 'emigrations' or 'immigrations' when they came to be seen as something to be regulated and even restricted by imperial- and then later nation-states.
8. As Thierry Tardy (2015) notes, the EU Council established "Operation Sophia" on 18 May 2015. "The operation's mandate," he documents, "is to contribute to the 'disruption of the business model of human smuggling and trafficking networks in the Southern Central Mediterranean' by 'efforts to identify, capture and dispose of vessels used or suspected of being used by smugglers.' The operation focuses on smugglers rather than on the rescue of the migrants themselves…".

References

Allen, R. B. (1999). *Slaves, Freedmen and Indentured Labourers in Colonial Mauritius*. Cambridge: Cambridge University Press.

Baines, D. (1994). European Emigration, 1815–1930: Looking at the Emigration Decision Again. *The Economic History Review, 47*(3), 525–544.

British and Foreign Anti-Slavery Society. (2014 [1842]), *Emigration from India: The Export of Coolies, and Other Labourers, to Mauritius*. New York: Cambridge University Press; London: Thomas Ward and Co.

Crépeau, F. (2003). The Fight Against Migrant Smuggling: Migration Containment Over Refugee Protection. In J. van Selm, K. Kamanga, J. Morrison, A. Nadig, S. Spoljar-Vrzina, & L. van Willigen (Eds.), *The Refugee Convention at Fifty: A View from Forced Migration Studies* (pp. 173–185). Lanham: Lexington Books.

Hochschild, A. (2005). *Bury the Chains: Prophets and Rebels in the Fight to Free an Empire's Slaves*. New York: Houghton Mifflin.

Linebaugh, P., & Rediker, M. (2000). *The Many-Headed Hydra: Sailors, Slaves, Commoners, and the Hidden History of the Revolutionary Atlantic*. Boston: Beacon Press.

Lowe, L. (2006). The Intimacies of Four Continents. In A. Stoler (Ed.), *Haunted by Empire: Geographies of Intimacy in North American History* (pp. 191–212). Durham: Duke University Press.
Macpherson, C. B. (1962). *The Political Theory of Possessive Individualism: From Hobbes to Locke*. Oxford: Clarendon Press.
Miles, R. (1993). *Racism After 'Race Relations'*. London and New York: Routledge.
Mongia, R. V. (2007). Historicizing State Sovereignty: Inequality and the Form of Equivalence. *Comparative Studies in Society and History, 49*(2), 384–411.
Mongia, R. V. (2018). *Indian Migration and Empire: A Colonial Genealogy of the Modern State*. Durham, NC: Duke University Press.
Potts, L. (1990). *The World Market for Labour Power: A History of Migration*. London: Zed Books.
Roediger, D. R. (1999). *The Wages of Whiteness: Race and the Making of the American Working Class*. London: Verso.
Scott, J. C. (2009). *The Art of Not Being Governed: An Anarchist History of Upland Southeast Asia*. New Haven, CT: Yale University Press.
Sharma, N. (2006). *Home Economics: Nationalism and the Making of 'Migrant Workers' in Canada*. Toronto: University of Toronto Press.
Steinfeld, R. J. (1991). *The Invention of Free Labour: The Employment Relation in English and American Law and Culture, 1350–1870*. Chapel Hill and London: University of North Carolina.
Tardy, T. (2015, September). *Operation Sophia Tackling the Refugee Crisis with Military Means*. European Union Institute for Security Studies. http://www.iss.europa.eu/uploads/media/Brief_30_Operation_Sophia.pdf. Accessed 14 Dec 2016.
Torpey, J. (2002). *The Invention of the Passport: Surveillance, Citizenship, and the State*. Cambridge, NY: Cambridge University Press.
Traynor, I. (2015, May 10). EU Draws Up Plans for Military Attacks on Libya Targets to Stop Migrant Boats. *The Guardian*. http://www.theguardian.com/world/2015/may/10/eu-considers-military-attacks-on-targets-in-libya-to-stop-migrant-boats?CMP=share_btn_fb. Accessed 10 May 2015.
Wood, E. M. (2002). *The Origin of Capitalism: A Longer View*. London: Verso.

Part II

Present

6

Prison Labour, Slavery, and the State

Genevieve LeBaron

Introduction

In the United States (US), prisoners today produce a vast array of products bought and sold in supermarkets. They milk cows and goats for artisanal cheeses sold at Whole Foods (Alsever 2014), pick and process Idaho potatoes and other fruits and vegetables (Millman 2011; Powell 2012), roast coffee beans (California Prison Industry Authority 2015), and farm trout and catfish (Colorado Correctional Industries 2015a). Prisoners also make clothes, shoes and other department store goods—like American flags or Prison Blues jeans (Prison Blues 2015; Baughman 2011). US prisoners are not alone in their production of commercial goods; prisoners in Russia, China, Thailand and other countries also labour for private firms, while countries like the United Kingdom are evaluating the possibility of expanding and diversifying their prison industries (Wright 2012). It remains to be seen how far

G. LeBaron (✉)
University of Sheffield, Sheffield, UK
e-mail: g.lebaron@sheffield.ac.uk

L. Brace and J. O'Connell Davidson (eds.), *Revisiting Slavery and Antislavery*,
https://doi.org/10.1007/978-3-319-90623-2_6

the prison industries will bleed into 'regular' industry in these different locales, but it is clear that the neoliberal era has been a boom period for prison labour and that in the US, prisoners are an increasingly important part of the labour market.

Most accounts of contemporary prison labour have tended to focus on its exploitation by private companies, describing prison labour as a form of 'modern-day slavery' fundamentally anchored in economistic concerns about profit (Schwartzapfel 2014). Scholars and media reports have depicted the problem as one in which corporations are exploiting prisoners as part of their 'eternal quest to maximize profit' (Khalek 2011; see also McCormack 2012; Winter 2008), emphasizing that prisoners are paid dramatically less than market rates for their labour. Furthermore, commentators note, the US prison system is characterized by staggering and notorious racial and class-based disparities. These dynamics are seen to interlock to create a cheap, easily disciplined labour force for American industry. In the words of one journalist, contemporary 'US prison labour pads corporate profits at taxpayers' expenses' (Walshe 2012). Another commentator argues that 'because businesses already realize that plentiful, dirt-cheap prison labor could be a panacea, prison labor is not only going to continue, but…it's likely to expand exponentially' (Macaray 2012).

Given that prison labour is—according to international legal definitions—forced and illegal,[1] critics of the corporate use of prison labour are right to question its use by firms. What is problematic about recent accounts, however, is their tendency to frame prison labour as an interchangeable form of corporate exploitation and 'modern-day slavery' that is fundamentally motivated by money and profit (Macaray 2012; Walshe 2012; Khalek 2011). There are a number of issues with this depiction, but this chapter focuses on four interrelated shortcomings. First of all, although corporate interest in prison labour may be motivated by financial interests, this cannot be assumed to explain why state and federal governments have raced to expand prison labour regimes. Second, the emphasis on prison labour as a cost-cutting strategy for firms has overshadowed its unique social, cultural and political purpose, which extends far beyond its value as a cheap source of labour for firms, and is rooted in a state strategy to discipline racialized and poor segments of the population. Third, in describing prison labour as analogous to 'slavery', contemporary accounts have tended to relegate slavery to the past, glossing over the real and highly significant links between prison labour and enduring legacies of slavery in the US context. And finally, the focus on corporate use of prison labour has overshadowed its much more endemic and widespread use by the state and federal government. In short, the tendency to reduce prison labour to a simple economic transaction obscures its role as a fundamentally state-imposed form of unfree labour driven by both economistic and racialized social logics.

After all, while it's no doubt true that some prison labour is pursued as a cost-cutting strategy for firms, the vast majority of US prisoners work for the government rather than for private corporations. Evidence indicates that government-exploited prisoners are likely to face worse conditions than those working for private firms. As a recent US Department of Justice investigation into a prison electronics recycling operation revealed (US Department of Justice 2010), for instance, many experience dangerous working conditions and exposure to toxic metals. Prisoners working for the state also tend to be paid less than those working for private corporations, with some states, including Texas, Georgia and Arkansas, reportedly paying prisoners nothing at all (Schwatzapfel 2014). Undoubtedly—although corporate use of prison labour has received the lion's share of attention—the government's cost savings and revenues accrued through prison labour vastly exceed the profits that it has helped to generate for private firms.

But most importantly, as noted earlier, the recent resurgence of state-imposed prison labour has been about far more than money. One needs only look to the re-institution of public chain gangs—an instrument that has been used to control and humiliate African-Americans throughout long stretches of US history—in states like Arizona and Alabama to recognize that governments are using prison labour for more than cost-savings (Maricopa County Sheriff's Office 2013; Schiller 2013; Gorman 1997). In the late 1990s, a prison in Alabama even used a publicly displayed 'hitching post'—'a reminder of racial terrorism' that 'consists of an iron collar that was closed by a bolt, attached to an upright bar or post' to punish prisoners who refused to join chain gangs (Gorman 1997: 442), though this practice was later declared unconstitutional by the Supreme Court (USA Today 2002). Just as it was historically, prison labour today is a highly racialized mode of domination and exploitation, and its imposition is deeply intertwined with broader state strategies to cultivate a disciplined workforce and market-based social order. These dynamics cannot be neatly reduced to profit margins, and have not been captured in the recent flurry of economistic media reports and articles centred on the use of prison labour by firms. In short, prison labour cannot be separated from the broader 'racial chattel logic' that animates the US prison regime (Rodriguez 2015).

So, what is the value of prison labour to governments, and why has it come to thrive in recent decades? Why has the US government come to promote exploitation of their prisoners—by states, federal corporations and private companies—and what are the consequences for prisoners, industry and the public? These questions remain very much unanswered in scholarly and popular accounts of contemporary prison labour regimes. There is, however, a vast historic literature on prison labour (as well as an emerging body of critical race scholarship, see: Childs 2015; Gilmore 2007; Rodriguez 2006) that contains useful engagement with these questions. This chapter will briefly revisit that body of work, and explore its significance to the political economy of US prison labour today.

The chapter proceeds in three sections. The first section provides an overview of the historic literature on prison labour, arguing that this rich body of work usefully highlights the key links between prison labour, slavery, and state policies to facilitate industrialization, and that these insights can be mobilized to mend analytical and empirical blind spots in contemporary debates. The second section provides an overview of the contemporary prison labour system, exploring how federal, state, and private forms of prison labour serve different social, economic and political purposes. In the final section, I conclude that prison labour continues to play an important role in anchoring the unequal, highly racialized and punitive social order that characterizes US society. Just as in historic systems of prison labour, I argue, the key architects and beneficiaries of prison labour remain federal and state governments.

Histories of Prison Labour in the United States

There is a rich body of scholarship on historic systems of US prison labour. This literature highlights the prison labour regime as a component of state strategies of capitalist development and industrialization (Oshinsky 1997; McLennan 2008; Lichtenstein 1996). It also identifies the political and social foundation of prison labour as a racialized and often violent form of productive power and discipline, enacted through complicity between multiple levels of government, police forces and employers (Oshinsky 1997; Blackmon 2008). A comprehensive review of this literature lies outside the scope of this chapter, but a brief overview of historic systems of prison labour will help to deepen our understanding of prison labour today, and the role of states in instantiating it. Contrary to its portrayal in many contemporary accounts, prison labour is not a new or 'modern' phenomenon. As a vast body of historiography makes clear, there have been at least two major waves of for-profit prison labour in the history of US capitalism prior to the system that prevails today.

The Northern Contracting System

The earliest prison labour regime reigned across the Northern states throughout the nineteenth century. In this system, prisoners toiling in large-scale industrial factories fulfilled capitalists' need for a productive and disciplined labour force in the context of labour scarcities and rebellions characterizing the rise of factory work. Amidst the breakdown of slavery and the rise of industrial manufacturing in the North, prison factories became penal-social laboratories where 'the whip made men living machines' as managers experimented with violent forms of labour discipline and divisions of labour (Gildemeister 1987: 15). As historian Rebecca McLennan has argued, these prison factories played an important role in quelling widespread resistance to the new industrial social order and in cultivating a wage-earning class (2008).

The prison factories were—by design—similar to the factories that the US became famous for during industrialization. Far from common perceptions of prisoners toiling in isolated workshops away from modern industry, the two systems of production were tightly intertwined. Prisons flourished rapidly during the industrial revolution and expanded in its wake, not just in the US but also in countries like Britain, Germany and France. The reasons for this are complex, but carceral institutions played an important role in anchoring the industrial social order, and from the outset were centrally concerned with putting inmates to work and habituating them into the disciplines of industry (Neocleous 2000; Rusche and Kirchheimer 2003; Ignatieff 1978; Garland 1990). Inmates during this period tended to be drawn from the poor and working classes, and were most commonly people who were not employed in waged work—either because they were unable to find any, or because they had resisted its imposition as a necessity to obtain the goods of life. As historian Joanna Innes has described it, 'The new prisons… were designed for a very specific clientele: for men and women drawn from the ranks of the laboring poor, guilty of no more than petty delinquencies considered to be especially characteristic of the poor: "idle and disorderly" behavior of various kinds, unlicensed begging, vagrancy and the like' (1987: 42).

In the US, as the upper classes protested against increasing 'disorderliness, chaos, and criminality' in society throughout the early nineteenth century, penitentiaries spread across the country. Their goal was to reform convicts and to habituate them into labour market participation by inflicting 'bodily pain, labor, watchfulness, and silence' (McLennan 2008: 36). These qualities—and especially discipline and routinized hard work—were perceived by elites and the government to be badly needed in the context of labour scarcities and rebellion, and the prison system was designed to reform individuals in this way. Simply put, one of the government's explicit purposes in creating a modern prison system was to produce a more reliable and stable wage-earning class, by replacing hangings, corporal punishments and fines with the same repetitive forms of factory work that were becoming the norm outside of prisons.

In this light, it is not surprising that productive labour thrived in the penitentiary system. Although private companies have had a role in prison labour regimes since the early days of the US prison system, the large-scale prison contracting system began to take firm hold beginning in the 1840s. Northern states transferred their property right in convict labour to private corporations, and in exchange, brought in sizable revenues. Prisons were transformed into large-scale textile and shoe factories that looked nearly identical to the factories that the US was becoming internationally famous for outside of prison walls. Upon visiting a US prison factory, British author Charles Dickens noted that it looked so similar to the other textile factories he'd seen that he found it 'difficult to persuade himself he was in a jail' (quoted in McLennan 2008: 66). By the time the system peaked in the 1870s, the prison industries were so monopolized that companies often held exclusive contracts lasting up to 20 years in duration for a state's entire prison population (Gildemeister 1987). The system was highly profitable; according to one study, in 1865–1866, 'American prisoners made goods or performed work worth almost $29 million—a sum equivalent, as a relative share of Gross Domestic Product, to over *$30 billion* in 2005 dollars' (McLennan 2008: 90, emphasis in the original).

Although the prison factories resembled factories in society at large, convicts were not accorded the same freedoms as ordinary workers. They were unable to refuse to work, due to their sentences and physical confinement, and were subjected to violent punishment including whipping and torture if they were deemed to be working too slowly or poorly. In one prison, convicts were 'strung to the ceiling by their thumbs and rendered unconscious' if their work was not considered satisfactory (McLennan 2008: 128–131). Injury rates and casualties were high. For instance, according to the Physician's Report to the warden at Indiana State Prison, in a single year there were 245 industrial accidents resulting in permanent disability or death for a population of 378 prisoners. These were caused primarily by contractors' failure to provide safeguards against the dangers of operating machinery (Gildemeister 1987: 96). The very high rates of production also played a role. Contractors tended to set two production levels: one bare minimum that convicts were required to meet at the penalty of whipping, and another 'bonus' target that prisoners were promised tobacco or other luxuries for meeting. As McLennan describes, however, prisoners were not physically capable of meeting these bonus targets, such that they often 'labored to the point of extreme exhaustion, producing significantly more than the required minimum but often much less than the bonus level' (2008: 120).

As historians have documented, industrial prison labour had important effects on labour and freedom outside of the prison (Foner 1970; Foner 1988). Throughout the second half of the nineteenth century, free shoemakers, tailors, textile makers and weavers went on strike and agitated against the wages and mechanization associated with industrialization. Prison labour was introduced and expanded as both a political and economic response to the resulting labour shortage and growing unrest. In the first case, states expanded the prison labour regime as a political response to labour market instability and the growing refusal of factory work. Following the Civil War, the Northern states faced a labour crisis and began adopting criminal sanctions for breaches of labour contracts (Steinfeld 2001). As Steinfeld describes, the law became 'the ultimate source of an employer's power to force a worker to choose between wage work and a more disagreeable alternative to work' (2001: 19). As people were imprisoned for breaching obligations to employers, the contract system became a strategy to habituate the poor into factory work as a permanent condition. Significantly, most prisoners in the North were people of colour—primarily immigrants, indigenous people and African-Americans—who were increasingly being barred from skilled employment, and pushed into the lowest paid, most dangerous and least skilled jobs in the burgeoning working class (Foner 1988: 479). States deployed prison labour as a tool to stabilize this increasingly racially bifurcated working class.

In the second case, prison labour was an economic response to costly delays in manufacturing sparked by strikes and agitation. In the face of labour market instability, companies imposed higher and higher productivity targets onto their prison workforces to make up the slack. By some estimates, at their peak, the prison industries were significantly more productive than 'free' factories. For instance, one study of a prison shoe factory found it could produce 25% more than a free factory of a similar size (McLennan 2008: 121). At a moment when capital worried the unstable labour force was inhibiting growth, higher productivity–in prisons became a crucial source of profits for both industry and states.

Northern states used the income from the prison industries to expand their carceral systems in order to instantiate an unequal race and class-based social order, while industrialists found that prison labour could be used to produce footwear and textiles at a higher profit margin (Gildemeister 1987). This sparked intense competition within the 'free market', as companies without access to the increasingly monopolized prison industries struggled to compete.

The Southern Convict Lease System

The second and overlapping system of prison labour—the convict lease system—emerged in the Southern states in the wake of the formal abolition of plantation slavery in 1865. Through this system of labour recruitment, control and exploitation, American states leased large blocks of prisoners to private companies, who forced prisoners to work picking cotton, in the mines, or laying railroad. Far from being a mere substitute for slavery, historians like David Oshinsky have argued that this system of unfree labour was 'worse than slavery': it was a brutal strategy to re-appropriate the labour of former slaves and their children (1997; see also Blackmon 2008). With convict death rates of over 40% in some states, it powerfully and publicly reinforced a racially bifurcated social order (Novak 2014).

Just as in the North, the South's prison labour regime played a complex role in the evolving social, political and economic order. The 13th Amendment to the US Constitution outlawed slavery 'except as punishment for crime'.[2] Its passage was shadowed by the creation of a number of new modalities of unfree labour, and the convict lease system figured centrally within these (Novak 1978; Oshinsky 1997; Foner 1988; Davis 1998). Although various forms of convict labour were used in the South prior to Emancipation, the 13th Amendment solidified states' and employers' use of convicts as an alternative to now-outlawed forms of slavery. Amidst social unrest and economic instability, Southern states sought to stabilize and reconstruct a white-supremacist social and economic order through restrictive laws known as the 'Black Codes' (Du Bois 1992; Lichtenstein 1996).[3] These Codes significantly constrained the mobility, activities and labour market opportunities of now legally free African-Americans, and seriously curtailed their substantive freedoms. At the same time, enterprising industrialists were rushing to provide goods for the national and global marketplaces, and began to put pressure on state and county governments to provide a reliable labour force in the form of leased convicts. In this context, carceral populations skyrocketed. In Georgia between 1868 and 1908, for instance, there was a tenfold increase in carceral population. In Mississippi between 1871 and 1879, the population quadrupled. Prisoners were overwhelmingly African-American: of Georgia's 1200 prisoners that year, over 1100 were black, and of South Carolina's 431 prisoners in 1880, only 25 were white (Oshinsky 1997: 63).

Just as in the North, entrance into the prison labour regime was highly coerced. Most convicts were arrested for committing very minor crimes or none at all, since previously permissible behaviours like 'vagrancy' and 'obscene language' were criminalized under the Black Codes as states sought to stabilize the white-supremacist social order and to amass prison workforces to be leased to corporations. There is ample evidence to suggest that—across many states and locales—arrest rates correlated with labour demands by major industrialists. For instance, Myers and Massey (1991) have noted that in Georgia, arrest levels responded to changes in labour demands. Similarly, Blackmon (2008) has convincingly argued on the basis of thousands of county jail records that spikes in arrest rates correlated to needs for cheap labour, and not to actual surges in crime. In Blackmon's words, 'By 1900, the South's judicial system had been wholly reconfigured to make one of its primary purposes the coercion of African Americans to comply with the social customs and labor demands of whites' (2008: 7).

Unlike the North, the South had very few penitentiaries, and those that were built tended to be reserved for whites. The South's carceral institutions, as Mancini describes, were 'great rolling cages that followed construction camps and railroad building, hastily built stockades deep in forest or swamp or mining fields, or windowless log forts in turpentine fields' (1996: 59; see also Childs 2015). Working conditions in the lease system were harsh, and by many accounts, far more brutal than slavery since employers had no incentive to keep convicts healthy as they had under the slave system (Oshinsky 1997). Convicts were routinely 'whipped into unconsciousness' and forced to work until they 'dropped dead in their tracks' (Oshinsky 1997: 61). Prisoners often worked 15–17 hours per day, and were otherwise kept shackled in iron cages on wheels, ready to be transported to the next job site. As Adamson describes, 'black convicts throughout the South were starved, chained to each other at night in overcrowded, dirty stockades, overworked and forced to continue working while sick, and whipped, occasionally to death' (1983: 561). Injury and casualty rates were alarming. In South Carolina, for instance, death rates among convicts leased to railroad companies averaged 45% from 1877 to 1879 (Novak 1978: 33). In Alabama, a doctor estimated that most convicts died within three years (Garvey 1998: 352). In Texas, the 'average life of a convict' was seven years (Oshinsky 1997: 61). States were contractually obliged to replace dead convicts with healthy convicts, and so death and injury rates rarely cut into profits. These brutal and violent conditions compelled high levels of productivity from convicts: according to one study, at the peak of the convict lease system, prisoners were 50% more productive than free workers in similar industries (Lichtenstein 1996).

As the system monopolized, it became highly profitable and indispensable to Southern modernization (Myers 1998; Lichtenstein 1996). The most significant and rapidly growing sectors of the economy—including logging, mining and farming—all came to heavily rely on convict labour and fought for the system's expansion. For example, in 1908, the US Steel Company paid the government of Alabama nearly US$60,000 (estimated to be over US$1 million today) to lease every prisoner it arrested (Blackmon 2008: 312). Individual industrialists commonly held 10–20-year-long leases for large numbers of prisoners (Myers 1998). The economic rationale for state institutionalization and expansion of the convict lease system certainly related to the need to meet these industrialists' requests for a disciplined labour force. Brutal as the system was, it played a critical role in fostering growth in the context of burgeoning industrialization.

As the convict lease system became tightly intertwined with Southern states' strategies for industrialization, it had an increasingly negative effect on working conditions and the labour market outside of the prison system. The system suppressed the wage levels of juridically free Southern workers (Mancini 1996: 52) and convicts were frequently used to break strikes (Lichtenstein 1996). In many important senses, convict labour immunized the South's largest companies against the growing strength of workers and unions, which was notable in other parts of the country (Blackmon 2008: 90; Lichtenstein 1996; Novak 1978). Convicts were also used to antagonize relations between white and black workers, and were strategically used to perpetuate racial division in the labour market. This not only drove down wages and working conditions, but more broadly, stabilized the post-emancipation structure of racial subordination (Du Bois 1992). As Du Bois noted, so-called free African-American labour was chained to convict labour, given that the low-skilled industries in which African-Americans sought employment—including brick-making, mining and road-building—were the same industries in which convicts were being leased from the state for US$3 per month (1992: 744–745).

In short, just as in the North, in the South prison labour was introduced and expanded as both a political and economic response to social instability and unrest. In the first case, as states sought to stabilize a restrictive racial and economic order and to curtail the substantive freedom of emancipated African-Americans, prison labour was enacted as a violent tool of social discipline. Linked to restrictive and racist laws, it became a powerful strategy to coerce free African-Americans into the worst and lowest-paid sectors of the economy, in part by curtailing their bargaining power as well as alternative forms of securing livelihoods. As states instituted and expanded convict leasing, they brought in sizable revenues to fund carceral expansion, which was in itself a strategy to stabilize the racial and economic order. At the same time, states heightened the profitability of burgeoning industries through the provision of a disciplined labour force. Forced labour was thus a deliberate state strategy of capitalist development and growth.

The role of prison labour in US capitalism has never been just about corporate profit. The key architects and beneficiaries of these prison labour systems were states, as they sought to generate power and revenue to impose social orders conducive to profitability through the construction of prison systems, and to facilitate industrialization. Viewed in this light, prison labour has historically played an important disciplinary role, both for individual prisoners and for society more broadly. It also, until it was outlawed during the Great Depression, helped to instantiate racialized and class-based social orders on which 'growth' was predicated in both the North and the South.

US Prison Labour Today

The third system of US prison labour—the contemporary system—needs to be understood in the light of this history. Today, prison labour is not a mere 'substitute for' plantation slavery or an interchangeable 'form' of corporate-led unfree labour. While there are obvious links between these systems of exploitation and domination, simplistic analogies blur the complex entanglements between slavery, prison labour, and other systems of unfree labour today, and throughout the history of US capitalism. Further, they too often relegate slavery to the past, overlooking its enduring social and cultural legacy in the US. This framing also overshadows the central role of states in perpetuating and profiting from prison labour, as part of a broader carceral system designed to anchor an unequal and unstable social and economic system of ever-deeper market rule. There is a need to understand the different types of prison labour at play today, the differential roles of states and governments in imposing these, and the role of prison labour within the broader carceral matrix that the state has imposed to instantiate market rule.

Who Do Prisoners Work For?

Prisoners in all 50 states and in the federal prison system are required to work during their time in prison. The legal requirement to work is often enforced through violence and punishment, which is increasingly compounded by economic coercion, since many states have recently imposed 'room and board' fees that charge inmates for their own incarceration. One recent study conducted by the Brennan Center for Justice at New York University Law School found that 49 states currently allow for prisoners to charge prisoners for room and board fees as well as medical expenses. These 'Pay-to-Stay' policies began to be introduced in the 1980s, with the rationale of lessening the costs of prison system expansion for taxpayers, and have resulted in over US $50 billion in charges to US residents for their involvement in the criminal justice system (Brennan Center 2016; see also Rawlings 2013). As has been widely documented by criminologists, the vast majority of prisoners are poor and working-class men of colour, and cannot pay these fees. In this context, while some prisoners have refused to work—such as the prisoners who participated in the 2010 Georgia prison work strike, shutting down several prisons for multiple weeks—most have worked, and have struggled to access the most remunerative work available in the prison to meet financial obligations to prisons, and their families, banks, courts, and others in the outside world. Before analysing the role of prison labour within the broader carceral regime, it is worth clarifying the contours and forms that prison labour takes today.

Compared to previous systems of prison labour, today, a relatively small number of prisoners work for private businesses. A wave of legislation—beginning with the Prison Industry Enhancement Act in 1979—re-authorized profitable prison labour and mandated that prisoners work during their incarceration. Today, most of the US' 2,220,300 prisoners (Glaze and Kaeble 2014) work directly for the state towards prison maintenance although roughly 6% of state prisoners and 16% of federal prisoners are incarcerated by and work for private companies (ACLU 2011: 5).

Others work for the Federal government-owned corporation UNICOR, who were reported in 2014 to employ 12,468 inmates across 78 prison factories (UNICOR 2014a). UNICOR runs a profitable toxic e-waste recycling business (US Department of Justice 2010), and manufactures goods ranging from the postal containers used by US

Postal Service to ballistic military gear, and provides services to private firms, such as by running call centres (UNICOR 2015a, b). UNICOR's total sales surpassed US$389 million in 2014 (UNICOR 2014b).

Still more inmates work for the booming state-level prison industries. States are not required to disclose information about their prison industries, making it difficult to estimate their exact scale. Yet, most state prison industries have marketing websites that advertise the types of products and services that prisoners can provide, which give a sense of the labour that prisoners in these industries perform. In states like California and Colorado, prisoners work at everything from building custom motorcycles that sell for over US$30,000 (Colorado Correctional Industries 2015b), to farming and roasting almonds, to making the diploma covers that college graduates buy in their University gift shops (California Prison Industry Authority 2015). Indeed, across the country, state-level prison industries have expanded rapidly in recent years, and appear to be quickly diversifying.

Although these prison industries are owned and operated by state governments, through 'joint venture programs' private businesses can partner with the state to exploit inmate labour through a variety of different management structures (Joint Venture Program 2015a). In many states, prisoners are leased or contracted directly to private firms. The Arizona Correctional Industries, for instance, claim to have 'provided over 2 million hours of labor to private sector companies' since the year 2000, including to Cargill, Hickman's Family Farms and ESB Modular Manufacturing (Arizona Correctional Industries 2015). Significantly, although these programmes appear to be expanding, still only about 6% of state inmates are estimated to work for private firms (Lipez 2006). And even in these schemes, the state benefits through revenue exchanged for prisoners' labour. In California, for instance, the state deducts 20% of inmate wages for 'room and board' at the prison and 20% for restitution fines (Joint Venture Program 2015b).

Table 6.1 provides a typology of contemporary prison labour. Given the serious challenges in obtaining reliable and up-to-date statistics on prison labour, inmate wages and numbers should be considered illustrative rather than definitive.

Table 6.1 Typology of US prison labour

Employer	Wages	Examples of tasks	Scale
Federal Government	\$0.12–\$0.40 per hour	Cleaning; landscaping; plumbing; food service; maintenance; laundry	As of 2014, the Federal Government had over 208,388 inmates. All able-bodied inmates are required to work
Federal Prison Industries (UNICOR)	\$0.23–\$1.15 per hour, but 80% of pay can be deducted towards prisoners' 'room and board' at the prison, family support and victim compensation	Metals; services including printing, data entry and call centres; textiles; energy conservation including electronics recycling	As of 2014, UNICOR employed 12,468 inmates
State Government	Varies by state, ranging from \$0.00 to \$2.00 per hour	Cleaning; landscaping; food service; maintenance; laundry; firefighting; underwater diving; production of commodities	States currently imprison approximately 2 million people. Most states require all able-bodied inmates to work 40 hours per week
Private company through State Prison Industries	Law requires that prisoners are paid minimum wage (\$7.25), but 80% of pay can be deducted towards prisoners' 'room and board' at the prison, family support and victim compensation	Production of commodities including roasting nuts and coffee; milk and cheese making; clothing manufacture; services including running call centres	States currently imprison approximately 2 million people. At least 37 states have enacted laws permitting corporate involvement in prison industries

(continued)

Table 6.1 (continued)

Employer	Wages	Examples of tasks	Scale
Private prison	Widely reported to be around $0.12 an hour	Cleaning; landscaping; food service; maintenance; laundry	According to the ACLU, private prisons are currently responsible for approximately 6% of state prisoners, 16% of federal prisons, and some inmates in local jails
Private company through private prison	Law requires that prisoners are paid minimum wage ($7.25), but 80% of pay can be deducted towards prisoners' 'room and board' at the prison, family support and victim compensation	Services including software testing; production of commodities including clothing and food	Private prisons are currently responsible for approximately 6% of state prisoners, 16% of federal prisons, and some inmates in local jails. Evidence indicates that the majority of these prisoners work directly for the private prison companies, while a smaller percentage work for additional private companies

Sources Federal Prison Industries website, State Prison Industry Association websites, and ACLU website

States as Architects of Contemporary Prison Labour

There is undoubtedly an economic logic to prison labour today. But most of the profits and cost-savings are not going to private corporations. Rather, they are going directly to states, and more specifically, towards funding the cost of the carceral matrix that is anchoring the US' increasingly unequal, racially bifurcated socio-economic order (Gilmore 2007; Alexander 2012; Rodriguez 2015). As Alexander has described it, 'the American penal system has emerged as a system of social control unparalleled in world history. And while the size of the system alone might suggest that it would touch the lives of most Americans, the primary targets of its control can be defined largely by race' (2012: 8). In this context, the state has sought both to exploit prisoners' labour power in an effort to fund and sustain the carceral lockdown, as well as to generate income through partnerships with private companies to offset the costs of incarceration.

Although corporations are often depicted as the key architects behind the prison labour regime, states heavily market their prison workforces to attract corporate customers. UNICOR's recent brochure advertises prisoners as an attractive alternative to offshoring. It asks, 'Tired of off-shore supply chains, logistics challenges and hidden costs, climbing transportation, freight and fuel costs, and communication challenges? We can help. Reshore with us and bring jobs back home!' The benefits of 'onshoring', include '"Made in USA" marketing advantage' (UNICOR 2016). The California Prison Industries Authority similarly markets its captive labour force to firms. Its Joint Venture Program website notes that it can help businesses to 'reduce costs, increase profits, and return operations from offshore' (California Prison Industries Authority 2016). The website features testimonials from firms confirming these benefits. A ground cover nursery business noted, 'Our profitability has increased by 15% since we became a joint venture', while an electronic contract manufacturer explained, 'we have an excellent workforce. They are easy to train and they are never late or absent' (Joint Venture Program 2015a).

As Table 6.1 makes clear, the majority of prisoners work directly for state and federal governments. As the costs of incarceration have skyrocketed in the recent decade, prison labour has become an important source of revenue for states coping with fiscal crisis. For instance, in California—which faced prolonged and dramatic budget crisis between 2008 and 2012—prisoners have increasingly performed skilled jobs including underwater diving and firefighting (CBS 2012; Helmick 2014b). In California, prisoner firefighters reportedly make $2 a day compared to a non-inmate firefighter's typical hourly mean wage of $34.44 (Helmick 2014a; United States Bureau of Labor Statistics 2015; see also: Kovensky 2014). While news reports indicate that prisoners experience greater satisfaction from skilled jobs than non-skilled jobs, there is little data to suggest that prisoners find skilled employment upon release (both because former prisoners face high levels of discrimination on the job market, and because the numbers of skilled jobs are reduced by reliance on prisoners) (LeBaron and Roberts 2012). Replacing unionized and well-paid government employees with low-paid prisoners has been profitable for states—California's inmate firefighter programme, for instance, reportedly saves the state $1 billion a year (Lewis 2014). Taken together, the cost-savings and revenues generated for the federal and state governments through these different modalities of prison labour are substantial. Much of this directly offsets the massive cost of keeping 1 in 35 American adults under correctional supervision (Glaze and Kaeble 2014).

Just as in historic systems of prison labour, the economic logic of prison labour is inseparable from its cultural and social logics. As documented in the previous sections, prison labour originated in the North as a political response to labour market instability and the widespread refusal of factory work, primarily amongst immigrants racialized as 'non-white', and in the South as a strategy to discipline, terrorize and exploit African-Americans in the wake of the 13th Amendment. Today, it is a strategy to discipline racialized and poor segments of society who have either refused or been unable to submit themselves to the dictates of the waged labour market, as part of a political response to the social insecurity generated by the disintegration of Keynesian-era social welfare protections. As the state has mass-incarcerated the poor, instantiating a 'racial, chattel logic' in US society (Rodriguez 2015), prison labour has served as a daily, corporeal and violent tool to discipline those already excluded from the labour market. Governments are explicit about their goals of ensuring that prisoners 'learn the habit of working', since 'many offenders have never been successful in securing or holding jobs in the free world' (Correctional Industries Association 1998).

Importantly, state-imposed and state-organized prison labour can take a public and humiliating form. For example, in Arizona's prison labour programme, prisoners are shackled individually, and prisoners' ankles are tied together with an 18-inch chain (Gorman 1997). Arizona also instituted the chain gang, a form of prison labour used widely during and in the wake of the convict lease system. One newspaper described Arizona's female chain gang's routine in 2003 as follows: 'At 6am, 15 women assemble for chain gang duty. They work padlocked together by the ankle, five to each chain, and marched military style to a van that transported them to their work site. The women had to bury the bodies of indigents who had died in the streets or in the hospital without family and without the money to pay for a proper funeral' (Elsner 2003). Arizona's prisoners work seven days a week, are fed only twice a day and 'get no coffee, no cigarettes, no salt, pepper or ketchup, and no organized recreation … they have to pay $10 every time they need to see a nurse' (CNN 2003). Sheriff Joe Arpaio, who oversees the programme, recently bragged that he 'got meals down to .40 a day per inmate. It costs $1.15 a day to feed the department's dogs. Now, I'm cutting prisoners' calories from 3000 to 2500 a day' (CNN 2003). This regime is clearly intended to discipline inmates into submission into a racially-bifurcated and unequal social order. As Tessa Gorman has described it, 'Chain gangs are a loaded symbol. They evoke the horror of countless racial indignities, from slave ships to forced labor. Since chain gangs have been used as instruments in such barbaric systems, they now cannot be used as part of a "legitimate" system seeking to administer justice' (1997: 443).

These blatantly race-based and violent elements of the prison labour regime make it clear that slavery is far from being safely confined to the past. In the Southern states, prison labour still operates according to explicit logics and practices of slavery. For instance, on Louisiana's infamous Angola prison farm:

> long rows of men, mostly African-American, till the fields under the hot Louisiana sun. The men pick cotton, wheat, soybeans, and corn. They work for pennies, literally. Armed guards, mostly white, ride up and down the rows on horseback, keeping watch. At the end of a long work-week, a bad disciplinary report from a guard- whether true or false- could mean a weekend toiling in the fields. (Schenwar 2008)

Prison labour, as part of a broader carceral matrix, is a social and cultural strategy enacted by states to anchor and instantiate market order, which just like the early days of US history, is predicated on deep and pervasive unfreedoms for large swathes of the population.

Conclusion: Slaves of the State

Just as in previous systems of prison labour, however, prison labour today is about far more than money. It plays an important role in anchoring the increasingly unequal, highly racialized, social order that characterizes US society. Like in previous eras of US history, the majority of prisoners are working class people of colour who have been incarcerated for minor offences including theft, selling drugs, or property-related crimes. If imprisonment is, as Loïc Wacquant has described it, 'the punitive regulation of poverty' (2011), then prison labour is one of the most corporeal forms of neoliberal discipline, routinizing the unemployed, disenfranchized, and discriminated against into the disciplines of precarious waged labour.

Crucially, the key architects and beneficiaries of prison labour remain federal and state governments. Governments have long been clear about their ownership of prisoners' labour, with the Virginia Supreme Court declaring in 1871 that prisoners were 'slaves of the state' (as quoted in Doran 2013: 1036). Representations of prison labour as yet another form of 'modern slavery' in which profit-hungry mega corporations exploit cheap, racialized workers shields these governments from blame. By championing its role in fighting 'modern slavery' overseas, the US government is distracting consumers and the American public from its role in institutionalizing forced labour on its own soil, and its ongoing use of the criminal justice system to discipline and exploit poor, racialized populations.

Notes

1. Private use of prison labour is prohibited in a number of international conventions and laws, including the ILO 1930 Convention Against Forced Labour. Its use is permissible in the US through a number of federal and state laws, anchored in the 13th Amendment to the US constitution, which abolished slavery except as a punishment for crime (see endnote two).
2. Section 1 of the 13th Amendment to the US Constitution reads, 'Neither slavery nor involuntary servitude, except as a punishment for crime whereof the party shall have been duly convicted, shall exist within the United States, or any place subject to their jurisdiction.'
3. For a description of the Black Codes, see: Du Bois, W. E. B. [1935] (1992) *Black Reconstruction in America, 1860–1880*. New York: The Free Press.

References

ACLU. (2011). *Banking on Bondage: Private Prisons and Mass Incarceration*. https://www.aclu.org/files/assets/bankingonbondage_20111102.pdf. Accessed 2 May 2015.

Adamson, C. (1983). Punishment After Slavery: Southern State Penal Systems, 1865–1890. *Social Problems, 30*(5), 555–569.

Alexander, M. (2012). *The New Jim Crow: Mass Incarceration in the Age of Color Blindness*. New York: The Free Press.

Alsever, J. (2014). Prison Labor's New Frontier. *Fortune Magazine*. http://fortune.com/2014/06/02/prison-labor-artisanal/. Accessed 2 May 2015.

Arizona Correctional Industries. (2015). *Labor Contracts*. https://www.aci.az.gov/labor-contracts/. Accessed 2 May 2015.

Baughman, J. (2011). Women Inmates Sew 1812 Flags for Bicentennial Celebration. *Baltimore Sun*. http://articles.baltimoresun.com/2011-06-14/news/bs-md-flag-day-prisons-20110610_1_sewing-machines-flags-state-buildin. Accessed 2 May 2015.

Blackmon, D. (2008). *Slavery By Another Name: The Re-Enslavement of Black Americans from the Civil War to World War II*. New York: Anchor Books.

Brennan Center for Justice. (2016). *Is Charging Inmates to Stay in Prison Smart Policy?* https://www.brennancenter.org/states-pay-stay-charges. Accessed 21 Mar 2016.

California Prison Industry Authority. (2015). *Products and Services.* http://catalog.pia.ca.gov/store.php?t=1432667692. Accessed 2 May 2015.

California Prison Industry Authority. (2016). *Joint Venture Program.* http://jointventureprogram.ca.gov/docs/files/JVP%20tri-fold%20Brochure.Revised%20Feb%202012-2.pdf. Accessed 21 Mar 2016.

CBS. (2012, February 6). *Program Offers California Inmates a Second Chance Through Diving.* http://sanfrancisco.cbslocal.com/2012/02/06/program-offers-california-inmates-a-second-chance-through-diving/. Accessed 2 May 2015.

Childs, D. (2015). *Slaves of the State: Black Incarceration from the Chain Gang to the Penitentiary.* Minneapolis: University of Minnesota Press.

CNN. (2003, October 29). *Sherriff Runs Female Chain Gang.* http://edition.cnn.com/2003/US/Southwest/10/29/chain.gang.reut/. Accessed 23 June 2015.

Colorado Correctional Industries. (2015a). *Fishery.* https://www.coloradoci.com/manufacturers/agriculture/fishery.html?intro. Accessed 2 May 2015.

Colorado Correctional Industries. (2015b). *Motorcycles.* https://www.coloradoci.com/manufacturers/tag/index.html?intro. Accessed 2 May 2015.

Correctional Industries Association. (1998). *1998 Directory: Producing Productive People.* Baltimore: Correctional Industries Association.

Davis, A. (1998). From the Prison of Slavery to the Slavery of Prison: Frederick Douglass and the Convict Lease System. In J. James (Ed.), *The Angela Y Davis Reader* (pp. 74–95). Oxford: Blackwell.

Doran, M. (2013). Lawsuits as Information: Prisons, Courts, and a Troika Model of Petition Harms. *The Yale Law Journal, 122,* 1024–1088.

Du Bois, W. E. B. (1992). *Black Reconstruction in America, 1860–1880.* New York: The Free Press.

Elsner, A. (2003). Sheriff Revels in Female Chain Gang's Misery. *The Sydney Morning Herald.* http://www.smh.com.au/articles/2003/10/31/1067566085163.html?from=storyrhs. Accessed 21 Mar 2016.

Foner, E. (1970). *Free Soil, Free Labor, Free Men: The Ideology of the Republican Party Before the Civil War.* Oxford: Oxford University Press.

Foner, E. (1988). *Reconstruction: America's Unfinished Revolution, 1863–1877.* New York: Harper & Row.

Garland, D. (1990). *Punishment and Modern Society*. Chicago: Chicago University Press.

Garvey, S. (1998). Freeing Prisoners' Labor. *Stanford Law Review, 50*, 339–398.

Gildemeister, G. (1987). *Prison Labor and Convict Competition with Free Workers in Industrializing America, 1840–1890*. New York: Garland.

Gilmore, R. (2007). *Golden Gulag: Prisons, Surplus, Crisis, and Opposition in Globalizing California*. Berkeley: University of California Press.

Glaze, L., & Kaeble, D. (2014). Correctional Populations in the United States, 2013. *US Department of Justice Bulletin*. http://www.bjs.gov/content/pub/pdf/cpus13.pdf. Accessed 2 May 2015.

Gorman, T. (1997). Back on the Chain Gang: Why the Eighth Amendment and the History of Slavery Proscribe the Resurgence of Chain Gangs. *California Law Review, 85*(2), 441–478.

Helmick, A. (2014a). Thousands of Inmates Serve Time Fighting the West's Forest Fires. *Natural Product Reports*. http://www.npr.org/2014/07/31/336309329/thousands-of-inmates-serve-time-fighting-the-wests-forest-fires. Accessed 2 May 2015.

Helmick, A. (2014b, July 25). California Leans Heavily on Thousands of Inmate Firefighting. *KQED Science*. http://blogs.kqed.org/science/2014/07/25/california-leans-heavily-on-thousands-of-inmate-firefighters/. Accessed 2 May 2015.

Ignatieff, M. (1978). *A Just Measure of Pain: The Penitentiary in the Industrial Revolution, 1750–1850*. New York: Pantheon Books.

Innes, J. (1987). Prisons for the Poor: English Bridewells, 1555–1800. In F. Snyder & D. Hay (Eds.), *Labour, Law and Crime: An Historical Perspective*. London: Tavistock Publications.

Joint Venture Program. (2015a). *Program Models*. http://jointventureprogram.ca.gov/Program-Models/. Accessed 2 May 2015.

Joint Venture Program. (2015b). *Free Venture Program*. http://jointventureprogram.ca.gov/Free-Venture-Program/. Accessed 2 May 2015.

Khalek, R. (2011). *21st Century Slaves: How Corporations Exploit Prison Labor*. http://www.alternet.org/story/151732/21st-century_slaves%3A_how_corporations_exploit_prison_labor. Accessed 2 May 2015.

Kovensky, J. (2014). It's Time to Pay Prisoners the Minimum Wage. *The New Republic*. http://www.newrepublic.com/article/119083/prison-labor-equal-rights-wages-incarcerated-help-economy. Accessed 2 May 2015.

LeBaron, G., & Roberts, A. (2012). Confining Social Insecurity: Neoliberalism and the Rise of the 21st Century Debtors Prison. *Politics & Gender, 8*(1), 25–49.

Lewis, A. (2014). The Prisoners Fighting California's Wildfires. *BuzzFeed News*. http://www.buzzfeed.com/amandachicagolewis/the-prisoners-fighting-californias-wildfires#.hxWOMLLmK. Accessed 5 May 2015.

Lichtenstein, A. (1996). *Twice the Work of Free Labor: The Political Economy of Convict Labor in the New South*. New York: Verso.

Lipez, J. (2006). *A Return to the "World of Work": An Analysis of California's Prison Job Training Programs and Statutory Barriers to Ex-Offender Employment*, California Sentencing & Correctional Policy Working Papers Series, Stanford University, Stanford.

Macaray, D. (2012). Prison Labor as a Business Model. *The Huffington Post*. http://www.huffingtonpost.com/david-macaray/prison-private-business_b_2234243.html. Accessed 2 May 2015.

Mancini, M. (1996). *One Dies, Get Another: Convict Leasing in the American South, 1866–1928*. Columbia: University of South Carolina Press.

Maricopa County Sheriff's Office. (2013). *Turning Back the Hands of Time: Chain Gangs*. https://www.google.co.uk/webhp?sourceid=chrome-instant&ion=1&espv=2&ie=UTF-8#q=arpario%20chain%20gangs. Accessed 20 May 2015.

McCormack, S. (2012). Prison Labor Booms as Unemployment Remains High; Companies Reap Benefits. *The Huffington Post*. http://www.huffingtonpost.com/2012/12/10/prison-labor_n_2272036.html. Accessed 2 May 2015.

McLennan, R. (2008). *The Crisis of Imprisonment: Protest, Politics, and the Making of the American Penal State, 1776–1941*. Cambridge: Cambridge University Press.

Millman, J. (2011, October 18). Captive Labor on the Farm: Growers Rely on More Convicts to Harvest Crops as Field Hands Dries Up. *Wall Street Journal*. http://www.wsj.com/articles/SB10001424052970204774604576630972860034248. Accessed 2 May 2015.

Myers, M. (1998). *Race, Labor and Punishment in the New South*. Columbus: Ohio State University Press.

Myers, M., & Massey, J. (1991). Race, Labor and Punishment in Postbellum Georgia. *Social Problems, 38*(2), 267–286.

Neocleous, M. (2000). *The Fabrication of Social Order: A Critical Theory of Police Power*. London: Pluto Press.

Novak, D. (1978). *The Wheel of Servitude: Black Forced Labor After Slavery*. Lexington: University Press of Kentucky. First publication.
Novak, D. (2014). *The Wheel of Servitude: Black Forced Labor After Slavery*. Lexington: University Press of Kentucky.
Oshinsky, D. (1997). *Worse Than Slavery: Parchman Farm and the Ordeal of Jim Crow Justice*. New York: Free Press.
Powell, B. (2012). The Law of Unintended Consequences: Georgia's Immigration Law Backfires. *Forbes*. http://www.forbes.com/sites/realspin/2012/05/17/the-law-of-unintended-consequences-georgias-immigration-law-backfires/. Accessed 2 May 2015.
Prison Blues. (2015). *Work Jeans & Denim Apparel*. http://www.prisonblues.net/. Accessed 2 May 2015.
Rawlings, N. (2013). Welcome to Prison. Will You Be Paying Cash or Credit? *Time Magazine*. http://nation.time.com/2013/08/21/welcome-to-prison-will-you-be-paying-cash-or-credit/. Accessed 21 Mar 2016.
Rodriguez, D. (2006). *Forced Passages: Imprisoned Radical Intellectuals and the U.S. Prison Regime*. Minneapolis: University of Minnesota Press.
Rodriguez, D. (2015). The Present Tense of (Racial) Slavery: The Racial Chattel Logic of the US Prison. *openDemocracy.net*. https://www.opendemocracy.net/beyondslavery/dylan-rodr%C3%ADguez/present-tense-of-racial-slavery-racial-chattel-logic-of-us-prison. Accessed 23 June 2015.
Rusche, G., & Kirchheimer, O. (2003). *Punishment and Social Structure* (5th ed.). London: Transaction Publishers.
Schenwar, M. (2008). Slavery Haunts America's Plantation Prisons. *truthout.org*. http://www.realcostofprisons.org/blog/archives/2008/09/slavery_haunts.html. Accessed 2 May 2015.
Schiller, B. (2013, May 24). "America's Toughest Sheriff": Why Joe Arpaio's Days May Be Numbered. *Toronto Star*. http://www.thestar.com/news/world/2013/05/27/joe_arpaio_americas_toughest_sheriff_still_believes_in_pink_underwear_and_harsh_justice.html. Accessed 3 May 2015.
Schwartzapfel, B. (2014). Modern Day Slavery in America's Prison Workforce. *American Prospect*. http://prospect.org/article/great-american-chain-gang. Accessed 3 May 2015.
Steinfeld, R. (2001). *Coercion, Contract, and Free Labor in the Nineteenth Century*. Cambridge: Cambridge University Press.
UNICOR. (2014a, November 12). *Federal Prison Industries, Inc.: Fiscal Year 2014. Annual Management Report*. http://www.unicor.gov/information/publications/pdfs/corporate/2014%20FPI%20Annual%20Management%20Report_C.pdf. Accessed 2 May 2015.

UNICOR. (2014b). *Section I- FY 2014 FPI Sales By 4-Digit FSC Code and Customer 10/01/13 to 9/30/14*. http://www.unicor.gov/information/publications/pdfs/corporate/FY14_Sales_Report_all_sections_c.pdf. Accessed 2 May 2015.

UNICOR. (2015a). *Case Study: Unicor Industrial Products Designs Next-Generation Postal Container*. http://www.unicor.gov/information/publications/pdfs/industrial/CATMI1800_C.pdf. Accessed 2 May 2015.

UNICOR. (2015b). *Contact Center Solutions (Inbound and Outbound)*. http://www.unicor.gov/shopping/viewcat_m.asp?iStore=UNI&idCategory=1429. Accessed 2 May 2015.

UNICOR. (2016). *Bringing Jobs Home: Investing in America*. http://www.unicor.gov/Reshoring.aspx. Accessed 2 Mar 2016.

United States Bureau of Labor Statistics. (2015). *Occupational Employment and Wages, May 2014, 33–2011 Firefighters*. http://www.bls.gov/oes/current/oes332011.htm. Accessed 2 May 2015.

United States Department of Justice. (2010). *A Review of Federal Prison Industries' Electronic-Waste Recycling Program*. https://oig.justice.gov/reports/BOP/o1010.pdf. Accessed 2 May 2015.

USA Today. (2002, June 27). Court Calls Prison Punishment Unconstitutional. *USA Today*. http://usatoday30.usatoday.com/news/washington/2002/06/27/scotus-prison-punishment.htm. Accessed 2 May 2015.

Wacquant, L. (2011, August 1). The Punitive Regulation of Poverty in the Neoliberal Age. *openDemocracy.net*. https://www.opendemocracy.net/5050/lo%C3%AFc-wacquant/punitive-regulation-of-poverty-in-neoliberal-age. Accessed 5 May 2015.

Walshe, S. (2012). How US Prison Labour Pads Corporate Profits at Taxpayers' Expense. *The Guardian*. http://www.theguardian.com/commentisfree/2012/jul/06/prison-labor-pads-corporate-profits-taxpayers-expense. Accessed 20 May 2015.

Winter, C. (2008). What Do Prisoners Make for Victoria's Secret? *Mother Jones*. http://www.motherjones.com/politics/2008/07/what-do-prisoners-make-victorias-secret. Accessed 2 May 2015.

Wright, O. (2012, June 5). Plan for Cheap Prison Work 'May Cost Thousands of Jobs'. *The Independent*. http://www.independent.co.uk/news/uk/politics/plan-for-cheap-prison-work-may-cost-thousands-of-jobs-7815140.html. Accessed 2 May 2015.

7

From Victims of Trafficking to Freedom Fighters: Rethinking Migrant Domestic Workers in the Middle East

Mark Johnson

Introduction

Throughout the Middle East several million migrant women, from Asia and Africa especially, are employed routinely to work in people's homes as cooks, cleaners and caregivers for children and older people. While some experience good working relations with employers, others experience forms of abuse and labour coercion. More specifically, migrant women working in the home may be confronted by citizen employers who, enabled by the state, convert what is nominally a contractual relationship of wage labour into one construed as indebtedness on the part of the employee and beneficence on the part of the employers.

Responding to that, migrant women who describe themselves as 'freelancers', exit their original employer's home both to escape that relation and in hopes of securing a better situation outside of the regular system of sponsorship. Defined variously by some as contract slavery

M. Johnson (✉)
Goldsmiths, University of London, London, UK
e-mail: m.johnson@gold.ac.uk

L. Brace and J. O'Connell Davidson (eds.), *Revisiting Slavery and Antislavery*,
https://doi.org/10.1007/978-3-319-90623-2_7

or bonded labour, we now have a reasonable understanding of the state system of migrant labour sponsorship known commonly as the *kafala* system that produces and enables this particular form of unfree labour and of its consequences for many migrants, female domestic workers in particular, in that part of the world. We have much less knowledge about or understanding of 'freelancing' and 'freelancers'. What does freelancing entail and what does it mean to describe oneself as a freelancer in a situation of severe constraint?

The term freelancing reportedly originates in the early nineteenth century and was used initially in English literature to designate the freelance knights and mercenaries of medieval Europe, those who had escaped 'lordship', owned their own armour and exercised, 'de facto independence and freedom of movement', even if in practice their situation was far more constrained, and as the notion of mercenary suggests, also were sometimes regarded as morally suspect (Scammell 1993). In contemporary times, the term, including its recent variation 'elancer', is now frequently associated with a growing number of 'contract professionals' engaged in contingent work including artists, writers and computer engineers (Osnowitz 2010).

In beginning to think about the possible meanings of freelancing as used by migrant domestic workers in the Middle East especially, I start with Laura Brace's work (2002, 2010, 2013) who draws on Wood's (1990: 242) use of the term 'freelance hustler' to evoke eighteenth- and nineteenth-century gendered ideologies about morally suspect and disreputable persons engaged in inappropriate market behaviour, such as gamblers and women. Good liberal subjects were men who not only owned their labour but also were ethically self-possessed and exhibited public virtue. Women, by contrast, did not fully own their labour and were considered virtuous only to the extent that they concerned themselves primarily with the family and the management of her husband's private property. Those women who participated in the market were deemed to be self-seeking women who repudiated the bonds and obligations of family and civil society and became chancers, vagabonds and 'working women'. Extending that work Brace (2013) argues that a contemporary analogy of those 'freelance hustlers' are to be found in discourses that simultaneously constrict and deny some groups of 'unskilled', 'economic' migrants, women especially, the possibility of citizenship and ascribes that lack of belonging to their perceived moral failings as people who have through choice or compulsion cut their ties with families, place and cultures in order to pursue a better life elsewhere.

The discourses that produce the precarious and morally suspect migrants that Brace seeks to unravel are certainly resonant with the discourses that shape and attach to the women who are migrant domestic workers in the situations I am concerned with here, especially those who openly challenge the systems of unfree labour under which they work. On the one hand, migrant domestic workers are often regarded as being driven by necessity to take on work routinely cast as both dirty and degrading. On the other hand, migrant domestic workers are also, as Brace suggests, cast routinely as women who violate the natural bonds of family and kinship in order to inappropriately sell their reproductive and intimate labour to others.

Significantly, however, the term 'freelancer', which is now generally associated with contingent and own account professional work, has been appropriated by many migrant domestic workers as a category of self-identification. First, and most importantly, the term freelancing, as in its original usage, denotes that the freelancer has, quite literally in the case of many migrant domestic workers, escaped their employer's lordship and claimed de facto independence; more specifically, it refers to those who seek employment outside of the formal sponsorship system known as *kafala*. Second, appropriating the term freelancing asserts a professional status for themselves as domestic workers against their ascribed status as downwardly mobile maids, helpers or servants who 'do the dirty work'. Thirdly, I suggest that claim to independence complicates and troubles contemporary accounts of migrant domestic workers as victims of trafficking and forced labour.

Methodologically, the chapter draws on and brings together a growing body of research, including my own, on migrant domestic workers in Arab countries across the Middle East, some of which is discussed below (e.g. de Regt 2008, 2010; Fernandez and de Regt 2014; Frantz 2008, 2013; Gamburd 2000; Johnson 2010; Johnson and Wilcke 2015; Jureidini and Mourkarbel 2004; Longva 1997; Mahdavi 2011;

Mourkarbel 2009; Silvey 2004, 2006; Vlieger 2012). The first part of the chapter reviews arguments put forward for categorizing migrant domestic work in that region as a form of modern-day slavery and/or system of trafficking. More specifically, I suggest that while there is some merit to describing migrant domestic work in Frantz's (2013) terms as a form of 'state sponsored bonded labour', the use of the term trafficking elides rather than illuminates complex processes through which agency is shaped and exercised in situations of constraint. Moreover, the implicit and explicit comparisons to the violent and forcible movement of people in the historical slave trade actually obscures and reinforces the key loci of power, state-enforced employer control over people's labour and mobility. If analogies between contemporary migrants and older forms of enslavement are to be sought it is not in the system of transportation, but rather in the various and persistent actions people take against the very different systems of constraint that they face (O'Connell Davidson 2015).

The second part of the chapter describes how women who work as freelance migrant domestic workers challenge directly that state-enforced control over their mobility, refiguring their ascribed status as either compliant workers or victims of trafficking by reorganizing social relations through an act of political prefiguration; that is through the defiant insistence on acting as if they were already free (Graeber 2009, 2014: 5). Describing the action of freelancers as a sort of direct action and political prefiguration might at first glance be seen as stretching the sociological definition of those terms. However, if, as others contend, the notion of prefiguration is not about people deciding in advance what counts or qualifies as an act of freedom or agreeing about what the aims of freedom should be, but rather simply about people reconstructing social relations by acting as if they were free, then it seems reasonable to suggest that freelancers are a sort of (non-violent) social movement (Maeckelbergh 2011; Graeber 2009). I refer to freelancers as a social movement despite the fact they rarely coalesce into formally organized collectives, though freelancers have taken a leading role in the recent founding of the first union of domestic workers in Lebanon (Kobaissy 2015). Just as importantly, freelancers are aware of, create and experience a sense of solidarity with other freelancers through discursive acts of identification, affirming and asserting that they are people who practice freedom, despite and because of the system of constraints they face. In that way freelancing is more than simply a form of resistance or weapon of the weak. Rather, as I demonstrate in this paper, freelancers are on the vanguard of those migrants who are seeking through their own actions to effect social change.

Migrant Domestic Workers in the Middle East: A Form of Modern-Day Slavery?

The first systematic scholarly attempt at linking migrant domestic labour in the Middle East to modern-day slavery was by Jureidini and Moukarbel (2004, cf. Haddad 1999) who argued that the situation of Sri Lankan domestic workers in Lebanon approximated what, following Bales (1999), they describe as an example of modern-day 'contract slavery' and 'debt bondage' characterized not by ownership but by control. Contract slavery is deemed to be a situation in which people voluntarily enter into a contractual relation of employment but where the contract is merely a ruse to cover over and sanction an employer's almost limitless control over employees. Jureidini and Moukarbel contend that is the case for many domestic workers in Lebanon whose contracts of employment neither adequately specified employer responsibilities nor were they backed up in law or in practice. Additionally, employees were sometimes unaware they had signed a contract or did not comprehend the content of the contract that they had signed because it was written in a language that they did not understand. In that situation, migrant domestic workers entered a situation of employment ungoverned by employment legislation that effectively placed them at the mercy of employers and their beneficence.

Debt bondage is a situation where servitude is attached to the loan of money and where the length and nature of that servitude is indeterminate. Migrant domestic workers are nominally protected from debt bondage by a system that normally requires employers to pay the fees charged by recruitment agencies to find employees, oversee employment contracts, process paper work and arrange for travel. Jureidini and

Moukarbel contend that on arrival migrant domestic employees were effectively placed in a situation of debt bondage by employers who held their employees responsible for the fees that they paid to recruitment agencies. Employers restricted their employee's movements by confiscating their passport and physically confining them to the home on the grounds that this was an important means of safeguarding their investment. They also note that despite the fact that employers are meant to pay recruitment agency fees, migrant domestic workers routinely contract debts to pay for agency fees in the home country.

Whether it is deemed contract slavery or debt bondage, Jureidini and Mourkarbel (2004: 597) suggest that migrant domestic workers in Lebanon face three conditions that are, 'sufficient to categorise their status as one of slavery', including abuse or threat of abuse and violence by employers or the employment agency; denial of freedom by employers and/or the state, including forced confinement, confiscation of passports and restrictions on changing employers; and exploitative working conditions with no formal employment rights and little legal recourse. What they significantly add to and revise in terms of Bales' original definition of modern-day slavery is their insistence on the racialized nature of migrant domestic work and the forms of exploitation and abuse that characterize those relations.

The situation that Jureidini and Mourkarbel describe for Sri Lankan migrants in Lebanon, especially those who are 'live in' domestic workers (the distinction between live in and freelancers is discussed further below) is one that has been widely reported and confirmed in the literature on migrant domestic workers in that region including scholarly accounts, and a number of important Human Rights Watch reports (Human Rights Watch 2008a, b, 2010a, b, 2011a, b).

One important aspect that both HRW reports and anthropological work on migrant domestic labour highlight that was to a certain extent downplayed in Jureidini and Mourkarbel's original account is the *kafala* system of sponsorship put in place by countries throughout the region as a way to transfer responsibilities for the management of migrants onto their populace. The role of the *kafala* in relation to expatriate workers, including domestic workers, was first systematically described in the scholarly literature by Longva (1997) in her seminal study of transnational migrants in Kuwait, where she outlined among other things transformations in and differences between former relationships of indentured labour and contemporary relations between migrant workers and their sponsors. More recently, Elisabeth Frantz (2013) building on those and other insights about *kafala* (Gardner 2010) extends and refines the initial arguments made by Jureidini and Mourkabel (2004) suggesting that migrant domestic work in that world region may best be conceived as a form of state-sponsored bonded labour.

Frantz suggests that bonded labour is the best way to characterize the situation of migrant domestic workers who are effectively bound to their employers in multiple ways including indebtedness and the *kafala* system for a specified period of time at the end of which they are expected to return home rather than granted settlement rights. The key point for Frantz is that this form of unfree labour is neither simply the result of states turning a blind eye to practices hidden from sight nor of failing to extend employment protection or preventing people from being enslaved, but rather is about the way the system is, 'facilitated and enforced by the state and plays a fundamental role in the economy' (2013: 1073; see also Johnson and Wilcke 2015). Crucially Frantz suggests that it is not just receiving states but also sending states who facilitate this form of unfree labour. The latter do so both by actively 'brokering' their citizens as migrant labour (Rodriguez 2010) and by enforcing conditions of bonded labour in destination countries through complicity and compliance by, for example, reporting employees who have escaped abusive employers.

An important corollary of Frantz' argument is that this system of unfree labour depends on a regular, if selectively regulated, system of internationally mobile labour. It is precisely for that reason that Frantz suggests that recent and growing emphasis on 'trafficking' and other forms of irregular migration are misguided. In what follows, I examine in more detail two recent contrasting arguments about the applicability of the term 'trafficking' to migrant domestic workers in this situation.

Trafficking is, following UN conventions and the Palermo Protocol, sometimes used to describe the situation of migrant domestic workers who are deemed to have been recruited through duplicitous means and hence transported without their consent for the purposes of exploitation. One of the strongest scholarly statements in support of that view is by Vlieger (2012: 182, 185) who, writing about Saudi Arabia and the Emirates, suggests that because forced labour and practices similar to slavery are 'general market conditions' and because migrant domestic workers are 'misinformed or deceived about the most important working conditions' then many migrant domestic workers ought properly to be regarded as the victims of trafficking.

Drawing on survey questionnaire research with Indonesian and Filipino migrants prior to departure, Vlieger reports that half of her Filipino respondents said that they were told they would not, or probably would not, be allowed to leave the home, while the other half were either not told anything or were told that they would be able to leave. The majority of Indonesian respondents reported that they were told that they would not be able to leave their employers' households, but Vlieger surmises based on interviews with recruitment agents that their knowledge of that was likely based on what was reported by other migrant domestic workers rather than disclosure by recruiters. Vlieger suggests likewise that migrants are misinformed about other aspects of employment including salary, rest periods and days off.

The question of deception in relation to securing migrants' consent is crucial here because despite the evocative language of trafficking, this is not a case of people being physically coerced and transported for labour: rather, in quite the opposite manner, this is a system that requires migrants in one way or another to choose to migrate and to invest time, resources and personal effort and energy to become a migrant to undertake employment abroad. Vlieger's argument that migrant domestic workers are the victims of trafficking is premised on the claim that migrant domestic workers are systematically misled by duplicitous recruiters and employment agents about the exploitative conditions of employment that they will face. Jureidini (2010) by contrast contends that designating this as trafficking by deception hinges both on establishing deliberate acts of deception on the part of individual recruiters, employment agencies and employers, etc., and establishing that a particular individual was a victim of their deception. As Jureidini makes clear, the process through which migrant domestic workers are produced, recruited and transported is complex and not infrequently involves a range of both state and non-state actors (see also Frantz 2013; Lindquist 2012). In that situation, it is virtually impossible to distil out and identify who the individual traffickers are that might be held responsible since it is also the case that while some migrant domestic workers do experience exploitative working conditions amounting to forced labour and slavery-like practices, others do not. Vlieger (2012: 189) claims that the difficulty of assigning or apportioning individual culpability and intent is not salient when, 'one switches the focus from individual cases towards the fact that exploitation of domestic workers in Saudi Arabia and the Emirates is the rule, not the exception'.

There is a general agreement that the system of transnational migrant domestic labour in the Middle East is a particularly exploitative form of unfree labour. The problems with labelling that system 'trafficking' are several and extend beyond the question of whether or not it is possible to establish individual culpability, to whether internationally agreed definitions of trafficking may appropriately in their own terms be used to designate the entire system of migrant domestic labour from recruitment in country of origin to deployment in host country. As descriptive categories, trafficking, contract slavery and debt bondage are all limited in so far as they hone in on one aspect or set of agents for targeted interventions, be it duplicitous recruitment practices, the inadequacy of employment contract or the ways that employers hold employees responsible for the recruitment fees incurred by employers. The notion of state-sponsored bonded labour used by Frantz (2013) comes closest to describing the system of unfree labour as a whole. In doing so, it foregrounds both sending and receiving states' involvement and investment in producing that system and highlights the need for state-led reforms that minimally include the enactment of enforceable employment law for domestic workers and amendment of the *kafala* system of sponsorship to remove employer control over their employees' movement and residential status.

Further, as Vlieger and Jureidini's discussion illustrates, the discourse of trafficking in particular tends to reduce the issue to a question of choice versus compulsion or deception at the point of entry and movement. As others have suggested, that focus on the process of arrival may result in restricting further people's freedom of movement internationally rather than addressing the basis for people's exploitation in work situations in the countries in which they live and labour (Anderson and O'Connell Davidson 2004; Andrijasevic 2007; O'Connell Davidson 2010). The discursive structure and legal frameworks of trafficking effectively turn what is a complex process and set of relationships into a simple binary of people either voluntarily undertaking labour migration or becoming victims of trafficking subject to exploitation and forced labour. Following Brace (2013) what we see again here in respect of women who are migrant domestic workers are certain gendered presumptions about different sorts of people's capacity to act based on liberal notions of individual self-possession, including the possession of all the facts, that underpins economistic and legalistic models of rational social actors.

Conceptualizing Migrant Domestic Worker Agency Beyond 'Compulsion by Necessity'

Just as some scholars have argued that 'contemporary labour relations often cannot in any useful sense be positioned on one side or other of a clear dividing line between "free" and "unfree" labour' (Barrientos et al. 2013: 1038), so too the line between free and involuntary movement is rarely as neat as the discourse of trafficking may suggest. One way of addressing the issue of agency that begins to move beyond the simplistic binary of forced and voluntary movement and labour is to conceptualize people's choice as 'compulsion by necessity' (O'Neill 2011: 16, cited in Fernandez 2014: 54). Fernandez (2014) describes how in straightened economic times migration has become an important household diversification strategy within which Ethiopian women elect to become migrant domestic workers. The reference to the household is indicative also of the way that agency is relationally constituted in ways that troubles notions of an autonomous liberal self (Mahdavi 2014), whether those relations are conceived of as familial, households, inter-generational or sibling set kinship obligations (Aguilar 2013) or, more broadly, in terms of membership in the imagined national community (Anderson 2006).

Existing scholarship on the gendering of Filipino migrant domestic workers as 'new heroes' has shown, for example, how successive governments in the Philippines have mobilized a discourse that links and transforms the needs and aspirations of individual migrants into those of the nation as a whole in ways that exert a disciplining power on them (Parreñas 2001; Rodriguez 2002). In that way, as Rodriguez (2010) contends, it is impossible to understand the situation of migrants who choose to work abroad without first comprehending the production of workers in and by the state in the home country.

Though the notion of compulsion by necessity combined with a more nuanced understanding of the relations involved in producing and enabling migrant 'agency' complicates considerably stories about trafficking, there are two further points that need to be made here. The first is that in the case of the Philippines and in some other migrant sending countries also, migrants are rarely from the poorest and most impoverished groups of people and migrant domestic work is as often about aspiration as it is necessity. The second point is that just as a focus on the duplicitous actions of recruiters reduces women to victims of trafficking, so too it is possible to overemphasize the work and agency of others, be that the sending state, kinship group or household, in producing women who are able and willing to migrate. Women's choice to migrate may be part of a household's or wider kinship group's economic strategy, but it is noteworthy that electing to become a migrant is in fact often initiated by women against the wishes or despite the initial reluctance of husbands, fathers and brothers. In a pre-migration study of legal migrant workers in 2004 conducted by the Scalabrini Centre for Migration in the Philippines, that included both a survey of 990 migrants, mainly women, as well as focus group discussions (FGD), the investigators concluded, 'that migrants are the ones who decide to migrate. The FGDs, in particular, highlighted that migrants, including women migrants, would even defy their spouses' or parents' wishes because they were convinced that working abroad was the only way to improve their family situation' (Asis 2005: 23).

Undertaking domestic work abroad evidently lacks the status that women who secure professional work abroad may obtain and that at least partially ameliorates objections based on gender norms about absent mothers. Domestic work by contrast is not only regarded as a lowly occupation and the economic rewards and social mobility that migrant domestic work potentially confers is often accompanied by downward social status. Just as significantly it also is perceived to entail exiting, at least temporarily, their ascribed positions of daughter, sister, wife and/or mother and converting their nominally gifted labour into a commoditized relation in which they are expected to perform or undertake some of the same intimate labours for strangers in exchange for a wage. That particular configuration of gendered and classed ideologies positions women who are migrant domestic workers simultaneously as both 'new heroes' and in Brace's (2013) terms, 'freelance hustlers'. Women continually negotiate that transgressive, victim and new hero position within family and household, both prior and subsequent to departure across the course of their migrant careers (Gibson et al. 2001).

Anju Paul (2015) describes in more detail the household- and family-level negotiation processes that Filipino independent women labour migrants undertake in order to secure the necessary financial backing and emotional support needed to undertake mobility. Filipino women as elsewhere are more likely than men to encounter resistance to their independent migration. They are nonetheless able to secure familial support if not wholehearted endorsement by casting migration as fulfilment rather than transgression of gender appropriate roles as devoted wife, dutiful daughters and caring mother. Her conclusion is that, while 'women migrants break gender barriers when it comes to their independent labor migration, they do so by "doing," rather than "undoing," gender' (2015: 1).

Gender may not be 'undone' entirely, but it is important not to underestimate what those women accomplish by redefining spatially and conceptually normative practices of femininity and masculinity: left behind men with migrant wives can and do redefine masculinity and husbandry at least partially (Pingol 2001) and women are able to redefine and reformulate femininity in and through migration (Johnson 1998). Moreover, while women may claim in response to formal interview questions that their primary motivation in undertaking migrant domestic work abroad is to meet perceived material needs, invest in new homes or businesses, enhance a sibling or child's life chances, what anthropological work drawing on informal ethnographic encounters demonstrates is that women cite many reasons for migration that include among other things, adventure, opportunity for travel and to experience new places, religious pilgrimage, leaving abusive husbands and failed marriages, beginning new relationships and acquisition of new skills. The journeys that women embark on and undertake may also be conceived of in different ways and frequently evolve en route. For some women, initial and temporary sojourns as domestic worker in Saudi Arabia or Hong Kong may be imagined as a 'stepwise' process leading on eventually to opportunities for immigration and permanent settlement abroad in places like the USA or Canada (Paul 2011). For others, what may have begun as a simple temporary journey may either become one part of a longer journey going on and on (Liebelt 2008) without any fixed or final destination, or may lead to feelings of attachment and a desire for settlement in new places even those where settlement and permanent residency is impossible, as is the case with countries throughout the Middle East region (Elyas and Johnson 2014).

In sum, the decision to become a migrant domestic worker may be a sort of compulsion by necessity and in conditions where the person choosing to migrate is not given all the facts and/or may be subject to deliberate duplicity. In many other cases, women choose to become migrants and undertake domestic work not because necessity demands it but because it is deemed to be the best available option to pursue what may in fact be a variety of contradictory claims and aspirations. In doing so, as the results of Vlieger's own survey suggests, many if not the majority, are aware of the different sorts of conditions that they might potentially face. It is also entirely plausible and hardly surprising that, as Vlieger suggests, most people's information about the actual conditions of employment come not from recruiters but from fellow migrants. To be sure, as Gardner (2012) contends, stories told by migrant returnees will always be selective and may downplay personal exploitation in order to accentuate personal success in ways that can create misleading impressions of life and work in the Gulf. It is that prospect of success that many people cling on to at the same time that they are aware that securing an employer who is fair and reasonable, if not generous, is always a matter of luck, rather than a legally guaranteed certainty. That is the gamble that most migrants that I have encountered in the Philippines as in Saudi Arabia were willing to take. Moreover, as I describe below, just as for some women the act of departure required negotiating the reluctance and sometimes resistance on the part of other household and family members to secure their exit, so too there are those who do not rely solely on fate or the decency of employers but on their own direct action to ensure that even if they do end up with an abusive or exploitative employer, they will not remain there: exit always remains a possibility despite the systems of symbolic violence and structural constraints that seek to keep them in their place.

Freelancing

Recent writing and research on migrant domestic workers in the Middle East frequently distinguishes between contract and freelance workers. As summarized by Fernandez and de Regt (2014: 9–13), contract workers enter into formal employment contracts with employers through employment agencies that nominally specify salaries, hours of employment, duration and other rights. These contracts, first signed in the sending country, are often not legally binding and are frequently altered in the destination country. Contract workers are also subject to the *kafala* sponsorship system in which an employee's residency permit is tied to their employers who act also as their visa sponsor. They can neither seek alternative employment nor leave the country without the consent of their employer, who often confiscates their passport. Contract workers normally live with their employers as a condition of employment and residency: their mobility is thus constrained legally, physically and socially.

Freelancers are workers who exit their formal contract, their employer's home and, as a consequence, their conditions of stay to become irregular residents who enter informal contractual arrangements with a new employer and, if possible, live outside of the new employer's home. In some cases, freelancers may pay their original employer so they can live outside of the latter's home and work for someone else while remaining tied nominally to their visa sponsor who is named on their residency papers. The practice is not legal, though it is reportedly wide spread. Freelancers may work for more than one household or in other part-time jobs. Just as there is some variation in the specificities of contract work under the *kafala* system in different countries in the Middle East, so too there is some variation in the organization of freelance work, the conditions that lead to migrant domestic workers' exit from their original employer and the situations that they encounter on leaving. Nonetheless, there are a number of general points about freelancing that are widely reported from across the region.

First, many women who exited formal contracts often did so to escape acute forms of exploitation and abuse (Johnson and Wilcke 2015; Mahdavi 2011), whether that is long term withholding of salaries, physical coercion or sexual violence. They subsequently became 'freelancers' who sought better living and working conditions. However, there is also evidence to suggest that other women see formal contracts as initial staging posts to seek work as freelancers, or whose initial entry into the host country as irregular migrant requires and facilitates direct entry into freelance contracting (Fernandez 2014: 69; de Regt 2008). Second, it is important to clarify that for those individuals in existing formal contracts the threat of going 'freelance' does not appear to be a bargaining chip in negotiations between domestic workers and their regular employers/sponsors. Rather, it is only after one has left that regular employment and become a 'freelancer' that opportunities arise to seek out and bargain for an improved situation. As reported widely from across the region, and elsewhere, women working as 'freelancers' and who lived outside of their employers homes were likely to report better pay and working conditions and greater autonomy than those employed on a regular contractual basis (Fernandez and de Regt 2014; Frantz 2008).

Third, while 'freelancers' generally enjoy better working conditions, leaving an employer without their consent or complicity is risky for a variety of reasons. The women are likely to be reported to the authorities and if apprehended, will be treated as in violation of residency laws, and possibly even as criminals (Fernandez and de Regt 2014; Strobl 2009). They are often forced to leave without any formal residency papers or their passports, which remain in the possession of their employer. In that way, as Lan (2007) observed about the situation of undocumented migrant domestic workers in Taiwan, the trade-off is sometimes perceived to be between 'legal servitude' and a form of 'free illegality'. Moreover, freelancing is not just an unintended consequence of the state sponsorship system. Rather the state is also part of, and profits from, the production of this form of irregular labour. As Johnson and Wilcke (2015: 146) suggest elsewhere,

> In the regular system of contract employment and state sponsorship, the gendered notion of privacy functions to protect a system that is heavily slanted in favour of the employer. In the system of irregular migrant work that is its corollary, privacy is also the basis on which the state can conveniently turn a blind eye to employer violations of the state sponsorship system, while using a system of fines to heavily penalize those migrants whose residential status is deemed to be irregular. That selective vision paradoxically provides migrant domestic workers who have left their original employer some small opening to negotiate better pay and working conditions outside of the formal sponsorship system, but it does so at a price.

Freelancing as Political Prefiguration

Having outlined some of the contours of freelancing among migrant domestic workers in the Middle East, I set out the reasons for suggesting that freelancing might be deemed an act of political prefiguration. It is important to be clear first of all about the symbolic and subjective significance of migrant domestic workers' use of the term 'freelancing' and 'freelancer' as a label of self-identification. As I describe elsewhere, being able to leave an employer and become a freelancer is partly enabled by and dependent on the social networks of kin and compatriots they, and others, are able to access and mobilize on their behalf (Johnson 2010). One of the social costs of that mobilization, especially when it depends on compatriots who occupy a higher class position, is the stigma of being labelled a runaway or escapee.

Filipinos, for example, commonly refer to migrant domestic workers who are living irregularly as *takas*, a word that describes someone who has taken flight to escape confinement and/or an abusive employer. Identifying someone as *takas* conveys pity for a victim of difficult circumstances whose only option is to take flight and run. One Filipino woman who routinely employed irregular Filipino workers in her beauty parlour described her business as 'an orphanage for takas' (Johnson and Wilcke 2015: 151). Especially as applied to domestic workers, *takas* may also suggest some moral failing on the part of the person so identified, and in the case of women is linked either to an assumption that they have been sexually violated and/or to judgment about their presumed sexual promiscuity. Identifying as a freelancer is a conscious refusal of the label *takas* and other status categories variously ascribed to, and occupied by, domestic workers—be it the putatively good and compliant servant, absconder, criminal, victim, or runaway charity case and conveys the capacity to take positive action the aim or goal of which is more than simply escape or flight. In a situation where migrant domestic work generally is associated with downward social mobility in terms of occupational status, identifying oneself as a 'freelancer' is also a way of affirming the value, worth and skill of the work that one does in domestic employment.

I contend, however, that the significance of freelancing, as both a relation of employment and a category of identification, extends beyond the opportunities and subjective meanings it carries for particular people. More specifically I argue that freelancing transforms a workers' exit from their employer from an act of resistance and weapon of the weak (Scott 1985) into an act of political prefiguration. It is important to be clear here that rather than try to specify sociologically the precise characteristics or features that count or qualify in order to designate a movement or action 'prefigurative' (see Yates 2015), I take a more minimalist approach that understands prefigurative politics as any form of direct action that simultaneously challenges existing structures and that creates alternatives in the present (Maeckelbergh 2011; Graeber 2009) without any necessary collective agreement on what those alternatives are, or should be, or on the best ways to achieve them. In that way prefigurative politics clearly includes aspects of resistance, but extends both beyond hidden transcripts and overt challenges and acts of insubordination to secure in some way, however partial and temporary, the reorganization of relations. On that basis, I think we can reasonably suggest that freelancing is a kind of direct action and form of political prefiguration for the following reasons.

First, as Fernandez (2014) notes, writing about Ethiopian migrant domestic workers in Lebanon and Kuwait, while governments and employers' routinely cite absconding employees as justification for constricting mobility and in the latter case confiscating passports, the threat of exit continues to exist despite, and precisely because of, the constraints in place to prevent it. The possibility of exit, moreover, 'generates a fundamental instability in the relationship' and makes evident the 'structural contradiction that has transformative potential' (Fernandez 2014: 69). As Johnson and Wilcke (2015) writing about Saudi Arabia suggest, freelancing makes explicit the temporally and materially contingent basis of women's intimate labour in a situation where there is otherwise a presumption of ownership and control over their bodies and the work that they do. It also reveals the gaps between the state-sanctioned cultural fictions that publically legitimate and sustain the system of sponsorship and the more variable social practices of employees and employers. Regional governments routinely claim that cultural norms underpin the legal requirement for employees to live in, be part of and be restricted to the family home in which they labour. Freelancers who are more likely to 'live out' than 'live in' demonstrate that employers will accept alternative living and working arrangements that apparently transgress those state sanctioned conventions.

Second, and following on from that, exit is not just escape from a situation of abuse and constraint but movement to, and at least the partial reorganization of, the relationship between employee and employer in the relationship of domestic labour. That scholars writing about migrant domestic work in the Middle East now describe that as being organized in one of two major ways, i.e. as either contract or freelance (Fernandez and de Regt 2014, see above), is a testament to the fact that migrant domestic workers have through practice created an alternative set of social arrangements. As Vlieger (2011: 108) observes, 'while "freelancers" contrast themselves to those migrants who are nominally "contract workers", [...] it is the freelancer whose labor relation [based on verbal agreement] is more contractual, whereas the position of the live-ins is more status-based and patriarchal'.

Third, migrant domestic workers have not only creatively appropriated the term 'freelancing' to nominate this alternative form of relationship but also are widely reported to be involved in circulating the idea of freelancing as an alternative form of working among fellow migrants employed in domestic workers in host society and among prospective migrants in home country. They may also assist fellow domestic workers to leave abusive employers and provide contacts to enable them to enter into freelance working arrangements.

Amrita Pande (2014) writing about migrant domestic workers in Lebanon, for example, notes that women working as freelancers frequently gather on Sundays and form 'informal' support groups. The members of the support groups pay dues, appoint committees and provide financial assistance, as well as advice and contacts for new runaways seeking freelance work.

Also, in Lebanon in the early part of 2015, a group of women, led by freelancers, established the first migrant domestic workers union in the region (Kobaissy 2015). Kobaissy (2015) provides the earliest systematic account of the formation of that union and shows how the emergence of the union grows out of, and to some extent brings together, prior sites of migrant advocacy and solidarity, including religious groups and national communities on the one hand, and NGOs in conjunction with the ILO and a national federation of labour organizations, FENASOL, on the other. Significantly she describes how many of the most active militants in the union were freelancers drawn from across different national communities. For Kobaissy what made freelancers ideal leaders in that movement was the relative duration of their stay in Lebanon (between 7 and 30 years) and their greater mobility than live in domestic workers, coupled with their wealth of experience in assisting fellow migrant domestic workers in Lebanon, and for some, previous experience of labour activism in their country of origin. Kobaissy likewise suggests that the formation of the union may be seen as evidence that domestic workers have opened a new political front beyond that of the everyday forms of resistance. I agree and would only add here that the opening of that front commenced the moment that a migrant domestic worker first exited the home of her employer to become a freelancer, and it is that experience of taking direct action that positions freelancers as ideal leaders of this new union.

Conclusion: Fashioning Futures Beyond *Kafala*

Promises to reform the *kafala* system have been made repeatedly by Arab countries in the Middle East. Confronted by increasing media attention to the precarious situation of workers preparing for FIFA's troubled World Cup, the Qatari government promised to bring forward reforms in 2015.[1] What exactly those reforms will be and whether they will ever be delivered is an open question there and in the rest of the region. One of the key stumbling blocks that reportedly remain is reluctance to remove employer control over their domestic employees' movements since more than any other element of the potential reform, this is deemed by regional governments to work against both conventional gender norms and the perceived interest of their citizens who might otherwise have to contend with employees free to take their labour elsewhere and subsequently drive up wages (see Johnson and Wilcke 2015). In the meantime, there remain women who continue to act as if they were free despite and precisely because of the system of constraints that they face, acts of individual and collective civil disobedience and political prefiguration that, more than international media coverage or human rights reports, make the argument for freedom of movement in a courageously concrete manner.

There are four final points that I wish to make in conclusion. First, while the media increasingly latches on to stories about *kafala* as an exotic Arab system of modern-day slavery, it is important to recall that a system that ties migrant domestic workers conditions of stay to their employers and restricts their freedom of movement is found in a variety of more and less extreme forms across the world, including in Britain (see e.g. Anderson 2000). Second, the discourse of modern-day slavery and trafficking picked up in the media casts migrants, especially migrant domestic workers, in the role of victims. They appear as women who have been forced, by necessity or duplicity, to leave their homeland, cultures and families to inappropriately, if tragically, (s)eek out an existence elsewhere (Brace 2013). Such a view not only obscures migrant agency and capacities to act but also just as importantly elides the fact that it is migrant sending states, as much if not more than migrants themselves, whose participation in facilitating forms of bonded labour may appropriately be deemed 'compulsion by necessity'. That is to say, dependence on migrant remittances by some governments in the global south is at least indirectly the product of external demands imposed by indebtedness and subordination to the IMF (Enloe 2000).

Third, international organizations and transnational migrant alliances have often intervened to offer support and succour for migrant domestic workers. They have also been instrumental in exerting pressure on receiving states to reform the *kafala* system and on sending countries to ensure that the remittances they rely on (to meet their external obligations) are not at the expense of those who are both 'inflexible citizens' and 'flexible noncitizens' (Constable 2009; Mahdavi 2014). However, the discourse of slavery that is sometimes mobilized by the former, especially to press for that change systematically ignores and misrepresents forms of direct action taken by the latter to challenge daily the system of constraints that they face: that is to say, the dominant image is of women who, having through their own efforts escaped abuse and exploitation, sit passively awaiting their salvation and repatriation. Such a view replays European abolitionist accounts of emancipation in the past that likewise systematically underplayed the actions taken by the enslaved to liberate themselves. It also creates a situation where proposals brought forward to reform the existing sponsorship system are unlikely to enshrine or guarantee as legal rights the hard won benefits that domestic workers achieve currently through exit from formal employers and entry into informal contracts of employment as freelancers. Freelancers, in other words, have set the bar by which any formal reorganization of the sponsorship system and extension of employment legislation ought to be measured.

Finally, it is important to note that while the actions of freelancers are directed against the structural violence that they face and combat on a daily basis, this is not, as indicated at the outset, part of a common political project or agreed upon programmatic framework. For some, including those in the nascent union in Lebanon documented by Kobaissy (2015) who have previous experience of workers' rights advocacy in their home countries, becoming a freelancer or encouraging others to do so may be tied to a broader anti-global capitalist discourse or identifiably 'progressive' politics (see also Constable 2009 on migrant domestic worker activist in Hong Kong). For others, becoming a freelancer is primarily about asserting their liberty to participate and sell their labour in more favourable circumstances and reorganizing social relations in such a way that compels recognition by states and employers that they are more than disposable people.

Note

1. See e.g. http://www.aljazeera.com/news/2015/09/uae-announces-labour-reforms-protect-foreign-workers-150929143336000.html (accessed 7 April 2016) and https://www.hrw.org/news/2015/11/15/saudi-arabia-steps-toward-migrant-workers-rights (accessed 7 April 2016).

References

Aguilar, F. (2013). Brother's Keeper? Siblingship, Overseas Migration, and Centripetal Ethnography in a Philippine Village. *Ethnography, 14*(3), 346–368. https://doi.org//10.1177/1466138113491674.

Anderson, B. (2000). *Doing the Dirty Work? The Global Politics of Domestic Labour*. London: Palgrave Macmillan.

Anderson, B. (2006). *Imagined Communities: Reflections on the Origin and Spread of Nationalism*. London: Verso Books.

Anderson, B., & O'Connell Davidson, J. (2004). *Trafficking—A Demand Led Problem?* Stockholm: Save the Children.

Andrijasevic, R. (2007). Beautiful Dead Bodies: Gender, Migration and Representation in Anti-trafficking Campaigns. *Feminist Review, 86*, 24–44. https://doi.org//10.1057/palgrave.fr.9400355.

Asis, M. B. (2005). *Preparing to Work Abroad: Filipino Migrants' Experiences Prior to Departure*. Manila: Scalabrini Migration Centre.

Bales, K. (1999). *Disposable People: New Slavery in the Global Economy*. Berkeley: University of California Press.

Barrientos, S., Kothari, U., & Phillips, N. (2013). Dynamics of Unfree Labour in the Contemporary Global Economy. *The Journal of Development Studies, 49*(8), 1037–1041. https://doi.org//10.1080/00220388.2013.780043.

Brace, L. (2002). The Tragedy of the Freelance Hustler: Hegel, Gender and Civil Society. *Contemporary Political Theory, 1*(3), 329–347.

Brace, L. (2010). Improving the Inside: Gender, Property and the 18th-Century Self. *The British Journal of Politics & International Relations, 12*(1), 111–125.

Brace, L. (2013). Borders of Emptiness: Gender, Migration and Belonging. *Citizenship Studies, 17*(6–7), 873–885. https://doi.org//10.1080/13621025.2013.834143.

Constable, N. (2009). Migrant Workers and the Many States of Protest in Hong Kong. *Critical Asian Studies, 41*(1), 143–164. https://doi.org//10.1080/14672710802631202.

de Regt, M. (2008). High in the Hierarchy, Rich in Diversity: Asian Domestic Workers, Their Networks, and Employers' Preferences in Yemen. *Critical Asian Studies, 40*(4), 587–608. https://doi.org//10.1080/14672710802505307.

de Regt, M. (2010). Ways to Come, Ways to Leave: Gender, Il/legality and Mobility Among Ethiopian Domestic Workers in Yemen. *Gender and Society, 24*(2), 237–260. https://doi.org//10.1177/0891243209360358.

Elyas, N., & Johnson, M. (2014). Caring for the Future in the Kingdom of Saudi Arabia: Saudi and Filipino Women Making Homes in a World of Movement. In B. Fernandez & M. de Regt (Eds.), *Migrant Domestic Workers in the Middle East: The Home and the World* (pp. 141–164). London: Palgrave Macmillan.

Enloe, C. (2000). "Just Like One of the Family": Domestic Servants in World Politics. In M. Zimmerman, J. Litt, & C. Bose (Eds.), *Global Dimensions of Gender and Care Work* (pp. 118–122). Palo Alto: Stanford University Press.

Fernandez, B. (2014). Degrees of (Un)Freedom: The Exercise of Agency by Ethiopian Migrant Domestic Workers in Kuwait and Lebanon. In B. Fernandez & M. de Regt (Eds.), *Migrant Domestic Workers in the Middle East: The Home and the World* (pp. 51–74). New York: Palgrave Macmillan.

Fernandez, B., & de Regt, M. (2014). Making a Home in the World: Migrant Domestic Workers in the Middle East. In B. Fernandez & M. de Regt (Eds.), *Migrant Domestic Workers in the Middle East: The Home and the World* (pp. 1–26). New York: Palgrave Macmillan.

Frantz, E. (2008). Of Maids and Madams: Sri Lankan Domestic Workers and Their Employers in Jordan. *Critical Asian Studies, 40*(4), 609–638. https://doi.org//10.1080/14672710802505323.

Frantz, E. (2013). Jordan's Unfree Workforce: State-Sponsored Bonded Labour in the Arab Region. *The Journal of Development Studies, 49*(8), 1072–1087. https://doi.org//10.1080/00220388.2013.780042.

Gamburd, M. (2000). *The Kitchen Spoon's Handle: Transnationalism and Sri Lanka's Migrant Housemaids*. Ithaca, NY: Cornell University Press.

Gardner, A. (2010). Engulfed: Indian Guest Workers, Bahraini Citizens and the Structural Violence of the Kafala System. In N. de Genova & N. Peutz (Eds.), *The Deportation Regime: Sovereignty, Space, and Freedom of Movement* (pp. 305–349). Durham, NC: Duke University Press.

Gardner, A. (2012). Why Do They Keep Coming? Labor Migrants in the Gulf States. In M. Kamrava & Z. Babar (Eds.), *Migrant Labour in the Persian Gulf* (pp. 41–58). New York: Columbia University Press.

Gibson, K., Law, L., & McKay, D. (2001). Beyond Heroes and Victims: Filipina Contract Migrants, Economic Activism and Class Transformations. *International Feminist Journal of Politics, 3*(3), 365–386. https://doi.org//10.1080/14616740110078185.

Graeber, D. (2009). *Direct Action: An Ethnography*. London: AK Press.

Graeber, D. (2014). Anthropology and the Rise of the Professional-Managerial Class. *HAU: Journal of Ethnographic Theory, 4*(3), 73–88. https://doi.org///10.14318/hau4.3.007.

Haddad, R. (1999). A Modern-Day "Slave Trade": Sri Lankan Workers in Lebanon. *Middle East Report, 211*, 39–41.

Human Rights Watch. (2008a). *"As If I Am Not Human": Abuses Against Asian Domestic Workers in Saudi Arabia*. New York: Human Rights Watch.

Human Rights Watch. (2008b). *Perpetual Minors: Human Rights Abuses Stemming from Male Guardianship and Sex Segregation in Saudi Arabia*. New York: Human Rights Watch.

Human Rights Watch. (2010a). *Without Protection: How the Lebanese Justice System Fails Migrant Domestic Workers*. New York: Human Rights Watch.

Human Rights Watch. (2010b). *Walls at Every Turn: Abuse of Migrant Domestic Workers Through Kuwait's Sponsorship System*. New York: Human Rights Watch.

Human Rights Watch. (2011a). *Saudi Arabia: Country Report*. New York: Human Rights Watch.

Human Rights Watch. (2011b). *Domestic Plight: How Jordanian Laws, Officials, Employers, and Recruiters Fail Abused Migrant Domestic Workers*. New York: Human Rights Watch.

Johnson, M. (1998). At Home and Abroad: Inalienable Wealth, Personal Consumption and Formulations of Femininity in the Southern Philippines. In D. Miller (Ed.), *Material Cultures: Why Some Things Matter* (pp. 215–238). Chicago: University of Chicago Press.

Johnson, M. (2010). Diasporic Dreams, Middle Class Moralities and Migrant Domestic Workers Among Muslim Filipinos in Saudi Arabia. *The Asia Pacific Journal of Anthropology, 11*(3–4), 428–448.

Johnson, M., & Wilcke, C. (2015). Caged in and Breaking Loose: Intimate Labor, the State and Migrant Domestic Workers in Saudi Arabia and Other Arab Countries. In S. Friedman & P. Mahdavia (Eds.), *Migrant Encounters: Intimate Labor, the State and Mobility Across Asia* (pp. 135–159). Philadelphia: University of Pennsylvania Press.

Jureidini, R. (2010). Trafficking and Contract Migrant Workers in the Middle East. *International Migration, 48*(4), 142–163. https://doi.org//10.1111/j.1468-2435.2010.00614.x.

Jureidini, R., & Moukarbel, N. (2004). Female Sri Lankan Domestic Workers in Lebanon: A Case of "Contract Slavery"? *Journal of Ethnic and Migration Studies, 30*(4), 581–607. https://doi.org//10.1080/13691830410001699478.

Kobaissy, F. (2015), *Organizing the Unorganized: Migrant Domestic Workers Labor Union Organizing in Lebanon*. Unpublished MA thesis, American University Cairo, Cairo.

Lan, P.-C. (2007). Legal Servitude and Free Illegality: Migrant "Guest" Workers in Taiwan. In R. S. Parreñas & L. C. D. Siu (Eds.), *Asian Diasporas: New Formations, New Conceptions* (pp. 253–277). Stanford: Stanford University Press.

Liebelt, C. (2008). On Sentimental Orientalists, Christian Zionists, and Working Class Cosmopolitans: Filipina Domestic Workers' Journeys to Israel and Beyond. *Critical Asian Studies, 40*(4), 567–585.

Lindquist, J. (2012). The Elementary School Teacher, the Thug and His Grandmother: Informal Brokers and Transnational Migration from Indonesia. *Pacific Affairs, 85*(1), 69–89. https://doi.org//10.5509/201285169.

Longva, A. N. (1997). *Walls Built on Sand: Migration, Exclusion, and Society in Kuwait*. Boulder, CO: Westview Press.

Maeckelbergh, M. (2011). Doing is Believing: Prefiguration as Strategic Practice in the Alterglobalization Movement. *Social Movement Studies, 10*(01), 1–20. https://doi.org/10.1080/14742837.2011.545223.
Mahdavi, P. (2011). *Gridlock: Labor, Migration and Human Trafficking in Dubai*. Stanford, CA: Stanford University Press.
Mahdavi, P. (2014). Immobilized Migrancy: Inflexible Citizenship and Flexible Practices Among Migrants in the Gulf. In B. Fernandez & M. de Regt (Eds.), *Migrant Domestic Workers in the Middle East: The Home and the World* (pp. 75–94). New York: Palgrave Macmillan.
Moukarbel, N. (2009). *Sri Lankan Housemaids in Lebanon: A Case of 'Symbolic Violence' and 'Everyday Forms of Resistance'*. Amsterdam: Amsterdam University Press.
O'Connell Davidson, J. (2010). New Slavery, Old Binaries: Human Trafficking and the Borders Of "Freedom". *Global Networks, 10*(2), 244–261. https://doi.org/10.1111/j.1471-0374.2010.00284.x.
O'Connell Davidson, J. (2015). *Rights Talk, Wrong Comparison: Trafficking and Transatlantic Slavery*. Beyond Trafficking and Slavery, Open Democracy. https://www.opendemocracy.net/beyondslavery/julia-o%27connell-davidson/rights-talk-wrong-comparison-trafficking-and-transatlantic-sl. Accessed 1 July 2015.
O'Neill, J. (2011). *The Varieties of Unfreedom* (Manchester Papers in Political Economy, No. 4/11). Manchester: University of Manchester.
Osnowitz, D. (2010). *Freelancing Expertise: Contract Professionals in the New Economy*. Ithaca, NY: ILR Press, An Imprint of Cornell University Press.
Pande, A. (2014). Forging Intimate and Work Ties: Migrant Domestic Workers Resist. In B. Fernandez & M. de Regt (Eds.), *Migrant Domestic Workers in the Middle East: The Home and the World* (pp. 27–50). New York: Palgrave Macmillan.
Parreñas, R. (2001). Transgressing the Nation-State: The Partial Citizenship and "Imagined (Global) Community" of Migrant Filipina Domestic Workers. *Signs: Journal of Women in Culture and Society, 26*(4), 1129–1154. https://doi.org/10.1086/495650.
Paul, A. (2011). Stepwise International Migration: A Multistage Migration Pattern for the Aspiring Migrant. *American Journal of Sociology, 116*(6), 1842–1886. https://doi.org/10.1086/659641.
Paul, A. (2015). Negotiating Migration, Performing Gender. *Social Forces, 94*(1), 271–293. https://doi.org/10.1093/sf/sov049.

Pingol, A. (2001). *Remaking Masculinities: Identity, Power, and Gender Dynamics in Families with Migrant Wives and Househusbands*. Quezon City: University of the Philippines-University Center for Women's Studies.
Rodriguez, R. M. (2002). Migrant Heroes: Nationalism, Citizenship and the Politics of Filipino Migrant Labor. *Citizenship Studies, 6*(3), 341–356. https://doi.org//10.1080/1362102022000011658.
Rodriguez, R. M. (2010). *Migrants for Export: How the Philippine State Brokers Labor to the World*. Minneapolis: University of Minnesota Press.
Scammell, J. (1993). The Formation of the English Social Structure: Freedom, Knights, and Gentry, 1066–1300. *Speculum, 68*(3), 591–618. https://doi.org//10.2307/2864967.
Scott, J. (1985). *Weapons of the Weak: Everyday Forms of Peasant Resistance*. New Haven, CT: Yale University Press.
Silvey, R. (2004). Transnational Domestication: State Power and Indonesian Migrant Women in Saudi Arabia. *Political Geography, 23*, 245–264. https://doi.org/10.1016/j.polgeo.2003.12.015.
Silvey, R. (2006). Consuming the Transnational Family: Indonesian Migrant Domestic Workers to Saudi Arabia. *Global Networks, 6*(1), 23–40. https://doi.org//10.1111/j.1471-0374.2006.00131.x.
Strobl, S. (2009). Policing Housemaids: The Criminalization of Domestic Workers in Bahrain. *British Journal of Criminology, 49*(2), 165–183. https://doi.org//10.1093/bjc/azn071.
Vlieger, R. (2011). *Domestic Workers in Saudi Arabia and the Emirates: A Socio-Legal Study on Conflicts*. Ph.D. thesis, University of Amsterdam, Amsterdam.
Vlieger, R. (2012). Domestic Workers in Saudi Arabia and the Emirates: Trafficking Victims? *International Migration, 50*(6), 180–194. https://doi.org//10.1111/j.1468-2435.2012.00785.x.
Wood, A. (1990). *Hegel's Ethical Thought*. Cambridge: Cambridge University Press.
Yates, L. (2015). Rethinking Prefiguration: Alternatives, Micropolitics and Goals in Social Movements. *Social Movement Studies, 14*(1), 1–21. https://doi.org//10.1080/14742837.2013.870883.

8

"Back Home, It Would Have Been Worse Anyway…": Vietnamese Wives' Perspectives on Their 'Arranged' Marriages with Chinese Men

Caroline Grillot

This chapter presents and analyses data on Vietnamese women's life trajectories. This case study supports the idea that "southeast Asia demonstrates very well the fundamental contradictions always inherent in slavery. The slave is a commodity and yet a human being; exploited and yet trusted to be loyal; inferior and yet intimate. The contradictions have ensured that no system of slavery can be "pure" or free from anomalies" (Reid 1983: 36). It shows that despite clear evidence of deception, abduction, exploitation and abuse in the Sino-Vietnamese borderlands, personal narratives and local residents' perceptions challenge the conventional victimizing discourse on arranged cross-border marriages.

In early summer 2006, I went to the town of Hekou (Yunnan, China), one of the main international border gates between China and Vietnam, to find out about cross-border marriages between Vietnamese women and Chinese men. I had in mind numerous accounts of human trafficking cases related in media reports, as well as in reports from various international organizations, and more rarely, academic analyses that

C. Grillot (✉)
Lyon Institute of East Asian Studies, Lyon, France

L. Brace and J. O'Connell Davidson (eds.), *Revisiting Slavery and Antislavery*,
https://doi.org/10.1007/978-3-319-90623-2_8

focused on these specific borderlands. In these accounts, South Yunnan and South Guangxi were portrayed as infamous spots for all sorts of illegal activities, including smuggling of people. Most testimonies relating to marriages emphasized dramatic trajectories of poor, uneducated rural women from northern Vietnamese provinces lured by brokers into China, and sold to local peasants in need of a wife, a womb or a sex slave. I was determined to conduct research on these marriages to discover how severe the actual life conditions of these women were; hence, I decided to start my enquiries in this border town. Driven by empathy for those presented as victims of money seekers and morally questionable males, I began my research fieldwork by asking around about mixed Chinese–Vietnamese couples whose marriages had been arranged, and about Vietnamese women who had experienced human trafficking. The responses to my questions were unexpected and challenging:

> — What trafficked women? You won't find any here. Don't trust them, they'll tell you moving stories. You'd better ask Chinese men around what they think of Vietnamese women…

These comments marked the beginning of a long process of deconstructing established public discourses on cross-border marriages and particularly the sensationalistic accounts circulated by activists, international organizations and, from time to time, national authorities. They also reoriented my research focus towards the locality's history in terms of local migration, and the social representation of marriage migration's recent development. Later on, long-term exchanges with Hekou's Chinese dwellers (locals and migrants), members of the Vietnamese community and individuals involved in cross-border marriages at some stages of their life trajectories all confirmed that the human trafficking prism that brought me to the field was insufficient to embrace the complex and ambiguous realities on the ground (Grillot 2010; Ford et al. 2012).

The ethnographic material informing this chapter was collected between 2006 and 2009 in two Sino-Vietnamese border twin cities, Hekou (Yunnan province) and Lào Cai (Lào Cai province, Vietnam) in the eastern mountainous section of the frontier, and Dongxing

(Guangxi province) and Móng Cái (Quàng Ninh province, Vietnam), on its western maritime section. Semi-structured conversations with members of local communities, participant observation and specific life-stories sessions with Chinese men and Vietnamese women involved in cross-border marriages constitute the main ethnographic sources that intend to enlighten a limited, yet relevant, historical corpus with contemporary perspectives. This chapter presents and analyses data on Vietnamese women's life trajectories. It shows that despite clear evidence of deception, abduction, exploitation and abuse in the Sino-Vietnamese borderlands, personal narratives and local residents' perceptions challenge the conventional victimizing discourse on arranged cross-border marriages. They reveal alternative perspectives in which questions of belief, personal emancipation and the pursuit of freedom are highlighted, and so challenge the relevance of categories such as 'slavery', 'trafficking' and even 'marriage' as frames for the intimate histories of couples who participated in my research.

Before turning to these personal narratives, the chapter opens with a brief historical overview of slavery and the sale of women in the nineteenth- and early twentieth-century Sino-Vietnamese context, for this is the history that, for some commentators, is continued in contemporary cross-border marriages.

Slavery in Vietnam and China: Some Historical Background

Even before the French established the Indochinese Union in 1887, the border cities of Dongxing and Móng Cái were thriving trading areas. Indeed, Dongxing had long been devoted to trade of all kinds. Historical accounts from the French colonial period reveal that in former times—more than a century ago—handicrafts, manufactured goods and agricultural products were not the only objects of transaction between the Vietnamese and Chinese. 'Human livestock' was openly negotiated as well:

> Before the Chinese Republic [before 1912], the Tong-hing [Dongxing] market where the Yellows [Asians] are traded, displayed a barbaric and grotesque spectacle. Girls, boys and women for sale were brought to the market the night before the sale to avoid being seen by the public. The next morning [at a time when the market was about to open] they were made to sit on a stool. One covered their entire upper body, up to their knees, by a sort of large conical basket, showing in an apparent manner the price, age and sex of the person to be sold. The buyer, therefore, only relied on the legs to get an idea of the 'goods' he wanted to buy. (…) Mostly, these markets of Tong-hing are self-supplying at the deposits of Cat-ba [Cát Bà] and Ké-bao [Kê Báo] islands. The Chinese come with their junks and choose the most beautiful subjects who are stored in the caves and in the forest dens. The price is negotiated after the selection. (Baudrit 1943, republished in 2008: 138–139, *translation by the author*)

Baudrit (1943, republished in 2008) in his time, and more recently Lessard (2009), are among the few historians who have written on the topic of 'human trade' or slavery during the colonization of Indochina, especially in North Vietnam—in Tonkin. More particularly, they have documented the widespread practice of selling Vietnamese women to China for purposes of prostitution, marriage or domestic work. The incredibly detailed information provided in these accounts finds a strong echo in contemporary Vietnamese women's stories, especially as regards the very similar ways by which they reached China, namely through kidnapping, sale of daughters by poor families, trickery, smuggling and so on. According to Lessard (2009: 26–28), the Confucian system, the development of the colonial economy, the improvement of the transportation system, rural impoverishment, colonial rule, and border conflicts and chaos were the main factors that contributed to the continuity and even the expansion of this 'human trade' from northern Vietnam [Tonkin] to China, from the pre-colonial period up to the middle of the twentieth century.

On the Chinese side, recourse to the work of several European observers of Chinese society under the imperial regime and the Republic of China (pre-1949) also reveals a trade in women within as well as without China's frontiers, through acts of piracy and kidnapping (Cooper and Gallieni, cited in Baudrit 2008). In South China, for example, slavery was practised until the middle of the twentieth century as James Watson's research into the Cantonese region—including Guangxi—has shown:

> Until the foundation of the People's Republic in 1949 China had one of the largest and most comprehensive markets for the exchange of human beings in the world. In many parts of China, notably in the south, nearly every peasant household was directly or indirectly affected by the sale of people. (1980: 223)

This, however, mostly concerned the *mui tsai*, young girls sold to families for domestic work, and most scholarship focuses on the Cantonese region of China (including Hong Kong) where it was an institutionalized form of slavery. In her account on 'homes for slaves' that Western missionaries introduced in Yunnan, Jaschok (1994: 173) reminds us that the Qing dynasty had already proscribed public and private slavery in 1910 and that soon after, the newly established Republic of China began to take action by opening institutionalized homes for runaway slaves and by framing laws against the sale of women and children in 1928. But the author also sheds light on the ambiguous implementation of the new law and the way it dealt with the rescued slaves. On the one hand, "The Chinese officials saw it as their duty to marry off these girls as wives to the poor, or as concubines into comfortably-off families," and on the other hand, it also "distinguished between the 'legitimate' rights of the *pater familias* to transfer women and their illegitimate appropriation by persons other than the head of the family or the appointed guardian (175)". Offering former slaves a chance to enjoy a new social life did not prevent them from being commodified and negotiated, under the customary prerogatives still in practice. Along with local resistance to the legal abolition of slavery, the few defenders of slaves' rights—Chinese activists and Western missionaries—encountered great difficulties in raising their voices:

> On the whole, missionary accounts of the inmates tell of callous abandonment of little girls by guardians and relatives and of their sale for reasons that include the need for money to buy coffins, to finance weddings

> and to buy expensive opium. They tell of buyers whose disregard for the humanity of a slave girl led to brutal treatment and callous neglect, in 'a heathen society' in which respect for the rights of ownership made public intervention very rare – even where a death occurred. (Jaschok 1994: 179)

In the introduction of their edited volume *Women and Chinese Patriarchy: Submission, Servitude and Escape*, Jaschok and Miers also mentions other forms of exploitation of women in China besides the *mui tsai* in the Cantonese region. The *san po tsai* were girls sold by their families at a very young age to the family of their future husbands, while the *pipa tsai* were sold to be entertainers in musical venues, which could include the provision of sexual services. Speaking of these girls, the authors add that "[t]he boundaries here between outright exploitation, emotional dependence, servitude, and filial submission are especially fluid" (Jaschok and Miers 1994: 12). All these forms of slavery vanished after 1949, with the new government, a new Marriage Law, more education and more job opportunities for young people, as well as greater prosperity in rural areas.

It should also be noted that other ethnic groups from China and its Southeast Asian borders historically maintained, as did Han Chinese, practices associated with a system of slavery. In Yunnan province, in the nineteenth century, for example, a European traveller reported the following scenes:

> Tali-foo [Dali], as well as Yunnan-foo [Kunming], were also famous as slave markets to which dealers from Canton, Soo-Chow [Suzhou], near Shanghai, and even Pekin itself, resorted for the purchase of female children, numbers of whom were brought for sale by the different tribes visiting the annual fairs, who in their wars look upon women and girls as valuable booty. Caravans, sometimes numbering several hundreds of girls purchased in the neighbourhood of these cities, started regularly every year for the different places I have mentioned. (Cooper 1870–1871: 165)

Yunnan and also Guangxi have long histories as 'uncontrolled' regions, dominated by local mandarins who enforced the laws according to their own interpretation and benefits. The regions were highly connected with the rest of Southeast Asia and mainly populated by various ethnic groups spread over the boundaries of the empires. The Wa and the Yi, for instance, were infamous for capturing slaves among their neighbours until the Chinese Government imposed new laws and took control over the population in the early 1950s (Fiskesjö 2011). Their social structure and system of land exploitation, which included practices of slavery, earned them the label of "primitive" or "slave" societies in the Marxist classification of ethnic groups. Whether individual were sold by their parents to pay debts, captured to work as miners or commodified as trading goods, slave trading was a reality in these border regions of the Empire, then the Republic, of China until the mid-twentieth century.

According to some commentators, these practices continue, albeit in slightly changed forms:

> Today, as in the past, the powerful forces of the market and their ideological commodification of everything progressively infect the practice of kinship, and in the absence of open, legalized, mass slavery, kinship in fact has become the only convenient cover for a "trade in people" such as house slave or wives retained against their will. (Fiskesjö 2011: 13)

Indeed, as the world entered a new phase of globalization at the turn of the millennium, interest and concern about this kind of 'trade in people' were renewed, now framed more in terms of a problem of 'human trafficking', as opposed to 'slavery'.

Comparing old patterns of slavery with contemporary practices termed 'human trafficking' in China may seem reasonable and straightforward if we focus merely on "the logic and shared rules of the global marketplace in which labour is exploited as a commodity" (Fiskesjö 2011: 13). But evaluating the continuities between past and present, and importantly, the impact of given historical legacies on the local population and their perception of 'human trade' is more complicated, especially when our focus is on migrants recently settled in borderlands, who may not even be aware of previous local practices. The sections below explore some of this complexity.

The Sino-Vietnamese Borderlands Today

Dongxing, Móng Cái, Hekou and Lào Cai, the four border cities where many Sino-Vietnamese couples live in either more or less stable marital relationships, share many economic and social features in common.

Lào Cai (Vietnam) and Hekou (China), which are linked by a long bridge above the Nanxi River, are located in a mountainous once-secluded region. They have combined to establish an area called the 'Hekou – Lào Cai economic cooperation district.' The area enjoyed its first substantial development during the nineteenth century, as a result of economic exchanges between Vietnam and China. These exchanges accelerated at the beginning of the twentieth century with the activities of the French-built railway line that connected Hanoi with Kunming. Trade continued to grow thereafter, despite the military and political conflicts that have regularly closed the border and prevented crossings (the Independence War, the Vietnam War and the Sino-Vietnamese conflict). The year 1992 saw the twin cities reopen to the outside world, officially becoming a transit port for international trade and an international border gate for tourists. Further east on the frontier line, the bustling twin cities of Dongxing and Móng Cái share a similar status to that of the twins Hekou and Lào Cai. They constitute one of the areas known as 'cross-border economic cooperation districts', officially named the 'Dongxing - Móng Cái-Free Trade Zone', another strategic node of regional economic development and transnational integration common to several countries in the Greater Mekong Subregion. They benefit from the proximity to the Cantonese region, one of the most economically developed and active areas of China. There as well, Chinese and Vietnamese traders exchange goods and natural resources, restoring to this small port damaged by history its role of intermediary.

Connected to major provincial capitals by rail and regular bus lines, the four cities support a large population of migrants, who come in their thousands to these cities in search of work, especially jobs related to the cross-border trade. Each day sees new cohorts of migrants eager to find jobs, and new visitors eager to have a curious glance on China across the river. Since the reopening of the border, a micro and mixed society of migrants have settled here, hoping to make their fortunes from cross-border trade. This heterogeneous population originates from diverse ethnic, regional and social backgrounds. However, most of them struggle to make a living from risk-taking business and adventurous entrepreneurship: wholesalers specializing in ready-to-wear garments, groceries, investors in natural resources trade, workers in construction, mining, catering, accommodation and low-paid service work. Many are very mobile, and use formal as well as informal channels to go back and forth across the border. This allows for all sorts of trade in both directions, including smuggling of wildlife species, protected natural resources, forbidden commodities and flows of products that evade the tax system. Like many other borderlands in the world, drug, currencies, arms trafficking and other illegal activities also take place under the rather indulgent eye of the local authorities.

On both sides of the border, many workers employed in the cross-border trade-related sectors involving low-range physical activities and time flexibility come from Vietnam. Young men become carriers, handlers, or motorcycle taxi drivers while women work as carriers, vendors or interpreters in shops, wholesale markets or streets. It is within this segment of the population that we find the young women who are most likely to cross the border to meet Chinese men after a period of professional activity that familiarizes them with the frontier community. Border cities also tend to host many marginalized individuals searching for opportunities to make a living because this has become difficult for them elsewhere. Among these people are hundreds of young Vietnamese prostitutes living mainly in small brothels, on the second floor of the Vietnamese market in Hekou, for instance (Grillot and Zhang 2017). And there are many other persons present in the border cities simply hoping to acquire an improved social position in a competitive yet more 'open' setting.

These border towns thus host a population of migrants and 'floating' individuals, thereby providing ideal conditions for some to meet and form couples, on a more or less voluntary basis, including mixed Chinese–Vietnamese couples who start or end their migration trajectories there, grasping opportunities to improve their lives. The border is thus a site in which mutually desired encounters and pragmatic alliances that could not otherwise take place are forged. However, it also constitutes a space in which exploitation by the opportunistic and the unscrupulous is possible. And this is the context in which contemporary cross-border marriages are set.

Cross-Border Marriages and Problems of Definition

The Sino-Vietnamese matrimonial alliances arranged all along the 1306 kilometres land border between China and Vietnam, deep into the provinces of Guangxi and Yunnan, and as far as the Northern provinces of China[1] are occurring at a significantly visible level. Though some reports offer estimates of tens of thousands of unions, they do so without much explanation of the methods employed to arrive at these figures. Moreover, it is hard to say how extensive this phenomenon is nowadays compared to the past, given the illegal nature of many of these unions and the absence of historical data. Nonetheless, such unions are a significant and visible feature of social life in the region. In my own fieldwork, I found that the backgrounds of cross-border marriages were extremely various in virtually all respects, and only some of the marital relationships obviously entailed coercion. Because this chapter is concerned with the question of whether 'slavery' and 'trafficking' provide useful frames for understanding cross-border marriages that could be described as coerced, it pays extra attention on couples whose alliance was arranged by go-betweens, including brokers who lured and smuggled Vietnamese women into China. But even here, there is diversity and great caution is therefore required when attempting to sketch a typical profile of the spouses involved.

In fact, cross-border marriages are difficult to classify and analyse for other reasons. To describe particular marriages as 'coerced', 'forced' or 'slavery-like' is to draw a conceptual line between them and 'normal' marriages, but the marriages with which I am concerned in this chapter challenge the normative structure of marriage in Southwest China and Vietnam in ways that have nothing to do with the forced/voluntary binary. First of all, they defy the administrative rules that, in both China and Vietnam, require foreign partners of nationals to provide documents such as proof of unmarried status and a valid residential permit to proceed with marriage regularization. However, many of the Sino-Vietnamese couples, unable to provide this documentation, choose not to register their marriage. Thus, they fail to comply with marriage and family laws, as well as migration policies of both the People's Republic of China and the Socialist Republic of Vietnam. They also often ignore local practices, as despite local custom, these Sino-Vietnamese marriages do not necessarily entail the formal payment of a bride price.

In addition to often being illegal and/or transgressing social norms and conventions, cross-border marriages are frequently based on pragmatism rather than romance, and a number of different actors may play a role in arranging them (Jones 2012). How then are they to be classified? Whose point of view is to be taken as defining in these circumstances? Should the status of the marriage as 'good'/'legitimate'/'normal' be judged according to the standpoint of a satisfied husband, a suffering woman, a family member who has arranged it, a devious broker, a suspicious community member or a local authority figure? How do these marriages differ from arranged marriages between nationals, i.e. those that do not involve foreign citizens?

Similar problems arise in relation to the classification of Vietnamese women as 'cross-border brides', 'marriage migrants' or 'trafficked wives' for the purpose of research on the phenomenon. The label that we attach as researchers, such as "marriage migrant" for instance, may not fit with the researched individual's own definition of her/his status at a certain period of his/her life. How, for example, should we classify a woman from a remote village in Northern Vietnam, who is deceived and sold to a Chinese man, but escapes and back to her village, officially marries a Vietnamese man, then divorces him and returns to China where she turns to prostitution to survive, then enters into cohabitation with a Chinese client whom she sees as her temporary boy-friend, and then later becomes the long-term unregistered de facto spouse of a Chinese worker, before returning to Vietnam as a regular worker in Hanoi, ultimately single? Is she a victim of human trafficking, a prostitute, an illegal migrant, a marriage migrant, a returnee or a regular rural migrant within Vietnam, or all of the above? Many of the women who confided their stories in me had experienced life journeys so complicated that they defied simple categorization. Their alliances have to be placed in an historical and temporal context, as well as a social context. Only then can one understand the heterogeneity and blurriness of individual women's shifting status, social position and even their image/credibility in the eyes of the community that is hosting them (Phung 2006).

Most alliances occur across the border, without any 'professional' intermediaries and, in many cases, without any initial plan. In fact, a large space is left for interaction between coincidence, calculation, serendipity and individual strategies, which distinguish each case from the next and, above all, make relationships evolve in different directions despite their similar beginnings. Each stage of a marriage sees various factors influencing the relationship between a man and a woman: one union may fit different models throughout different periods of time. A woman forced to marry a foreign man might accept her situation when she realizes that she will be well treated. After bonding with her husband, the passage of time sees her rejecting the label of coerced union. Thus, analysing a particular, fixed moment of a marriage can neither accurately capture the full experience of a relationship and the way it transforms over time, nor can tell us into which definitional category the marriage should be placed.

There is, however, one common characteristic of cross-border marriages. In most cases, they challenge the commonly accepted notion that marriage, in particular in Chinese and Vietnamese societies, unites two families and that this function is more important than the feelings and agency of the bride and groom. In cross-border marriages, by contrast, the two families rarely, if ever, interfere with the choice of each partner; indeed, they are commonly the missing link, being overwhelmingly absent from the whole arrangement. So, for example, the Vietnamese family may be party to the migration or the departure of a daughter—whether or not there is a clear understanding of what might be the consequence of a journey towards and across the Chinese border—but is unlikely consulted about her marriage, especially regarding the choice of the husband. Meanwhile, the Chinese family may be involved in an arrangement with a broker, but not necessarily in the choice of the bride. It is only after a marriage is settled, or following the birth of a child, or if the bride journeys back to Vietnam to visit her family long after her entry in her Chinese family, that both Chinese and Vietnamese families may become linked through the marriage. At this stage, exchanges may happen, through gifts or intended greetings. Arranged Sino-Vietnamese alliances in the borderlands are often settled irrespective of whether both partners *all* have a say in the process or not because they mainly occur in a context of migration that isolates individuals and puts them in a vulnerable position. Some Chinese men may decide to partner with Vietnamese women in the place they both migrated for the sake of convenience, regardless of their families' opinion, and for the option to terminate the relationship whenever its conditions change. Others living in their native place might think that 'marrying' Vietnamese women who are separated from their acquaintances and families, often illegally entered into China, is a both a means to keep control over them, and a way to avoid the necessary negotiations between families that sustain a conventional marriage arrangement. This is, among other reasons, why the English term 'alliance,' with its large meaning seems more appropriate here to define pragmatic and informal unions than the more formal word 'marriage' that entails the implication of a particular range of actors, including family members, rituals, formalities, transactions and projects.

Arguing against a tendency to lump migrant women together under the heading 'victims of trafficking', Nicole Constable (2006: 1, original emphasis) calls for a new approach to the categorization of migrants: "Instead of arguing that the three separate literatures on what I prefer to call domestic workers, sex workers, and correspondence brides are too separate and would benefit from being combined, I am concerned with the potential for *unwarranted blurs* – or fuzzy shadow lines between the three categories". In keeping with her argument, I suggest that the three categories Constable identifies may already be more convenient than relevant. For instance, many of my female informants were neither domestic workers nor prostitutes when I met them. Yet, they could all have been engaged in one of these activities at one time or another in their lives. So far as their mobility was concerned, while in some cases people had undoubtedly deceived them, in others, they had decided themselves to cross the border and work illegally. None of them had gone through a process such as correspondence to meet their husbands; yet, they were all involved in various forms of cross-border marriage at some point in their trajectories, not necessarily as a consequence of a coerced match. Were they trafficked women coerced into marriage, regular foreign spouses, or migrant women in long-term relationships with Chinese partners? And how can this question be answered without reference to the ways in which the women concerned articulate their own experiences and their ongoing lives (Kim 2010)? As Constable observes, "[i]dentifying whom we are talking to and about by the labels they would recognize and respect, would seem be a fundamental step in the right direction for scholars, activists, and policy makers" (Constable 2006: 21–22). The narratives of two of my research participants provided below flesh out and illustrate all of the points made in this section.

Vietnamese Women's Fate: Mai and Oanh's Perspectives[2]

Amongst the Vietnamese women whose narratives have informed this study, some have left their hometown and/or country as a consequence of coercion or deception, but have later agreed on staying where they ended: a choice driven by pragmatism. Others, in contrast, may have chosen to leave their home to experience something new, but were then forced by circumstances to remain where they arrived. The whole process of building a life out on a given socio-economic ground once again blurs the dichotomy between 'agent' and 'passive' (or 'trafficked') migrant. I propose to call the choice emerging from the interstices 'choice by default,' a situation that one of my research participants, Mai, experienced when she was young.

When I first met Mai, a woman from Haiphong, she was working as an interpreter for a couple of Guilin shop owners in Dongxing. The mother of two teenagers was still living with the man who bought her from a broker 17 years earlier. After weeks of silence during which she observed me interacting with other Vietnamese women, she eventually disclosed her identity and story to me. She recalled how she met her husband in 1989:

— I had a girlfriend, Thanh, who spoke *baihua* [the Cantonese dialect spoken in the south of Guangxi province]. We had a small business selling vegetables together. One day, with another friend, Nan, we decided to go to Móng Cái to buy fresh supply. A male friend of Thanh came with us. But, once we arrived, there were no cucumbers. Then, Thanh suggested crossing the border to see what might be available on the Dongxing side. An old Vietnamese woman joined us to take us all to visit her married daughter in Qinzhou. From there, we went to Fangcheng[3] to have lunch with one of her friends. This is where our guests and guides' [started to make] suggestions about finding a local husband [in China] and this made us realize that we had no money and didn't know our way back to the frontier: we found ourselves trapped. Much later, I realized the bottom of the story: Thanh's male friend was actually her lover whose wife had threatened to disfigure Thanh with acid if she didn't disappear. So Thanh asked her lover to take her to China where she would find a husband; he was her accomplice… it was easier [this] way to rebuild her life. But, she couldn't leave alone and therefore, she cheated Nan and me. It was the son of the old Vietnamese woman who found us our husbands. He first introduced me to an old man who had a three-storey house, and tried to convince me that it was his own son that I could marry. But the son was away, working in Shenzhen [in Guangzhou province]. So the proposition could be a trick. Then the old woman's son took the three of us to a village near Qinzhou where he introduced me to my current husband. But I refused the same way: I didn't want to get married! But the guy was young and my girlfriend convinced me: "If you don't want him, I'll take him!" So it was this young guy or the old man I had met earlier. Anyway, the people who had brought us to this village refused to take us back to town, leaving us at an impasse. The woman was a broker; she could have taken us to a brothel back in Fangcheng, because she had connections in this field. So I finally agreed, thinking the situation would be temporary. My two girlfriends and I asked to stay together. They both agreed to marry two other men from the village, and then things turned out right. I learned from my husband's family that I was sold for 1200 yuan.[4]

But the unfortunate circumstances that Mai faced at this point of her life were not only due to her friend's betrayal. Another element had already weakened her social position in her hometown, changing the interpretation of the choice she eventually made in this Chinese village, and challenging the "coercive" label one could use to define her situation. Back home, Mai had previously refused a marital match her father had arranged for her:

> — I am the eldest of four children, and I was fifteen when my father, who was alcoholic, decided to marry me to a young man from my village without my consent. He was only sixteen years old. Our fathers were friends, and made a deal. Neither the boy nor our mothers agreed, but on an auspicious day, the boy's father brought to my family a chicken that they sacrificed, and money that my father spent on alcohol quickly. I refused to accept the gifts, but he didn't care. This family was rich. As I refused to submit, I found myself at an impasse: either I gave in, or I worked to reimburse the bride price. Since I was already out of school because our family was too poor, I started to do business to repay my debt. Time passed, the boy who treated me as if I were his bride was waiting for me to decide. Meanwhile, I dated a boyfriend. I guess the boy was jealous, he began to stop me from flirting with my boyfriend. In fact, the boy was waiting for me to grow old so I would finally give into the impossibility of marrying elsewhere. I managed to reimburse the bride price, but the boy's family refused it, and gave back the money to my father who spent it again on alcohol. My situation was hopeless. At 21 years of age, I left with a friend [Thanh]. Until today, both the boy and my boyfriend are still single.

Mai paid for her misconduct and lack of respect towards her family's decision when she found herself trapped in China, due to a friend's plot. Defying her family's authority prompted this family to sully her personal reputation by representing her as non-submissive. Mai's account also raises the question of affective pressure and sexual harassment, which in Vietnamese society, is also a factor of exclusion. Her reputation then became her stigma and led her to China where she married, even though this was not her original wish.

Many other Vietnamese women who ended in arranged marriages in China experienced similar trajectories. They sometimes escaped a life in brothels by using their tears, their threats to commit suicide or by relying on their friends to impose their will and swing a position of powerlessness in their 'favour,' to change the course of their lives, and win a measure of power over their destinies. If it took Mai a period of time to acknowledge (to me) that she had been forced into marriage with her husband, it may also be because nearly two decades after the event, her perspective on her personal life had changed. She was still married to her Chinese man, was raising two teenagers and said she was rather satisfied with her life. And, so it was with many similar life stories I have collected. Even though 'forced marriage' seems relatively easy to identify in such stories as an event, the temporal factor and the phenomenological experience raise doubt about any attempt to conveniently classify relationships initiated by coercion and deception as necessarily 'forced'.

Oanh, a Vietnamese woman in her fifties lives in Hekou, and her narrative blurs the picture even further. Living on the western side of the Sino-Vietnamese border, Oanh was a young married mother in Vietnam when she was smuggled to China and sold. Now, a street bike repairer in Hekou, she decided to stay with the Chinese man in a Guangxi village to whom she was sold because she pitied him:

> — In 1992, I was 31 years old and I was married in Vietnam, with two kids. One day, a woman lured me into China and sold me to a peasant in Guangxi. His wife had died in the hospital, and he was left with three children, so he wanted to remarry. But he was too poor to pay the bride price that local families were asking. So he decided to marry a Vietnamese woman. When I met him, he had already bought three Vietnamese women who all escaped from him. He was poor, but he spent again 4000 yuan to have me[5] and I felt sorry that he had lost so much money before, for nothing in return but abandonment. I stayed with him. His living conditions were modest but good. Anyway, I was there already, and my Vietnamese husband did not wait long before divorcing me and remarrying. My Chinese husband agreed to adopt my Vietnamese children whom I brought to China later on. I have spent twenty years living and working with him and we have had three more children together. I learned to love him; he is a responsible man. We spent ten years in his village but work in the field was hard and we decided to come to Hekou. We've repaired bicycles for several years now near the market. Business is ok, so we may stay. I think about Vietnam everyday, I cry often but I don't want

> to return there, life is too tough. Anyway, my son does not want to go and I want to stay with him. And my husband is good to me; he neither insults me nor hits me.

Certainly, one cannot deny the dramatic circumstances that frame the formation of some Sino-Vietnamese couples and families in borderlands. Some women are lured and sold by smugglers/brokers to third parties, be they individuals or families. But as the two stories above illustrate, within this, women can exercise a degree of agency that distinguishes their situation from the position of a "slave" historically. Two other points are crucial to distinguishing these exemplary cases from slavery. First, there is the question of time and temporality: at what point in a life trajectory should we consider that conditions obtain which allow us to define an individual as a slave? Watson (1998: 151) actually raises this very issue in relation to the evaluation of *mui tsai*: "[F]emale servants often played multiple roles in the kinship system: They could be purchased as surrogate daughters in infancy, exploited like slaves in adolescence, and married to their buyer's male relatives in adulthood." Second, there is the fact that women coerced into marriage can nonetheless speak of that event as having led to benefits. Such marriages are associated with the acquisition of rights through entry into Chinese families and society, rights that despite being informal and limited by administrative non-existence still often represent advancement from the perspective of a Vietnamese woman.

Unintended Marriage as Destiny, Not Slavery

Destiny is the word that constantly emerges in their narratives, be these as dramatic as Mai and Oanh's or not. Mai and Oanh did not choose to go to China and marry a Chinese man. But there have certainly been room for personal agency in the direction these women's lives took, despite the difficult conditions under which their life in China began. According to their narratives, i.e. the way they articulate their life experience, one simply wanted to avoid prostitution and the other took pity on a man she perceived as a victim of trickery and bad faith. Whether or not they were also strategically considering the potential advantages of the marital relationship they were being pressed into is difficult to judge. This is part of their intimate world, their own articulation of their plight, and very likely, a traumatic episode they did not want to recall and confide to the life-story collector I represented. However, the rest of their stories illustrate how time transformed their plight, thanks to their determination to make an acceptable life out of their initial predicament, along with a complaisant husband, and children soon appeared in the marriage picture. Above all, they adopt a comparative perspective that helps them to relativize their position. Both Mai and Oanh explained, as well as other Vietnamese women sharing similar life trajectories, that had they had the chance to remain in Vietnam in the first place, their social position and private life would have not necessarily been better: "Back home, it would have been worse anyway…" as one of my research participants put it.

Some might interpret such hypothesizing as an emotional strategy to reassess their current situation, and console themselves about being deprived of their liberty. But were they really free in Vietnam? Women's comments on their life often focus on what they regard as significant details about a form and degree of emancipation that their marriage in China encompasses: a husband who is willing to work hard, even sometimes to cook and do domestic chores from time to time, who does not demand to have many children, who does not take drugs, and above all, who is responsible. This contrasts with what Vietnamese women often depict as the typical life of a wife in Vietnam: hard, unfair and demanding. In other words, marriage to a Vietnamese man is perceived as a passage to adult life that will generally imply loss of personal emancipation and lack of respect.

Even though there were elements of the condition of my Vietnamese women research participants that could be described as similar to elements of the condition of slavery, their subjective understanding of their own life-stories indicates another perspective. The centrality of the concept of destiny is especially noteworthy. I would suggest that, at least in this region and among individuals whose regular migrations expose them to additional external and uncontrollable risks and disturbances, the belief in destiny makes sense of the vicissitudes of one's life, including the consequences of risk-taking behaviours. In his work on the psychocultural approach of the concept of destiny in Confucian families in East Asia, Slote (1998) summarizes the state of mind resulting from the strong conviction in destiny that was also reflected in my Vietnamese informants' sighs and smiles. He states "The Vietnamese operate upon the premise that there are forces, external to themselves, that are very influential in determining their destiny. It is true that other cultures also live with the certainty of external determination—God, Christ, Mohammed. What is unique about the Vietnamese is the nature of their beliefs, the power that is assigned to the forces that govern their destiny, the panoply of elements that combine to determine fate, and the high degree to which these external forces are internalized within the conscious and unconscious life of the Vietnamese people" (1998: 320). As a matter of fact, many of my Vietnamese informants invoked this concept to explain their plight—rather than bad luck—but also to cope with the challenges and the anxiety encountered caused by their current situation, and their tendency to adjust with rather than resist their life conditions in China.

Integration of Vietnamese women into Chinese society through marriage remains limited, but it is important to note that this is in part due to the negative representations of Vietnamese women that circulate locally. Proximity with borderland's prostitution, local rumours on business cheat involving Vietnamese women, media accounts of vanishing Vietnamese brides and general distrust towards Vietnamese people due to Chinese resentment towards their former brother-then-enemy neighbour inform the ambiguous social representations of these women and affect their personal reputation (Grillot 2012).

Among the research participants, life stories like those from Mai and Oanh prove that some Vietnamese women eventually found some consolation in their arranged—or forced—alliance with a Chinese husband. However, many other have confided hardship and difficulties in coping with their precarious relationship and status, even though they have eventually accepted their plight. Their narratives articulate a sense of disillusionment behind a face of satisfaction, due to the common reality they share: they know that the range of alternative options is narrow, and they remain convinced that, at least, they escaped or avoided a worse scenario in Vietnam. Vietnamese women who choose to stay, to remain married, to raise their child(ren) and to work in China with a Chinese man need to accommodate both the impossibility of return, and the limited possibilities for fully integrating into their host society, and the absence of documents to secure their marriage (Grillot 2015). Nonetheless, they often develop strategies and tactics that allow them to express their own agency and to some minimal powers of decision-making. Greater control over the details of their lives often comes with the birth of a child; motherhood makes women's presence obviously needed within a family and it empowers them. This is unlikely the case where a purchased woman only 'serves' the purpose of bearing a child, becomes exploited or even chased away afterwards. The use they make of the interstices between being free and being controlled strongly differentiates their condition from that of the slave, which would imply vulnerability to being treated as a commodity throughout the entire life course. And this is very clearly not the case among the Vietnamese women whose trajectories were documented in my study.

Conclusion

If slavery is understood to entail extreme restrictions on individual freedom, natal alienation and the impossibility of exerting one's own agency and determining one's life condition, then marital relationships between the Vietnamese female migrants and Chinese men I studied are not slavery, even though there may often be highly coercive aspects to the arrangement. Indeed, my research suggests that local definition, personal agency, temporality and pragmatic benefits should be included as crucial elements in any evaluation of specific cases of arranged marriage—embedding various forms of exploitation—in the Sino-Vietnamese borderlands. Two decades ago, Jaschok (1994: 17) called for "writing which gives women voices from within their native milieu, from within the tension, the harmonies and dissonances which shape individuals as tradition and modernity impinge on each other." This chapter aimed to provide greater insight into Vietnamese women's subjective interpretations of imposed marital relationships by showing how, thanks to their belief system and determination to keep their plight in perspective, they can also sometimes manage to take advantage of a condition that might have otherwise been associated with that of slaves.

Notes

1. In recent years, the phenomenon of Sino-Vietnamese marriages has extended further than the borderlands and reaches every corner of China where demands in brides lead cohorts of bachelors to search for available women from Southeast Asian countries. Organizational patterns of these marriages are more diversified and the phenomenon is constantly evolving. My study only involved data collection in semi-urban settings, and this chapter does not, therefore, include data related to these new developments.
2. All names in this chapter are pseudonyms.
3. Qinzhou is about 100 kms from Dongxing; Fangcheng is 50 kms from Qinzhou, and 55 kms from Dongxing. The three towns belong to the prefecture-level city of Fangchenggang.
4. Mai did not say who received the money but according to all testimonies of this kind in the region, the money never goes to the bride's family, as would be the case were it bride price. The money is simply shared between the various intermediaries who brought a woman from Vietnam to a groom's village.
5. In 1992, 4000 yuan was a large sum of money, especially for a peasant. But Oanh assessed that the average bride price for a Chinese bride was approximately 10,000 yuan. This information, although difficult to verify, seems suspicious since my informants in Guangxi informed me twenty years later that 10,000 yuan is the minimum amount of money that Chinese families ask nowadays for marrying their daughter. Oanh wanted to stress that she was a cheap investment compared to a local bride.

References

Baudrit, A. (2008). *Bétail Humain. La traite des femmes et des enfants en Indochine et en Chine du sud, suivi de onze documents sur l'esclavage (1860–1940)*. Textes réunis et présentés par N. Lainez & P. Le Roux. Paris: Connaissances et Savoirs.

Constable, N. (2006). Brides, Maids, and Prostitutes: Reflections on the Study of "Trafficked" Women. *Journal of Multidisciplinary International Studies, 3*(2), 1–25.

Cooper, T. T. (1870–1871). On the Chinese Province of Yunnan and Its Border. *Proceedings of the Royal Geographical Society of London, 15*(3), 163–174.

Fiskesjö, M. (2011). Slavery as the Commodification of People: Wa "Slaves" and Their Chinese "Sisters". *Focaal: Journal of Global and Historical Anthropology, 59,* 3–18.

Ford, M., Lyons, L., & van Schendel, W. (Eds.). (2012). *Labour Migration and Human Trafficking in Southeast Asia: Critical Perspectives*. London and New York: Routledge.

Grillot, C. (2010). *Volées, Envolées, Convolées… Vendues, en fuite ou re-socialisées: les "fiancées" vietnamiennes en Chine*. Paris: Connaissances et Savoirs.

Grillot, C. (2012). Between Bitterness and Sweetness, When Bodies Say It All: Chinese Perspectives on Vietnamese Women in a Border Space. *Journal of Vietnamese Studies, 7*(1), 106–148.

Grillot, C. (2015). The Creation of a Nonexistent Group: Sino-Vietnamese Couples in China's Borderlands. *Cross-Currents: East Asian History and Culture Review, 15*(15), 30–56.

Grillot, C., & Zhang, J. (2017). Ambivalent Encounters: Business and the Sex Markets at the China-Vietnam Borderland. In P. Nyíri & D. Tan (Eds.), *How Chinese Engagements Are Changing Southeast Asia: People, Money, Ideas and Their Effects* (pp. 143–168). Seattle and London: University of Washington Press.

Jaschok, M. (1994). Chinese "Slave" Girls in Yunnan-Fu: Saving (Chinese) Womanhood and (Western) Souls, 1930–1991. In M. Jaschok & S. Miers (Eds.), *Women and Chinese Patriarchy: Submission, Servitude and Escape* (pp. 171–197). Hong Kong, London and New Jersey: Hong Kong University Press, Zed Books Ltd.

Jaschok, M., & Miers, S. (1994). Introduction. In M. Jaschok & S. Miers (Eds.), *Women and Chinese Patriarchy: Submission, Servitude and Escape* (pp. 1–24). Hong Kong, London and New Jersey: Hong Kong University Press, Zed Books Ltd.

Jones, G. W. (2012). *International Marriage in Asia: What Do We Know, and What Do We Need to Know?* (Working Paper, No. 174). Singapore: National University of Singapore, Asia Research Institute.

Kim, M. (2010). Gender and International Marriage Migration. *Sociology Compass, 4*(9), 718–731.

Lessard, M. (2009). "Cet Ignoble Trafic": The Kidnapping and Sale of Vietnamese Women and Children in French Colonial Indochina, 1873–1935. *French Colonial History, 10,* 1–34.

Phung, V. T. [Vũ Trọng Phụng]. (2006). *The Industry of Marrying Europeans* (T. Tranviet, Trans.). Ithaca, NY: Cornell University Press.

Reid, A. (1983). Introduction: Slavery and Bondage in Southeast Asian History. In A. Reid (Ed.), *Slavery, Bondage and Dependency in Southeast Asia* (pp. 1–43). St Lucia, London and New York: University of Queensland Press.

Slote, W. H. (1998). Destiny and Determination: Psychocultural Reinforcement in Vietnam. In W. H. Slote & G. A. DeVos (Eds.), *Confucianism and the Family* (pp. 311–328). Albany: State University of New York Press.

Watson, J. L. (1980). Transactions in People: The Chinese Market in Slaves, Servants, and Heirs. In J. L. Watson (Ed.), *Asian and African Systems of Slavery* (pp. 223–250). Oxford: Basil Blackwell.

Watson, J. L. (1998). China. In S. Drescher & S. L. Engerman (Eds.), *A Historical Guide to World Slavery* (pp. 149–152). New York and Oxford: Oxford University Press.

9

Moral Economies and Child Labour in Artisanal Gold Mining in Ghana

Samuel Okyere

Introduction: 'Modern (Child) Slavery'

To what extent do institutions and social movements reproduce or entrench the problems they set out to challenge? During his debate with Noam Chomsky on human nature, Foucault (1974: 171) observed:

> It seems to me that the real political task in a society such as ours is to criticize the working of institutions which appear to be both neutral and independent; to criticise them in such a manner that the political violence which has always exercised itself obscurely through them will be unmasked, so that one can fight them.

Foucault's statement invites us to consider the paradox and bring into focus 'the ruptural effects of conflict and struggle that the order

S. Okyere (✉)
Sociology and Criminology, University of Nottingham, Nottingham, UK
e-mail: Samuel.okyere@nottingham.ac.uk

L. Brace and J. O'Connell Davidson (eds.), *Revisiting Slavery and Antislavery*,
https://doi.org/10.1007/978-3-319-90623-2_9

imposed by functionalist or systematizing thought is designed to mask' (Foucault 1980: 82). In his opinion, no ideas, institutions or conventions should be deemed beyond critique; especially those that are presented as benign, apolitical, natural or indispensable to social order. Anatomising the politics, ideologies and practices of normative institutions is not only essential to democratic debate and the practice of freedom itself, but it is also indispensable to our understanding of the social world and the production of alternative (and perhaps more credible) ways of conceptualising social phenomena (Foucault 1980).

Application of this critique to international children's rights conventions and discourses on child labour has revealed their oppressive, superficial and normalising qualities (Myers 2001; Pupavac 2001) which became evident again in a conversation with a fellow participant at a recent African Studies conference in Paris. My fellow conference participant worked for an international human rights NGO which had produced a documentary film on human rights violations in gold and cassiterite mining in the Democratic Republic of Congo. The involvement of children in this activity, an issue of mutual interest, was the main topic of our conversation. He intimated that many of the children in the film had been orphaned by the country's civil war and had therefore taken on mining work to fend for themselves in the absence of support from the Congolese government and dwindling humanitarian aid from the UN now that war had ended. Other children, he said, were working alongside 'irresponsible' parents and carers who 'looked on unconcerned while their children as young as 5 slaved away'. He was especially critical of these parents and adults, questioning their conscience and morals for allowing children to work in that sort of environment. He concluded that in response his organisation was lobbying stakeholders against the exportation and sale of 'dirty minerals' produced by children in Congo. They were also in talks with the Congolese government to apprehend and punish parents and adults working with children in the country's mines, to serve as deterrent to others. Palpably missing was a social welfare strategy or response.

I had no doubt about his organisation's commitment to children's rights and about their conviction that the actions they were promoting were in the best interests of children featured in their film. However, as I told him, given that the major causal factors he had himself identified for children's involvement in Congolese small-scale mining were the civil war, dwindling humanitarian assistance and non-existent social welfare support, I was dubious of his NGO's responses. They were representative of the ineffective and oppressive responses which have been promoted by the International Labour Organisation (ILO) for nearly a century. Supported by national governments, trade unions, human rights activists, NGOs and myriad of other actors, the ILO has been at the forefront of efforts to abolish children's participation in WFCL, notably through creation of the Worst Forms of Child Labour Convention (Convention 182) in 1999. The abolitionist campaign has been galvanised in the last two decades by NGOs which have emerged as part of the modern slavery abolishment movement. Notable among these 'neo-abolitionists' are the Global Alliance against Child Labour, Walk Free Foundation and Free the Slaves (FTS). For neo-abolitionists, children's involvement in artisanal mining and other WFCL is consonant with 'child slavery', for the two occur in tandem, as FTS (2014: 8) has argued. The term is therefore employed by neo-abolitionists as shorthand for virtually any scenario deemed to constitute a WFCL.

This observation is most evident in FTS' campaigns in Ghana over the last five years. Following a study of children's involvement in the country's artisanal gold mining sector between 2012 and 2013, the NGO declared that it had found evidence of 'child enslavement'. On its web pages and other publicity materials, FTS claimed that 12-year-old boys were found working with dangerous chemicals without rest and unable to escape[1] while girls aged 10 were found working as 'sexual slaves' at the mining sites where the studies were carried out (FTS 2014: 6). Paradoxically, in contrast to these sensational headlines, a more detailed project report makes clear that the study did not actually find any child whose' involvement in artisanal mining work was due to violence, force, trickery or coercion (FTS 2014: 8). The 'child slavery' headlines appear all the more astonishing as the report again indicates that the research fieldworkers neither visited nor collected data at the artisanal gold mining sites where FTS publicity materials indicate that children had been 'found' in conditions of abuse and 'sexual slavery'. Citing ethical concerns, the report further indicates that none of the child research participants were asked questions which could serve as basis for determining whether their work could be defined as child slavery. The mere fact of their involvement in artisanal gold mining work seemed to have been taken at face value by FTS as evidence of child slavery; ignoring findings in their own research report. Such sensational (mis)representations of children's participation in what are without doubt difficult working conditions reflects the primary strategy employed by FTS and other neo-abolitionist groups in their child and human rights advocacy.

In what follows, this chapter subjects such characterisations and the wider WFCL abolitionist discourse to critical interrogation using evidence from a study I conducted of children's income-seeking activities in the Ghanaian artisanal gold mining sector. I argue that the 'child slavery' and WFCL abolitionist discourses on this activity largely ignore the narratives of affected children and communities. They draw on melodrama, sensationalism and problematic assumptions about children's involvement in WFCL to proffer responses which suture, but do not actually take on the factors underpinning and necessitating children's entry into artisanal mining work in Ghana and elsewhere. The originality of this work is that it is one of the first known ethnographic studies focused principally on using working children's own narratives as basis for understanding their work and lived experiences and for critiquing both the nascent neo-abolitionist 'child slavery' and mainstream WFCL discourses on children's involvement in artisanal mining work. It is a distinct and crucial intervention in international child and human rights debates and agendas such as efforts to eliminate WFCL as articulated in Target 8.7 of the United Nations Sustainable Development Goals.

Definition of Key Terms: 'Modern Slavery', 'Child Slavery', 'WFCL'

A major criticism levelled against neo-abolitionist groups relates to their attempts to distinguish what they class as 'modern slavery' from other statuses or conditions with similar features that are not typically imagined as slavery (McGary and Lawson 1992; Lott 1998; Clarke

2003). Given that there are no slave societies or places in the modern world where the status of slavery still exists as a distinct category as was the case in eighteenth-century American and Caribbean colonies, it is actually very difficult to agree on a distinct or precise measure with which 'slaves' can be separated from 'non-slaves' (Salafia 2013; O'Connell Davidson 2015). Thus, in seeking to define 'modern slavery' or 'modern child slavery', abolitionist point to a range of international instruments including, but not limited to the 1926 Slavery Convention; the 1957 Supplementary Convention on the Abolition of Slavery, the Slave Trade, and Institutions and Practices Similar to Slavery; the ILO Forced Labour Convention No. 29, and the United Nations' Protocol to Prevent, Suppress and Punish Trafficking in Persons, Especially Women and Children 2000.

For some, the 1926 Slavery Convention definition, 'the status or condition of a person over whom any or all of the powers attaching to the right of ownership are exercised' does not fully capture the 'essence' of child slavery in modern times (Kooijmans and van de Glind 2010). Thus, the term 'slavery-like practices' is also employed to describe conditions deemed to violate various articles of the United Nations Convention on the Rights of the Child (UNCRC). In this context, neo-abolitionists suggest that child slavery is where children's rights under Article 32, the right for children (defined as anyone under age 18 by the UNCRC) to be shielded from economic exploitation; Article 33, the right for children to be protected from drug trafficking and other illicit activities; Article 34, which prohibits child sexual exploitation; and Articles 35 and 38, which calls for children to be protected against trafficking and involvement in armed conflict, respectively, are violated. Reference is also made to Optional Protocols of the UNCRC, such as the Optional Protocol on the Sale of Children, Child Prostitution and Child Pornography in attempts to classify various phenomena as modern cases of child enslavement (Buck and Nicholson 2010; Craig 2010; Kooijmans and van de Glind 2010).

Reference is also made to the UN Trafficking Protocol, 2000 in attempting to define 'child slavery'. Under the Palermo Protocol as it is commonly called, the movement of a child 'for purposes of exploitation' counts as 'child trafficking'. A very low threshold has been set for the identification of child trafficking primarily because policymakers do not accept that a person under the age of 18 is capable of consenting to his or her movement for work and other activities that may be considered 'exploitative', as Hashim (2005) and Bastia (2005) have both identified. The ILO Convention No. 182, commonly referred to as the Worst Forms of Child Labour Convention is yet another notable source to which abolitionists have frequently turned in attempting to define child slavery. Article 3 of Convention 182 defines WFCL as:

> (a) all forms of slavery or practices similar to slavery, such as the sale and trafficking of children, debt bondage and serfdom and forced or compulsory labour, including forced or compulsory recruitment of children for use in armed conflict; (b) the use, procuring or offering of a child for prostitution, for the production of pornography or for pornographic performances; (c) the use, procuring or offering of a child for illicit activities, in particular for the production and trafficking of drugs as defined in the relevant international treaties; and (d) work which, by its nature or the circumstances in which it is carried out, is likely to harm the health, safety or morals of children. (Article 3, ILO Convention No. 182)

Noting the potential for confusion about what constitutes 'work likely to harm a child's health, safety or morals', the ILO passed Recommendation No. 190 to specify such jobs as:

> (a) work which exposes children to physical, psychological or sexual abuse; (b) work underground, under water, at dangerous heights or in confined spaces; (c) work with dangerous machinery, equipment and tools, or which involves the manual handling or transport of heavy loads; (d) work in an unhealthy environment which may, for example, expose children to hazardous substances, agents or processes, or to temperatures, noise levels or vibrations damaging to their health; and (e) work under particularly difficult conditions such as work for long hours or during the night or work where the child is unreasonably confined to the premises of the employer. The WFCL Convention itself thus amalgamates elements of what is elsewhere defined in international law as both 'slavery' and 'slavery-like' conditions.

Despite this panoply of sources and definitions, some neo-abolitionists have formulated proprietary ideas for identifying a 'child slave' or 'modern slave'. Notable among these is FTS, which primarily relies on a definition provided by Kevin Bales, one of its founders. For Bales, (1999) the historic understanding of slavery as ownership or property rights over another person is inadequate in contemporary times. As he argues, instead of owning people outright as the case has been historically, 'slave owners' today simply appropriate 'the economic value of individuals while keeping them under complete coercive control' (Bales 1999: 25). Bales and FTS therefore define 'modern slavery' as the situation where a person (or child in this case) is held through force, fraud, violence or coercion to provide services that enable the slaveholder to extract profit or some form of benefit (Bales 1999, 2005; FTS 2014[2]).

Critics have described this definition as deficient for deviating from the international legally recognised definition of slavery (Allain and Hickey 2012) and for promiscuously conflating virtually any form of human suffering with slavery (Patterson 2012: 1). Indeed, using FTS' definition, thousands of migrant workers on sponsorship visas around the world, such as those on overseas domestic worker visas in the UK, could be classed as 'modern slaves'. Their visas legally tie them to their employers; many are subjected to potential and actual wholesale coercive control, violence and various forms of exploitation by their employers or employers' associates and many are unpaid or subjected to wage theft with virtually no means of walking away in some cases. Yet, neo-abolitionists discount such cases from their accounts modern slavery.

Putting its definitional deficiencies aside, Bales' (1999, 2005) definition of 'modern slavery' is also discordant with FTS' classification of children's work in the Ghanaian artisanal mining sector as a form of 'child slavery'. The essential ingredients of Bales (1999, 2005) slavery definition, force, fraud or coercive control are non-existent in the circumstances surrounding the children's work, as the FTS (2014) report concedes. As the next section demonstrates using the narratives of children working in this sector, the situation is far more complex than the sensational claims of child slavery and child exploitation presented by neo-abolitionists and mainstream WFCL discourse. Hearing these complexities may bring us closer to lasting responses to the problem.

The Research

My study of children's involvement in the Ghanaian artisanal gold mining sector aimed to critically examine the extent to which the narratives of children in this sector squared with dominant discourse and policy directives on occupations deemed to be WFCL. The study was guided by an interpretivist framework focused on understanding the reality of children's work in this sector from the vantage position of children working in it rather than relying on NGO and ILO accounts which dominated the field at the time of the research. The ethnographic fieldwork was carried out at an artisanal gold mining site at Kenyasi, Ghana, for 15 weeks between June and September 2010. A total of 57 children (30 girls and 27 boys aged 14–17) generously provided information for the research. Information was also collected from adult miners, community leaders, officials of Newmont Ghana Gold Limited, government officials, parents and guardians of the children and other actors. Data were collected through the use of unstructured and structured interviews, participant observation and photo-elicitation at the artisanal gold mining site, participants' homes and other spaces in the community.

Understanding of the history of the Kenyasi artisanal gold mining site is crucial for understanding the narratives of the children and adults who work there, for circumstances behind the site's creation encapsulate the wider socio-economic and political circumstances within which the research participants accounts and lived experiences are embedded. In the early 1980s, facing economic ruin, Ghana sought financial assistance from the IMF and World Bank. IMF structural adjustment conditionalities and other economic reforms imposed on the country since then have compelled Ghana to open up sectors such as energy, mining, water and telecommunication to the private market (Brune et al. 2004; Hutchful 2002). It is within this context that 10,000 residents of Kenyasi and surrounding areas were dispossessed of their lands, houses and farms in 2005 to make way for the establishment of a gold mine owned by Newmont Ghana Gold Limited (NGGL), a subsidiary of the Newmont Mining Corporation, one of the world's largest gold mining companies.

Previous to the land dispossession, farming had been the mainstay in Kenyasi for generations. Residents faced socio-economic challenges, as some of the adults acknowledged, but, until they lost their lands, most were self-sufficient living off the land. With the loss of their lands, the community was thrust into severe hardship overnight. The elderly found it especially hard to cope, given that subsistence farming was the only livelihood activity they had known all their lives. Their hardships were further compounded when the derisory compensation packages paid for their lands run out (Okyere 2013; Armstrong 2008). The situation eventually reached a crises point when the youth realised that jobs promised them by NGGL were not going to materialise. Now aware that their lands were rich with gold, some started small-scale gold mining activities on family lands which were now legally owned by NGGL. The company was dissatisfied with this encroachment on its property and sought to put a stop to it with the support of the Ghanaian military and police. For almost a year, there were clashes between the town's youth and NGGL security personnel supported by Ghanaian security agents. Some Kenyasi youth were arrested, beaten or harassed, with their rudimentary mining equipment seized and destroyed. For their part, the youth also led demonstrations against the company, some of which turned violent and resulted in destruction of the company's property and sabotage of its operations.

Eventually, in a truce which largely helped to settle the matter, NGGL decided to turn a blind eye to small-scale mining activities on an area of its concession about 3 acres in size, as long as the small-scale miners did not extend their activities beyond this territory. This space thus became the Kenyasi artisanal gold mining site, which was the source of livelihood for an estimated 4000 people at the time of the fieldwork. Many of these men, women and children were from Kenyasi, neighbouring villages and the country at large, but others were migrants Burkina Faso and other neighbouring West African countries. Geographically, in addition to the numerous pits dotted across the site, the site was also populated by huts and wooden shacks used as sleeping areas, restaurants and machine repair spaces. Some of these shacks were also used as shops of various sorts including a 'cinema' cum entertainment centre; a space with a generator-powered TV and DVD player where films were screened at night.

The Kenyasi artisanal gold mining site was, during the fieldwork, a largely self-sufficient space. Many of the workers, particularly migrants, lived within the site for months on end without need to visit the main Kenyasi town for supplies or services. Nonetheless, as it was located in a forest area that was previously used for farming, it was generally bushy. Scorpions, rats and other rodents were not uncommon at night. The site's environmental hazards were worsened by the huge volume of stones, sharp rocks, soil and debris scattered across the place following pit excavations and mining operations. Again, as the fieldwork was carried out towards the end of the rainy season, there were stagnant pools of water at various locations which served as breeding grounds for mosquitoes and other insects. The site's generally unhygienic and hazardous environment was one of numerous observations which deeply troubled me during the fieldwork. It was clear to see why the ILO and international children's rights policymakers reason that an artisanal gold mining site is no place for a child to work. However, as the chapter discusses later, the child research participants in whose interests these claims are made reject it because it showed superficial understanding of their circumstances and range of 'hazards' they were confronted with. Also, the site's harsh physical appearance belied the fact that *socially*, it was very orderly, peaceful and well-organised. Given the circumstances under which NGGL had allowed them to use the land, the workers were wary that antisocial conduct or behaviour might cause the company to rescind its decision. This concern led to the formation of a site governing committee to enforce rules and guidelines for behaviour. Notable among these standards of conduct was a zero tolerance stance on all forms of violence; all disputes had to be brought before the site committee for arbitration. Those who resorted to violence or took matters into their own hands were banished from the site. Given that there were no lands for farming or other notable employment opportunities and artisanal gold mining work was the town's mainstay, hardly anyone violated this code of conduct. Reflecting on my own situation as an outsider asking sensitive questions in the community, I feel not feel at risk or threatened at any point during my three months stay at the site.

The site's very organised, friendly and disciplined nature was one of many observations which challenged the popular assertion that artisanal gold mining sites are violence-prone, lawless domains teeming with criminals and social misfits who have no qualms about abusing children or corrupting their morals. This was one of a number of normative assumptions informing dominant representations of children's involvement in artisanal mining work, which the study sought to scrutinise. Among these widely held assumptions are the following:

(a) *Age*: International children's rights policymakers' and neo-abolitionists' attempts to prohibit the involvement of children in jobs they class as WFCL or 'child slavery' are primarily premised on the assumption that anyone under 18 years is incompetent or lacks the capacity to take up such work. Abolitionist literature reviewed around the period of the fieldwork argued that a 'typical child mine worker' was aged 12 (Jennings 1999; ILO 2005: 8). Indeed, some texts asserted that it was not uncommon to find toddlers; 3- and 4-year-old children, labouring at small-scale mining sites (ILO 2011: 33). The belief is that children are unlikely to take up such dirty, difficult and dangerous work unless compelled by an adult third party through coercion, force or trickery (Amin et al. 2007: 18; Hentschel et al. 2002).
(b) *Unquestionable victimisation and exploitation*: Another normative abolitionist assumption which the study aimed to subject to critical interrogation was a widely held belief that children in artisanal gold mining work are necessarily victimised or exploited. Policymakers and abolitionists reason that because of children's relative immaturity, they are unlikely to protest against maltreatment or challenge adults at mining sites (ILO 1999, 2001, 2002, 2011). They are also said to be regarded as disposable and thus exposed to the most hazardous or dangerous jobs which adults cannot or may not want to perform:

> Some of the most dangerous extraction tasks are set aside for children, whose smaller, more nimble bodies enable them to go down into mining shafts to extract minerals that are difficult to access. Young, numerous, cheap (if not free) and often without a parent or guardian to look out for them, these children are seen as expendable. (Free the Slaves 2010: 1)

Linked to this is the assumption that children working in artisanal mining are either not paid or given paltry rewards if it all:

> Many children in mining and quarrying do not get any remuneration for their work; they only receive basic sustenance (in-kind payment). Besides, when they do receive payment for their work, the wages of children are normally inferior to the wages of adults. (ILO 2005: 16)

(c) A third normative assumption in the WFCL abolitionist discourse which the study sought to examine is a suggestion that participation in work at artisanal gold mining sites corrupts or risks corrupting children's morals. The discourse places special emphasis on girls' safety and morals, with the argument that they are at risk of sexual violence or of being called upon to provide sexual services to men and boys in mining communities. In fact, this largely unquestioned belief that moral turpitude and 'sexual slavery' of girls, as FTS (2014: 8) puts it, is a dominant feature of children's involvement in artisanal mining forms basis for the ILO's argument that small-scale mining involves 'unconditional' WFCL:

> Some children are engaged in prostitution and they are also confronted by problems related to alcohol and drug abuse, and violence. So small-scale mining also involves aspects of the unconditional worst forms of child labour. (ILO 2005: 8)

Two key questions which guided the study's aim of scrutinising these dominant abolitionist assumptions were whether these widely held claims were representative of children's work at all artisanal mining sites, and, related to this, whether the reality at one artisanal mining site could reliably serve as basis for a blanket policy on children's involvement everywhere. I was concerned that policymakers and WFCL abolitionists were extrapolating from evidence at individual artisanal gold mining sites (often the worst examples) and also drawing on particular assumptions and definitions of childhood, harm, development, exploitation and 'slavery' for policies and interventions on children's involvement at all other sites. What perspectives and potential solutions were foreclosed by this strategy? As discussed in the next section, the evidence from Kenyasi lends credence to these concerns.

Children's Labour and Working Conditions at the Kenyasi Artisanal Gold Mining Site: A Case of Force, Coercion, Exploitation and Slavery?

Children's work at the site took two forms. They were either self-employed in roles such as hawking, head porterage, fetching of water and other supplies for the processing of gold ore, or they sold their labour on a day-by-day basis to 'buyers'. Buyers were often adults, and occasionally children or groups of children, who had purchased gold ore and needed assistance to process it. I have avoided describing the relationship between the children and buyers as that of 'employee' and 'employer' because this characterisation would be a misnomer. Everyone who was seeking income earning opportunities at the Kenyasi artisanal gold mining site could best be described as a hustler in an 'economy of makeshifts' (Brace 2004; Williams 2005). The site was populated by adults and children collaborating in an attempt to scrape out a living on the margins of society in the face of mutual hardships arising locally from the loss of lands and nationally from decades of enforced austere socio-economic reforms. Social relations at the site were therefore characterised primarily by mutual dependence in recognition of their limited or non-existent opportunities and livelihood alternatives.

Another notable factor guiding children's work avenues and roles at the site was superstition or spirituality. There was strict adherence to a superstitious belief that if women were allowed direct involvement in gold extraction or the gold processing chain, yields would be low, or worse still, serious accidents may occur. Consequently, roles which were directly linked to the extraction and processing of gold were reserved for boys and men, while women and girls were permitted jobs traditionally regarded as females'; kitchen work in restaurants or serving customers, hawking of various wares at the site, head porterage, fetching water and other supplies for the processing of gold ore, but not directly participating in that activity itself.

To find work, those who were not self-employed relied on a system outlined by 'Ayesha' during the fieldwork:

> ...we turn up in the morning and go 'door knocking'..., we move from one spot to the other to find out the sorts of work available and who the owner [buyer] is. If we are interested, we ask the owner if they want to work with us for the day. When we finish, he pays us and we go our way.

There was no third party involvement in the entry of children into work at this site. Self-employed children went around the site by themselves soliciting for work, while those who preferred to work with others went to look for such work on their own, as Ayesha's quote shows. Her account, which was repeated by her friends and further corroborated through prolonged observation during the research cast doubt on the abolitionist assumption that children's participation in work at such spaces was necessarily the product of force, trickery, coercion or other 'unfree' actions by adult third parties. Indeed, the evidence also raised questions about views that no child would choose this sort of work because it is exploitative, dirty and dangerous.

Further evidence on the mechanisms through which children entered into work at site and the conditions surrounding their work also raised questions about FTS (2010) claims of widespread 'child slavery' in the Ghanaian gold mining sector. Besides the lack of third party involvement in their entry into work, the child research participants were neither kept in employment nor compelled to work with anybody at the site. The working day typically began at 8 a.m., with an hour break at noon, and ended by 4 or 5 p.m.; whereupon workers were paid. However, this was applicable to adults only, for if a child decided to withdraw his or her labour before 4 p.m. for whatever reason, as part of exclusive protections for children instituted by the site governing committee, the 'buyer' or person who had contracted the child's labour for the day was still obliged to pay him or her for the period worked. This and other measures discussed elsewhere (Okyere 2013) ensured that contrary to WFCL abolitionists claims of wholesale victimisation and exploitation of children at artisanal mining sites, those at Kenyasi were not only shielded from the most hazardous jobs at the site, but also they were not cheated or exploited in terms of remuneration. Although abolitionists insist that child labour is cheap labour, the principle of equal payment for equal work enforced by site governing committee ensured that as long children performed the same roles as adults, their age and maturity was immaterial to their earning potential.

The gendered nature of work and experiences at artisanal gold mining sites was an abolitionist claim supported by the research findings. Work at the site was indeed highly gendered due to the community's superstitious beliefs about work men and women can and cannot do in artisanal mining. However, the assertion that such gendered roles fuels sexual exploitation of girls and women (see ILO 2011; ILO/IPEC 2004; Mwami et al. 2002) or 'sexual slavery' as FTS (2014) calls it, could not be substantiated. There was no evidence whatsoever of girls trading sexual favours for money at or near the site, as the literature would lead one to expect. The site's superstitions included the belief that a 'gold goddess' and other spirits who kept workers safe abhorred sexual activity of any kind in their presence. Consequently, there was a strong taboo against prostitution and any sexual activity of any sort at or near the site. These were among a number of activities that were believed to lead to dire consequences for all if practised at the site and were therefore strongly prohibited and policed as part of the site's code of conduct. In fact, instead of prostitution or sexual abuse of girls, the most telling impact of the site's gendered division of work for both adults and children was that boys earned more than women; another research finding that raised questions about abolitionists' claims that children working at mining sites are unconditionally paid less than adults due their relative immaturity.

On the whole, the research findings contradict key assumptions which inform FTS 'child slavery' and WFCL abolitionists' claims on children's involvement in artisanal mining. For sure, the environment and aspects of the children's work exposed them to severe hazards. But, as discussed in the next section, the child research participants in whose' interests abolitionists claim to be working strongly rejected the argument that banning them from accessing earning opportunities at the mining site was the best way to safeguard their rights or best interests.

Why Had Children Taken up Artisanal Gold Mining Work at Kenyasi?

A range of motivational factors informed the child research participants' decisions to seek income earning opportunities at the Kenyasi artisanal gold mining site. Their work formed part of their attempts to feed themselves and their loved ones. It was also a means of purchasing other basic life necessities, accessing healthcare and pursuing development opportunities such as education, apprenticeships and skills training. I am mainly going to address the education–child labour nexus in this section not only because education was the reason most cited by the children as motivation for taking up work at the site, but also because this finding sheds new light on how we think of the connections between child labour and education. This finding forms part of the significant original contributions the study makes to international children's rights debates. The commonly held view is that children in WFCL are mostly illiterate or school dropouts (Jennings 1999; ILO 2005). The ILO's designation of jobs such as artisanal gold mining as WFCL is not only due to concern about harm and exploitation, but it is also premised on the belief that such work denies children education and other development opportunities. More broadly, child labour is said to 'allow no room for dreams' as Wahba (1998: 1) has argued, and children working at places such as artisanal gold mining sites are described as having 'no educational or future perspective' (ILO 2009: 12) and therefore condemned 'to a harrowing present and hopeless future' (UNICEF 2001: 11).

So pervasive are these assumptions that prior to undertaking fieldwork, I translated copies of the consent form, participant information sheet and other ethics documents into the local language in anticipation of reading and explaining this information to illiterate children. It was therefore a surprise to discover that 50 of the 57 child research participants were in full-time education and could all speak, read and write in the English (which is the language of instruction in Ghanaian schools) very well. Of the 50, 40 had taken up work at the site principally in an attempt to secure funds for their education as exemplified by these abstracts:

> My father cannot give us money for school and my elder sister has stopped school because of this. I came here with some girls to see if I can get some money for myself and continue school next term. (Adams, aged 14);

> I have been coming here for 3 vacations now. There is nobody to help me [with money to attend school] and that is why I do this. (Rocky, aged 16);

> Sometimes I need money urgently and my mother cannot afford [to give me money]. That day I don't go to school or maybe I don't do extra classes and I come here to work and find the money to go back to school the next day or when I can afford to do so. (Albert, aged 17)

These child participants' predicament underline a wider problem faced by many poor families in the space where this study was carried out. Government officials interviewed during the fieldwork insisted that all Ghanaian children have free access to education as a result of schemes such as the Free Compulsory Universal Basic Education (FCUBE) and the Capitation Grant (CP). Under these schemes, education is, in theory, free until Junior High School level (JHS); the level that most of the child participants were at. Despite the absence of school fees, Eugene's comments below show that many children are still unable to attend due to household financial constraints:

> It is true that we don't pay fees, but that is not the only problem. There is no money at home; there is even nothing to eat. That is also a problem; you can't go [to school] if you can't eat. (Eugene, aged 17)

Osei et al. (2009) have examined this problem in more detail and similarly concluded that the fee component is just one of many financial burdens schooling in Ghana imposes on parents:

> School fee abolition is not just about tuition fees (which do not necessarily constitute the main bulk of fees). School fee abolition must take into

> consideration the wide range of costs of schooling to families and households. This means any direct and indirect costs/charges (tuition fees, costs of text books, supplies and uniforms, PTA contributions, costs related to sports and other school activities, costs related to transportation, contributions to teachers' salaries, etc. (2009: 4)

In a country with a deprivation score of nearly 50% and 28.6% of the population living below the poverty line, according to the most recent available statistics captured in the 2014 Human Development Report, many families are simply unable to meet these additional costs. Thus, although attendance is 'free' as officials insisted, school remains inaccessible to children from poor families or communities. Many drop out as a result, but other children try to support their parents' efforts to fund their education and in many cases do so entirely by themselves through work and other income earning activities. This was the story of many children working at Kenyasi. They mostly worked at the site after school or during vacations, which was the period during which the fieldwork was carried out.

Their educational ambitions coupled with how work was organised and remunerated at the site served to shield them from the most hazardous jobs, contrary to the popular abolitionist assumption that children working at such places are unquestionably lumped with the most hazardous jobs because of their relative immaturity or because they are seen as 'disposable'. The hardest and most dangerous jobs, such as underground work, require long-term commitment, months in most cases, because workers are not paid until they had started hauling gold ore from below the pits. As the longest school holidays lasted for just about six weeks, the child participants were in a race against time to earn as much money as possible to tide them by over the next three-month school term. Waged labour in the 'fringe' and comparatively easier roles which required no long-term commitment assured them of daily payments. Jobs on the fringes of the core mining work provided the security that the child participants could end their stay at the site at any point the need arose, without the risk of going back home empty handed. These considerations coupled with the fact that work in artisanal mining gave them the best chance of earning a decent amount of money in the short vacation period were the key reasons for their preference of artisanal gold mining work over others such as agricultural labour and head porterage at market centres; jobs which are also targeted for elimination by abolitionists anyway.

In discussing what they saw as the relative advantages of working in artisanal gold mining compared to other options open to them, it was evident that the child research participants were not entirely bereft of agency and choice. For sure, their decisions to undertake paid work at the site was driven by the harsh socio-economic conditions they and their families were facing. Nonetheless, even within this constrained circumstance, they were making rational decisions about the sort of work they preferred to do, where they wanted to do such work, who they wanted to work with and the hours they wanted to work. They were essentially making decisions about their own lives under conditions Klocker describes as 'thin agency': 'decisions and everyday actions that are carried out within highly restrictive contexts, characterised by few viable alternatives' (2007: 85).

On the substantive matter of the education–WFCL nexus, the findings firstly call into question the idea that engagement in WFCL automatically deprives children of education. While the study was unable to go into the impact of their work on their school results, attendance or performance, what was without doubt was that the participants' access to schooling was made possible by their earnings from their work at the site. Secondly, and linked to the first point, the findings trouble the notion that schooling is of itself a panacea to disengaging children from dangerous or hazardous work. The paradox in this example is that the children's desire to access education and the challenges they faced with this objective had become a direct causal factor for their entry into work classed by the ILO as a WFCL. Their educational and developmental opportunities were not being threatened or deprived them by their work. Rather, whatever limited access they had was by virtue of it. The barriers they faced in accessing education and other developmental opportunities, much like their participation in work at the artisanal mining site, were the result of socio-economic hardships and structural insecurities facing the country as a whole rather than the actions of uncaring parents or callous adults seeking to exploit children's labour as abolitionists tend to argue.

All in all, the children's accounts and other evidence from the research showed a clear divergence between how they, their families and wider community visualised their involvement in artisanal gold mining work and how policymakers and abolitionists also perceive the same situation. For policymakers and abolitionists, there can be no question about it; WFCL must be banned because it is 'hazardous to children'. It threatens them with physical and psychological harms and also deprives them of their childhood. In neo-abolitionist rhetoric, children's participation is without doubt exploitative and evidence of child slavery, because children are tricked, forced or coerced into such work by adults who pay them a pittance, if at all, for their hard labour. And yet, the accounts of this group of children involved in the phenomenon show a highly complex situation than these popular narratives suggest. The child participants agreed with some abolitionist claims about the difficulties and hazards surrounding their work:

> This is very dirty work. The sand and dust gets in your face, your mouth and everywhere, even your eyes. (Jude, aged 15)

> Sometimes after work, it feels like somebody has beaten you up. Your whole body pains you, but you know everyone is feeling the same and so you only think of the reason why you came here and forget about the pains. (Esi, aged 15)

> If you are not careful, you can get injured at any time. I have not been injured before, but I have seen a man who smashed his hand with a hammer when he was working. (Ebo, aged 16)

And yet, pressed on why they still kept coming back to the site to find work each day, particularly when during discussions many of them told me that they knew, (from media reports, advocacy campaigns and abolitionist literature I had shown them during the fieldwork), that their work was forbidden by international children's rights policymakers and the Ghanaian government (through the country's Child Rights Act and its ratification of ILO Conventions 138 and 182), a very different narrative often emerged:

> people say this work is bad and so we should stop and go to school,...but if I can't buy books, shoes and other things I need, how can I go to school?...I will go to school but I can't eat school if I am hungry. (James, aged 15);

> I don't need anybody [those calling for a ban on their work] to come and tell me about this work and why I should stop, because I do it myself and know everything. I know that it is difficult and dangerous but if anyone wants me to stop just like that, then the person must give me school money before. (Cynthia, aged 16)

Children's voices, much like those of adults, must be considered critically in research. It is crucial to understand the complexity in their narratives instead of taking them at face value or uncritically presenting everything they say as truth. To this end, careful, repeated and extensive interactions coupled with data triangulation strategies were employed to corroborate their assertions. Their claims were challenged where necessary and at the end critical discourse and thematic analyses were used reflexively to extract and decode both superficial and latent messages in their narratives. Application of these techniques revealed that in the children's own eyes and in that of the community in which they lived and worked, the hazards described by policymakers and neo-abolitionists were of lesser significance than the hazards of humiliating poverty, hunger, lack of clothing, shoes and other personal effects. They considered the potential physical, medical or physiological injuries and hazards associated with their work to be no less hazardous and injurious than the social and economic hazards or harms linked to being unable to access education, healthcare, skills training, apprenticeships and other reasons for which they were toiling at the site. The moral judgements and understandings of deviance, exploitation and harm on the basis of which WFCL abolitionists make pronouncements about the children's work were very different to those held by the children themselves.

This discord between the two assessments brings into focus the fact that while the United Nations Convention on the Rights of Children guarantees children the right for their views to be elicited and taken into account in the formulation of policies that affect them, in reality, children's rights policymakers are themselves only willing to take children's views on board if these views are in consonance with theirs. The long-standing refusal by the ILO to engage with organised groups of working children from Peru, Bolivia, Senegal, Burkina Faso, India and elsewhere stems from the fact that these working children's unions insist on their right to take up any form of work necessitated by their socio-economic, political and cultural circumstances; the same arguments made by their peers at Kenyasi. This view directly contradicts the ILO's perspectives on children's work as enshrined in Conventions 138 and 182 notably. A crucial question thrown up by this dilemma concerns the lack of accountability to children by key actors in the international child rights framework. Are the ILO and neo-abolitionists legitimately representing working children and their best interests, as they claim, when they sideline working children and deny them a meaningful role in deliberations about the rights of working children and children's work? This question has become especially poignant in the last decade following statements by organised unions of working children and youth (such as UNATSBO, MANTHOC, ENDA and AMCWC) that they now speak for themselves and represent their own best interests after years of having their voices, much like those expressed by their peers at Kenyasi paternalistically marginalised or ignored by the ILO.

Discussion and Conclusion

This chapter set out to question the depiction of children's involvement in the Ghanaian artisanal gold mining sector as a form of 'child slavery' by FTS and to scrutinise the wider abolitionist discourse on this phenomenon using the accounts of children involved in income seeking activities in the sector. The children's narratives and other evidence presented by the chapter problematise the characterisation of this phenomenon as a form of 'modern slavery' or 'child slavery' and also undermine key normative assumptions that underpin the wider WFCL abolitionist discourse spearheaded by the ILO. Judged even by Bales' (1999) definition of modern slavery, which has been adopted by FTS, the chapter has demonstrated that the neo-abolitionist NGO's portrayal of such scenarios as child slavery is misguided. Far from being compelled through force or other coercive means to work in this sector, children at the study site take up work without any third party involvement or compulsion and similarly face no obstacles in withdrawing their labour whenever they wish to. Far from being denied payment or cheated out of their wages, as the abolitionist discourses suggests as the norm, the children's wages were the same as adults', and boys could actually earn more than women in some instances because of the gendered nature of labour at the site. Their wages are also mainly used for their own education and benefit instead of being used by a third party 'exploiter' or beneficiary. The work done by children and the conditions of their labour were the safest and most secure within the precarious setting in which adults and children alike were compelled to toil; a finding that also troubles the assumption that children in artisanal mining are forced to undertake the most hazardous tasks because of their relative immaturity. Without seeking to idealise their work, the chapter contends that the reality of children's work in artisanal mining at Kenyasi, similar to findings in Northern Ghana by Hilson (2010) bear no resemblance whatsoever to chattel slavery, or any form of slavery. Thus, FTS (2010) suggestion that about '*10,000 Ghanaian children are forced to work in hazardous conditions, and child slavery in the form of debt bondage and forced prostitution also occur in the country's mining communities*', without evidence of how this number was obtained and names of specific communities in which such enslavement occurs is at best a wild exaggeration. It follows the trope of neo-abolitionist advocacy which harness the language of slavery, melodrama and sensationalism to draw attention to their work.

The problem, however, is that such sensationalism and allegations of 'child slavery' or 'modern slavery' can draw public attention to the problem without doing much in practical terms to support the purported slaves and their communities. In the case of children in the Ghanaian artisanal gold mining sector, the solution proposed by FTS, policymakers and WFCL abolitionists to such assertions of slavery is the extraction of individual children from work and a blanket ban on all children's participation in the sector. Such solutions are not only rejected by the children themselves but they also highlight a number of problems that attend on global efforts to eliminate WFCL.

The first is whether informed judgements can be made about children's work without adequate knowledge or consideration of the social, economic and political specificities surrounding the work. The decision by international children's rights policymakers to enforce a blanket ban on jobs deemed to be WFCL may be well-intentioned. However, this sweeping approach misses the variation and nuance of children's experiences in such jobs. Children working in artisanal gold mining work in Ghana, for example, may have patently different motivations, conditions of work and other experiences from their peers undertaking similar work in India or Senegal or even at different sites in the same country. WFCL abolitionists' totalising discourse and children's rights policymakers' tendency to formulate policy for all forms of children's work based on evidence from specific places or instances is therefore inherently problematic. The default abolitionist position to view children's work at places such as Kenyasi only in terms of harm and exploitation obscures the equally important fact presented by this chapter: that in some cases these jobs are also the only available means through which working children attempt to access schooling and other development opportunities or eke out the most basic survival.

To be clear, this chapter is not arguing in favour of the children's continued involvement in hazardous work. Rather its main concern is with child rights policy makers and neo-abolitionists diagnosis of the problem and the solution they proffer. Ignoring the complexity of the issue and presenting it only in terms of exploitation, harm or slavery, in order to support abolitionist or rescue agendas largely omits from the equation the deficits this particular group of children will suffer if they are deprived access from their work while the underlying issue of individual, household and communal socio-economic deprivation remain untouched. The entry of Free the Slaves, Walk Free Foundation and other neo-abolitionist groups into the WFCL advocacy arena has further deflected attention from the crucial need to address the structural factors at the heart of the heart of the problem as an alternative to the abolitionist model the ILO has been pursuing for nearly a century. Neo-abolitionist reformulation of the problem in terms of child slavery or modern slavery produces the false narrative that extracting or 'rescuing' children from their alleged 'slave masters' is all that is required to address the problem. Consequently, the need to take on local and global forces which have created and continue to shape the adverse socio-economic conditions that necessitate the entry of children into precarious and hazardous work largely remains unexamined.

"To call on Wright Mills (1959) then, the approach adopted by neo-abolitionists and the international children's rights policy makers for addressing this phenomena is characterised by a rupture of the connections between the biographies or circumstances of the child research participants and their histories, which are in turn enmeshed with the history of their communities and the country at large". As discussed earlier in the chapter, creation of the Kenyasi site where the entire community was attempting to secure their livelihoods was a direct outcome of obligations placed on Ghana to open up its mining sector to the private market as part of IMF structural adjustment conditionalities imposed on the country in the 1980s. These conditionalities and other forced market liberalisation measures have exposed millions of Ghanaians to abject socio-economic deprivation. The 'child slavery' discourse obfuscates understanding of the fact that for decades, to be able to access aid, loans, debt relief and other assistance from the IMF, World Bank and richer nations, poorer countries such as Ghana have been compelled to pursue economic policies and socio-economic reforms that are patently deleterious to the social welfare and other interests of their own citizens. As the NGO Action Aid argues in a report on the impact of IMF economic reforms in Ghana, while there have been improvements in macro-economic stability in successive years:

> Stability has been achieved against the backdrop of high unemployment, poverty and increased inequality. IMF policies have thus not contributed to shared growth and income redistribution in Ghana. IMF required Government of Ghana to reduce spending on health, education and development. In effect, the IMF demands the poor in Ghana to have lower standard of living. (2010: 45)

Ghana's underdevelopment and her inability to provide an accessible, viable and sustainable welfare safety net for children and families is also largely due to her colonised past and current weak position on the global economic and political stage. Faced with the lack of a state welfare safety net such as those available in Britain and elsewhere, residents of Kenyasi, like millions of other Ghanaians are left with no option than to seek out jobs they themselves readily recognise as undignified, dirty, difficult and dangerous. Martin Verlet echoes this point, when he argues that the worsening of living conditions in Ghana and children's uptake of precarious work can be attributed to 'domestic deregulation' in the country:

> the break-up of family units combined with the increasing fragility and destabilisation of households which has been gathering pace and becoming more serious under the impact of the polices of liberalisation through structural adjustment. A connection exists between the deregulation of the labour market and what we call domestic deregulation. Clearer still is the correlation between both these processes and the general spread of child labour. (2000: 67)

I conclude by reasserting Foucault's point on the urgency of holding up to scrutiny the practices, discourses and work of institutions which appear to be both neutral and independent, in such a manner that the political violence which they perpetuate can be unmasked and challenged (1974: 171). FTS and WFCL abolitionists' calls to eliminate children's work at Kenyasi and similar spaces appear uncontroversial. Who can argue, afterall, that they are in support of children's work in artisanal mining, child slavery or child exploitation? The 'child saving' rhetoric is largely unquestioned, for it is presumed to be wholly in children's best interests. But, it is precisely this kind of discourse which Foucault argues we ought to critically scrutinise. This undertaking by the chapter shows that the 'child saving' or emancipatory goals FTS and WFCL abolitionists envisage are undermined by their failure to question global economic forces which prioritise profits over human need and shape systems of inequality affecting many over the world. The conceptualisation of children's work in artisanal mining exclusively in terms of harm and exploitation (which they also mainly attribute to children's own parents and communities) forecloses understanding of the nuances surrounding it as well as the structural causes underpinning it.

By attributing the problem to individual 'slave masters' or 'exploiters' instead of bringing into focus the need for socio-economic and political structural reforms and action against the deleterious aspects of global capitalism, many children and their families may remain trapped in the precarious work and existence conditioned by these factors. By localising or individualising the causes, neo-abolitionist and mainstream rhetoric unwittingly or deliberately depoliticise and avoid the intrinsically political task of campaigning for fairer trade deals, debt relief, reparations for historic wrongs and a more equal playing field on the global economic stage so that poorer countries like Ghana can meet their welfare obligations to their citizens, improve their livelihoods and ultimately reduce the need for children to take on hazardous work. It is this paradox which Foucault's philosophy of normativity, highlighted at the start of this chapter, invites us to consider.

Notes

1. http://www.freetheslaves.net/where-we-work/ghana/.
2. http://www.freetheslaves.net/about-slavery/faqs-glossary/.

References

ActionAid Ghana. (2010). *Implications of IMF Loans and Conditionalities on the Poor and Vulnerable in Ghana*. Accra: Actionaid. http://bit.ly/28Slcqi. Accessed 23 June 2016.

Allain, J., & Hickey, R. (2012). Property and the Definition of Slavery. *International and Comparative Law Quarterly, 61*(4), 915–938.

Amin, S., Quayes, S., & Rives, M. (2007). Are Children and Parents Substitutes or Complements in the Family Labor Supply Decision in Bangladesh? *The Journal of Developing Areas, 40*(1), 15–37.

Archard, D. (2004). *Children: Rights and Childhood*. London: Routledge.

Armstrong, A. T. (2008). *Gold Strike in the Breadbasket: Indigenous Livelihoods, the World Bank and Territorial Restructuring in Western Ghana*. A Report for the Institute for Food and Development Policy Development (IFDPD). http://goo.gl/VXqEZ. Accessed 1 June 2010.

Bales, K. (1999). *Disposable People: New Slavery in the Global Economy* (2nd ed.). Berkeley: University of California Press.

Bales, K. (2005). *Understanding Global Slavery: A Reader*. Berkeley: University of California Press.

Bastia, T. (2005). Child Trafficking or Teenage Migration? Bolivian Migrants in Argentina. *International Migration, 43*(4), 57–89.

Brace, L. (2004). *The Politics of Property: Labour, Freedom and Belonging.* Edinburgh: Edinburgh University Press.

Brune, N., Garrett, G., & Kogut, B. (2004). The International Monetary Fund and the Global Spread of Privatization. *IMF Staff Papers, 51*(2), 195–219.

Buck, T., & Nicholson, A. (2010). Constructing the International Legal Framework. In G. Craig (Ed.), *Child Slavery Now: A Contemporary Reader* (pp. 43–60). Bristol: Policy Press.

Clarke, S. (2003). Slaves, Servility and Noble Deeds. *Philosophical Inquiry, 25*(3–4), 165–176.

Craig, G. (Ed.). (2010). *Child Slavery Now: A Contemporary Reader*. Bristol: Policy Press.

Foucault, M. (1974). Human Nature: Justice Versus Power. In E. Fons (Ed.), *Reflexive Water: The Basic Concerns of Mankind* (pp. 135–197). London: Souvenir Press.

Foucault, M. (1980). Two Lectures. In C. Gordon (Ed.), *Power/Knowledge: Selected Interviews and Other Writings by Michel Foucault* (pp. 1972–1977). New York: Pantheon Books.

Free the Slaves. (2010). *Findings of Slavery Linked with Mineral Extraction in Eastern DRC. Free the Slaves Research Brief.* https://bit.ly/2IHDkzO. Accessed 1 May 2016.

Free the Slaves. (2014). *Child Rights in Mining Pilot Project Results & Lessons Learned.* https://www.freetheslaves.net/wp-content/uploads/2015/03/ChildRightsinMiningPilotProjectOverview.pdf. Accessed 1 November 2016.

Hashim, I. (2005). *Exploring the Linkages Between Children's Independent Migration and Education: Evidence From Ghana* (Migration DRC Working Paper WP-T12). http://bit.ly/28QSktn. Accessed 23 June 2016.

Hentschel, T., Hruschka, F., & Priester, M. (2002). *Global Report on Artisanal and Small-Scale Mining* (Report Commissioned by the MMSD project of IIED). http://goo.gl/A3KNC. Accessed 3 January 2017.

Hilson, G. (2010). Child Labour in African Artisanal Mining Communities: Experiences from Northern Ghana. *Development and Change, 41*(3), 445–473.

Hutchful, E. (2002). *Ghana's Adjustment Experience: The Paradox of Reform.* Oxford: Oxford University Press.

ILO. (1999). *Social and Labour Issues in Small-Scale Mines. Report for the Tripartite Meeting on Social and Labour Issues in Small-Scale Mines.* Geneva: ILO.

ILO. (2001). *Anatomy of a Prohibition: ILO Standards in Relation to Night Work of Women in Industry*. Geneva: ILO.

ILO. (2002). *A Future Without Child labour*. Geneva: ILO.
ILO. (2005). *A Load Too Heavy: Children in Mining and Quarrying*. Geneva: ILO.
ILO. (2011). *Children in Hazardous Work: What We Know What We Need to Do*. Geneva: ILO.
ILO/IPEC. (2004). *Action Against Child Labour and Quarrying: A Thematic Evaluation*. Geneva: International Labour Organization.
ILO/IPEC. (2016). *World Day Against Child Labour: End Child labour in Supply Chains—It's Everyone's Business!* Geneva: ILO.
Jennings, N. S. (1999). *Small-Scale Gold Mining: Examples from Bolivia, Philippines and Zimbabwe. Sectoral Activities Programme* (Working Paper, SAP 2.76/WP.130). Geneva: ILO.
Klocker, N. (2007). An Example of 'Thin' Agency: Child Domestic Workers in Tanzania. In R. Panelli, S. Punch, & E. Robson (Eds.), *Global Perspectives on Rural Childhood and Youth: Young Rural Lives* (pp. 83–94). Routledge.
Kooijmans, J., & van de Glind, H. (2010). Concept of Child Slavery: Historical Background. In G. Craig (Ed.), *Child Slavery Now: A Contemporary Reader* (pp. 21–41). Bristol: Policy Press.
Levison, D. (2009). Child Labour Policy for Developing Nations. In H. Hindman (Ed.), *The World of Child Labour: An Historical and Regional Survey* (pp. 10–17). London: M.E. Sharpe.
Lott, T. (1998). *Subjugation and Bondage: Critical Essays on Slavery and Social Philosophy*. Lanham, MD: Rowman & Littlefield.
McGary, H., & Lawson, B. E. (1992). *Between Slavery and Freedom: Philosophy and American Slavery*. Bloomington and Indianapolis: Indiana University Press.
Mwami, J. A., Sanga, A. J., & Nyoni, J. (2002). *Investigating the Worst Forms of Child Labour No. 15. Tanzania Children Labour in Mining: A Rapid Assessment*. Geneva: ILO.
Myers, W. E. (2001). The Right Rights? Child Labour in a Globalising World. *Annals of the American Academy of Political and Social Science, 575*, 38–55.
O'Connell Davidson, J. (2015). *Modern Slavery: The Margins of Freedom*. London: Palgrave Macmillan.
Okyere, S. (2013). Are Working Children's Rights and Child Labour Abolition Complementary or Opposing Realms? *International Social Work, 56*(1), 80–91.
Osei, R. D., Owusu, G. A., Asem, F. E., & Afutu-Kotey, R. L. (2009). *Effects of Capitation on Education Outcomes in Ghana*. Accra: Institute of Statistical, Social and Economic Research.

Patterson, O. (2012). Trafficking, Gender and Slavery: Past and Present. In J. Allain (Ed.), *The Legal Understanding of Slavery: From the Historical to the Contemporary* (pp. 322–359). Oxford: Oxford University Press.
Pupavac, V. (2001). Misanthropy Without Borders: The International Children's Rights Regime. *Disasters, 25*(2), 95–112.
Salafia, M. (2013). *Slavery's Borderland: Freedom and Bondage Along the Ohio River*. Philadelphia: University of Pennsylvania Press.
Tzannatos, Z. (2003). Child Labour and School Enrolment in Thailand in the 1990s. *Economics of Education Review, 22,* 523–536.
UNICEF. (2001). *Beyond Child Labour, Affirming Rights*. New York: UNICEF.
Wahba, J. (1998). *Child Labour and Poverty Transmission: No Room for Dreams. ERF Working Papers Series* (Working Paper No. 0108). Available at http://goo.gl/neBLi. Accessed 1 January 2016.
Williams, S. (2005). Earnings Poor Relief and the Economy of Makeshifts: Bedfordshire in the Early Years of the New Poor Law. *Rural History, 16,* 21–52.
Wright Mills, C. (1959). *The Sociological Imagination*. New York: Oxford University Press.
Yakovleva, N. (2007). Perspective on Female Participation in Artisanal and Small-Scale Mining: A Case Study of Birim North District of Ghana. *Resources Policy, 32*(1–2), 29–41.

Part III

Revisiting the Politics of Antislavery

10

Abolitionist Anti-politics? Capitalism, Coercion and the Modern Anti-slavery Movement

Neil Howard

Introduction

'Slavery', 'trafficking' and 'forced labour' are crimes that sit at the far end of what Jens Lerche calls the 'spectrum' of labour exploitation (2007: 435). As Bridget Anderson (2007) observes, they are to 'badness' what Apple Pie and Motherhood are to 'goodness'. And by most media or political accounts, they are getting worse. Barely a day now passes without stories of 'trafficked people' here or 'modern slaves' there. Governments everywhere are passing anti-slavery laws, modern abolitionist NGOs are mushrooming, and millions of consumers now call for products that are 'slavery-free' (see, for example, Slavery Footprint 2011). Yet this trend poses major problems. For although exploitation merits our attention, the focus on its extreme forms obscures more than it reveals. Concentrating on extremes seen to lie *outside* of capitalism

N. Howard (✉)
University of Bath, Bath, UK
e-mail: n.howard@bath.ac.uk

L. Brace and J. O'Connell Davidson (eds.), *Revisiting Slavery and Antislavery*,
https://doi.org/10.1007/978-3-319-90623-2_10

hides the fact that this 'outside' is actually *part* of capitalism, and represents nothing other than its worst excesses.

In this chapter, I will make three main arguments. The first expands on the above point. I suggest that we need to understand 'outside-the-system' extremes as helpful for maintaining the system itself. This is because the discursive-ideological work that the *idea* of them does sustains both the fictitious binaries and the foundational principles upon which the system rests. It also shields the system from legitimate critique.

The second argument is that 'modern abolitionists' play a paradoxical role in relation to the status quo. I understand 'modern abolitionists' and 'the modern anti-slavery movement' to include all those governmental, inter-governmental and non-governmental bodies seeking to prevent or protect against 'slavery', 'trafficking' and 'forced labour'. These range from government agencies such as the US Departments of State and Labor, to UN bodies such as UNICEF, the International Labour Organization (ILO) and the UN Office on Drugs and Crime (UNODC), labour unions such as the International Trades Union Confederation (ITUC), and civil society actors such as Free the Slaves, Walk Free and The Freedom Fund. I have spent a decade working with and on these organisations, combining participant observation inside them, professional work for them, and interviews with current and former staff members. On this basis of this research (see, for example, Howard 2013, 2016), I argue that although choosing to ally with people they see as exploited, 'modern abolitionists' end up serving the interests of their exploiters, not least through their complicity with the notion that severe exploitation exists only outside the capitalist system, and that it can be overcome without systemic changes.

Finally, I present an alternative. If exploitation under capitalism is necessarily contingent on the economic vulnerability deriving from propertylessness, then a genuine abolitionist response to that exploitation must strive to eliminate this vulnerability. I argue that one policy with the potential to achieve this is the Unconditional Basic Income (UBI). Should abolitionists be bold enough to reject the strictures of their donors and advocate UBI, they are in fact well placed to play a revolutionary role in the advancement of global social justice, instead of merely reinforcing the status quo.

Capitalism and Coercion

Two core dualisms structure capitalist thinking, between *consent* and *coercion,* and *freedom* and *force*. Each derives from what may be understood as capitalism's twin foundational principles—self-ownership and private property (Cohen 1994; Brace 2004). The capitalist interpretation of the human condition centres on the notion of self-ownership—'nothing is more bourgeois than this principle—it is *the* principle of the bourgeois revolution' (Cohen 1994: 259)—or what Brace terms the 'territorial understanding of self' (2004: 4). Thinkers from Locke to Nozick begin from the premise that 'every man has a property in his own person', which 'nobody has any right to but himself' (Locke in Cohen 1994: 209). From this it follows that each individual is an ontologically discrete island of autonomy, that stewardship over this island must be a matter of individual discretion, and that this discretion should extend up to the point at which it encounters the limits of another's.[1]

Importantly, in this capitalist world of meaning, the sphere of discretion includes (control over) the use of one's labour-power (man's 'original property'—and it is usually, implicitly a man, who is also white and wealthy), as well as the material property that one may acquire with that labour-power. Man is understood to be 'free' when he disposes of his energy and his property as he pleases, and 'unfree' when he is forced by another to dispose of his energy or his property according to that other's preferences. This in turn means that the exchange of goods or labour may be 'legitimate'—capitalist—when both parties to the exchange consent to it, and 'illegitimate' when at least one of them does not. Moreover, it implies that coercion can only ever be *individual*, for in a(n a-historical) world of self-owning individuals exercising their right to self-ownership, only a legal or moral person can impinge upon the ability of another to actualise this right. Just as it is impossible for an act of God to steal your car, so circumstance cannot render you a slave. And we should note that this understanding of coercion has been formalised everywhere in law. Even the ILO makes this clear in its own interpretation of the Forced Labour Convention: 'An external constraint or indirect coercion interfering with a worker's freedom to "offer himself voluntarily" may result not only from an act of the authorities, such as a statutory instrument, but also from an employer's practice...However, the employer or the State are not accountable for all external constraints or indirect coercion existing in practice: *for example, the need to work in order to earn one's living could become relevant only in conjunction with other factors for which they are answerable*' (ILO 2007: 20–21, emphasis added).

For capitalist thinkers, then, 'capitalism' denotes the universe of self-owning persons freely exchanging their property, including their labour. Exchanges that do not correspond to these conditions—in other words, which are subject to individualised force or coercion—are those that lie *outside* the putative world of capitalism. With material goods, this includes theft, larceny or looting[2]; with labour it includes 'trafficking', 'slavery' or 'forced labour', since each crime boils down, in definitional terms, to the presence or absence of consent or coercion in the exchange.

Yet there are obvious problems with these binary criteria. For one thing, they fail to reflect the messy realities that we find in the real world. For another, they cannot account for the pre-existing, property-based inequalities that structure these messy realities, or, as I shall argue below, for the historic 'primitive accumulation' generating those very inequalities (Marx, Capital Vol. 1; 1977). To give a concrete example, take the mother who is so poor and so lacking in social protection that she chooses to accept the proposal of a brothel owner who promises to feed her children if she will commit to a period of 'sexual servitude'. Who is guilty of coercion here? And where is the line between freedom and force? Or what of the subsistence farmer, so indebted and so limited in his options that he agrees to 'sell himself' into debt-bondage in order to pay off what he owes? Is his contract illegitimate simply because we find it morally unpleasant, and even though he consents to his 'coercion'?

It is important to recognise that these are *not* mere rhetorical or philosophical questions. A wealth of research now shows that people at the margins of the global economy routinely choose—and probably have always routinely chosen—to submit to this kind of exploitation as their best available option. In Steinfeld's terms, it is the lesser of the two 'disagreeable alternatives' that face them (1991: 19). These alternatives are not always as stark as between death or destitution. And those making the choice are often not the very poorest. As Nicola Phillips has recently shown, even the working poor often elect to accept exploitative, coercive or abusive labour conditions as a tactical necessity in the pursuit of their livelihood goals, since the adverse terms under which they have been incorporated into the global economy preclude any superior option (Phillips 2013; Phillips et al. 2014). Crucially for our purposes, however, a great many of those faced with such choices are subsequently classified as victims of trafficking, slavery or forced labour. I found this clearly in my own research in West Africa, where I interviewed dozens of adolescents officially labelled as 'victims of trafficking'. Although depicted in official circles as agency-less innocents kidnapped by unscrupulous gangmasters, in reality almost all of these young men had exercised what we would commonly understand as their 'choice' in the decision to migrate from their southern Beninese villages to Abeokuta's artisanal gravel quarries for work. They did so on two-year 'apprentices' and almost universally in order to earn some money—which each of them actually did (Howard 2016; see also Howard and Morganti 2014; Sharma 2003; Andrijasevic 2010).

What does this mean? There are three important points to be drawn out. First is the fact that in the messiness of real-world practice it is impossible to sustain the fictitious, arbitrary binaries between consent and coercion or freedom and force that structure the idealised notion of individual capitalist exchange. There are myriad workers who both consent to their treatment *and* experience coercion. The fact that their coercion is not of the individual, criminal, contract-abrogating type does not make it any less real, or any less brutal.

This brings us to our second point. Although capitalist ideologues maintain that in a free world populated by self-owning individuals, coercion can only ever be individual, this is clearly false. Indeed, at best it is incoherent, and at worst bad faith (Banaji 2003). As Robert Hale aptly puts it:

> [The worker] must eat. Yet while there is no law against eating in the abstract, there is a law which forbids him to eat any of the food which actually exists in the community—and that is the law of private property. (in Steinfeld 1991: 20)

The Nozickian formulation of market freedom works if everybody has property; it fails miserably if they do not. Because in very simple terms, for consent to be meaningful, you need to be able to withhold it. Saying yes means *being able to say no* (Van Parijs 1997; Widerquist 2013). But in order to say no, you have to have property to sustain yourself when you do. And if you do not, your formal freedom is substantively meaningless, because you will be coerced by the force of circumstance to say yes. Most workers cannot really say no to a job. Capitalism is ultimately premised on this exploitative reality, as Marx long ago showed us (1977), and despite what its apologists may claim. This is why Jairus Banaji asks: 'When is a contract "voluntary"? The answer is, probably never… [B]ecause economic coercion is pervasive under capitalism' (2003: 69–70).

It is precisely this foundational hypocrisy of the free market that is hidden by the idea of 'slavery', 'trafficking' and 'forced labour'. This is our third and most important point. Recall that even people—such as my Beninese teenage interviewees—who are engaged in labour officially labelled as 'trafficked' or 'modern slavery' often consent to that work. This means that, according to the principle of self-ownership, even work that is supposedly outside of capitalism actually exists within it—and, indeed, *because of it*. Yet what talk of 'slavery', 'trafficking' and 'forced labour' does is to take these labour experiences that express capitalism's moral and theoretical failings and present them as existing *outside of capitalism*. It thereby obscures the arguably constitutive role played by property-based inequalities in securing the coerced consent that most people would intuitively understand as exploitation (Cohen 1994). In doing so, it re-inscribes capitalism's fictitious binaries, protects its underlying commitment to unfettered private property and diverts the moral outrage that might otherwise challenge its hegemony.

The Hegemonic Function of Modern-Day Abolitionism

What role do the 'modern abolitionists' play in this process? 'Modern abolitionists' are those international agencies, academics, government departments, NGOs and charities whose self-appointed mission is to 'rid the world of slavery, trafficking and forced labour'. I have spent the past ten years working with these people and their organisations, in Europe, Australia, Africa and North America. I have mixed professional engagement *with* them, with detailed, anthropological research *of* them (2012, 2016). I have observed them at work, analysed the interactions across and between their different bureaucracies and quizzed many on why they do what they do. They are, as David Kennedy (2004) would put it, very often just 'good, well-meaning people' who (at least think they) wish to improve the lives of the world's most exploited workers (see also Heron 2007; Kempadoo 2015). Yet although (at least some of) their hearts reside in the right place, their contribution to the workers of the world is at best highly limited and at worst very problematic. This is because they are central to promoting *precisely* the story that everyday exploitation under capitalism actually lies outside of it, and thus that it can be prevented by market-friendly policies.

Kemala Kempadoo's recent article taking stock of the past two decades of contemporary abolition illustrates this point perfectly (2015). In examining the discourse and practice of the world's major abolitionists, she concludes that most faithfully reflect and repeat the capitalist mantra that the world can be divided into 'free' and 'forced' labourers, and that these groups are separated by the vanishing line between individualised consent and coercion. For abolitionists, she asserts, 'legitimate' capitalist exchange is the norm, outside of which we find extreme 'anomalies' such as trafficking or slavery. Furthermore, as her example of the Walk Free Foundation makes clear, contemporary abolitionists 'individualize' the dividing line between one and the other, claiming that 'it involves one person depriving another person of their freedom' (2015: 14). Causality is therefore abstracted from relations of property and reduced either to individual criminality or to the empty signifier that is 'poverty' (about which we shall have more to say below). As Elizabeth Bernstein puts it, contemporary abolitionism locates 'all social harm outside of the institutions of corporate capitalism and the state apparatus', such that 'the responsibility for slavery is shifted from structural factors and dominant institutions onto individual deviant men' (in Kempadoo 2015: 16).

This tragic farce is echoed in the policies that abolitionists commonly advocate. For those policies consist predominantly of a-political, technical, market-friendly strategies that leave the market and its unequal property relations entirely un-cha(lle)nged. These include persuading businesses to behave better, pushing governments to better police the bad apples or encouraging consumers to 'shop more responsibly'. In this regard, Slavery Footprint are paradigmatic. Slavery Footprint represent what Allison Page describes as 'an analog to green consumption's carbon footprint' (2014: 1)—in other words, a green-washing device that allows consumers to 'feel better about feeling bad'. They purport to measure consumers' reliance on slave labor by analysing their consumption habits. They do *not* encourage a reduction in consumption, or bring into question wider relations of consumer capitalism. As their founder clearly states: 'Our torches and pitchforks are out for the slave traders, not the multinationals' (Page 2014: 6). What they therefore do is encourage consumers to write letters to the companies with poor supply chain governance records and 'urge' them to do better, or simply to shop with companies certified as 'slavery-free'.

Why is it that modern abolitionists remain so anodyne? Even when activists are seemingly so dedicated to social justice? On the basis of my research with them, I would argue that there are three interrelated reasons. The first is an ideologically conditioned simple *lack of understanding/refusal to understand*. The majority of the abolitionist staff I have interviewed do not have a nuanced grasp of how capitalism works or of the economic vulnerability that is central to it. Although declaring themselves to be outraged by exploitation and injustice, very few have ever actually met a 'forced labourer', and most see exploitation through the reductive binary prism of consent or coercion. As a result, when confronted with data showing that the coerced often consent to their coercion, the common response is one of denial or baffled silence. That silence is echoed when asked why they think that people have to make this choice. While some will identify 'poverty' as the reason, none are able to explain what poverty is, what causes it, or what relation it has to property.

In my analysis, this reflects the sheer hegemony of capitalist ideology over their thinking. Here I am using 'ideology' in the three-dimensional way proposed by Žižek (1994: 11–18). His first dimension is 'ideology as a doctrine, a composite of ideas, beliefs, concepts, and so on, destined to convince us of its "truth", yet actually serving some unavowed power interest'. This corresponds to the more traditional Marxist notion of 'ideology'. His second dimension is 'the materiality of ideology', which corresponds more to the Althusserian 'Ideological State Apparatus' (ISA). His third is what he terms 'ideology-in-and-for-itself… neither ideology *qua* explicit doctrine… nor ideology in its material existence… but the elusive network of implicit, quasi-"spontaneous" presuppositions and attitudes that form an irreducible moment of the reproduction of non-ideological [practices]'. With the abolitionists I interviewed and observed in the course of my research, the power of ideology's first and third dimensions became clear in the fact that it was *literally* un-thinkable for them that severe labour exploitation could be part of, or caused by, capitalist social relations. Their denial and silence it were genuine *aporia*, a real expression of the fact that their mental framework could not account for such disturbing realities. As Mark Fisher (2010) and Jodi Dean (2012) have rightly noted, this is not uncommon in the age of 'capitalist realism'. Ideology is at its most powerful when at its most opaque (Žižek 2012), and under conditions of capitalist realism, it has become so opaque and so naturalised that these abolitionist figures simply cannot see through its fog.

This does not mean, however, that abolitionists do not experience distress. On the contrary, their denial reflects their distress clearly, while the invocation of the word 'poverty' is surely a doomed attempt by those who reject denial to fill the void which erupts when their framework is confronted by its own contradictions. Here we may turn instructively to Lacan and Laclau.[3] Lacan shows that the human psyche is irredeemably primed to seek narrative closure, because absences of meaning are too disquieting for us to entertain. In order to cope, therefore, we identify ourselves with closed, narrative totalities that build meaning for us. Crucially, when these break down (when, in Lacanian terms, the 'Real' irrupts into our narrative Reality), we are thrust into the disturbing position of having to respond. Our response can either be to confront the ultimate impossibility of total narrative closure, to adopt a new narrative, or to seek to reconstruct the old. The abolitionist invocation of poverty falls into this latter camp. As Laclau would have it, it is an attempt to suture the tear in the capitalist imaginary by using the patch of poverty. This is a capitalist ideological response *par excellence*. For what the word 'poverty' does is to locate the cause of 'forced labour' again *outside* of capitalism, rather than as both a consequence and a part thereof. This is nothing other than a deferral, for poverty is itself an empty signifier that has no positive content of its own—it is an a-historical description of what is, rather than an historicised account of *why*. In this respect, the invocation of 'poverty' as causal represents a parallel to the very creation of the concepts of 'modern slavery', 'trafficking' and 'forced labour' in the first place. Indeed, it represents the next step in the psychic-conceptual self-defence strategy of which their creation is the beginning. Both are attempts to preserve the integrity of the capitalist imaginary and its foundational principles, in the face of real-world experiences that manifest their practical-theoretical impossibility. 'Modern slavery', 'trafficking' and 'forced labour' thus arguably represent what may be understood as capitalism's Real, its un-symbolisable 'constitutive outside'. When they force their way back 'inside', 'poverty' comes to the rescue to fill the necessary conceptual void.

The pathos of this may be lost on most abolitionists, but not all. Some of those I interviewed or have worked with are troubled by their *aporia* and others do have a sense of where it comes from. Yet despite their understanding, many are prevented from saying or doing anything about it, phenomena I have elsewhere described as the *politics of silence* and the *politics of representation* (Howard 2012). In brief, these politics operate as follows: either (1) abolitionist staff may be forbidden by their (capitalist) donors from identifying the political-structural forces that sustain the poverty (propertylessness) that I have argued in this chapter's first section underpins exploitation, or (2) they may self-censor in the knowledge that the truth does not sell, whereas sensationalist stories of outside-of-the-system suffering do.

On the first point, *I do not wish to suggest that abolitionists are corrupt, at least not in the conventional sense of that term. Rather, the problem is that those* who pay their wages and fund their work are the very same governments or corporations with greatest stake in the status quo (Kempadoo 2015). The latter are virtually all neoliberal. For them, inequality is almost entirely off the table. And when it is on the table, it is (to be) understood as a problem of exclusion from the (benefits of) the market, rather than as a consequence of differential and adverse *inclusion* within it (Phillips 2013). Their discourse constructs wealth as a consequence of endeavour. It admits no challenge to its legitimacy and denies that it could rely on profiting from the fact that some people are too poor to say no to exploitative work. What this in turn leads to is the propagation of a sensationalist, simplistic narrative depicting trafficking, slavery or forced labour as existing entirely *outside of capitalism*, the straightforward consequence of bad men choosing to abuse innocent victims (and again, it is usually men, even if these particular men are implicitly non-white and non-wealthy). As one very senior abolitionist bluntly told me: 'we must avoid discussion of politics'. Or, in the words of another: 'this story is "sexy", it raises money, and it mobilises support'.

Many abolitionists are thus caught in a catch-22 situation. Squeezed on one side *by their paymasters and on the other by the rigours of fundraising, they are reduced to peddling a story that protects the very injustices responsible for what they stand against. If they say otherwise and mobilise around alternatives that challenge foundational inequalities, they risk losing the money that enables them to do anything at all.* Under these circumstances, the rise of such an a-political, *technical*, consumer-centred version of abolitionism must be understood as a perfect hegemonic coup by the forces of the established order.[4] Its corporatised co-optation of dissent channels outrage at systemic injustices away from any collective, politicised resistance to them (Dauvergne and LeBaron 2014).

Basic Income as a Potential Way Forward

So what, then, is to be done? If the modern abolitionist movement wishes to be more than a mere fig-leaf for injustice and wants to achieve more than simply making consumers and activists feel better about feeling bad, what options does it have? Does it have any at all? In this chapter's final section, I will argue that its most promising option is to politicise its analysis of labour exploitation, to unite as a field against donor restrictions, and to rally behind a policy that could have genuine emancipatory potential, precisely because it seeks to overcome the economic vulnerability pertaining to propertylessness. This policy is the UBI.

UBI has a long and respected pedigree. Thomas Paine advocated a version of it in *Agrarian Justice*, it has had modern supporters ranging from Russell to Rawls, and now even established progressive political parties are taking it up (Blaschke 2012). What does it entail? The idea is as simple as it is disarming: give everyone a regular stipend sufficient to guarantee survival, with no strings attached. The amount is not intended to make you rich, but to prevent you from going hungry (Van Parijs 1992: 1). In this regard, it represents a good faith response to the economic vulnerability characterising a world of unequal property relations. For if, as we have seen, control over private property is necessary for survival, then it is crucial that everybody possesses a necessary minimum. In seeking to ensure that they do, UBI aims to actualise what Philippe Van Parijs (1992) calls 'real freedom'—that is, the ability to say 'no' to labour, to withhold one's consent, and to resist what Marx termed 'the dull compulsion of economic relations' (see also Widerquist 2013).

Importantly for our purposes, UBI is no longer simply utopian theory. It has also been explored in practice. UNICEF have recently completed a large-scale pilot study with the Self-Employed Women's Association in India to trial UBI among thousands of villagers in the state of Madhya Pradesh (Davala et al. 2015). The findings attest to the policy's multi-dimensional emancipatory potential. In this case, it led to an increase in economic activity among the poor, generated improvements in things ranging from nutrition to sanitation, and had egalitarian outcomes that saw greater benefits for women than for men and for the poorest vis-à-vis the wealthy. Most significant of all, however, it had profoundly liberatory consequences. It engendered a clear decrease in debt bondage, as poor villagers were able either to pay off their debts or to accumulate sufficient cash reserves to avoid indebting themselves in the first place.

The importance of this cannot be overstated. As I have argued throughout this essay, the labour exploitation denoted by the terms 'trafficking', 'slavery' and 'forced labour' often results when people lack suitable alternatives to that exploitation. Yet by guaranteeing that all people possess a sufficient monetary minimum, UBI has the potential to ensure that no one finds themselves in this position. This is equivalent to replacing the patchy existing social safety-nets—through the gaps in which many will always fall—with an unconditional floor on which everybody can stand (Van Parijs 1992: 5).

Conclusion

The argument I have sought to make in this essay turns on a very simple premise—that the 'freedom' held so dear by capitalist ideologues can only be substantively meaningful when every 'yes' is backed by a potential 'no'. Despite professing their allegiance to self-owning liberty, the architects of the market economy have designed it in such a way as to deny that liberty to most people. This is why the arbitrary division between 'free' and 'forced' labour is so dishonest. In reality, many people have no alternative to the exploitation offered by their 'employers'. This is capitalism's original sin. And although it is re-enacted every day on the body of the exploited worker, that re-enactment is hidden precisely by the idea contained in the terms 'slavery', 'trafficking' and 'forced labour'.

The modern abolitionist movement exists officially to put an end to the exploitation denoted by this terminology. Yet in its current guise it hinders more than it helps. For by positioning exploitation as an anomaly lying *outside* of capitalism, instead of representing capitalism's major failings, it stifles any possible conversation about how we might organise things differently. This reduces modern abolitionists to the status of unwitting accomplices, blindly defending the unjust status quo.

One alternative to this sad state of affairs would be for abolitionists to unite in calling for a worldwide UBI. This of course requires them to be far more *politicised* than they currently are and, once this politicisation has taken place, for them to unite in resistance against existing donor restrictions. Such a move would be bold, and there can be no doubt that implementation of a successfully advocated UBI would pose technical and political challenges—not least how to ensure that its introduction did not come at the expense of other public goods provision (Bergmann 2005), or with non-recipient migrants being reduced to denizen status (Wright 2005: 7; Cruz 2013). But humanity surely possesses the collective wherewithal to suitably answer these questions if only sufficient political will can be mobilised.

Intriguingly, for all their current failings and for all we may rightly assume that a politicised abolitionism remains a long way off, abolitionists are uniquely well placed to lead that mobilisation, since they enjoy quite unrivalled discursive power. Nobody is *for* what is commonly understood as slavery; everybody is against it. This is why the abolitionist call to 'end slavery within a generation' goes entirely unopposed and garners allies ranging from the global business elite to the Pope himself (Jenkins 2011). If abolitionists were to channel this discursive energy into an advocacy effort behind basic income, might the idea not shift rapidly from the margins to the mainstream? Moreover, might it not conceivably bring 'the enemy' on board? The idea has, after all, been described as 'the capitalist road to communism' (Van der Veen and Van Parijs 1986). Because what self-respecting capitalist could possibly object to a policy that enhances 'free labour', or that makes consent real by giving people the chance to withhold it?

Notes

1. As Cohen has it, 'Self-ownership ensures that my right to use my fist as I please stops at the tip of your nose, because of your rights, under maximal self-ownership, over your nose' (1994: 215).
2. In the more extreme, Nozickian formulation, it even includes even redistributive taxation, since Nozick sees taxation as incompatible with self-governing liberty in the same way that slavery is incompatible with liberty. Unsurprisingly, Nozick concedes the legitimacy of a tax that pays for the police force, even as he rejects the same tax being spent on 'welfare' (1974).
3. Here I draw variously on: Stavrakakis (1999), Laclau and Mouffe (2001), Critchley and Marchart (2004), Glynos and Stavrakakis (2004).
4. Itself a parallel to the many other ways that neoliberalism's major powerbrokers render technical problems that are eminently political—as indeed tragically evidenced by the European discourse around Greek exit from the Euro.

Acknowledgements Research for this essay was funded by European Union Marie Curie Actions, and by the EUI's Migration Policy Centre. Neil is grateful for this funding, and for the generous editorial assistance provided by this volume's editors, as well as by Asha Amirali. Portions of the essay were previously published as media articles with *Al-Jazeera* and *openDemocracy*.

References

Anderson, B. (2007). *Motherhood, Apple Pie and Slavery: Reflections on Trafficking Debates* (COMPAS Working Paper Series 47). Oxford: Centre on Migration, Policy and Society.

Andrijasevic, R. (2010). *Migration, Agency and Citizenship in Sex Trafficking*. Basingstoke: Palgrave Macmillan.

Banaji, J. (2003). The Fictions of Free Labour: Contract, Coercion, and So-Called Unfree Labour. *Historical Materialism, 11*(3), 69–95.

Bergmann, B. R. (2005). A Swedish-Style Welfare State or Basic Income: Which Should Have Priority? In E. O. Wright (Ed.), *Redesigning Distribution* (pp. 130–142). London: Verso Books.

Blaschke, R. (2012). *From the Idea of a Basic Income to the Political Movement in Europe: Development and Questions*. Berlin: Rosa Luxemburg Siftung.

Brace, L. (2004). *The Politics of Property: Labour, Freedom and Belonging*. Edinburgh: Edinburgh University Press.

Cohen, G. A. (1994). *Self-Ownership, Freedom and Equality*. Cambridge: Cambridge University Press.

Critchley, S., & Marchart, O. (Eds.). (2004). *Laclau: A Critical Reader*. Abingdon and New York: Routledge.

Cruz, K. (2013). Unmanageable Work, (Un)liveable Lives: The UK Sex Industry, Labour Rights and the Welfare State. *Journal of Social and Legal Studies, 22*(4), 465–488.

Dauvergne, P., & LeBaron, G. (2014). *Protest Inc*. Cambridge: Polity.

Davala, S., Jhabvala, R., Mehta, S. K., & Standing, G. (2015). *Basic Income: A Transformative Policy for India*. London: Bloomsbury.

Dean, J. (2012). *The Communist Horizon*. London: Verso Books.

Fisher, M. (2010). *Capitalist Realism: Is There No Alternative?* London: Zero Books.

Glynos, J., & Stavrakakis, Y. (2004). Encounters of the Real Kind: Sussing Out the Limits of Laclau's Embrace of Laclan. In S. Critchley & O. Marchart (Eds.), *Laclau: A Critical Reader* (pp. 201–216). Abingdon and New York: Routledge.

Heron, B. (2007). *Desire for Development: Whiteness, Gender and the Helping Imperative*. Waterloo, ON: Wilfred Laurier University Press.

Howard, N. (2012). Accountable to Whom? Accountable to What? Understanding Anti-trafficking Discourse and Policy in Southern Benin. *Anti-Trafficking Review, 1*(1), 43–59.

Howard, N. (2013). Promoting 'Healthy Childhoods' and Keeping Children 'At Home': Beninese Anti-trafficking Policy in Times of Neoliberalism. *International Migration, 51*(4), 87–102.

Howard, N. (2016). *Child Trafficking, Youth Labour Mobility and the Politics of Protection*. London: Palgrave Macmillan.

Howard, N., & Morganti, S. (2014). (Not!) Child Trafficking in Benin. In E. Van der Meulen & M. Dragiewicz (Eds.), *Global Human Trafficking: New Research in Context*. London: Routledge.

International Labour Organization (ILO). (2007). *General Survey on Forced Labour*. Geneva: ILO.

Jenkins, J. (2011). 'Pope Francis' Plan to Rescue Millions from Modern-Day Slavery. *Think Progress*. http://thinkprogress.org/economy/2014/12/11/3602687/pope-francis-modern-slavery/.

Kempadoo, K. (2015). The Modern-Day White (Wo)Man's Burden: Trends in Anti-trafficking and Anti-slavery Campaigns. *Journal of Human Trafficking, 1*(1), 8–20.

Kennedy, D. (2004). *The Dark Sides of Virtue*. Princeton: Princeton University Press.

Laclau, E., & Mouffe, C. (2001). *Hegemony and Socialist Strategy: Towards a Radical Democratic Politics* (2nd ed.). London: Verso.

Lerche, J. (2007). A Global Alliance Against Forced Labour? Unfree Labour, Neo-Liberal Globalization and the International Labour Organization. *Journal of Agrarian Change, 7*(4), 425–452.

Marx, K. (1977). *Capital* (Vol. I). Middlesex: Harmondsworth.

Nozick, R. (1974). *Anarchy, State, and Utopia*. New York: Basic Books.

Page, A. (2014). "How Many Slaves Work for You?" Race, New Media, and Neoliberal Consumer Activism. *Journal of Consumer Culture, 17*(1), 1–16.

Phillips, N. (2013). Unfree Labour and Adverse Incorporation in the Global Economy: Comparative Perspectives from Brazil and India. *Economy and Society, 42*(2), 171–196.

Phillips, N., Bhaskaran, R., Nathan, D., & Upendranadh, C. (2014). The Social Foundations of Global Production Networks: Towards a Global Political Economy of Child Labour. *Third World Quarterly, 35*(3), 428–446.

Sharma, N. (2003). Travel Agency: A Critique of Anti-trafficking Campaigns. *Refuge, 21*(3), 53–65.

Slavery Footprint. (2011). How Many Slaves Work for You? http://slaveryfootprint.org/.

Stavrakakis, Y. (1999). *Lacan and the Political*. Abingdon and New York: Routledge.

Steinfeld, R. J. (1991). *The Invention of Free Labor: The Employment Relation in English and American Law and Culture, 1350–1870*. Chapel Hill: University of North Carolina Press.

Van der Veen, R., & Van Parijs, P. (1986). A Capitalist Road to Communism. *Theory & Society, 15*(5), 635–655.

Van Parijs, P. (1992). *Arguing for Basic Income*. London: Verso.

Van Parijs, P. (1997). *Real Freedom for All: What (if Anything) Can Justify Capitalism?*. Oxford: Oxford University Press.

Widerquist, K. (2013). *Independence, Propertylessness, and Basic Income: A Theory of Freedom as the Power to Say No*. Basingstoke: Palgrave Macmillan.

Wright, E. O. (Ed.). (2005). *Redesigning Distribution*. London: Verso Books.

Žižek, S. (1994). *Mapping Ideology*. London: Verso Books.

Žižek, S. (2012). *Living in the End Times*. London: Verso Books.

11

Empowering Women: The Contradictions of Feminist Governance

Srila Roy

We have today a vast apparatus of discourses, practices and strategies aimed at empowering women. This assemblage has made possible the kinds of institutionalised power that feminists increasingly wield in what has come to be known as 'governance feminism'. This chapter looks at a range of sites and practices—all of which would broadly fall under the remit of 'governance feminism'—to extend some of the critiques of the 'modern slavery' paradigm presented in this book from a feminist perspective. In so doing, my observations also expand—I hope—these critiques from being strictly about modern-day abolitionism to a host of other interventions and governmental practices (and their underlying rationalities) in the name of 'saving' women and upholding their rights.

In what follows, I interrogate the rationality and practice of feminist government in the broad context of feminist empowerment strategies especially in the Global South. I move onto the ubiquity that

S. Roy (✉)
University of the Witwatersrand, Johannesburg, South Africa
e-mail: srila.roy@wits.ac.za

L. Brace and J. O'Connell Davidson (eds.), *Revisiting Slavery and Antislavery*,
https://doi.org/10.1007/978-3-319-90623-2_11

rights have come to assume in (neoliberal) development and how the presumption of the rights-bearing subject legitimates contemporary practices of 'saving' women from unfreedom or slavery. I end with a slightly unusual site of feminist intervention but one that echoes many of the rationalities at work on the terrain of (neoliberal) development and human rights, namely the public protest. I use the 2012 Delhi rape case—that has come to be understood as a 'critical event' in terms of shifting the public debate on sexual violence in India—as an instance of constraining women's lives in the name of their protection and further exceptionalising violence against women. All the sites of feminist government considered here make obvious the wider argument at stake in this book, namely, the production of 'unfreedom' in the name of freedom and rights.

Governance Feminism and the Will to Empower

'Governance feminism' is a term coined by Janet Halley and colleagues (Halley et al. 2006) to describe the ways in which transnational feminist advocacy—particularly around trafficking, prostitution and sexual violence—has led to actual tangible change in, for instance, international human rights law. It also refers to the 'mainstreaming' of feminist demands and ideas in the institutions and practices of the state and civil society actors implicated in 'good governance' agendas. For Halley, in particular, governance feminism references the power that feminists have come to wield in domestic, national and supranational agencies with respect to regulating—in the name of bettering—women's lives.

Halley et al. (2006) focus on the key areas in which feminist advocacy has effected institutional change, namely prostitution, sex trafficking, and more recently, wartime sexual violence. They find a common punitive or even carceral tendency in all three instances of governance feminism that is a tendency to 'empower' women through law enforcement and criminalisation, whether partial or complete (as in the case of sex work). Halley et al. (2006: 341) underscore how governance feminism has gained most success in preventing violence against women and protecting its victims 'in the form of, very state-centered, top-down, sovereigntist feminist rule preferences' manifest in the use of criminal law and criminal law enforcement.

It is especially in the area of anti-trafficking interventions that we see the carceral character of governance feminism or what Elizabeth Bernstein (2010) calls 'carceral feminism'. She uses the term to refer to feminism's reliance on statist tools of policing, prosecution and incarceration as punishment and deterrence in order to protect women from (gender-based) violence and to further women's human rights. Bernstein identifies carceral feminism as a subset of both governance feminism and military humanitarianism, which is the deployment of military technologies to secure human rights as in the case of the war on terror (see Grewal 2005). She also understands it in the wider context of neoliberal governmentality that posits market-based as opposed to redistributive solutions to contemporary social problems. This 'neoliberal turn' (Oksala 2013: 32) is especially evident in contemporary development discourse and practice to which, as I discuss further below, women and women's human rights have emerged as key.

A number of key studies show the confluence of different rationalities—be they liberal, neoliberal, punitive and paternal—in the context of anti-trafficking advocacy and activism, whether undertaken by conservative abolitionists or radical feminists. In her reading of the infamous International Justice Mission (IJM), an American Christian non-profit organisation that has pioneered the use of 'raid and rescue' of trafficked women, Padma Govindan (2013) shows how such coercive and carceral strategies are rooted in deeply paternalistic beliefs with respect to victimised women of the Global South. Gretchen Soderlund, also analysing the IJM, remarks how the constitution of 'women as victims in need of protection from harm rather than as subjects deserving of positive rights' (2005: 82) underlies such strategies of rescue. Once 'rescued', women victims are invariably rehabilitated through the offer of low-paid employment or, more and more, through neoliberal economic measures such as 'small-scale business enterprises to manufacture goods that are advertised as having been produced by trafficked victims' (Kapur 2013: 335). Kapur argues that ultimately the solutions posed and practised in the name of women's freedom from this so-called form of modern-day slavery end up serving the conjoint interests of the state, the family and the market, but not those of the trafficked women themselves. It is also interesting to note that women who reject such forms of rehabilitation are presented as suffering from false consciousness in ways that further legitimate the use of punitive measures (cf. Soderlund 2005; Govindan 2013).

The carceral dimension of governance feminism thus raises the following dilemma: whether empowerment strategies intended to protect and enhance the rights of subaltern groups like women are actually coercive and work against their interests? This apparent contradiction is not merely manifest in the most obviously punitive forms of governance feminism namely, those that make explicit use of the criminal justice system and state's security apparatus. The double-edged nature of 'empowering women' can, in fact, be discerned in a range of statist and non-statist interventions in women's rights, their development and in ways that eventually work against their freedom.

Women have emerged as key subjects and objects of contemporary development regimes premised on the global understanding that 'meeting the needs of women [is] key to removing inequalities around the world' (Grewal 2005: 131). National and supranational agencies like the World Bank and the UN have made it a truism that 'development could only work well if women were given help; micro-lending, literacy, and contraception and other health services were all seen as means to this goal' (ibid.). Notwithstanding the progressive lineages of current empowerment speak (see Sharma 2008 for a discussion of the lineages of 'empowerment'), 'empowerment' has come to be seen, by its feminist critics, as paradigmatic of the neoliberal turn in development (Leve 2014; Madhok 2013; Karim 2011; Sharma 2008; Rankin 2001, 2004). These critics map a shift from a liberal feminist emphasis on women's economic inclusion and productivity to a neoliberal discourse of entrepreneurship and privatisation in contemporary development practice. While using a leftist and feminist language of empowerment and agency, neoliberal development is said to enact a form of agency that is opportunistic and, via microcredit, instrumental.

Microfinance is not merely being used in the rehabilitation of those 'freed' from forms of slavery like trafficking but has become a development panacea for resolving gendered poverty. Based on stereotypical cultural and gendered premises that posit women as being better and more reliable investors than men, 'third world women' are the targets and beneficiaries of microcredit (Rankin 2001). Feminist analyses of microcredit have critiqued its deep imbrication with narratives of individualism and entrepreneurism alongside the avoidance of 'structural analyses or critiques' (Moodie 2008: 455). They have also uncovered their problematic and sometimes violent outcomes of microcredit such as the further deepening of rural indebtedness and the gendered vulnerability this gives rise to (see, for example, Karim 2011). For Gayatri Spivak (2000), gender and development programmes, spearheaded by NGOs, impart quick-fix solutions like microfinance and gender training to make subaltern women 'appropriate receivers and servicers of credit'. Poor rural women of the South—the 'new subalterns', as she calls them—are thereby integrated into the circuits of power and capital that remain gendered and racialised. In the absence of wider structural change, the emphasis on microcredit to manage—and not reduce—poverty and that too, via the instrumentalisation of poor women's agency can only be, Spivak (2000: 322) argues, a form of 'credit-baiting'.

In sum, this critical mass of commentary on 'empowering' poor and victimised women, whether undertaken by state or non-state agents including feminist and human rights organisations and advocates, makes the following apparent: that technologies of empowerment that are aimed at liberating women from violence, harm and deprivation are at once technologies of control, surveillance and disciplining. While this duality might be most obvious in the carceral side of governance feminism (in anti-trafficking interventions), it is implicit in attempts to regulate poor and 'rescued' women's entry into a free market that remains riven with asymmetrical gendered power relations. As Jason Hickel (2014: 1356) remarks in relation to the current emphasis not just on the empowerment of women but that of adolescent girls: 'Women and girls are made to bear the responsibility for bootstrapping themselves out of poverty that is caused in part by the very institutions that purport to save them'. Taking together the carceral and neoliberal side of governance feminism, the use of gender to advance market-based interests and solutions as well as to strengthen domestic and international security discourses suggest how empowerment technologies, whether undertaken by the state or progressives, can create as many spaces of unfreedom for women as they (purportedly) enable their freedom.

Sexual Governance in Early and Forced Marriage

A site upon which we can observe the convergence of such developmental interventions into women's lives and the discourse around modern slavery is that of early and forced marriage. Recent studies (Hickel 2014; Koffman and Gill 2013) observe the increasing focus on adolescent girls or young women as key catalysts for social change in the Global South. As opposed to women per se, it is now young women who are presented as being key to economic growth and poverty eradication in low-income countries while also having the potential to 'contribut[e] to family health and slow[ing] the growth of the population' (Hickel 2014: 1356). In what the Nike Foundation has termed the 'Girl Effect', major development agencies including the World Bank and IMF in partnership with corporations like Nike, Coca Cola and Goldman Sachs are now investing specifically in the skills and labour of adolescent girls (Hickel 2014; see Koffman and Gill 2013). This includes focusing on their schooling and delaying marriage. Hickel (2014) shows how the remaking of kinship and family structure is part of the rationality of the 'girl effect' project/discourse. For, in order for individuals—women and men—to be full participants in a free market, they must be freed from the shackles of family, society and culture, which are identified as 'pre-modern'. In other words, the current developmental goal of empowering adolescent girls is not only about the aggressive integration of such subjects into the market but also about transforming ideas of personhood, kinship, family and relationships such that these 'less developed' societies can evolve from being pre-modern to modern. Besides this evolutionary rationality, Hickel identifies the demands of Western liberalism—the ideals of individual freedom and the rights-bearing citizen-subject—as key drivers of this transformation of the status of the girl ('personal empowerment') and the wider structure in which she finds herself ('economic growth') (Hickel 2014: 1359).

Personal empowerment is the explicit aim of eradicating 'child marriage' when it comes to organisations like Anti-Slavery International and Girls Not Brides. Needless to say, these organisations and campaigns understand child marriage as a form of modern-day slavery. In their media reportage and campaign materials, they present child marriage as preventing girls—strictly from the Global South given the 'cultural' dimension to this practice—from fulfilling their true potential 'to play, to go to school, to dream about what their futures might hold for them' and become instead 'child brides, child mothers, domestic servants' (Warner 2014). They also compare child marriage to slavery because of the assumed lack of informed consent, the inability to leave the marriage and enforced domesticity. Child marriage is thus distinguished from 'normal' marriage, which is equated with mutual consent, respect and equality. Although campaigners often note that adults too suffer experiences that amount to slavery and that 'child marriage' is not always slavery, these qualifiers are quickly set aside to declare the following: 'our study suggests that a potentially high proportion of the millions of children in marriage globally could be in slavery as a result' (Turner 2013). For these organisations, ending this form of slavery is tied to current development logics and ends: empowerment. Their campaign materials present alternatives to marriage such as education or work or savings and loan activities.

Both the rhetoric around 'modern slavery' and on 'underdevelopment' use 'culture', 'gender' and 'tradition' as substitutes for understanding power relations and structural determinants for the low or 'backward' status of women and girls in particular societies of the Global South. Poverty and the lack of mobility and resources—to which the development institutions committed to 'empowerment' have ironically played no small role (see Hickel 2014)—are often greater drivers than custom or tradition when it comes to the choices open to poor families in matters of marriage. Given, however, the attachment that both governance feminism and the modern slavery movement have to economic growth as a key strategy of 'saving' women, 'culture' assumes easy explanatory power in place of a serious appraisal of the feminisation of poverty and women's underdevelopment. Not surprisingly, Hickel (2014: 1369) notes how—as in the case of microcredit, discussed above—'initiatives designed to empower girls by encouraging their participation in the labour market often end up placing them in new forms of subservience as workers in a context wherein wages are unfair and conditions unsafe'. A similar critique can be applied to the self-help and micro-credit fads so popular among development institutions today. These approaches seek to empower women to participate in the market and thus lift themselves out of poverty, but they ignore the fact that this kind of self-help is impossible on a large scale without market regulations and state subsidies that favour small enterprises, and without welfare arrangements to support people when they fail. Yet these arrangements are being rolled back, through structural adjustment, by the same organisations that promote micro-credit.

Besides the lack of viable alternatives to marriage, both the modern slavery and 'Girl Effect' movement presume a clear divide between consensual and non-consensual marriage, largely based on the category of the child. While this divide is, as I discuss in greater detail below, less than sustainable, the discursive transformation of 'child marriage' into 'slavery' entirely obliterates from view the difficult question of what choice a young girl in fact has in marriage. In countries like India, child marriage has long attracted a series of domestic interventions whether by the state or civil society activists like NGOs or even feminist activists. Even though it is illegal for girls under 18 and boys under 21 to get married in India,[1] child marriage persists in large parts of the country where it is perfectly normal on the grounds of practical necessity and tradition for minor girls to be married and even sold into marriage. The practice is especially widespread amongst the poor, dalits and Backward Castes[2] but also amongst minority communities like Muslims (Agnes 2013; Sunder Rajan 2003). Law enforcement is negligible and no one has ever been prosecuted under the Prohibition of Child Marriage Act (2006), the recently revamped version of the 1929 Child Marriage Restraint Act.

While civil society advocates—whether local-level NGOs or transnational anti-slavery organisations—call for more draconian laws and more stringent law enforcement to abolish child marriage (Dhareshwar as discussed in Sunder Rajan 2003), the feminist legal scholar, Flavia Agnes (2013) not only points to the failure of the law to curb early marriage at the community level but to the fact that the law has actually strengthened patriarchal paternal power and control over young women's sexuality, diminishing their potential for exercising choice in intimate matters. Agnes turns to 'elopement cases' or to marriages of choice by young people that are policed and curbed through the force of the legal provision around child marriage, especially when they are seen to transgress caste and communal boundaries.[3] In other words, girls are falsely projected as minors—by the family and state representatives alike—to dismiss their choice to marry partners of their own and ultimately to regulate their sexuality. Such 'elopement marriages', as Agnes (2012) calls them, have recently been the focus of international media attention given their association with 'honour killings' at the hands of caste-based *khap* panchayats [caste and clan-based councils] in rural north India.[4] More routinely, elopement cases are transformed, often through the active support of the police in collusion with parents and community heads, into cases of abduction thereby blurring the distinction between consensual sex and rape (Baxi 2014), love and seduction (Baxi 2014; Mody 2008), force and consent (Mody 2008) and effectively criminalising 'contentious' (Chowdhry 2007) forms of love, intimacy and marriage.

Given such a complicated matrix of power and powerlessness, can progressive—especially feminist—intervention into this arena be purely carceral, which is to say, simply entail criminalising all such marriages? The call upon the state to protect women's rights is deeply problematic in a context where the state's sexual security regime is powerfully manifest in the routine regulation of women's sexuality, especially when it is expressed through choice in matters of marriage and love. Feminist governance around gender and sexual rights, as in the case of child marriage, thus has to thus exercise great caution in inviting the state to 'protect' women from harm.

But even in the case of community-based forms of feminist government such as feminist grassroots NGOs, one finds the confluence of state and market interests in the service of protecting women. I recently observed the politics around developmental interventions into forms of gendered oppression—'child marriage'—in the Indian state of West Bengal and centred on the actions of a self-identified feminist NGO.

In its dealings with cases of early marriages in the operational area, NGO workers adopted distinctly carceral approaches in their deliberate use of the legal sanction against child marriage as a strategy of deterrence and fear. On least one observable instance, the NGO even threatened to stop the microfinance programme that it ran in the area, threatening to withhold scarce economic resources from an entire community of women, in the name of saving young women. At the same time, NGO workers adopted paternal and protective dispositions towards the young women who were the subjects of such gender-based violence. Young women who 'chose' to marry early were infantilised, their expressed agency and desire to get married dismissed as they were reduced to objects—and not agents—of rescue and reform by NGO workers. Other solutions that the NGO proposed to the problem of early marriage—such as employment and education—were also limited to neoliberal visions of gender justice without a broader sense of or attempt at redistribution of resources and wealth.

In the case of early marriage, it is the category of 'force', unfreedom or the lack of consent and agency that places such practices alongside those of 'modern slavery' under consideration in this book. And, as in the case of practices like trafficking and forced migration, bonded and indebted labour, and sexual commerce, the division between freedom and unfreedom becomes less than sustainable in the context of marriage. Julia O'Connell Davidson (2015) has argued that 'modern slavery' discourse and activism fails to recognise or address the structures that constrain the choices of *all* women and not just minority women or those from the 'third world'. Given that new abolitionist writings and campaign materials hinge on the category of consent as marking the line between 'marriages that are free and those that are a form of modern slavery', how easy is it, she (ibid.) asks, 'to draw a clear line between 'forced' and 'voluntary' marriage in the contemporary world [...]?'

In the context of 'forced marriage' in the UK, Anitha and Gill (2009) focus on how 'force' forms the basis of a presumed divide between arranged and forced marriages in legal and policy discourses. A polarised understanding of consent and coercion based on the (Western) privileging of free will prevents an appreciation of the varying levels of expectations, pressures and constraints that all—and not only minority—women face in matters of marriage. As a consequence of universalist *and* culturalist assumptions, the law not only remains inadequate in capturing women's ambivalent agency but also ends up further constraining it in the name of protection. Such statist and legalistic responses reinforce culturally-based and racially-inflected gendered stereotypes, and ultimately they do little to uphold women's rights. As in the case of anti-trafficking interventions, they have ramifications that extend far beyond the remit of women's rights such as strengthening immigration control and extending the remit of the securocratic state (see also Gangoli and Chantler 2009).

For several critical commentators writing in the area of sex work and early and forced marriage, the agency-oppression and concomitantly, consent-coercion binary cannot represent the experience of the vast majority of women that lies in the grey area between these absolutes, for whom consent is potentially a product of necessity but for whom necessities or compulsions cannot be straightforwardly read as 'coercion' (Anitha and Gill 2009; Gangoli and Chantler 2009; Agnes 2012; Shah 2014). This polarisation stems from the particular kind of imagined subject that contemporary empowerment strategies rely on, namely the sovereign autonomous subject of liberalism.

Rights and the Liberal Subject

A 'rights-based' approach to development has become more and more normative since it was proposed in the late 1990s. In a nutshell, the attempt was to embed concerns around human—political and civil—rights upon the economic and social terrain that development practitioners concerned themselves with, especially given the high levels of discrimination, inequality and violence that particular subjects of development face globally. It is thus no surprise that women (and not gender; see Grewal 2005) have emerged as key sites for the 'conceptual marriage of human rights with development' (Madhok 2013: 171).

There is already considerable criticism of rights-based approaches to development. It is fair to say that much of the initial enthusiasm with which academic, activists and development experts—especially those working on women and gender—received this approach as progressive and potentially politicising of otherwise depoliticised development is now muted. These critiques echo more general feminist ones around the liberal underpinnings of rights discourses, such as their easy co-option by the state or market, their universalising and homogenising tendencies, and their abstraction from particular social contexts that often mean that they only serve rhetorical functions (see Madhok 2013; Grewal 2005; Cornwall and Molyneux 2007 with respect to development). While it is beyond the scope (and aim) of this essay to rehearse these arguments here, I focus on two recent critiques of the liberal underpinnings of rights talk and practices that have a direct bearing on the kind of rights-based feminist governance at stake in this essay. The two critiques I draw on—respectively concerned with the politics of neoliberal development and the global sex trade—also suggest the similarly contested ways in which normative liberal ideas of rights and the rights-bearing subject have travelled to the distinct domains of feminist governance and human rights with similar effects.

Underlying both Sumi Madhok and Julia O'Connell Davidson's critiques of rights-based interventions into developmental problems and sex work respectively is the particular kind of subject that these assume, namely the sovereign autonomous subject of liberalism (see also Hickel 2014). For Madhok (2013) whose ethnographic site is the unique state-cum-feminist Women's Development Programme in Northern India, the autonomous subject linked to notions of individualism, voluntarism, free-will and action makes it impossible to view subjects of development (poor and marginalised women development workers or *sathins*, in her case) as inhabiting more complex subjectivities: as being socially embedded, relational, precariously positioned and engaging in development work in a not straightforwardly agentive manner. In effect, Madhok criticises the manner in which the agency of women—particularly subaltern women from the Global South—has become central to the moral legitimacy and political gravitas that neoliberal developmentalism in particular affords itself (see also Wilson 2008). The rhetorical foregrounding of women's agency in development has two related and politically troubling effects: first, it diverts attention away from the actual contexts of oppression and inequality that inform the workings of individual agency; second, it eclipses from view agential acts that subjects might engage in but that do not conform to its model of voluntarist, individualised and autonomous agency. Modalities of empowering poor subaltern women or protecting their rights thus end up ascribing new forms of vulnerability over existing ones in ways that metropolitan feminists implicated in such developmental projects have not always considered.

If Madhok is worried about the assumed existence of fully sovereign subjects in development discourse and interventions at the cost of recognising their complexity and actively reinforcing their vulnerability, O'Connell Davidson (2005, 2015) is concerned with the presumption of fully coerced subjects in anti-sex trafficking strategies. While Madhok indicts developmental interventions for not seeing subaltern agency as situated in and moulded by oppressive contexts, O'Connell Davidson indicts abolitionists for not recognising the presence of agency, albeit situated and conditioned, in the sex industry. Children, in particular, are constituted as objects of rescue and salvation, entirely evacuated of agency and autonomy, and removed from the particular social political context in which trading in sex presents itself as an option. O'Connell Davidson shows how children exhibit agency in highly oppressive contexts (such as sex work) where it is literally inconceivable as per the liberal parameters of agency. In place of protectionist and punitive strategies that are legitimated in the name of 'saving' the powerless, she forwards 'a more complex vision of autonomy, moral agency and human sociality than that provided by liberalism' (O'Connell Davidson 2005: 151): one that recognises that we are all simultaneously objects and subjects, agents and victims, and resists the false oppositions between agency and coercion that the production of 'sovereign selves' relies on.

The two different kinds of assumptions about subjects and agents that are under critique in Madhok's and O'Connell Davidson's work converge in standard liberal conceptions of the rights-bearing subject: the rights-bearing individual is either perceived to be capable of acting on the basis of and in accordance with her own free will ('pure' consent) *or* as having her free will curbed or effaced by external forces and thus being subject to pure force. Mobilised in the context of feminist governmentality, such conceptions of the subject inform technologies of empowerment that manifest in the form of (a) a refusal to recognise forms of agency that deviate from liberal expectations of 'authentic' agency and (b) an expectation that subaltern women will—given an appropriately enabling environment—make choices that are sovereign and autonomous and thus present a challenge to existing power relations. As previously noted, victims of early and forced marriage are invariably placed upon this terrain as occupying one or the other extreme of this binary. As Svati Shah (2014) notes in researching sex work in Western India, the 'broad dichotomies of "choice" and "force" have come to define the limits of what can be asked about the experience of selling sexual services' thereby eclipsing from view 'a complicated matrix of decisions, and of power and powerlessness, in which people aim to negotiate their best option for economic survival'.

There is thus a demand to abandon the coercion-consent binary and frame these debates in terms of the contextual complexity and particularity of women's lives 'for careful, historically situated analyses of women's struggles to gain power in a world rarely of their own choosing' (Parpart et al., cited in Madhok and Rai 2012). Beyond its inability to grasp, then, the empirical reality of most women's lives, the presumption of the rights-bearing or sovereign autonomous subject of liberalism underscores the contradictions inherent to feminist governance. This is because the 'governed' individual is presumed, in a classically liberal sense, to have the capacity to act freely and rationally but to be prevented from doing so by external constraints. The task of external agents of governance is, from this perspective, simply to enable the actualisation of individual autonomy, free of external dictates of custom, tradition or direct coercion (Mahmood 2001). The removal of external constraints on freedom in order to enable the individual to exercise free choice and will is ultimately what legitimates the will to empower and its practices, both punitive or paternal.

The next and final section looks at a site outside of the remit of governance feminism and one that has traditionally been the locus of feminist optimism: the public protest. I turn to the unprecedented public protests that took place after the 2012 gang rape and murder of a young student in Delhi. These were informed, I argue, by the same rationalities that are at work in institutionalised forms of feminism and were expressed in similarly carceral and neoliberal ways.

Protesting Publics: The 2012 Delhi Rape

The brutal gang rape and murder of 23-year-old Jyoti Singh Pandey in Delhi in December 2012 has come to constitute a 'critical event' in contemporary India (Roy 2014). This is largely ascribable to the unprecedented public protests around sexual violence that the event propelled. A large constituent of the protests were politically unorganised and unaffiliated young people, rightly described as an 'otherwise indifferent middle-class youth' (Dutta and Sircar 2013: 294). These protests transformed the judicial and discursive landscape by forcing a new legal response (the 2013 Criminal Law Amendment Act) and by 'mainstreaming' the experience and politics of rape that had hitherto functioned as a 'public secret' in India, known but not spoken of (Baxi 2012, 2014). What is also well known of the mass movement that followed the Delhi rape was that it was comprised of different and fairly divergent publics, not all of which were exclusively informed by the vocabularies of India's vibrant and long standing women's movement: 'the 2012 protests were, and are, yet to become feminist', as one set of commentators put it (Dutta and Sircar 2013: 297). Indeed many self-identified Indian feminist activists recoiled with horror at some of the calls for chemical castration and death of rapists that were heard on the streets of the capital more loudly than the more progressive calls for *azadi* or freedom for women.[5] Manisha Sethi (2012) voices these feminist anxieties when she says:

> While we applaud the sudden centrality of sexual violence in our public discourse, the outpouring of rage and anger has in fact reinforced and reiterated many of the things that democratic movements have been struggling hard against: tough laws, jettisoning of due process, securitisation of our spaces and lives, and stigmatisation of the rape victim (fate worse than death). But most of all, the very dangerous idea that revenge is an alternative to justice.

Justice as retribution was concretised not only in the state's handing out of the death penalty to four of the accused in Pandey's case but more viscerally, in the death of one of the accused while in the custody of the Indian government. Ram Singh, the bus driver, was found hanging in his cell in Tihar jail while awaiting trial. His death was seen as divine retribution by most sections of India's urban public.

There have been several recent and rich readings of what Anupama Roy (2014) has called the *izzat* or masculinist honour strand of the Delhi protests (in contrast to the feminist *azadi*/freedom strand) and the state response it legitimated: namely, stringent sentencing including the use of the death penalty, greater policing, calls to contain women's freedom and mobility in the name of protection, criminal as opposed to social justice, and ultimately the strengthening of the state's sexual security regime. For Kapur (2013), it is the continued focus on and appeal to the state as the chief custodian of women's rights by feminists and human rights advocates alike that enables largely statist, carceral and securatised responses to violence against women as opposed to—and against—securing their rights and liberties. Equally, for Dutta and Sircar, it is the feminist faith in the law that—in spite of limited material efficacy in the Indian context—has served to 'strengthe[n] state power to police women's sexuality' and in the name of protecting some subjects (heterosexual women/good/chaste/respectable) while casting others as outside of its protective reach (Dutta and Sircar 2013: 300). Even as the 2012 Delhi protests led to the constitution of the three-member Justice Verma Committee that recommended changes in the criminal law on sexual violence that were far-reaching and feminist, the government chose to disregard these. The 2013 Criminal Law Amendment Act that it passed based on the committee's recommendations fixed the age of consent at 18, exempted marital rape, retained the death penalty, immunised from prosecution (and thereby exceptionalised) sexual violence at the hands of the army and refused to recognise violence against transgender persons (Dutta and Sircar 2013). Not only has the failure of legal reform post the Delhi rape, then, led to renewed feminist dilemmas about the law's potential to achieve gender justice but it served to limit legal, political and ultimately wider common sense understandings of sexual violence and its subjects and objects to visions of criminal justice. Kapur (2013) juxtaposes such a discursive framing of sexual violence—that promotes, she says, 'protectionism and infantilism'—with the framework of rights that was foregrounded in the Justice Verma Committee report.

Anupama Roy (2014) further notes that what was evoked in the *izzat* strand of public protest—and materialised in the legal reform that was subsequent to it—was not simply the punitive power of the state but also its pastoral or paternal power. Gender was articulated within a framework of 'victimhood' invoking the 'logic of masculinist protection' to demand strong action from the state (Roy 2014: 61). This is not surprising given that the masculinist ideology of the state is manifest, she argues via the political theorist Iris Marion Young, through coercion and paternal protection. Coercion and protection serve the same purpose: 'to launch an unprecedented reinforcement of its coercive apparatus through the enactment of new extra-ordinary laws, vigorous application of existing ones, establishment of surveillance systems and repression of dissent' (ibid.: 61). Women are brought with greater force as 'obedient, docile and consenting citizens' under the 'disciplinary power of the state'. Roy goes onto show how, in the idioms of honour, shame, nationalism and Indian womanhood deployed in narratives around sexual violence since the Delhi rape, the state allied itself with the heteronormative family to 'protect' women through strategies of disciplining.

The caste-class politics of the Delhi rape were the final locus of reflections in its wake. Many commented on the selective mourning of rape victims on caste-class, metropolitan and non-metropolitan lines given the excessive (national and international) media attention that Pandey's case got as against the erasure—and thereby normalisation (Ramdas cited in Dutta and Sircar 2013: 299)—of the routine forms of violence that dalit and adivasi women in India face. For Roychowdhury (2013), however, mediatised representations of the victim and her assailants did not simply voice long-standing class-based and urban Indian interests but were closely tied to neoliberal ideologies. Jyoti Singh Pandey came to be presented—and partly mourned—as a quintessential neoliberal subject in being aspirational, independent, rights-bearing and standing in for a globally resonant 'modern' female subjectivity in the Third World. In sharp contrast, her assailants came to represent a 'backward' India rooted in the rural, tradition and working class subjectivity. Why, ultimately, we are able to mourn for Pandey in ways that we are not for other (dalit, adivasi,

Muslim) victims of India's rape culture is, Roychowdhury (2013: 285) seems to argue, because her representation:

> fits easily into a growing consumer-oriented, neoliberal economy. The violence inflicted on her body becomes legible as a violation because it fetters her desire for modernity and its accoutrements. And as such, her violation rationalizes a set of politicized claims.

Unlike Kapur for whom carceral responses to violence against women diminish women's rights, for Roychowdhry women's rights are themselves being secured in problematic ways: on behalf of protecting the rights and liberties of particular subjects, mostly elites who can participate in a neoliberal economy *and* at the expense and exploitation of those who cannot, and who are further disenfranchised from it.

Conclusion: The Limits of Freedom

From the discussion of the 2012 Delhi rape and the protests that ensued around it, some things clearly converge with the wider terrain of feminist governmentality that has been under consideration in this chapter.

First, feminist governance, including rallying around violence against women, has not precluded the deployment of technologies that are both punitive and paternal. In fact, in all the instances of governance feminism at stake here—from anti-trafficking interventions to the regulation of early and forced marriage—the punitive and paternalistic character of feminist governmentality is manifest. We see how relations of empowerment can be both voluntary and coercive insofar as they seek to elicit the voluntary support and compliance of individuals and groups, but also to coerce them, even through punitive and carceral means, when they are unwilling to act in their own 'best interests' (Cruikshank 1999). In the Delhi protests, those who called upon criminal justice did so in the name of women's protection, while the state also responded in carceral ways in the name of 'protecting' women and upholding their rights. Carceral and paternal technologies of empowerment are thus in service of securing women's rights such that rights cannot be juxtaposed as being outside of these governmental rationalities (as Kapur (2013) seems to suggest). The feminist and sexual governance undertaken by states and non-state actors alike is in the name of rights, and rights talk and work is part of such governance.

Second, governance feminism serves the current neoliberal focus of sovereign states and major development agents and corporations alike. In a neoliberal context where self-empowerment is intended to free the individual from dependence on the state, feminist actors posit solutions to social problems that advance state and donor agendas in being market-based rather than redistributive. Subalterns are disciplined into the rationalities and practices of the purportedly free market in order to help themselves. Johanna Oksala (2013) reminds us how women could not traditionally inhabit the quintessential liberal subject—individual, autonomous, self-interested—given their near conflation with the domain and ideology of marriage, kinship and family. However, with the neoliberal turn where all domains of social life come to be rationalised through cost-benefit calculation, women can be fully liberal—not only as individual subjects of rights but as 'egotistical subjects of interest' (Oksala 2013: 42). The public outrage against Pandey's working class assailants bespeaks an overarching governmental rationality in which 'the measure of women's liberation has become individual economic success and the choices women are able to make' (ibid.: 44).

Third, empowerment strategies do not straightforwardly 'empower' women and girls and enhance their freedom. In fact, they often have the opposite effect of reducing their mobility and freedom and increasing their vulnerability to power and violence. This (unintended) effect can be seen in the explicit use of punitive and carceral means in anti-trafficking policies that 'do not empower the women who are the primary objects of concern, but strengthen the state's regulatory apparatus and intensify the sexual surveillance of women's lives' (Kapur 2013: 335). It can also be seen in the use of market-based and non-redistributive solutions to women's vulnerability and victimisation in the context of the feminisation of poverty. Part of the problem here is the liberal rationality underpinning 'empowerment' which constitutes women as sovereign subjects of rationality, autonomy and choice. Such a rationality is unsustainable and constantly brought to its knees when it encounters 'real' women and the complexities of their lives. Consequently, governance feminism fails to respond to the actual contexts of women's vulnerability and powerlessness which may have little to do with whether subjects are wholly free and consenting or wholly coerced and unfree, as per the binaries available to classical liberal thought.

The last point brings us to the slippery nature of freedom. The line between freedom and unfreedom—as the critiques of 'modern slavery' forwarded in this book have made clear—is difficult to draw, particularly in the case of women. And yet—as with modern abolitionism—governance feminism remains committed to drawing such a line, one that sequesters 'unfreedom' into particular spaces, associated with particular practices and subjects. Violence against women is thereby exceptionalised in 'cultural' practices of early and forced marriage while the institution of marriage is normalised. The 'development' of subaltern women rests on their integration into—and thereby normalisation of—capitalism. Carceral demands of public protestors and the state (as in the case of the Delhi protests) exceptionalises (some forms of) violence against women, thereby normalising its daily, routine manifestation in women's lives. In creating zones of normality and exceptionalism, such instances of 'empowering' women show an inability to truly appraise the wide constraints on *all* women's lives. Instead of 'freeing' women from forms of unfreedom and slavery, they end up justifying their unfreedom in marriage, in the market, in the securocratic state, and in the violence of the routine and everyday.

Notes

1. There is a long—well-documented—history as to the age of consent and marriageable age in India which also accounts for this gender-based difference. The reasons that historians list are both rooted in colonial legacies (the English common law) around difference in age of puberty, and 'indigenous' gender and caste-based expectations and anxieties around delaying marriage for girls past childbearing age. All of these broad reasons remained up till the 1970s when Child Marriage Restraint Act was amended. My thanks to Ashwini Tambe for clarifications; see Tambe (2009).

2. Backward Castes is a specific constitutional designation of caste groups in post-independence India which includes castes that are below the higher caste groups but above dalits (formerly, 'untouchables') in the Hindu caste hierarchy, largely for the purposes of affirmative action.
3. Sen and Sengupta (2012) also observe that elopements by school-going girls are fairly common and accepted in West Bengal especially as it frees poor parents from having to pay dowry.
4. Elopement cases are being policed in more controversial if not straightforwardly violent ways by the Hindu right who have recently launched a 'Love Jihad'. The campaign attempts to 'save' young Hindu women from being lured into marriage and eventual conversion into Islam by Muslim men. It turns out that many of the unions under the campaigns hateful purview were ones of 'love' between Hindu women and Muslim men (see Sarkar 2014). The political use of love in this manner has long constituted a mobilising platform for right-wing propaganda (see Mody 2008).
5. One of the slogans raised during the 2012 anti-rape protests was that of *Bekhauf Azaadi*, or Fearless Freedom for all women. It was meant to challenge the inevitable control of women's mobility and freedom in the name of her own safety and 'protection' thereby using the fear of sexual violence to justify the patriarchal control of women's bodies (see Statement by Women's and Progressive Groups available on http://kafila.org/2015/12/15/three-years-later-women-struggle-for-justice-and-freedom-from-fear-statement-on-the-eve-of-december-16th/).

References

Agnes, F. (2012). Consent, Age and Agency: Reflections on the Recent Delhi High Court Judgment on Minors and Marriage. *Kafila*. Available at http://kafila.org/2012/06/12/consent-age-and-agency-reflections-on-the-recent-delhi-high-court-judgement-on-minors-and-marriage-flavia-agnes/.

Agnes, F. (2013). Controversy Over Age of Consent. *Economic and Political Weekly, 48*(29), 10–13.

Anitha, S., & Gill, A. (2009). Coercion, Consent and the Forced Marriage Debate in the UK. *Feminist Legal Studies, 17,* 165–184.

Baxi, P. (2012). Rape Cultures in India. *Kafila.* http://kafila.org/2012/12/23/rape-cultures-in-india-pratiksha-baxi/.

Baxi, P. (2014). *Public Secrets of the Law: Rape Trials in India*. New Delhi: Oxford University Press.

Bernstein, E. (2010). Militarized Humanitarianism Meets Carceral Feminism: The Politics of Sex, Rights, and Freedom in Contemporary Anti-Trafficking Campaigns. *Signs, 36*(1), 45–71.

Chowdhry, P. (2007). *Contentious Marriages, Eloping Couples: Gender, Caste, and Patriarchy in Northern India*. New Delhi: Oxford University Press.

Cornwall, A., & Molyneux, M. (Eds.). (2007). *The Politics of Rights: Dilemmas for Feminist Praxis*. London: Routledge.

Cruikshank, B. (1999). *The Will to Empower: Democratic Citizens and Other Subjects*. Ithaca: Cornell University Press.

Dutta, D., & Sircar, O. (2013). India's Winter of Discontent: Some Feminist Dilemmas in the Wake of a Rape. *Feminist Studies, 39*(1), 293–306.

Gangoli, G., & Chantler, K. (2009). Protecting Victims of Forced Marriage: Is Age a Protective Factor? *Feminist Legal Studies, 17*, 267–288.

Govindan, P. (2013). Rethinking Emancipation: The Rhetorics of Slavery and Politics of Freedom in Anti-Trafficking Work in India. *Interventions, 15*(4), 511–529.

Grewal, I. (2005). *Transnational America: Feminisms, Diasporas, Neoliberalisms*. Durham and London: Duke University Press.

Halley, J., Kotiswaran, P., Shamir, H., & Thomas, C. (2006). From the International to the Local in Feminist Legal Responses to Rape, Prostitution/Sex Work, and Sex Trafficking: Four Studies in Contemporary Governance Feminism. *Harvard Journal of Law and Gender, 29*(2), 335–423.

Hickel, J. (2014). The "Girl Effect": Liberalism, Empowerment and Contradictions of Development. *Third World Quarterly, 35*(8), 1355–1373.

Kapur, R. (2013). Gender, Sovereignty and the Rise of a Sexual Security Regime in International Law and Postcolonial India. *Melbourne Journal of International Law, 14*(2), 1–29.

Karim, L. (2011). *Microfinance and Its Discontents: Women in Debt in Bangladesh*. Minneapolis: University of Minnesota Press.

Koffman, O., & Gill, R. (2013). 'The Revolution Will Be Led by a 12-Year-Old Girl': Girl Power and Global Biopolitics. *Feminist Review, 105*, 83–102.

Leve, L. (2014). Failed Development and Rural Revolution in Nepal: Rethinking Subaltern Consciousness and Women's Empowerment. In V. Bernal & I. Grewal (Eds.), *Theorising NGOs: States, Feminisms, and Neoliberalism* (pp. 50–92). Durham and London: Duke University Press.

Madhok, S. (2013). *Rethinking Agency: Developmentalism, Gender and Rights*. London and New York: Routledge.
Madhok, S., & Rai, S. (2012). Agency, Injury, and Transgressive Politics in Neoliberal Times. *Signs, 37*(3), 645–669.
Mahmood, S. (2001). Feminist Theory, Embodiment, and the Docile Agent: Some Reflections on the Egyptian Islamic Revival. *Cultural Anthropology, 16*(2), 202–236.
Mody, P. (2008). *The Intimate State: Love-Marriage and the Law in Delhi*. New Delhi and Abingdon: Routledge.
Moodie, M. (2008). Enter Microcredit: A New Culture of Women's Empowerment in Rajasthan? *American Ethnologist, 35*, 454–465.
O'Connell Davidson, J. (2005). *Children in the Global Sex Trade*. Cambridge: Polity Press.
O'Connell Davidson, J. (2015). *Modern Slavery: The Margins of Freedom*. London: Palgrave.
Oksala, J. (2013). Feminism and Neoliberal Governmentality. *Foucault Studies, 16*, 32–53.
Rankin, K. (2001). Governing Development: Neoliberalism, Microcredit, and Rational Economic Woman. *Economy and Society, 30*(1), 18–37.
Rankin, K. (2004). *The Cultural Politics of Markets*. Toronto: University of Toronto Press.
Roy, A. (2014). Gender and Citizenship in India. In L. Fernandes (Ed.), *Routledge Handbook of Gender in South Asia* (pp. 55–69). Abingdon and New York: Routledge.
Roychowdhury, P. (2013). "The Delhi Gang Rape": The Making Of International Causes. *Feminist Studies, 39*(1), 282–292.
Sarkar, T. (2014). Love, Control and Punishment. *The Indian Express*. Available at http://indianexpress.com/article/opinion/columns/love-control-and-punishment/.
Sen, S., & Sengupta, N. (2012). Marriage, Work and Education Among Domestic Workers in Kolkata. *Economic and Political Weekly, 47*(43), 67–77.
Sethi, M. (2012). So What Are We Demainding at India Gate? *Hardnews*. Available at http://www.hardnewsmedia.com/2012/12/5749. Accessed 5 Aug 2015.
Shah, S. (2014). *Street Corner Secrets: Sex, Work, and Migration in the City of Mumbai*. Durham: Duke University Press.
Sharma, A. (2008). *Logics of Empowerment: Development, Gender, and Governance in Neoliberal India*. Minneapolis and London: University of Minnesota Press.

Soderlund, G. (2005). Running from the Rescuers: New U.S. Crusades Against Sex Trafficking and the Rhetoric of Abolition. *Feminist Formations, 17*(3), 64–87.
Spivak, G. C. (2000). Discussion: An Afterword on the New Subaltern. In P. Chatterjee & P. Jeganathan (Eds.), *Community, Gender and Violence: Subaltern Studies* (Vol. XI, pp. 305–334). London: Hurst and Company.
Sunder Rajan, R. (2003). *The Scandal of the State: Women, Law and Citizenship in India*. Durham, NC: Duke University Press and New Delhi, Permanent Black.
Tambe, A. (2009). The State as Surrogate Parent. *Journal of the History of Childhood and Youth, 2*(3), 393–427.
Turner, C. (2013). When Does Child Marriage Become Slavery? *Girls Not Brides*. Available at http://www.girlsnotbrides.org/when-does-child-marriage-become-slavery/. Accessed 4 Aug 2015.
Warner, A. (2014). How Empowering Girls Can Help End Child Marriage. *Girls not Brides*. Available at http://www.girlsnotbrides.org/empowering-girls-can-help-end-child-marriage/. Accessed 4 Aug 2015.
Wilson, K. (2008). Reclaiming "Agency", Reasserting Resistance. *IDS Bulletin, 39*(6), 83–91.

12

Abolition Terminable and Interminable

Jared Sexton

Against the Global Comeback

How are we to understand the seemingly contradictory regard for the history of racial slavery and black freedom struggle in the early twenty-first century? The concept of slavery has of late undergone bifurcation in political and intellectual discourse in the West. On one side, there are those who assert that our thinking about possibilities for radical social

This article draws its title from one of Sigmund Freud's late works, the1937 essay 'Analysis Terminable and Interminable'. There he is exploring the difficulty of determining the proper end of a psychoanalytic treatment. According to Péran (2005): 'A terminated analysis supposes that two conditions are fulfilled: first, the patient must be relieved of symptoms, inhibitions, and anxieties, and second, enough of the repressed must be made conscious and elucidated, and enough of the resistance conquered, so as to banish the risk of repetition'. Grandin (2015) suggests something akin to the repression of slavery in the political culture of the modern world, an epoch-making violence that has, across the centuries, taken on the stalled dynamic of collective trauma. If this much is plausible, then it makes some sense to approach the question of the end of abolition with respect to both the matter of relief and the matter of repetition.

J. Sexton (✉)
University of California, Irvine, CA, USA
e-mail: jcsexton@uci.edu

L. Brace and J. O'Connell Davidson (eds.), *Revisiting Slavery and Antislavery*,
https://doi.org/10.1007/978-3-319-90623-2_12

change and transformation today is obstructed by an undue focus on the history of racial slavery, the international abolitionist movement and its post-emancipation cognates throughout the Atlantic world. The claim here is that the critical sensibilities and political energies borne by people of conscience have been practically absorbed by the centuries-long black freedom struggle against racial slavery, or what Nahum Chandler has described as 'the double articulation since the sixteenth century of the history of slavery and its aftermath in the Americas and the Caribbean and the emergence of a global practice of racial distinction' (1996: 78).[1] Framing our political and intellectual efforts through the matrix of racial slavery, on this account, eclipses equally pressing problems arising since the sixteenth century from distinct yet related histories of capitalism, colonialism, and settler colonialism as well as the diverse movements for socialism, decolonization and settler decolonization arrayed against them. Within the milieu of the Anglophone world at least, entire fields of academic inquiry, professional journalism, policy analysis, political lobbying, and service provision, and much community organizing and activism as well, have for a full generation or more advocated an end to 'the black-white binary' analysis of race and racism thought to be the essential byproduct of a conceptual framework reductively oriented by racial slavery. The call for paradigm shift has become the hallmark of the post-civil rights era United States especially, in which the initiatives of anti-racism, immigrant rights, indigenous sovereignty, liberal multiculturalism and conservative colour blindness operate uneasily—often unwittingly—within a broad-based strategic integration (Cole and Parker 2004; Dzidzienyo and Oboler 2005; Fernandez 2009; Lee and Bean 2010; Márquez 2014; O'Brien 2009; Pascoe 2009; Rodriguez 2000). That is to say, while these diverse and divergent political phenomena are characterized by serious conflicts of interest as they span the left–right spectrum, they nonetheless share a basic assumption about the ostensible limits that black movements impose upon their work.

On the other side, there are those who assert that the progressive causes to which they are dedicated are, in fact, *extensions* of the same black freedom struggle otherwise thought to have run its course in the mid-twentieth century (or, for some, the mid-nineteenth century) and whose residual pride of place continues to obfuscate and distort movements for justice and equality in the present. Indeed, even some of those urging us to move beyond 'the black-white binary' employ key terms and concepts, and not a little of the style, tone and timbre of black movements as they seek to decenter, subordinate or supersede them altogether. So, for example, the largely Latino immigrant rights movement in the U.S. seeks to battle the new 'Juan Crow' (a play on the colloquial name of the notorious 'Jim Crow' system of legal segregation arising after the Civil War) and Arab Americans facing the depredations of Homeland Security challenge the new 'racial profiling' (borrowing a concept from the longstanding resistance in black communities to the post-civil rights era War on Crime). I wrote elsewhere on that score: 'The metaphoric transfer that dismisses the legitimacy of black struggles against racial slavery … while it appropriates black suffering as the template for nonblack grievances remains one of the defining features of contemporary political culture' (Sexton 2010: 42). But the 'new abolitionists', fighting 'slavery's global comeback' a century and half after emancipation proclamations echoed throughout the western hemisphere, are surely the most curious of the lot. The new abolitionists, including those working for the United Nations, the U.S. State Department and human rights groups like Anti-Slavery International, are worried that interventionist approaches couched in terms of 'human trafficking' and 'forced labour' to ameliorate the condition of some 30 million people in question are euphemizing relations of power that amount to slavery here and now. For this emerging cohort, the problem is not too much talk of slavery, but far too little (O'Connell Davidson 2015). The rub, of course, is that the contemporary slavery they seek end is now, as it were, de-racialized.

To restate, then, our opening question: How are we to understand this seemingly contradictory regard for the history of racial slavery and black freedom struggle in the early twenty-first century? As a point of departure, we might interrogate the implied or stated definition of racial slavery held in common by these various and sundry 'post-black' political phenomenon. In each case, racial slavery is disavowed, which is to say that it is acknowledged and denied at once. It is acknowledged insofar as it is that historical experience most responsible for the production of the African Diaspora and definitive for the history of African-derived people in the Americas and the Caribbean especially. As such, it is the predicament properly associated with such groups; racial blackness and modern slavery were, across the better part of a millennium, mutually constitutive and materially and symbolically soldered in the historic instance. It is denied insofar as it is thought that racial blackness and modern slavery, once soldered, could be materially and symbolically separated without another epoch of catastrophic violence commensurate with their joint historical formation; an abolition without revolution. Hence, according to the new abolitionists, we face a global slave population in the current conjuncture whose 'highest ratios…worldwide are from South and Southeast Asia, along with China, Russia, and the former satellite states of the Soviet Union' (Gould 2012). J. J. Gould (2012), former Yale University lecturer and now editor of *The Atlantic* online, notes in a widely-read feature article on the issue: 'Though now universally illegal, slavery still exists, and it's common … around the world'. This assertion about slavery as both illegal and commonplace is at the heart of the problem, though not.

There's the rub, and neither for the reasons the new abolitionists propose nor even those offered by most of the new abolitionists' progressive and radical critics.[2] For the new abolitionists, the problem of slavery's illegality demands redoubled efforts at law enforcement and compliance monitoring throughout the global commodity supply chain, alongside humanitarian aid and economic development projects in the poorest and most vulnerable regions of the world and ethical consumption practices and immigration policy reform in the richest and most protected. All such approaches, as various critics have amply demonstrated, mistake the symptoms for the cause, leaving intact the whole infrastructure of neoliberalism. For critics of the new abolitionism, the rhetoric of contemporary slavery mystifies the genesis of 'human trafficking' and 'forced labour' and euphemizes relations of production that amount to exploitation here and now, all while insisting we can and should resolve the problem by pursuing what liberal political commentator Sally Kohn (2012) has called, *pace* Bill Gates, a 'kinder, gentler capitalism'.

Rethinking Racial Slavery

The new abolitionists and their critics, across an acute debate about how to address extreme exploitation today, may nonetheless share a common misunderstanding of (racial) slavery and (black) freedom, past and present. I am taking a cue here from the researches of historian James Oakes at the CUNY Graduate Center, who argues in his recently reprinted study, *Slavery and Freedom: An Interpretation of the Old South*, that such misunderstanding has to do centrally with a problematic indistinction between the economic and political domains. The result is, for Oakes, an all-too-common conflation of slavery with the most severe conditions of material deprivation, including the basic conditions requisite for life itself. Oakes, however, is careful to distinguish the economic question of material well-being from the political question of standing within a social order. He writes to that end in the opening pages of the text:

> I have no desire to dismiss the benefits of longevity or the importance of decent standards of material comfort in the alleviation of human misery. But I do wish to emphasize that these have little to do with slavery. To some degree the standard-of-living issue is universal: it applies to feudalism as well as to capitalism, to slave as well as free societies. But a slave was a slave, whether he lived a healthy hundred years or a sickly forty, whether she was better fed than a Polish peasant or more miserably housed than an American yeoman … *'slavery' and 'freedom' do not refer to material well-being* … Freedom and slavery are at bottom political categories; they refer to the distributions of power in society. (Oakes 1990: xv–xvi, emphasis added)

Power, in this sense, was and is at stake in the determination of slavery and freedom. A slave, no matter how elevated in role or material circumstance, was and is nonetheless a slave. Even the well-fed, long-lived slave. Even the royal advisor or military leader. Even, perhaps, the manumitted slave as well. Even one attaining the income and educational levels of the mythic American middle class, the celebrity of a Hollywood icon or the office of the so-called leader of the free world.

Though the latter examples may strike the reader as hyperbolic, we are, in the light shown by literary critic and cultural theorist Hortense Spillers, ultimately examining 'how *status* is made' (2003: 21). Oakes makes a related point along these lines, in response to those who might insist there are differences only of degree between the enslaved and the exploited.

> Because no society is completely free of coercion or inequity, it is possible to define slavery as the furthest point on a spectrum of social relationships ranging from the most to the least free. But to be a slave, whether in the American South or in classical Athens, was to suffer a deprivation of freedom so extreme as to be qualitatively distinct from all other forms of unfreedom. (Oakes 1990: 4)

I previously argued that 'it is not *labor* relations, but *property* relations that are constitutive of slavery' (Sexton 2010: 36). I would maintain now that this is a crucial first discrimination for understanding histories of slavery in relation to histories of labour. Only slavery involves the invention of 'propertized human being', to borrow a phrase from legal scholar Cheryl Harris (1993). I realize in retrospect, however, that this is a somewhat misleading conclusion to draw. Property relations are constitutive of slavery, to be sure, even if those relations are more complicated than we might first assume (Schroeder 1998). But the more salient point has to do with the novel *political* standing that racial slavery brings into the modern world: racial blackness as a status ascribed to the essence of the enslaved and to all those thought to be eligible for enslavement by virtue of a shared and inheritable social category, creating negative ties along horizontal and vertical axes to any and all contemporaries or to past and future generations. Hence, the uncanny resemblance between Oakes' historiographic rejoinder—'a slave was a slave, whether …'—and Frantz Fanon's trenchant observation in his post-war classic, *Black Skin, White Masks*—"*wherever … a negro remains a negro*" (2008: 133). And it is important to repeat that racial slavery was never the predicament of any one imperial endeavour or aspiring nation-state but rather was, from its inception, a globally articulated system. One cannot speak of racial slavery in one place without raising this always more expansive geography. Not only does racial slavery exceed the bounds of the national or regional context, it also precedes the historic emergence of any such form. It is, as Jason Moore argues regarding what he terms the 'world ecology' of capitalism, *local* but not *localized*.[3]

A more adequate history of the rise of racial slavery, one that would allow for an appreciation of its novelty, would take us back to something approaching the fourteenth century CE in an examination of the social, political and economic developments unfolding in historical outline within and between Africa, Asia and Europe. As there is not yet anything but speculation about the existence of the Americas in this hub of early global encounter, we see that the racial thematics of the 'New World' begin in and as transformations well prior to the Columbian advent. Three massive shifts deserve mention in this respect. First, the shift in the principal vector of trade in enslaved Africans, from the trans-Saharan and Indian Ocean basin toward the newer transatlantic circuit—what historian Patrick Manning (1990) calls, respectively, the 'Oriental' and 'Occidental' slave trades—whose pivot entailed an intensification of the internal slave trade throughout most of the African continent as well. It is crucial to remark that the transatlantic Occidental slave trade launched its maritime enterprise along a north–south axis, centred about the Mediterranean region, in the fifteenth century, well before European imperial expansion to the Americas (Green 2012; Hunwick and Powell 2002; Moore 2009; Segal 2001). Second, the related shift in mode of production from feudalism toward mercantilism in Europe, including the systematic enclosure of the commons so crucial to the incipient stage of capitalism in the early modern period (Solow 2014, Wood 2002). Third, the stirrings of Renaissance human ism throughout European intellectual life, unleashing historical, philosophical, theological, and scientific debates that would reconfigure long-standing notions of slavery and freedom for the subsequent formulation, and eventual consolidation, of the idea and practice of racial differentiation (Brotton 2006; Goldenberg 2005; Isaac 2004).

We thus begin to understand, following economist Elizabeth Donnan's four-volume documentary history of the transatlantic slave trade, whose landmark 1930s study for the Carnegie Institution Spillers consults assiduously, that by the mid-1400 s at least 'the magic of skin color is already installed as a decisive factor in human dealings' (Spillers 2003: 212). In this zone of convergence—where the European's nascent relation of predation toward the African *en masse* is mediated by long-standing relations of competitive coexistence with the peoples of the Maghreb, the Mashriq and the Arabian Peninsula—slavery as a legal, political and economic institution becomes progressively *circumscribed* to the populations of sub-Saharan Africa, *concentrated* in the West and Central regions, and *racialized* as black. Concomitantly, the status of the enslaved is *degraded* relative to its pre-modern and ancient variants across most of the inhabited world (Black 2015; Lovejoy 2012). This triadic structure of racialization—white, brown, black—is then repeated with a difference in the Spanish colonization of the Caribbean islands from the early 1500s onward, drawing together and structuring-in-dominance the mobile populations of Europe, the captive populations of Africa, and the displaced populations of the Americas. These would become the ties that bind with profound and lasting ramifications, as indicated by novelist, dramatist and essayist Sylvia Wynter's astute observations. I quote at length from her magisterial effort to reframe the matter on the occasion of the Columbian quincentenary:

> Not only would [large numbers of peoples of African descent] be used … as the totally disposable, coercible, and unpaid labor force that alone made possible the accelerated economic development of the Americas. They would also play a central role in the instituting of the bases of the new social structure. In this role they would not only serve to free the indigenous peoples from the outright slavery to which many had been reduced in the immediate decades after 1492 … As the liminal category whose mode of excluded *difference*, based on the hereditary slave status of its members as the only *legitimately enslavable* population group, they would also generate the principle of similarity or of conspecificity that would come to bond, if on the terms of sharply unequal relations, the incoming Spanish settlers with the indigenous peoples. From the mid-sixteenth century on, this principle would come to bond the latter as members of a category whose status was that of *hereditarily free* subjects of the Spanish state. This third population group, therefore, would come to embody the new symbolic construct of *Race* or of innately determined

> difference that would enable the Spanish state to legitimate its sovereignty over the *lands of the Americas* in the post-religious legal terms of Western Europe's now-expanding state system. It would do so by instituting by means of the physical referent of the group's enslaved lives and labor the empirical basis of, in [*Newsweek* journalist Gregory] Cerio's terms, the "moral and philosophical foundations" on which the Spaniards "accepted" the indigenous peoples "into their societies, however rudely". (1995: 11–12)

The 'principle of similarity' is inscribed thus not in any presumed identity, much less any presumed equality, between European colonists and the indigenous peoples of the Americas, but instead in the recognition of a shared 'hereditary freedom' over against the embodied difference of legitimate enslavement. Though slavery is an ancient institution with provenance in nearly every major form of human society, we are concerned here with the more specific emergence of freedom—as economic value, political category, legal right, cultural practice, lived experience—from the modern transformation of slavery into what historian Robin Blackburn (1997: 585) terms the 'Great Captivity': the convergence of the ascendant private property regime and the invention of racial blackness, which is also to say the invention of anti-blackness in the invention of whiteness, where the latter cannot but become immediately a more generalized non-blackness. For Blackburn: 'That slaves were sold in Africa or bought by merchants was not new. The novelty of New World slavery resided in the scale and intensity of the slave traffic and the plantation trades. Earlier forms of slavery had been geared to household service, or the strengthening of a lineage, or the construction of a military apparatus, or to relatively modest enclaves of estate or mine labor' (1997: 585). He continues in terms echoing Wynter, but with an additional turn of the screw: 'The New World slave plantations, by contrast, had established a *permanent and hereditary* slavery of the most onerous sort, *breaking with any geographical constraint* and displaying an unquenchable thirst for slave labor and slave lives' (1997: 585, emphasis added).

We have at this point a detonation of the spatiotemporal coordinates that characterized the history of slavery throughout the millennia.

The space of slavery is rendered infinite and the time of slavery eternal, whereas the source of eligibility for slavery was rendered immutable and specific, implanted in the body and soul, an inherent property of 'blackness' itself. 'Traditional defenses of slavery, and established racial notions', as a result, 'were inadequate to the task of explaining this Great Captivity … New World slavery thus brought about a degradation of the slave condition, and of the ideologies which justified or explained it' (Blackburn 1997: 585). Let us recapitulate, then, the key features of the modern transformation of slavery: (1) enslaved status becomes permanent and hereditary, or trans-historical, rather than temporally restricted; (2) enslaved status breaks as well with geographical constraints, attaching to the bodies of the enslaved, rather than to any particular spatial arrangement; (3) this eternal and infinite enslaved status is restricted to those of African descent (however defined in the local context); and (4) the combination of these factors degrades enslaved status in an unprecedented and irreparable way. The subsequent meditation is pressed to consider what is the most robust understanding of slavery—past, present and future—and, on that basis, how to proceed in the practice of writing history otherwise. We must think, more to the point, about what constitutes the modern problem of *racial* slavery if we are to pursue the abolition of the Great Captivity in the proper sense and the present tense.[4]

The Slave's Cause

We are now in a position to see how the critique of the new abolitionism takes shape along three lines of stress. First, there is a serious concern about addressing the legacy of slavery *since* emancipation in the nineteenth century and challenging the ways that the metaphorical use of slavery to describe contemporary political campaigns and policy initiatives against extreme exploitation does a dual disservice: (1) to the ongoing struggle for black equality throughout the Americas, and not least in the United States, by mis-recognizing the historical context of its emergence; and (2) to the true source, scale and nature of the problems that define our moment. Historian James Brewer Stewart's (2015) recent essay for *openDemocracy* stands as a fine example of work drawing attention to these dual concerns. Stewart founded Historians Against Slavery (HAS) in 2011 as 'a group of scholars who bring historical context and scholarship to the modern-day antislavery movement in order to inform activism and develop collaborations to sustain and enhance such efforts' (Burin 2015). Discontented by the a-historical and largely moralistic framework of the new abolitionists affiliated with religious organizations, corporate-financed non-profit organizations, and international human rights groups, Stewart assembled a team of professional academics whose collective expertise might serve a pedagogical function *within* the burgeoning movement to end what Stewart et al. nonetheless agree to call slavery in the present tense. HAS represents a form of internal criticism for the new abolitionism and seeks thereby to lend genuine gravity and direction where there has been too much sentimentality and blind faith to date.

Second, there is a midrange concern about the continuation of the political conditions of slavery *despite* the (near) universal emancipation enshrined in the 13th Amendment to the U.S. Constitution and similar legislation in the region. On this note, legal scholar Guyora Binder reminds us that emancipation, far from providing a remedy for slavery, racial or otherwise, is actually a component part of its form and function, so much so that 'the institution of slavery could persist without any individual being lawfully held as a slave' in the usual meaning of the term (1996: 2064). Binder contends that, with respect to the U.S. as a principle case study, the legislative action and the preceding executive order of the mid-1860s served mainly to manumit slaves already effectively emancipated by the enormous dislocations of the Civil War. Thus freed, however, was the abolition of slavery a *fait accompli*? To the contrary, Binder finds that 'for reasons intrinsic to its subject … the Thirteenth Amendment confronts interpreters with multiple dimensions of ambiguity', most importantly 'which of the deprivations imposed on slaves to regard as essential to slavery and which to legitimize as incidental to slavery' and 'how the abolition of slavery redistributes the resources and power of the masters and what sort of historical narrative justifies those distributive consequences' (1996: 2070). We might say, more pointedly, that we are faced with the questions of how the status of the slave is to be transformed entirely and how that transformation is to be known. If that transformation is held to be central to the prospects for abolition and its very elusiveness is acknowledged, then it becomes far more plausible to think 'that slavery may persist to this day' (1996: 2064). Abolition would, accordingly, entail far more than universal manumission *ceteris paribus*, something I can only indicate here as the generalization, on a global scale, of the ex-slaves' demands for a radical reconstruction of society. Eric Foner (2014), building upon the grand example of W. E. B. Du Bois' 1935 magnum opus, *Black Reconstruction*, demonstrates exhaustively the chasm that separated the conceptions of freedom held by ex-slaves and those held by nearly everyone else in the postbellum U.S.

Where Binder seeks to 'provoke uncertainty about the meaning of freedom and slavery, at least insofar as the alternative to such uncertainty is a reductive definition of slavery that places it at a safe distance from contemporary American society', he is, perhaps ironically, all too right to claim that 'when we speak of freedom and slavery we *do not* know "what we are talking about" and *should not* speak with self-assurance' (1996: 2063). It is against that overwhelming tendency toward self-assurance that the third line of stress is expressed. It consists in a fundamental concern about the paradoxical 'perfection of slavery' *through* emancipation and the ongoing struggle for black equality. Critical race theorist Anthony Farley (2005) has articulated this thinking most prominently in the past decade, pulling together arguments regarding race, law and society that he has developed since the early 1990s. Farley, to be clear, is not arguing that the basic elements of slavery persist *despite* emancipation under cover of a triumphalist narrative of progress, though he surely would agree with Binder's insights to that effect. Neither is he at pains to track the cunning of political retrenchment and revanchist legal maneuvering *after* emancipation. Farley is not interested in the machinations of the slave power as such or its functional surrogates. The perfection of slavery issues forth, rather, from the slave's desire for equality itself, from the dreamwork aimed at any participation in slave society. In fact, the more strident the demands for reform, the more the perfect slavery, and the slave, becomes. 'We are strangers to ourselves', Farley writes. 'The dream of equality, of rights, is the disguised wish for hierarchy. The prayer for equal rights is the disguised desire for slavery' (2005: 224). He continues further along:

> It seems that after "a division of mental and manual labour appears" that the slave is assigned the latter and the master is assigned the former. All is not as it seems. The slave actually does the *mental* work that keeps the structure from falling apart. The slave dreams of rights and of equal justice under law. The production of dreams is the slave's true and secret function. The slave produces all of the equations that stabilize the system of death-over-life through its prayers for equal rights. The slave's prayer resolves all present contradictions into white-over-black, for white-over-black is all that equal rights or law can ever be or become. (2005: 227)

The production of dreams: we would not be unwarranted to read in this intervention that the slave uninterested in emancipation is actually closer, psychically, to freedom than the slave or even the nominal 'free person of color' seeking the route of petition, protest, or politics. Emancipation, in this view, is a desire bound to the dream of equality, a palliative, an opiate of the enslaved masses, that wards against the true thought of freedom and the destruction of the global system of slavery it requires: abolition of slavery is abolition of the terms of order. 'To wake from slavery is to see that everything must go, every law room, every great house, every plantation, all of it, everything' (2005: 222–3). What is more:

> Without the dreamwork of the slave, the many crises of the system of white-over-black blossom in revolution. The flames are wooed from their buds and continue to unfold until the entire plantation system is gone. The servile insurrection continues until it brings down the system of marks, the system of property, and the system of law. Slaves are trained to *not* think this way. (2005: 244)

This third line of stress in the critique of the new abolitionism rejects decidedly the now standard belittling of black movements, including especially those ongoing in and against the United States, a critical demeanour that would reduce them to small-minded anti-racism, reduce anti-racism to demands upon the state and reduce demands upon the state to statist politics.[5] The resultant caricature of black freedom struggle—which fails altogether to appreciate the 'extent to which radicalism … is a fundamental and enduring force in the black public sphere' (Moten 2008: 177)—would like to paint its vast and varied activity into the corner of irrelevance; whether restricted to an admirable historic victory against a specific set of lamentable conditions in the nineteenth or twentieth century or to an admirable campaign against a specific set of lamentable conditions in the present, or denigrated as an annoying fixation upon a specific set of conditions far less lamentable than those it blocks from sustained consideration. What this third line suggests, while acknowledging some points of interest in the first and the second, is that slavery is very much a contemporary problem 'all over the world', but not the de-racialized colour blind slavery of the global comeback narrative. Racial slavery does not simply persist in attenuated form as a legacy or aftermath demanding our continued vigilance. That would be problem enough. Neither does it persist in vacated institutional form post-emancipation as slavery without slaves. That would be problem enough. Rather, it persists as a problem compounded by every effort to eliminate it while preserving the fabric of the singular modernity it brought into being and has sustained ever since.

Slavery is the threshold of the political world and genuine abolition is the interminable radicalization of every radical movement against it. As a dynamical system, the ongoing black freedom struggle, contrary to the new abolitionism, is a strange attractor betraying a deterministic chaos, a determined unpredictability; a movement presenting an endless series of problems unsolvable except in the most approximate ways, solutions that cannot be written in formulae; a politics whose demand is, as the late anthropologist Michel-Rolph Trouillot said of the still incomplete Haitian Revolution, 'too radical to be formulated in advance of its deeds' (2015: 88).[6] But if the rich dynamics of black freedom struggle are its chief power, we must bear in mind equally that it is, for the same reason, too easily controlled or channeled to irreconcilable ends. We must, therefore, act, or wait, on the fortuitous phenomenon of freedom, holding open the negative prospects generated in and through the 'complete lysis' of the world we have inherited

(Fanon 2008: 3). We cannot offer closing prescriptions for political action, not because the perspective suggested above counsels inaction or quietude, but rather because such prescription would unduly burden the sensitive initial conditions of any local effort whatever. If, as Grandin (2015) demonstrates, racial slavery is that which in the modern world 'can't be transcended but also what can never be remembered', that which in the modern world abstract and concrete divisions over and over again, that which is repeated in intellectual and political practice; then its abolition must involve a protracted, perhaps interminable, process of working through that entails, above all, bringing into speech (that which resists life in) the lives of those who live out a politically valueless form of life, those whose value exists as potential in and of another world. For those who think such a 'talking cure' inadequate to the task, we need only keep in mind that such speech circumscribes the site of the political, 'the opening of a door through which we must make a step…without a prescription and without guarantee' (Dolar 2008: 29). The slave's cause, then, indicates not only the *radical* tradition of abolition and the *revolutionary* resistance to slavery (Sinha 2016), but also, more profoundly, 'that which disrupts the smooth functioning of law-like interactions…something that seems not to obey laws, remaining inexplicable from the standpoint of scientific knowledge' (Fink 1995: 64).

Notes

1. The focus on the forms of modern slavery in the so-called New World should in no way prevent our keen recognition of the long history of the 'peculiar institution'— its economy, politics and culture—as a *global* phenomenon with linked and multiple sites of genesis and development (Engerman et al. 2001; Miller 2012; Walvin 2014).
3. This is more than an analogy to the history of capitalism, as should be clear already. In highlighting the need to distinguish conceptually racial slavery and historical capitalism, we needn't think of them as separate, much less opposed to one another. Cedric Robinson (2000, 2001) has done much to disabuse us of that habit of thought with the formulation over the last generation or so of a notion of 'racial capitalism'.

The growing literature on slavery and the history of capitalism affords additional resources for thinking about this problematic (Baptiste 2014; Beckert 2014; Grandin 2014b; Johnson 2013). An even more succinct comment on these relations is found in Ngugi wa Thiong'o's (2009) *Something Torn and New*: 'The dismemberment of African occurred in two stages. During the first of these, the African personhood was divided into two halves; the continent and its diaspora. African slaves, the central commodity in the mercantile phase of capitalism, formed the basis of the sugar, cotton, and tobacco plantations in the Caribbean and [North, Central and South] American mainland. If we accept that slave trade and plantation slavery provided the primary accumulation of capital that made Europe's Industrial Revolution possible, we cannot escape the irony that the very needs of that Industrial Revolution—markets for finished goods, sources of raw materials, and strategic requirements in the defense of trade routes—led inexorably to the second stage of the dismemberment of the continent [i.e., its colonial division]' (5). In this way, the enterprise of racial slavery provides the ground for the emergence of the Eurocentric capitalist system and its attendant imperialism. By contrast, abolitionism provides the ground for dismantling it: 'Scholars have long known that modern racial slavery fostered the growth of early capitalism. If slavery is capitalism…the movement to abolish it is, *at the very least*, its obverse' (Sinha 2016: 3, emphasis added).

4. While space does not allow for the development of my ideas on this point, I should say that this pursuit requires a deranged relation, if you will, to historical temporality and political agency. We must consider at once the future anteriority that will have abolished racial slavery as the substance of our 'freedom dreams' (Kelley 2002) and the anterior futurity—a 'knowledge of freedom' before racial slavery—that provokes the violence of capture in the first place (Moten 2008). In the first instance, I am drawing from Jacques Lacan's (2006) famous commentary on the 'function and field of speech and language in psychoanalysis', known among his circle as his 1953 Rome Discourse: "What is realized in my history is neither the past definite as what was, since it is no more, nor even the perfect as what has been in what I am, but the future anterior as what I will have been, given what I am in the process of becoming" (247). We might allow this notion, though elaborated for clinical practice, to suggest the element of *anticipation* in black freedom struggle. This is not anticipation in the sense of expectation, however, but

rather as an effect of the assumption of *desire*. In the second instance, I am modifying that temporality to acknowledge that there is a futurity that inhabits black freedom struggle logically and ontologically, which is not to say chronologically, prior to racial slavery. This priority is without nostalgia and should not be confused for the remembrance of things past, not even the involuntary memory of African indigenous ways of knowing. Rather, what Moten (2006) terms 'the freedom drive that animates black performances' (12), including the performances of political struggle, represents, to my mind, less the active integration of past, present and future into a greater and more complex wholeness and more a creative response enabled by 'a force in life that resists life and that, instead of following a course of progression and development, consists in a production of antiproductivity' or 'forces that strive towards nothing else than a persistence in their motion', thereby undermining 'the Aristotelian idea', central to the civilizing mission, 'that self-development is at the heart of being, of life' (Moyaert 2013: 94, 102). We might allow this notion to suggest, in turn, the element of *reluctance* in black freedom struggle, that which has 'no tendency to move, no anima, no desire to live' (Moyaert 2013: 114), what is otherwise known as the *death drive*.

5. I have in mind not only the recent Black Lives Matter movement (Taylor 2016), but also a longer genealogy entailing slave resistance and revolts, abolitionism, and the various twentieth-century movements for 'freedom, justice, and equality' from civil rights to black liberation. Again, see Robinson (1997) for an overview. See also Sexton (2014) on the reductionist accounts of black movements in certain currents of decolonial thought and practice.
6. The full paragraph is even more illuminating: 'Not only was the Revolution unthinkable and, therefore, unannounced in the West, it was also - to a large extent - unspoken among the slaves themselves. By this I mean that the Revolution was not preceded or even accompanied by an explicit intellectual discourse. One reason is that most slaves were illiterate and the printed word was not a realistic means of propaganda in the context of a slave colony. But another reason is that the claims of the revolution were indeed too radical to be formulated in advance of its deeds. Victorious practice could assert them only after the fact. In that sense, the revolution was indeed at the limits of the thinkable, *even in Saint-Domingue, even among the slaves, even among its own leaders*' (emphasis added).

References

Baptiste, E. (2014). *The Half Has Never Been Told: Slavery and the Making of American Capitalism*. New York: Basic Books.

Beckert, S. (2014). *Empire of Cotton: A Global History*. New York: Knopf.

Binder, G. (1996). The Slavery of Emancipation. *Cardozo Law Review, 17*, 2063.

Black, J. (2015). *The Atlantic Slave Trade in World History*. New York: Routledge.

Blackburn, R. (1997). *The Making of New World Slavery: From the Baroque to the Modern, 1492–1800*. New York: Verso.

Brotton, J. (2006). *The Renaissance: A Very Short Introduction*. New York: Oxford University Press.

Burin. N. (2015, December 9). History Matters: Reflections on the Historians Against Slavery Conference. *Historians Against Slavery Blog*. http://www.historiansagainstslavery.org/main/2015/12/history-matters-burin/.

Chandler, N. D. (1996). The Economy of Desedimentation: W.E.B. Du Bois and the Discourses of the Negro. *Callaloo, 19*, 78.

Cole, S., & Parker, A. M. (Eds.). (2004). *Beyond Black and White: Race, Ethnicity, and Gender in the U.S. South and Southwest*. College Station: Texas A&M University Press.

Davidson, J. O. (2015). *Modern Slavery: The Margins of Freedom*. New York: Palgrave Macmillan.

Dolar, M. (2008). Freud and the Political. *Unbound, 4*, 15.

Dzidzienyo, A., & Oboler, S. (Eds.). (2005). *Neither Enemies Nor Friends: Latinos, Blacks, Afro-Latinos*. New York: Palgrave Macmillan.

Engerman, S., Drescher, S., & Paquette, R. (2001). *Slavery*. New York: Oxford University Press.

Fanon, F. (2008). *Black Skin, White Masks* (C. Markmann, Trans.). London: Pluto Press.

Farley, A. P. (2005). Perfecting Slavery. *Loyola University Chicago Law Journal, 36*, 101.

Fernandez, R. (2009). *America Beyond Black and White: How Immigrants and Fusions Are Helping Us Overcome the Racial Divide*. Ann Arbor: University of Michigan Press.

Fink, B. (1995). Science and Psychoanalysis. In R. Feldstein, B. Fink., & M. Jaanus (Eds.), *Reading Seminar XI: Lacan's Four Fundamental Concepts of Psychoanalysis* (p. 55). Albany, NY: SUNY Press.

Foner, E. (2014). *Reconstruction: America's Unfinished Revolution, 1863–1877*, Updated Edition. New York: Harper Perennial.
Goldenberg, D. (2005). *The Curse of Ham: Race and Slavery in Early Judaism, Christianity, and Islam*. Princeton, NJ: Princeton University Press.
Gould, J. J. (2012, December 12). Slavery's Global Comeback. *The Atlantic*. http://www.theatlantic.com/international/archive/2012/12/slaverys-global-comeback/266354/.
Grandin, G. (2014a, February 24). How Slavery Made the Modern World. *The Nation*. http://www.thenation.com/article/how-slavery-made-modern-world/.
———. (2014b). *The Empire of Necessity: Slavery, Freedom, and Deception in the New World*. New York: Metropolitan Books.
———. (2015, May 1). Capitalism and Slavery. *The Nation*. http://www.thenation.com/article/capitalism-and-slavery/.
Green, T. (2012). *The Rise of the Trans-Atlantic Slave Trade in Western Africa, 1300–1589*. New York: Cambridge University Press.
Harris, C. (1993). Whiteness as Property. *Harvard Law Review, 106*, 1707.
Hunwick, J., & Powell, E. (Eds.). (2002). *The African Diaspora in the Mediterranean Lands of Islam*. Princeton, NJ: Princeton University Press.
Isaac, B. (2004). *The Invention of Racism in Classical Antiquity*. Princeton: Princeton University Press.
Johnson, W. (2013). *River of Dark Dreams: Slavery and Empire in the Cotton Kingdom*. Cambridge, MA: Harvard University Press.
Kelley, R. D. G. (2002). *Freedom Dreams: The Black Radical Imagination*. Boston: Beacon Press.
Kohn, S. (2012, May 15). Calling for a Kinder Capitalism. *The American Prospect*. http://prospect.org/article/calling-kinder-capitalism.
Lacan, J. (2006). *Écrits: The First Complete Edition in English* (B. Fink, Trans.). New York: W. W. Norton.
Lee, J., & Bean, F. (2010). *The Diversity Paradox: Immigration and the Color Line in Twenty-First Century America*. New York: Russell Sage Foundation.
Lovejoy, P. (2012). *Transformations in Slavery: A History of Slavery in Africa* (3rd ed.). New York: Cambridge University Press.
Manning, P. (1990). *Slavery and African Life: Occidental, Oriental, and African Slave Trades*. New York: Cambridge University Press.
Márquez, J. (2014). *Black-Brown Solidarity: Racial Politics in the New Gulf South*. Austin: University of Texas Press.

Miller, J. C. (2012). *The Problem of Slavery as History: A Global Approach*. New Haven: Yale University Press.

Moore. J. W. (2009). Madeira, Sugar, and the Conquest of Nature in the "First" Sixteenth Century. *Review, 32,* 345.

Moten, F. (2006). *In the Break: The Aesthetics of the Black Radical Tradition*. Minneapolis: University of Minnesota Press.

Moten, F. (2008). The Case of Blackness. *Criticism, 50,* 177.

Moyaert, P. (2013). The Death Drive and the Nucleus of the Ego: An Introduction to Freudian Metaphysics. *The Southern Journal of Philosophy, 51,* 94.

Oakes, J. (1990). *Slavery and Freedom: An Interpretation of the Old South*. New York: Alfred A. Knopf.

O'Brien, E. (2009). *The Racial Middle: Latinos and Asian Americans Living Beyond the Racial Divide*. New York: NYU Press.

Pascoe, P. (2009). *What Comes Naturally: Miscegenation Law and the Making of Race in America*. New York: Oxford University Press.

Péran, R. (2005). Analysis Terminable and Interminable. *International Dictionary of Psychoanalysis*. In A. Mijolla (Ed.). New York: Macmillan Reference: 76.

Robinson, C. (1997). *Black Movements in America*. New York: Routledge.

Robinson, C. (2000). *Black Marxism: The Making of the Black Radical Tradition*. Chapel Hill: UNC Press.

Robinson, C. (2001). *An Anthropology of Marxism*. London: Ashgate.

Rodriguez, C. (2000). *Changing Race: Latinos, the Census, and the History of Ethnicity*. New York: NYU Press.

Schroeder, J. L. (1998). *The Vestal and the Fasces: Hegel, Lacan, Property, and the Feminine*. Berkeley: University of California Press.

Segal, R. (2001). *Islam's Black Slaves: The Other Black Diaspora*. New York: Farrar, Straus and Giroux.

Sexton, J. (2010). People-of-Color-Blindness: Notes on the Afterlife of Slavery. *Social Text, 28,* 31.

Sexton, J. (2014). The Vel of Slavery: Tracking the Figure of the Unsovereign. *Critical Sociology* December: 2.

Sinha, M. (2016). *The Slave's Cause: A History of Abolition*. New Haven, CT: Yale University Press.

Solow, B. (2014). *The Economic Consequences of the Atlantic Slave Trade*. Lanham, MD: Lexington Books.

Spillers, H. (2003). *Black, White, and In Color: Essays on American Literature and Culture*. Chicago: University of Chicago Press.
Stewart, J. B. (2015, April 21). The "New Abolitionists" and the Problem of Race. *openDemocracy*. https://www.opendemocracy.net/beyondslavery/james-brewer-stewart/'new-abolitionists'-and-problem-of-race.
Taylor, K. (2016). *From #BlackLivesMatter to Black Liberation*. Chicago: Haymarket Books.
Thiong'o, Ngugi wa. 2009. *Something Torn and New: An African Renaissance*. New York: Basic Civitas Books.
Troillout, M.-R. (2015). *Silencing the Past: Power and the Production of History, Twentieth-Anniversary Edition*. Boston: Beacon Press.
Walvin, J. (2014). *Atlas of Slavery*. New York: Routledge.
Wood, E. (2002). *The Origin of Capitalism: A Longer View*. New York: Verso.
Wynter, S. (1995). 1492: A New World View. In V. L. Hyatt & R. Nettleford (Eds.), *Race, Discourse, and the Origin of the Americas: A New World View*. Washington, DC: Smithsonian Institution Press.

Index

A
Abolition:
Of child labour 233–45
Of slave trade 10, 125–27, 145
Of slavery 8, 16–19, 36, 124–28, 145, 211, 235, 315–17
Abolitionism 5, 79, 86–88, 104–05, 268–69, 273, 276, 281, 300, 308, 314–18, 320–21
Abolitionists 4–5, 10–18, 85–88, 104–05, 115–16, 233–37, 241–45, 249–56, 264–76, 283, 293, 307–09, 315
Agency 12, 22–25, 71, 86, 90–93, 182–184, 188–89, 199, 218, 224, 227, 249, 267, 284–85, 290–94, 320
Agency vs coercion 23–25, 37, 43–59, 86, 133, 220–28, 243–45, 265–75, 286–300
American Revolution 99, 104–05
Anti-black racism 12–15
Anti-politics 263–79. *See also* depoliticisation
Anti-slavery activism 3–33
Anti-Slavery International 3, 287, 307
Apprentices 103, 130–32, 246, 251, 267
Aristotle 39, 42, 54–55, 71–73, 76
Artisanal gold mining 231–59. *See also* mining
Atlantic World slavery 8, 15

B
Bales, Kevin 4, 21, 37, 52, 237
Black Codes 13, 159–60, 172
Black freedom struggle 305–07, 318–21
Black Lives Matter 321

L. Brace and J. O'Connell Davidson (eds.), *Revisiting Slavery and Antislavery*,
https://doi.org/10.1007/978-3-319-90623-2

Blackness 9, 13–14, 23, 308–10, 313–14
Bonded labour 20, 43, 180–87, 199
Borderland 116, 207–09, 213–15, 219, 224–28
Borders 17, 77, 101, 125, 143–44, 212
Brides 53, 217–19, 226–28, 287
British colonialism 126
British Empire 16, 27, 93, 105, 124–29, 132–39

C

Canada 16, 65–66, 89–90, 93, 106–108, 120, 127, 139, 145, 191
Capitalism 8, 25, 28, 89–90, 142, 155, 162–163, 256, 263–75, 279, 300, 306–11, 319–20
Caste 13, 288–89, 297, 300–01
Chain gangs 153–54, 170
Chattel slavery 9–19, 42, 47, 70–72, 83, 99, 103–05, 253
Childhood 108–09, 114–15, 119, 242, 250
Child labour 5–6, 19–22, 24–25, 28, 88, 231–57
Child marriage 19, 287–90, 300
Child rights 250–254
Child slavery 231–37, 241, 244–45, 250–56
China 16, 21, 128–29, 140, 151, 207–28, 308
Chinese indentured servants 37, 48–51
Citizenship 13–15, 28, 69, 181, 205
Civil War, American 11–13, 43, 158, 232–33, 307, 315
Coercion 21–22, 29, 37, 40–44, 47–48, 51–52, 56–58, 86, 105–07, 133, 143, 160, 164, 179, 193, 216, 220, 223, 233, 237, 241–44, 263–97, 310
Colonial slavery 80, 87
Colonialism 26, 28, 72, 76, 89, 93, 126, 306
Colonization 22, 100, 210, 306, 312
Colour-blind 4
Commodification 213
Compulsion 11, 21, 24–25, 59, 142, 181, 187–91, 199, 253, 274, 291
Consent 24, 29, 37, 47–48, 52–54, 57–58, 84, 185–86, 192–93, 222, 236, 246, 265–70, 274–76, 287–300
Consumers 107, 171, 263, 270–73
Contemporary slavery 19, 307–08
Contract 36–43, 46–48, 51–52, 55–58, 124, 129, 133–40, 145–46, 157–58, 162, 180, 183–84, 187, 192–99, 266–68
Contract slavery 179, 183–84, 187
Control 5, 15–17, 20–21, 27–29, 41, 52, 58–59, 90, 123–35, 138, 141–45, 153, 159, 168, 182–83, 187, 196–98, 213, 219, 227, 237, 265, 274, 285, 289–301, 318
Convict lease system 13, 159–61, 170
Coolie system 16–18, 124–25, 128, 133, 138–39
Corporations 152–54, 157, 160, 168, 171, 272, 286, 299
Cross-border marriage 19, 207–09, 216–20

D
Debt bondage 19, 35, 38–41, 57–59, 126, 183–84, 187, 236, 253, 266, 274
Debt slaves 38
Defoe, Daniel 83–84, 93
Delhi rape 282, 295–98
Depoliticisation 22, 257, 292
Development 8, 26, 74, 84, 103, 130, 134, 155, 162, 208–10, 214, 228, 234, 242, 246–49, 254–55, 288–93, 299–300, 308, 311–12, 321
Diaspora 308, 320
Dishonour 23, 45, 69, 70, 73, 79
Dispossession 238
Domestic servants 43, 54–56, 287
Domestic workers 179–99, 219, 238
Domination 6, 9, 13–15, 27–28, 37, 47, 53–54, 57–59, 154, 163
Douglass, Frederick 11, 50
Du Bois, W.E.B. 14, 18, 159, 162, 172, 316

E
Emancipation 13–14, 17, 28, 60, 69, 103, 159, 162, 199, 209, 225, 306–07, 314–18
Emigration 16, 98–102, 105–08, 112–13, 133–37, 142, 146
Empowerment 281, 284–87, 291, 294, 298–99
Enlightenment 13, 38, 57, 73, 76, 103–04, 113
Enslavement 4, 15–16, 37–40, 47, 53–57, 69–71, 75, 78–79, 82–84, 87, 92, 182, 233–235, 253, 310, 313
Equality 10, 132, 287, 307, 313–17
Equiano, Olaudah 114–16, 119–20
Euro-colonialism 26, 72, 76, 93
Europe 3, 6–15, 18, 22, 26–27, 39, 44, 47–48, 67–68, 72–73, 76–77, 80, 84, 88–89, 99, 106, 109, 113, 116, 126–27, 134, 141–45, 180, 199, 269, 276–77, 311–13, 320
Europeans 9, 12, 44, 78–80, 84–92, 98–100, 116–17, 126, 137, 145, 210–12, 312–13
Exile 16, 27, 97–98, 108–11
Exilic vs diasporic memory 109–118
Exploitation 5–6, 15–17, 20–22, 29, 36, 41–43, 52, 59, 130, 134, 143–44, 152–54, 159, 163, 188–93, 199, 207–09, 212–13, 216, 227, 235–37, 241–46, 251, 254–56, 263–75, 298, 308–09, 314

F
Family 24, 110, 136, 165–67, 170, 180–81, 189–92, 196, 211–12, 217–22, 227–28, 239, 256, 284–86, 289, 297–99
Fanon, Frantz 310
Feminism:
Governance feminism 281–87, 294, 298–300
Carceral feminism 283
Figurative slavery 68, 71–72, 82
First Nations 65–66, 89
Forced labour 5, 18–20, 29, 125, 162, 171–72, 181, 186–88, 235, 263–75, 307–08

Forced marriage 5, 20–22, 223, 286, 290–91, 294, 298–300
Force vs choice 19–24, 40, 52–58, 142, 181–89, 220–22, 267–70, 288–94
Foucault, Michel 231–232, 256–57
Free labour 11, 59, 126–28, 139, 141, 276
Free the Slaves (FTS) 3–4, 21, 87, 233–34, 237, 241–45, 252–56, 264
Freedom 3–19, 22–28, 38, 41–42, 48–53, 56, 59, 67–76, 85–90, 97, 101–08, 117–18, 126, 133–36, 139–41, 144, 157–62, 179–99, 209, 227, 232, 265–69, 274–75, 282–84, 286, 290, 294–313, 316–18, 320–21
Freedom Fund 264
Freedom of movement 15–16, 27, 42, 97–119, 180, 187, 198
Freelancers 179–84, 192–200
Freelancing 180–83, 192–97

G

Gender 9–11, 25–28, 88, 92–93, 117, 142, 180, 189–90, 198, 283–92, 296–97, 300
Gendered work 24, 56, 141–42, 188–90, 194, 245, 253
Ghana 231–34, 237–39, 244–47, 250–57
Global South 22, 25, 199, 281–83, 286–87, 292
Governance feminism 281–87, 294, 298–300
Graeco-Roman freedom 69, 72–73, 78–79, 82, 91–92
Gravel quarries 267

H

Haiti 11–12
Haitian revolution 11–12, 318
Hazardous work 249, 254–57
Hegel, Georg 37, 46–47, 57–59, 134
Hobbes, Thomas 35–39, 42, 46–47, 52, 56, 59, 125, 134
Honour 69, 70, 73–79, 86, 93, 100, 289, 296–97
Human rights 7, 184, 198, 232–34, 282–85, 291–92, 296, 307, 315

I

Ideology 8, 13, 57, 87, 93, 139, 270–71, 297–99
Immigrant 99, 106, 138–41, 158, 169, 306–07
Immigration controls 17, 132–35, 141–43
Incarceration 49, 164, 168, 283
Indentured labour 16–18, 50, 124–26, 132, 135, 146, 185
India 14–17, 89, 93, 124–25, 128–41, 145, 252–54, 274, 282, 288–89, 292–301, 311
Injustice 35–36, 45, 52, 57, 67, 73, 77, 85–89, 270, 273
International Justice Mission (IJM) 283
International Labour Organisation (ILO) 18, 21, 172, 197, 233–42, 245–46, 249–54, 264–66
International Trades Union Confederation (ITUC) 264

J

Jim Crow 13, 90, 307

K

Kafala system 180, 184–87, 193, 198–99
Kidnap 52, 135, 210, 267
Kinship 54, 70, 181, 188–89, 213, 224, 286, 299

L

Labour exploitation 36, 263, 271–74
Labour market 27, 139–41, 144, 152, 156–62, 169–70, 256, 288
Labour recruitment 124–27, 133, 138–40, 159
Land 12, 27, 37, 42–43, 49, 74–75, 105–07, 110–11, 114–15, 118, 136–37, 213, 216, 238–40, 243, 313
Latin America 14, 43, 51
League of Nations Slavery Convention 1926 18–19, 235. *See also* Slavery Convention
Liberalism 5, 25, 68, 89–90, 276, 286, 291–94, 308
Locke, John 35–42, 46–50, 56–59, 101, 265
Locomotion 102

M

Manumission 42–43, 56, 60, 92, 99, 316
Marriage 5, 19–22, 25, 28, 37, 42–43, 53–56, 191, 207–12, 216, 217–28, 286–91, 294, 298–301
Marx, Karl 25, 266–68, 274
Masters and Servants Acts 141
Mauritius 16, 27, 48, 124–25, 129–38, 145
Memory 12, 97–99, 107–20, 321
Microcredit 284–87
Middle East 92, 179–83, 187–98
Middle Passage 48, 115, 118, 135
Migrants 5, 16–17, 22–28, 36, 52–53, 56, 60, 88, 99, 100, 106, 113, 117–20, 126, 131, 139–46, 179–99, 208, 213–20, 227, 237–39, 275
Migrant domestic workers 179–200
Migration 15, 24–25, 53, 84, 98, 124, 188, 290
  Cross-border 17, 27, 99–100, 103, 113, 131–44, 188–91, 208, 216–19, 225
  Internal 27, 185
Mill, John Stuart 37, 53–56
Mining 160–62, 215, 232–33, 238–45, 248, 253–55
Mobility 15–16, 22, 27, 46, 84, 97–146, 160, 182, 190–92, 195–97, 219, 287, 296, 299, 301
Modern abolitionism 300. *See also* new abolitionists
Modern slavery 3–6, 14–28, 35–36, 47, 51–52, 59, 67, 86–88, 171, 233–37, 252–54, 268, 272, 281, 286–90, 300, 308, 319
Modernity 17, 26, 227, 298, 318
Morality 104
Motherhood 54, 227, 263

N

Nation 12–14, 17, 26–27, 66, 71–77, 80, 104, 107, 112–13, 117, 124, 139, 140–46, 160, 188–89, 197, 208, 216–17, 233, 243, 255, 282–84, 297, 310–11

Nationalism 124, 139–41, 297. *See also* Nationalist
Nationalist 124, 139–41, 297. *See also* Nationalism
Natural rights 8, 36
Neoliberalism 276, 308
New abolitionists 4–5, 15–17, 88, 307–09, 315
Nozick, Robert 37, 56–58, 265, 268, 276

O

Ownership:
Self-ownership 265, 268, 276

P

Paid work 249
Pass system 15, 16
Paternalism 10, 252, 283, 289–90, 294, 297–98
Patterson, Orlando 18, 37, 44–46, 54, 93, 237
Penal transportation 99
Philippines 189, 192
Plantations 16–18, 37, 43, 47–48, 67, 76, 84–85, 90, 101–05, 116, 127, 130, 139, 159, 163, 313, 317, 320
Policy making 236, 241–42, 250–55, 264, 273–74, 276, 290, 308, 314
Political economy 140, 154
Political slavery 71–74, 79, 81–83, 90
Poverty 4, 22, 89, 136, 171, 248, 251, 255, 269–72, 288–99
Power:
Gendered 6, 70, 227, 282–289, 294–300
Racialised 10, 15, 38–40, 48–59, 74, 82–86, 116, 155, 162, 309, 315
Powerlessness 44–45, 86, 223, 289, 294, 300
Prison industrial complex:
Prison factories 155–57, 164
Prison industries 151–52, 157–59, 164–68
Prison labour 49, 151–52, 162–72
Prison labour regimes 152–60, 168–70
Prison labour system 154, 162
Prisoners 21, 70, 92, 151–71
Property 8, 15, 21–23, 26, 40, 76, 92, 157, 171, 180, 237–39, 264–74, 310, 313–14, 317
Prostitution 6, 19, 29, 53, 56, 210, 217, 224–26, 235–36, 242, 245, 253, 282. *See also* sex work
Protest 59, 80, 90, 117, 156, 241, 282, 294–301, 317

R

Race 11–17, 26–28, 55, 76, 89, 102, 140–42, 154, 159, 168–70, 248, 306, 312, 316
Racial slavery 28, 305–11, 314, 318–21. *See also* racialized slavery
Racialized slavery 68, 80, 83, 86–87, 90, 127–28, 140–42, 153–55, 163, 169–71, 184, 307, 312, 318. *See also* racial slavery

Racism 12–15, 22, 39, 89, 140, 306, 317–18
Rape 78, 243, 282, 289, 294–98, 301. *See also* Delhi rape
Recruitment
By deception 20–29
By force 20–29, 236
Of labour 124–27, 133–41, 159, 186–87
Rescue 12, 22, 56, 123, 138, 143–44, 146, 211, 254, 272, 283–85, 290, 293
Revolution 11–12, 23, 72, 76, 85, 99–101, 104–05, 117, 156, 265, 308, 317–21. *See also* American Revolution and Haitian Revolution
Runaway slaves 211
Running away 60

S

Sale of women 209–11
Saudi Arabia 186–87, 191–92, 196, 200
Self-employment 243–44, 274
Serfdom 19, 37, 42–47, 236
Servants 8–10, 37–40, 43, 48–51, 54–56, 78–85, 100–01, 117, 136, 141, 145, 181, 195, 224, 287
Servitude 8, 26–29, 35–41, 47–58, 72, 76–80, 84, 99, 102–03, 117, 128, 172, 183, 194, 212, 266
Settler colonialism 89, 306
Sex work 24–25, 52–53, 60, 127, 140–42, 219, 282, 291–94. *See also* prostitution
Sexual abuse 236, 245
Sexual slavery 53, 127, 233, 242, 245
Sexual violence 193, 242, 282, 295–97, 301
Shame 68–70, 74, 77–79, 83–85, 93, 297
Slave labour 18, 43, 48–49, 125–30, 134, 141, 145
Slave status 91, 312
Slave trade 7–14, 19, 39, 48, 85–86, 97–105, 125–27, 130, 135, 145–46, 182, 235, 270, 311, 320
Slavery:
And war captives 38–59
Ancient world 6–17, 44–49, 54, 56–57, 67–68, 73–77, 309–14
Definition of 17–23, 35–59, 183–88, 234–38, 252, 266, 307–08, 316
In international law 41–43, 234–38
In Vietnam and China, historical background 209–13
Slavery Convention 18–19, 235. *See also* League of Nations Slavery Convention 1926
Slavery-like practices 187, 235
Smuggling 20, 146, 208–10, 215
Sponsorship 13, 159
State-imposed forced labour 153, 170
Structural Adjustment 238, 255–56, 288
Subalterns 25, 76, 101–02, 284–85, 292–94, 299–300
Supply chains 135, 168, 270, 308

T

Thirteenth Amendment to the U.S. Constitution 315
Torture 16, 86, 90–92, 114, 157
Tradition 10–11, 18, 43, 74, 79, 113, 227, 243, 271, 287–88, 294, 297–99, 314, 319
Trafficking 3, 4, 20–28, 35–41, 45–53, 56–59, 87–88, 123–26, 143–44, 146, 179–99, 207–09, 213–19, 235–36, 263–69, 272–75, 282–85, 290–93, 298–99, 307–08
Transatlantic slavery 6, 14, 17, 23–24, 79, 85–87, 93, 97–99, 103, 118
Transgender 296
Tyranny 68, 71–76, 79, 88, 102

U

Unconditional Basic Income (UBI) 264, 273–75
Unfree labour 35–37, 41–50, 53, 57–59, 134, 153, 159, 163, 180–81, 185–88
Unfreedom 14, 28, 141, 171, 282, 286, 290, 300, 310
United Nations *Convention on the Prevention and Punishment of the Crime of Genocide* 66
United Nations *Convention on the Rights of the Child* 235, 251
United Nations Office on Drugs and Crime (UNODC) 264
United Nations' *Protocol to Prevent, Suppress and Punish Trafficking in Persons, Especially Women and Children* 235
United Nations' *Supplementary Convention on the Abolition of Slavery, the Slave Trade, and Institutions and Practices Similar to Slavery* (1956) 19
United Nations Sustainable Development Goals 234
United States 14, 59, 127, 139–42, 151, 155, 169, 172, 306, 314, 317
United States State Department 307

V

Vagrancy Laws 16
Victimhood 24, 86, 297
Victims of trafficking 25, 53, 59, 144, 179–205, 219, 267
Vietnam 207–10, 214–19, 223–28
Vietnamese wives 207
Violence 9, 12–14, 17, 21–23, 59, 66, 78, 89–92, 99, 163, 184, 192–93, 199, 231–33, 237, 240–42, 256, 282–85, 290–91, 295–301, 305, 308, 320
Voluntary slavery 39
Voluntary vs coerced movement 27, 98–142, 182–188, 235–236
Vulnerability 29, 82, 101, 227, 264, 270, 273–74, 285, 293, 299–300

W

Wage slavery 8, 105

Walk Free 3–4, 19–21, 233, 254, 264, 269
West Africa 239, 267
West Indies 8–10, 82, 135
West, Kanye 90
Whiteness 13–15, 118, 127, 313
Wilberforce, William 5, 10
Wives 22–24, 46, 53–55, 60, 70, 136, 190, 207, 211–13, 217
Working children 234, 252–54
Worst Forms of Child Labour (WFCL) 20–21, 233–38, 241–46, 249–54, 256

The manufacturer's authorised representative in the EU is Springer Nature Customer Service Centre GmbH, Europaplatz 3, 69115 Heidelberg, Germany. If you have any concerns regarding our products, please contact ProductSafety@springernature.com

Printed and bound by CPI Group (UK) Ltd, Croydon, CR0 4YY
05/10/2026
02228140-0011